BUSINESS PROCESS OUTSOURCING
PROCESS, STRATEGIES, AND CONTRACTS

**Subscriber
Update
Service**

BECOME A SUBSCRIBER!
Did you purchase this product from a bookstore?

If you did, it's important for you to become a subscriber. John Wiley & Sons, Inc. may publish, on a periodic basis, supplements and new editions to reflect the latest changes in the subject matter that you ***need to know*** in order to stay competitive in this ever-changing industry. By contacting the Wiley office nearest you, you'll receive any current update at no additional charge. In addition, you'll receive future updates and revised or related volumes on a 30-day examination review.

If you purchased this product directly from John Wiley & Sons, Inc., we have already recorded your subscription for this update service.

To become a subscriber, please call **1-800-225-5945** or send your name, company name (if applicable), address, and the title of the product to:

mailing address: **Supplement Department**
                                  John Wiley & Sons, Inc.
                                  One Wiley Drive
                                  Somerset, NJ 08875

e-mail: **subscriber@wiley.com**
fax: **1-732-302-2300**
online: **www.wiley.com**

For customers outside the United States, please contact the Wiley office nearest you:

Professional & Reference Division
John Wiley & Sons Canada, Ltd.
22 Worcester Road
Rexdale, Ontario M9W 1L1
CANADA
(416) 675-3580
Phone: 1-800-567-4797
Fax: 1-800-565-6802
canada@jwiley.com

John Wiley & Sons, Ltd.
Baffins Lane
Chichester
West Sussex, PO19 1UD
ENGLAND
Phone: (44) 1243 779777
Fax: (44) 1243 770638
cs-books@wiley.co.uk

Jacaranda Wiley Ltd.
PRT Division
P.O. Box 174
North Ryde, NSW 2113
AUSTRALIA
Phone: (02) 805-1100
Fax: (02) 805-1597
headoffice@jacwiley.com.au

John Wiley & Sons (SEA) Pte. Ltd.
2 Clementi Loop #20-01
SINGAPORE 129809
Phone: 65 463 2400
Fax: 65 463 4605; 65 463 4604
wiley@singnet.com.sg

Business Process Outsourcing
Process, Strategies, and Contracts

John K. Halvey
Barbara Murphy Melby

JOHN WILEY & SONS, INC.

New York   •   Chichester   •   Brisbane   •   Weinheim   •   Toronto   •   Singapore

For Colin and Grace Ann
—JKH
For GDM, Grayson and Garrett
—BMM

Copyright © 2000 by John Wiley & Sons. All rights reserved.

Published simultaneously in Canada.

To order books or for customer service please, call 1(800)-CALL-WILEY (225-5945).

Designations used by companies to distinguish their products are often claimed as trademarks. In all instances where John Wiley & Sons, Inc. is aware of a claim, the product names appear in initial capital or all capital letters. Readers, however, should contact the appropriate companies for more complete information regarding trademarks and registration.

This book and the accompanying software are designed to provide information about outsourcing business processes. While every effort has been made to make this book and the accompanying software as complete and accurate as possible, any use of the information and forms is at the reader's discretion. The authors and the publisher specifically disclaim any and all liability arising directly or indirectly from the use or application of the contents of this book and the accompanying software. This book and the accompanying software are not intended to serve as a replacement for professional legal, accounting, or financial advice. An attorney, an accountant, and a financial professional should be consulted regarding your specific situation. This product is sold without warranty of any kind, either express and implied, including but not limited to the implied warranty of merchantability or fitness for a particular purpose. (Some states do not allow the exclusion of implied warranties, so the exclusion may not apply to you.)

Library of Congress Cataloging-in-Publication Data:

Halvey, John K.
    Business process outsourcing: process, strategies, and contracts /
John K. Halvey, Barbara Murphy Melby.
       p.   cm.
    Includes index.
    ISBN 0-471-34821-X (alk. paper)
    1. Contracting out.   2. Procurement.   I. Melby,
Barbara Murphy. II. Title.
HD238.H35 1999   99-15790
658. 7'23—dc21   CIP

Printed in the United States of America.

10 9 8 7 6 5

ABOUT THE AUTHORS

John K. Halvey is a senior vice president at Safeguard Scientifics, Inc., an information technology holding company that develops and operates Internet-related companies. At Safeguard, Mr. Halvey is responsible for analyzing business opportunities, managing a select group of Safeguard partner companies in the enterprise applications space, and assisting partner companies with mergers and acquisitions. Prior to his position at Safeguard, Mr. Halvey was a partner at the international law firm of Milbank, Tweed, Hadley & McCloy, LLP, where he was the head of the Global Technology Transactions Group. At Milbank, Mr. Halvey practiced in all areas of technology law, with particular emphasis on information technology and business process outsourcing, technology joint ventures, strategic alliances, licensing agreements, acquisitions and financing, and venture capital transactions. Mr. Halvey's work has been the subject of numerous articles in national business and technology magazines, including *Forbes, Information Week, Computer World,* and *CIO Magazine*. In addition *Crain's* named Halvey to its list of the "40 Most Successful People under 40 in New York City" in 1995. An active participant in the technology community, Mr. Halvey was a founder and served as general counsel for the International Information Technology Group (IITUG). He has also authored several books on technology-related topics. He is the co-author of *Information Technology Outsourcing Transactions: Process, Strategies, and Contracts*.

Barbara Murphy Melby has a wide range of experience in structuring and negotiating outsourcing transactions in the United States and abroad. She has represented companies in many of the largest technology, telecommunications, and business process outsourcing transactions to date, including General Motors, DuPont, Hughes, Allied Signal, and Commonwealth Bank of Australia. Over the past eight years, Ms. Melby has been a member of the Global Technology Transactions Group in the New York, London, and Washington, DC, offices of Milbank, Tweed, Hadley & McCloy, LLP. Ms. Melby has lectured and written numerous articles on outsourcing, including articles on BPO published in the *New York Law Journal* and *High-Tech Industry*. Ms. Melby, along with Mr. Halvey, authored *Information Technology Outsourcing Transactions: Process, Strategies, and Contracts*.

CONTENTS

PREFACE

Business process outsourcing (BPO) is predicted to be a $282 billion industry by the year 2000, dwarfing the information technology outsourcing market.[1] In the hope of reducing cost, gaining efficiency, and improving service, customers are taking a hard look at their business processes to assess which areas would best be performed by an outside vendor. At the same time, vendors are restructuring or expanding their service offerings to accommodate the growing demand for BPO services.

The issues encountered by customers and vendors entering into BPO transactions run the gambit—from the more traditional outsourcing issues (e.g., defining scope, allocating responsibility, negotiating fees) to issues that are evolving as the BPO market matures (e.g., benchmarking, gainsharing, integration). The complexity of the issues that arise in connection with a BPO transaction vary depending upon the types of services outsourced, the geographic reach of the transaction and the degree of new project implementation that is included in the deal. The management of a BPO transaction—from inception to contract signing—is often a daunting task. Numerous areas of expertise will need to be tapped into when structuring a BPO transaction, such as tax, insurance, risk management, finance and information technology. As in most business transactions, familiarity with the key issues and knowledge of industry practices will aid both the customer and the vendor in navigating the BPO process and ensuring the execution of a successful and fair contract.

This book is intended to guide both the BPO customer and vendor through the many phases of a BPO transaction—from initial vendor selection to contract negotiation, execution and administration. Chapter 1 provides an overview of the BPO industry with highlights of recent deals, a listing of potential vendors and a look at the types of business processes being considered for outsourcing. Chapters 2 and 3 take the parties through the planning and vendor selection stages. Useful tools are included in these chapters, including sample requests for information and proposals. Chapter 4 gives a high-level look at contract negotiation and strategy, offering insight into weighing risks and benefits as well as negotiating a fair, balanced contract. Chapter 5 takes the reader through the nuts and bolts of the key contract provisions. Negotiating tips and sample contract provisions are provided to assist the customer and the vendor in the contract drafting and negotiation phase.

Chapters 6 through 10 move away from a general discussion of BPO and focus on more specific topics that arise in BPO transactions. Chapter 6 looks at both traditional and innovative ways to measure performance, including service levels, benchmarking, and gainsharing. Chapter 7 covers human resource issues, focusing primarily on the transfer of

---

[1] Kiely, Thomas, "Business Processes: Consider Outsourcing," *Harvard Business Review* (May/June 1997).

employees to the BPO vendor. Chapter 8 deals with the implementation of new projects as part of the outsourcing transaction, focusing on key contract terms and mechanisms for assuring on-time performance and delivery. Chapter 9 offers an overview of issues to consider in international transactions. Chapter 10 provides hints for structuring and negotiating the exhibits to the BPO transaction, as well as a summary of potential ancillary agreements that the parties may need to negotiate as part of the overall transaction.

Once the contract is signed, there are often a number of post-negotiation activities. These activities are discussed in Chapter 11, including internal and external communications and risk/benefit analyses. BPO relationships are continually evolving, with changes in corporate structure, directives and service requirements. Chapter 12 looks at the renegotiation and termination of the BPO relationship, as well as the activities associated with "winding down" the provision of services.

Chapters 1 through 12 are followed by a number of forms and checklists that take both the customer and the vendor through the many phases of the BPO process. As each BPO transaction is different, legal counsel should be consulted prior to using any contract form or checklist. The forms and checklists will need to be tailored to the particular transaction at hand.

A final note is that not all aspects of this book will apply to all BPO transactions. For example, not all deals will include the transfer of employees or have an international scope. This book is intended to be an overview of the many issues that may arise during the BPO process. The reader should use this book as a guideline and consult appropriate counsel to determine which sections are applicable to the particular transaction. In addition, while this book is intended to be comprehensive, it will not cover all of the issues that will arise in any BPO transaction. Again, appropriate counsel should be consulted when entering into any BPO arrangement.

ABOUT THE DISK

DISK CONTENTS

File Name	Title
APDX0201.DOC	2.1 Letter Agreement for Disclosure of Information in Connection with Evaluation of Possible BPO Transaction (Mutual Protection)
APDX0202.DOC	2.2 Questionnaire for Assessing Legal Resources Required (Customer Form)
APDX0203.DOC	2.3 Questionnaire for Assessing Legal Resources Required (Vendor Form)
APDX0204.DOC	2.4 Request for Information
APDX0205.DOC	2.5 Request for Proposal
APDX0301.DOC	3.1 Evaluation of Vendor Proposals Relating to the Provision of BPO Services
APDX0302.DOC	3.2 Letter of Intent (Customer Form)
APDX0303.DOC	3.3 Letter of Intent (Vendor Form)
APDX0401.DOC	4.1 Due Diligence Agreement
APDX0402.DOC	4.2 Model Term Sheet
APDX0501.DOC	5.1 Checklist: Key Issues in BPO Agreements (General)
APDX0502.DOC	5.2 Checklist: Key Issues in BPO Agreements (Accounting Services)
APDX0503.DOC	5.3 Checklist: Key Issues in BPO Agreements (Human Resource Services)
APDX0504.DOC	5.4 Checklist: Key Issues in BPO Agreements (Warehouse Management Services)
APDX0505.DOC	5.5 Checklist: Key Issues in BPO Agreements (Property Management Services)
APDX0506.DOC	5.6 Business Process Outsourcing Agreement (Customer Form)
APDX0507.DOC	5.7 Business Process Outsourcing Agreement (Vendor Form)
APDX0507A.DOC	5.7A Proprietary Rights Rider (Vendor Form)
APDX0601.DOC	6.1 Customer Satisfaction Survey Checklist
APDX0602.DOC	6.2 List of Reports

INTRODUCTION

The forms on the enclosed disk are saved in Microsoft Word for Windows version 7.0. In order to use the form, you will need to have word processing software capable of reading Microsoft Word for Windows version 7.0 files.

SYSTEM REQUIREMENTS

- IBM PC or compatible computer
- 3.5" floppy disk drive
- Windows 95 or later
- Microsoft Word for Windows version 7.0 (including the Microsoft converter*) or later or other word processing software capable of reading Microsoft Word for Windows 7.0 files.

*Word 7.0 needs the Microsoft converter file installed in order to view and edit all enclosed files. If you have trouble viewing the files, download the free converter from the Microsoft web site. The URL for the converter is:
http://officeupdate.microsoft.com/downloadDetails/wd97cnv.htm

Microsoft also has a viewer that can be downloaded, which allows you to view, but not edit documents. This viewer can be downloaded at:
http://officeupdate.microsoft.com/downloadDetails/wd97vwr32.htm

NOTE: Many popular word processing programs are capable of reading Microsoft Word for Windows 7.0 files. However, users should be aware that a slight amount of formatting might be lost when using a program other than Microsoft Word. If your word processor cannot read Microsoft Word for Windows 7.0 files, unformatted text files have been provided in the TXT directory on the floppy disk.

HOW TO INSTALL THE FILES ONTO YOUR COMPUTER

To install the files follow these instructions:

1. Insert the enclosed disk into the floppy disk drive of your computer.
2. From the Start Menu, choose **Run**.
3. Type **A:\SETUP** and press **OK**.
4. The opening screen of the installation program will appear. Press **OK** to continue.
5. The default destination directory is C:\HALVEY. If you wish to change the default destination, you may do so now.
6. Press **OK** to continue. The installation program will copy all files to your hard drive in the C:\HALVEY or user-designated directory.

USING THE FILES

Loading Files

To use the word processing files, launch your word processing program. Select **File, Open** from the pull-down menu. Select the appropriate drive and directory. If you installed the files to the default directory, the files will be located in the C:\HALVEY directory. A list of files should appear. If you do not see a list of files in the directory, you need to select **WORD DOCUMENT (*.DOC)** under **Files of Type**. Double click on the file you want to open. Edit the file according to your needs.

Printing Files

If you want to print the files, select **File, Print** from the pull-down menu.

Saving Files

When you have finished editing a file, you should save it under a new file name by selecting **File, Save As** from the pull-down menu.

User Assistance

If you need assistance with installation or if you have a damaged disk, please contact Wiley Technical Support at:

Phone: (212) 850-6753
Fax: (212) 850-6800 (Attention: Wiley Technical Support)
Email: techhelp@wiley.com

To place additional orders or to request information about other Wiley products, please call (800) 225-5945.

CHAPTER 1

OVERVIEW

1.1 THE EMERGING MARKET

Business process outsourcing (BPO)—the management of one or more specific business *processes or functions* (e.g., procurement, accounting, human resources, asset or property management) by a third party, together with the information technology (IT) that supports the process or function—is being heralded in the marketplace as the next generation of outsourcing. As IT outsourcing services become more "commoditized," customers and vendors alike are looking to BPO as a means to revitalize their organizations, reduce costs, or both. According to a recent study sponsored by PricewaterhouseCoopers, 46 percent of the individuals surveyed said that during the last three years the importance of BPO has increased at their organizations.[1] For the customer, the outsourcing of business processes would allow the customer to focus on its core competencies, while having a qualified third party focus on and add value to noncore processes. For the typical vendor, BPO, a natural extension of IT outsourcing, offers a possible means to expand its primary service offering, with the opportunity to introduce innovative service and pricing structures (and realize higher pricing margins) in a relatively untapped market.

G2R, a leading outsourcing and information services research firm, has noted that while IT costs equal 1 to 3 percent of revenues in most companies, a process like procurement management can cost companies 7 to 11 percent alone.[2] Therefore, the potential revenue that can be generated from outsourcing business processes (of which procurement management is just an example) is significantly greater than that generated by more traditional forms of outsourcing. Analysts are looking at the potential revenue to be generated from BPO transactions and are making astounding growth predictions for the BPO market in the next few years. If the predictions prove to be correct, the BPO market will dwarf the IT outsourcing market in the United States and abroad by the year 2000. Examples of some of the bold expectations for the BPO market include:

---

[1] *Global Top Decision Makers Study^SM on Business Process Outsourcing,* sponsored by PricewaterhouseCoopers, Yankelovich Partners and Goldstein Consulting Group (August 1998) (hereinafter referred to as the "Global Top Decision Makers Study^SM") at p. 8.

[2] Kiely, Thomas, "Business Processes: Consider Outsourcing," *Harvard Business Review* (May/June 1997).

- G2R estimates that by the year 2000, BPO will be a $282 billion industry, up from $138 billion in 1996, becoming 10 times the size for managing technology.[3] The worldwide demand for finance and accounting services alone will swell from $37 billion in 1998 to $89 billion in 2003.[4]
- The worldwide growth rate for BPO from 1996 to 2001 is expected to be 30 percent. The U.S. growth rate is expected to be 36 percent for the same time period.[5]
- The Yankee Group, another research firm, has noted that BPO will be a multiple of the worldwide outsourcing potential ($267 billion) by the year 2000.[6]
- Other analysts have placed the growth rate of the BPO market at 23 percent[7] and 26 percent[8] over the next five years. Much of the growth is expected to be in non-U.S. markets.

While BPO is emerging as a market in and of itself, it has also become more common for IT outsourcing vendors to market business process services, such as business process management and business process reengineering, as part of a comprehensive IT outsourcing deal. It is likely, therefore, that a large number of IT outsourcing deals will include some level of business process management in the next few years. As a result, the conventional IT vendor is being forced to realign its organizational structure, marketing strategies, and resource capabilities to account for the market's interest in business process and IT outsourcing services.

While the BPO market is expected to experience significant growth in the next three to five years, the concept of outsourcing some business processes is not new to most companies. The Global Top Decision Makers Study[SM] indicated that 63 percent of decision makers surveyed (out of a pool of 304 companies in 14 countries) said that their companies have already outsourced one or more business processes worldwide to external service providers.[9] A survey conducted by the American Management Association revealed that 75 percent of respondents outsource one or more human resources activities.[10] BPO, in many ways, dovetails with the growing idea of the "virtual" company, where the company offers limited core services and receives all non-core services from a third party, thereby reducing headcount and overhead. Although the concept of BPO is not new, the expected increase in the scope of the processes outsourced (e.g., a company may outsource only part of its benefits management today, leaving open the possibility of broadening the scope of its human resource outsourcing) and the various types of processes outsourced is new.

1.2 WHAT IS BPO?

As discussed earlier, BPO is becoming, if it has not already become, the hot topic in the outsourcing industry, receiving a good deal of attention in the press as well as outsourcing and industry-specific seminars. But what is covered by the term *BPO?*

---

[3] *Id.*

[4] "G2R Report Reveals Strategies for Maximizing Success in High-End Finance and Administration Outsourcing Market," *PR Newswire* (August 10, 1998).

[5] "Service, Please!" *Computer Industry Report* (July 1, 1997).

[6] "Outsourcing Works in a Virtual Industry," *National Underwriter* (Life and Health/Financial Services Edition) (March 17, 1997).

[7] "Outsourcing Growing Rapidly," *PR Newswire* (September 19, 1997).

[8] "European Outsourcing Market Will Reach $33B by 2001," *Computergram International* (November 25, 1997).

[9] *Global Top Decision Makers Study[SM]*, *supra* note 2 at p. 3.

[10] *Human Resource Department Management Report* (August 1997) at p. 8.

The typical IT outsourcing deal focuses mainly on the IT component of business operations, such as data center and desktop operations. The outsourcing of a customer's data center, for example, provides back-office support to a number of business functions thereby providing a service that is shared by several, often unrelated, business functions. Rather than providing IT support to multiple functions, BPO refers to the outsourcing of one or more specific *business processes or functions* to a third-party vendor, together with the IT that supports it. BPO focuses on how an overall process or function is run—from manager to end-user—rather than on the technology that supports such process or function. IT is only a component of the overall business process. A formal definition of BPO is set out in *The End-User Executive's Guide to BPO,* which defines BPO as "the delegation of one or more IT-intensive business processes to an external provider who, in turn, administrates and manages the selected processes based upon defined and measurable performance metrics."[11]

One of the challenges of discussing BPO is that it refers to the outsourcing of any "business process," which covers a wide spectrum of possibilities, from procurement to accounting to human resources to asset and property management. In the next section, we will try to place some parameters around the general categories of business processes that companies have focused on as potential targets for outsourcing.

1.3 AREAS TARGETED FOR BPO

(a) General Categories   Business processes that have come under close examination as potential candidates for outsourcing typically fall within one of the following six categories:[12]

1. Administration (audit, tax)
2. Asset and property management
3. Finance (accounting, billing, accounts payable, accounts receivable)
4. Human resources (benefits administration, payroll)
5. Miscellaneous (energy services, customer service, mailroom, food processing)
6. Procurement/logistics

These categories have been established to facilitate the discussion of the general types of business processes that are the subject of consideration for outsourcing. Since in many cases a business process touches different areas within an organization, customers and vendors may categorize certain business processes under different headings depending on the organization's internal structure. For example, in some companies, payroll is considered a human resource function, while in others it is considered a finance function. Similarly, tax compliance may be considered an administrative function in some companies and a finance function in others.

As the BPO market evolves, customers and vendors will undoubtedly identify more business processes that can—and will—be outsourced. The potential reach of BPO is evi-

---

[11] G2R, TPI, and Milbank, Tweed, Hadley & McCloy LLP, *The End-User Executive's Guide to Business Process Outsourcing* (1998) (hereinafter the "End-User's Executive Guide to BPO") at p. 9.

[12] The Global Top Decision Makers Study[SM] indicated that the processes that the participating companies have outsourced include: payroll (37 percent), benefits management (33 percent), real estate management (32 percent), tax compliance (26 percent), claims administration (24 percent), applications process (21 percent), human resources (19 percent), sourcing/procurement (15 percent), and finance/accounting (12 percent). *Supra* note 1 at p. 13.

denced by the scope of what is even now being considered for outsourcing. Business processes targeted for outsourcing are expanding beyond the traditional corporate support functions into the supply chain. For example, an increasing number of companies are considering outsourcing their customer service functions. The voice behind that toll-free customer service number may not be an employee of the manufacturer but an employee of a third-party outsourcing vendor.

(b) Administration   Since business processes that fall within the administration category are generally not considered core to a company's operations, more companies are examining processes such as tax compliance and internal auditing to assess whether they should be outsourced. Tax compliance has been the subject of outsourcing for longer than most other business processes. Companies have historically outsourced some or all of their tax compliance function to outside accounting firms. Since tax, in many ways like the practice of law, requires being constantly apprised of the laws, regulations, and rules in multiple jurisdictions, many companies have found it more efficient to rely on outside firms to effectively manage this process.

However, there are some administrative functions that companies are just beginning to consider for outsourcing. One example is internal auditing. Many companies have considered this function as one that should remain internal since it often involves looking closely at many of the company's sensitive operations. A potential problem is a possible conflict with the external audit function. However, with the negotiation of strict confidentiality provisions, companies are beginning to allow outside firms to manage this process.

(c) Asset and Property Management   An area that financial institutions, particularly investment companies, are considering for outsourcing is asset management. If, for example, an investment company manages a small amount of certain assets as part of a larger service offering or to be able to market itself as a full-service company, it may consider outsourcing the underlying business process to a more experienced company with larger portfolios of these types of assets and greater infrastructure and resources to manage such assets. An issue that arises with asset management outsourcing is the extent, if any, permission from or notice to the outsourcing customer's clients is necessary. Such an approval or notice requirement may dissuade certain financial institutions and investment companies from outsourcing for fear that clients may find it more cost effective to do business directly with the outsourcing vendor.

While asset management outsourcing has just begun to gain attention, property or real estate management operations have been the subject of outsourcing for some time. The management of property or real estate typically involves responsibility for such noncore functions as physical security, maintenance, customer service, cafeteria, parking, leasing, rent collection, and disaster recovery. Since in many cases the owner of real estate purchases property for investment purposes, the owner is often eager to turn over management responsibility to a third party.[13]

(d) Finance   Most of the big accounting firms and their consulting counterparts, such as PricewaterhouseCoopers, Arthur Andersen, Ernst & Young, Deloitte and Touche, and KPMG, offer outsourcing services that provide support for a company's financial functions. These functions may include:

---

[13] According to the Global Top Decision Makers Study[SM], 32 percent of the companies surveyed have outsourced property management. *Supra* note 1 at p. 13.

- General accounting
- Payroll
- Treasury/cash management
- Accounts payable
- Accounts receivable
- Credit
- Fixed assets
- Contract maintenance
- Collections
- Financial systems
- Tax compliance
- Budgeting
- SEC reporting

One survey revealed that only 12 percent of the respondents indicated that their organizations outsource "finance/accounting,"[14] while another survey indicated that 38 percent of the respondents indicated that their organizations outsource some or all of the finance function.[15] Dun & Bradstreet Receivable Management Services saw a 60 percent increase in outsourcing contracts in 1998, with its outsourcing portfolio increasing from $200 million in 1995 to $5 billion in 1998.[16]

Companies that do outsource all or part of their finance function often want to turn over managerial and operational responsibility of a finance function in conjunction with the reengineering of their financial methodologies and systems. Such reengineering may involve the development and implementation of new methodologies and/or systems or customization of off-the-shelf or standard third-party methodologies and/or systems (e.g., a SAP implementation). Outsourcing transactions that include business process reengineering and BPO are more complex, often involving multiple documents and requiring the parties to address issues such as cross-termination and cross-default.

(e) Human Resources   What is covered by human resources varies from company to company. For example, some companies consider payroll to be a human resource function, while others consider it a finance function. For the purposes of this discussion, the human resources category covers all employee-related functions, from recruitment to benefits management, claims administration, and payroll.

While some companies opt to outsource the entire human resource process to one vendor, it is more common to identify particular functions within the human resource process for outsourcing to different vendors, largely because different vendors have different expertise within this area. For example, if a company wanted to outsource payroll, it might consider a vendor with accounting expertise, while if it wanted to outsource benefits management, it might consider a vendor with more ERISA and insurance expertise. This outsourcing to multiple vendors may change as vendors develop—or more likely obtain through merger, acquisition, or strategic alliance/partnership—the expertise to become full-service human resource outsourcers.

A relatively new phenomenon is the offering of low-cost human resource services by Web-based outsourcers. The target of such outsourcers are generally smaller and start-up

---

[14] *Supra* note 1 at p. 13.

[15] *Supra* note 11 at p. 80.

[16] Old, Forrest, "Outsourcing as a Business Strategy," *Business Credit* (September 1998) at p. 24.

organizations that are typically not candidates for traditional outsourcing due to the size and scale of their service needs. Allegiance Telecom Inc., for example, disseminates human resource policies and benefits to its rapidly growing workforce via a password-protected Web site created by Online Benefits Inc.[17] Another Web-based outsourcer, Atlantic Media of Boston, creates online company directories for smaller organizations that are accessible to employees via the Internet. The directories may include such information as biographies, resumes, and skill listings.[18]

According to a number of surveys, human resources functions are among the most common business functions outsourced. The Global Top Decisions Makers Survey[SM] revealed that 37 percent of the respondents outsourced payroll, 33 percent of the respondents outsourced benefits management, and 24 percent of the respondents outsourced claims administration.[19] According to the End User's Executive's Guide to BPO, 54 percent of the respondents outsourced payroll and 54 percent outsourced benefits administration.[20] A 1997 study by Murray Hill, Dun & Bradstreet Corp., and The Outsourcing Institute revealed that human resource activities comprised as high as 12 percent of the outsourcing market in North America. According to Aon Consulting's 1997 Survey of Human Resource Trends, nearly 50 percent of respondents outsourced more human resource functions than they did three years before and more than 50 percent intended to outsource more functions during the following three years.[21]

Customers (and vendors) considering an arrangement that involves the outsourcing of one or more human resources functions will need to consult representatives from a variety of disciplines. Such disciplines typically include, at a minimum:

- Legal
- Audit
- Personnel
- ERISA
- Tax

(f) Miscellaneous In addition to the general business process categories discussed in this section, there are a number of other, less easily categorized, processes that companies are beginning to consider for outsourcing. Such business processes include energy services, customer service, mail and copying services, and food services (which, in some cases, may fall under the category of property management). The spectrum of business processes that are the subject of outsourcing will likely grow as companies identify noncore areas that may be effectively managed by a third party or, if outsourced, will lead to a reduction in costs.

Examples of transactions that involve the outsourcing of business processes that fall under the miscellaneous category include:

- A transaction between Duke Solutions and Kraft for energy services at 70 facilities in North America

---

[17] Raths, David, "Let the Net Do It," *Inc. Tech 1999,* No. 1 at p. 52.

[18] *Id.* At p. 54.

[19] *Supra* note 1 at p. 13.

[20] *Supra* note 11 at p. 80.

[21] Solomon, Charlene Marmer, "Protecting Your Outsourcing Investment," *Workforce* (October 1998) at p. 130.

- A transaction between Strategic Resources Solutions and Wachovia Bank of Winston-Salem to manage energy use at 708 sites
- A transaction between Flower Industries and Service Master for food processing
- A transaction between Merrill Lynch (UK) and Pitney Bowes Management Services for the outsourcing of interoffice mail
- A transaction between United HealthCare and Corporate Transfer Service, Inc. and PHH Relocation for the outsourcing of employee relocation services

(g) Procurement/Logistics   An area that is receiving significant attention, particularly in the vendor community, is procurement outsourcing. Procurement outsourcing covers some or all aspects of noncore purchasing and supplies management, including:

- Product selection
- Acquisition
- Delivery
- Inventory
- Packing
- Warehouse management
- Installation
- Moves, adds, and changes
- Refreshes
- Maintenance
- Help desk services

The types of goods and services that may be included in the procurement outsourcing arrangement depend largely on which goods and services the customer considers non-production goods and services. In some instances, the customer focuses the outsourcing on specific goods and services, such as office supplies or office equipment. In the typical procurement outsourcing transaction, the customer is typically looking to the vendor to standardize supply options and offer cost savings based on efficiency and economics of scale.

A business process that often overlaps with procurement is logistics. In addition to a number of midsize and smaller companies that focus primarily on logistics outsourcing, several of the large transportation and shipping companies, such as Ryder, Federal Express, and UPS, are offering logistics outsourcing services. Examples of recent logistics outsourcing deals include:

- An arrangement between Dow Chemical and Menlo Logistics for the outsourcing of inbound/outbound packaged goods transportation
- An arrangement between Ford Motor Company and Ryder Logistics for the design and management of a supply chain and transportation system
- An arrangement between Telstra Corp. and TNT Australia for management of warehousing and transportation functions

Since procurement and logistics outsourcing typically involves the acquisition, handling, and/or transportation of goods, a number of legal and regulatory issues specific to such services may arise, such as warehouse liens, security interests, insurance, and allocation of risk during transportation. As with any BPO transaction, the customer and the vendor should consult legal and other counsel, as appropriate, to flesh out all of the applicable legal and regulatory issues and assist in identifying the risks and benefits of the transaction.

1.4 REASONS FOR OUTSOURCING BUSINESS PROCESSES

Vendors are marketing BPO as an alternative to the typical IT outsourcing deal, encouraging customers to identify noncore processes that are inefficient, too costly, or difficult to manage. The entire process (except, in most cases, a high-level management position or positions) is then turned over to the vendor, who, in turn, agrees to productivity, customer satisfaction, and cost savings commitments.

As the IT outsourcing marketplace becomes more commodity based (e.g., number of CPUs provided, help desk calls answered), BPO customers are looking for innovative ways to increase the efficiency and quality of an entire business process through value-added services, customer satisfaction and, ideally, a direct, quantifiable impact on share price and profit. Since BPO focuses on an entire process rather than part of the process as with IT outsourcing, it is in many ways easier to identify the benefits derived from the BPO relationship. Some of the key business drivers for customers considering BPO include:

- Transferring the entire function (not just the IT component) out-of-house
- Enhancing/improving methodologies
- Benefiting from industry knowledge or experience
- Streamlining or standardizing processes across its organization
- Sharing resources or technologies
- Committing less upfront investment to new methodologies or technologies
- Obtaining flexibility with respect to the roll-out of methodologies or technologies
- Increasing productivity
- Quantifying savings or benefits more easily
- Tracking customer satisfaction
- Enhancing shareholder value

Obviously, a customer's objectives for outsourcing one or more business processes will vary on a deal-to-deal basis. The objectives are typically shaped by management's overarching goal in outsourcing (e.g., transition to new methodology or technology, reduction in costs or expenses).

1.5 INTEGRATION: MAKING BPO FIT

As customers are beginning to outsource one or more business processes, a number of issues are emerging with respect to the integration of the services and systems being provided by the BPO vendor with the services and systems used in connection with other business processes being provided internally or by a third party. Some of these "integration" issues are:

Systems integration. As part of the BPO transaction, the BPO vendor often introduces new, state-of-the-art systems that are specific to the business process being outsourced. The customer will need to consider how these systems will interrelate with the systems being used in connection with other business process. How will BPO impact the customer's move toward standardization?

Existing IT outsourcing arrangements. What impact will the BPO transaction have on existing outsourcing, particularly IT outsourcing, arrangements? Will there be a reduction or termination of services under existing outsourcing contracts? How do the customer's other outsourcing contracts deal with such reduction or termination?

Vendor management. How will responsibility be allocated among the outsourcing vendors if there is a service failure? How will the various outsourcing vendors be managed?

1.6 BPO VENDORS

When identifying vendors to provide BPO services, the customer's spectrum of possible vendors will depend on the particular process under consideration as well as the scope of the outsourcing. The vendor pool for payroll administration will in most cases be different than the vendor pool for procurement outsourcing. Similarly, the customer will probably consider different vendors if it wishes to simply have the vendor continue the operation of existing process service rather than a more complex outsourcing that requires the development, implementation, and management of new methodologies and/or technologies. Another factor to consider when selecting possible vendors is the geographic scope of the outsourcing. For multinational transactions or transactions in foreign countries, the customer should identify vendors with resources in the particular locations that are under consideration for outsourcing.

Many of the leading vendors in the BPO industry have capabilities and experience in process-related services (e.g., business process reengineering, management consulting, change management, consulting), as well as technology services. Often, the BPO transaction is preceded by or entered into in conjunction with a reengineering project. In addition to the conventional IT outsourcers, several of the top accounting firms—those with both process and technology capabilities—are leading the BPO market. To be able to provide the full scale of services that the BPO customer desires, many vendors are looking outside their own organizations to other companies with established service experience. The vendor who seeks to be a full-service BPO outsourcer may acquire the resources and experience offered by such an outside company through an outright acquisition or some type of teaming or "strategic alliance" relationship. For example, Affiliated Computer Services acquired Document Acquisition Services to enhance its data capture, imaging, and retrieval capabilities; Coventry Industries Corp. acquired BSD Healthcare Industries Inc. and People First LLC to expand the types of human resource outsourcing services that it offers; and Aspect Computing, Citibank Global Customer Solutions, and Manpower Services Australia formed a joint venture to offer a wide range of financial outsourcing services.

Another growing trend among BPO vendors is to team or form an alliance with a software provider with a product designed to serve particular business processes. For example, Arthur Andersen has teamed with J.D. Edwards to offer financial services,[22] and People-Soft has created a Certified Outsourcing Partner Program, which includes Computer Sciences Corporation (CSC) and KPMG as members, to break into the human resources outsourcing market.[23]

A relatively new but growing market is being forged by Web-based outsourcers that offer specialized services via the Internet. Such outsourcers are offering a wide range of low-cost services primarily to smaller and start-up organizations. Such services include document storage, payroll administration, data backup, and benefits management.[24]

Exhibit 1.1 provides a list of a number of BPO vendors.[25] (Please note that for the purposes of Exhibit 1.1, we have used the process categories identified in Section 1.3.)

---

[22] "Accounting Systems and Technology Briefs," *Managing Accounting Systems & Technology* (January 1999) at p. 1.

[23] "PeopleSoft Teams with CSC and KPMG," *Computergram International* (October 7, 1998).

[24] *Supra* note 17 at p. 52–58.

[25] The data contained in Exhibit 1.1 have been gathered from annual reports, press releases, and other public information. This list is not exhaustive by any means. It is intended to provide a sampling of vendors offering BPO services.

BPO VENDOR	PROCESS CATEGORY	NOTES
Adecco	Human resources	
Administaff, Inc.	Human resources	
Affiliated Computer Services (ACS)	Multiple categories	Acquired Document Acquisition Services (provider of data capture, imaging, and retrieval services) in July 1998
Ahead	Human resources	
Alliance Logistics	Procurement/logistics	Specific services: transportation/shipments
ALLTEL	Finance	Specific services: statement processing, deposit servicing
Andersen Consulting	Multiple categories	Specific services: payroll, accounting
Arthur Andersen	Multiple categories	
ASCo	Procurement/logistics	
AT&T Solutions	Human resources	
Atlantic Media	Human resources	Specific services: creation of company directories accessible via Internet
Automated Data Processing (ADP)	Human resources	Expanding beyond payroll services into other human resource–related services
Buck Consultants	Human resources	
Bruckner	Procurement/logistics	
Caliber Logistics	Procurement/logistics	
CAP Gemini	Finance	
Capita (UK)	Multiple categories	
CB Richard Ellis	Asset and property management	Merger between CB Commercial and REI Limited (UK)
Ceridian	Human resources	
CGI Group	Multiple categories	
CLW Realty Group	Asset and property management	
Computer Data Systems	Finance	Wholly owned subsidiary of Affiliated Computer Services
Computer Sciences Corporation (CSC)	Multiple categories	
Corporate Transfer Service	Multiple categories	Specific services: Employee relocation
Coventry Industries	Human resources	Acquired BSO Healthcare Industries and People First
COSI	Human resources	Specific services: payroll, tax filing
CSL (Deloitte & Touche)	Finance	Specific services: accounting
Cytex Systems Inc.	Miscellaneous	Specific services: document storage via Internet
Deloitte & Touche	Multiple categories	
Digital Work	Multiple categories	Specific services: external communications, salary/benefit research and debt collection via Internet
Dixie Carriers	Procurement/logistics	Specific services: barge fleet logistics
Duke Solutions	Miscellaneous	Specific services: energy services
Electronic Data Systems (EDS)	Multiple categories	Specific services: procurement, finance, human resources
Energy Information Centre (UK)	Procurement/logistics	Specific services: energy procurement
Enron	Miscellaneous	Specific services: energy services
Ernst & Young	Multiple categories	
Federal Express	Procurement/logistics	
First Data Corporation	Multiple categories	

(Continued)

Exhibit 1.1   BPO Vendors

BPO VENDOR	PROCESS CATEGORY	NOTES
Fiserv	Multiple categories	Specific services: tax filing; human resources
GATX Logistics	Procurement/logistics	
Genesys	Human resources	Specific services: payroll, benefits
Global Payment Systems	Accounting	
Grubb & Ellis	Asset and property management	
Healthcare Realty	Asset and property management	
IBM	Multiple categories	
Integrated Process Solutions	Finance	Joint venture between Aspect Computing, Citibank, Global Customer Solutions, and Manpower Services Australia Specific services: purchase order processing, fixed asset register, order taking, accounts receivable, customer service
Intellisource	Multiple categories	Specific services: accounting, auditing, communications, human resources, facility management, purchasing
ITNET (UK Based)	Multiple categories	Former IT Services Division of Cadbury Schweppes Specific services: benefits, payroll, pension administration, tax administration
JP Morgan Investment Management	Asset and property management	
KFPW PTY Ltd. (Australia)	Asset and property management	Joint venture between PricewaterhouseCoopers and Knight Frank of Australia
KPMG	Multiple categories	
Konsortium Perkapalan	Procurement/logistics	
LINFOX (New Zealand)	Procurement/logistics	Specific services: transportation, warehousing
Logix Services (formerly TNT Contract Logistics)	Procurement/logistics	Specific services: inventory management
Mailroom Management Services	Miscellaneous	Interoffice mail
Mark VII (Memphis)	Procurement/logistics	Specific services: transportation
Matrix	Miscellaneous	Specific services: customer service
Menlo Logistics	Procurement/logistics	Subsidiary of CNF Transportation
NovaCare Employee Services	Human resources	Specific services: payroll management, risk management, benefits administration
Novistar	Multiple categories	Subsidiary of Torch Energy Advisors Specific services: procurement, financial services
Online Benefits Inc.	Human resources	
Outsource International	Human resources	
Pay Maxx Inc.	Human resources	Specific services: payroll administration via Internet
PCS Health Systems, Inc.	Human resources	Employee health benefits
Perot Systems	Multiple categories	
PHH Relocation	Miscellaneous	Employee relocation
Pitney Bowes Management	Miscellaneous	Specific services: mailroom, duplicating, facility management *(Continued)*

Exhibit 1.1   BPO Vendors *(Continued)*

BPO VENDOR	PROCESS CATEGORY	NOTES
PricewaterhouseCoopers	Multiple categories	Specific services: finance/ accounting, internal audit, tax compliance, applications process, procurement, human resources, property management
Pro Business Services	Human resources	
Rebus HR Services	Human resources	Wholly owned subsidiary of Rebus Group PLC
REMITCO Management Corp.	Miscellaneous	Created by US Postal Service Specific services: remittance processing
Resource Partners	Human resources	
Ryder (Logistics Unit)	Procurement/logistics	
Schneider National	Procurement/logistics	
Schroder Capital Management	Asset and property management	
SEB Asset Management	Asset and property management	
Sema (Europe)	Multiple categories	
Service Master	Miscellaneous	Specific services: food processing
Shell Services	Multiple categories	Specific services: human resources and finance and accounting services
Siemens Business Services (Europe)	Miscellaneous	Specific services: airport baggage handling
Sodexho Marriott Services	Miscellaneous	Specific services: food services
SS&C Direct	Finance	Specific services: accounting and reporting
Strategic Resources Solutions	Miscellaneous	Specific services: energy services
Tasco	Finance	Joint venture between Shell and Ernst & Young
TNT Australia	Procurement/logistics	Specific services: warehousing, transportation
Torch Energy Advisors Incorporated	Multiple categories	Specific services: oil and gas accounting and transaction processing, procurement
Trigen	Miscellaneous	Specific services: energy services
Unisys	Multiple categories	
United Parcel Service of America Inc. (UPS)	Procurement/logistics	
Wackenhut Corporation	Miscellaneous	Specific services: security personnel

Exhibit 1.1 BPO Vendors (*Continued*)

1.7 BPO TRANSACTIONS

As noted earlier, in many companies one or more business processes are already being out-sourced to a third-party vendor. Exhibit 1.2 lists a number of recent BPO transactions by type of process.[26] (Please note that for the purposes of Exhibit 1.2, we have used the "process categories" identified in Section 1.3.)

---

[26] The data contained in Exhibit 1.2 have been gathered from annual reports, press releases and other public information. This list is not exhaustive by any means. It is intended to provide a sampling of recent BPO transactions.

CUSTOMER	VENDOR	PROCESS CATEGORY	ESTIMATED CONTRACT VALUE IN U.S. DOLLARS (MILLIONS)	TERM IN YEARS	POINTS OF INTEREST
Acordia	Fiserv	Administration			Tax filing
London Borough of Honnslow	ITNET	Administration		7	Council tax collection, administration of housing and council tax benefit
Ogelthorpe Power Corp.	Intellisource	Administration			Administrative and auditing services
AETNA	CLW Realty Group	Asset and property management			Real estate management
AT&T	JP Morgan Investment Management	Asset and property management			
CitiCorp.	Grubb & Ellis	Asset and property management			
Columbia/HCA Healthcare	Healthcare Realty	Asset and property management			Management of 98 properties
IBM	Grubb & Ellis	Asset and property management			
John Alden Life Insurance	CLW Realty Group	Asset and property management			
National Australia Bank (Australia)	KFPW PTY Ltd. (JV owned by PricewaterhouseCoopers and Knight Frank of Australia)	Asset and property management		5	Care and Maintenance of approx. 2,000 buildings and 13,000 real estate leases and licenses
Ogelthorpe Power Corp.	Intellisource	Asset and property management		10	Real estate management
Spartan Insurance Co.	SEB Asset Management America (SEB)	Asset and property management			25% of Spartan's general account outsourced to SEB
Spartan Insurance Co.	Schroder Capital Management (SCM)	Asset and property management			75% of Spartan's portfolio outsourced to SCM
The Traveler's Group	CLW Realty Group	Asset and property management			Real estate management
United HealthCare	CLW Realty Group	Asset and property management			Real estate management
BBC (UK)	EDS/Pricewaterhouse-Coopers	Finance			Accounting services

(Continued)

Exhibit 1.2.   BPO Transactions

CUSTOMER	VENDOR	PROCESS CATEGORY	ESTIMATED CONTRACT VALUE IN U.S. DOLLARS (MILLIONS)	TERM IN YEARS	POINTS OF INTEREST
British Airways	EDS	Finance	$56	10	Global accounting center
British Petroleum (Columbia, Venezuela)	PricewaterhouseCoopers	Finance	$25	5	Accounting and financial services
British Petroleum (Poland)	PricewaterhouseCoopers	Finance			Accounting services
British Petroleum (US)	Andersen Consulting	Finance	$120	10	Pension fund management, short-term investment management, accounts payable/receivable, accounting, treasury management
California Earthquake Authority					
CGA Investment Management	SS&C Direct	Finance			Accounting and reporting
Chittenden Bank	Global Payment Systems	Finance	$4		Merchant accounting
Dublin Corporation (Ireland)	CAP Gemini	Finance			Management of payments, IT infrastructure, inquiries, correspondence and financial reporting for ticketing/traffic control
ELF Oil UK Limited	PricewaterhouseCoopers	Finance		7	Most accounting functions; 45 accounting staff employees transferred to PWC
Investors Research Fund	ND Holdings	Finance			Accounting and distribution
Laurentian Bank of Canada (Canada)	CGI Group	Finance	$20	5	E-commerce and electronic funds transfer services
Lord Chancellor Dept. (UK)	CSL (Deloitte & Touche)	Finance	$200	9	Accounting services
Ogelthorpe Power Corp.	Intellisource	Finance		10	Accounting services
Saga Petroleum (Norway)	Andersen Consulting ANS	Finance			Accounting and financial reporting
Sears	Andersen Consulting	Finance		10	Accounting and logistics
Sheffield City Council (UK)	Deloitte & Touche	Finance	$210		Tax, billing, payroll and accounting services
Shell	Tasco (joint venture between Shell and Ernst & Young)	Finance			

(Continued)

Exhibit 1.2 BPO Transactions (Continued)

CUSTOMER	VENDOR	PROCESS CATEGORY	ESTIMATED CONTRACT VALUE IN U.S. DOLLARS (MILLIONS)	TERM IN YEARS	POINTS OF INTEREST
Sunlite Casual Furniture		Finance			Pension fund management, short-term investment management, accounts payable/receivable, accounting, treasury management
TIG Insurance	PricewaterhouseCoopers	Finance			Accounting and financial reporting
Thomas Weisel Partners	ReSource/Phoenix	Finance			Information technology management, accounting, financial reporting and transaction processing
U.S. Small Business Association	Computer Data Systems (wholly owned subsidiary of Affiliated Computer Services)	Finance	$20	1	Disaster home loan servicing; three one-year renewal options
Wilmington Savings Fund Society	Alltel	Finance			Item and statement processing, deposit servicing, overdraft processing
Acordia	Fiserv	Human resources			Payroll and human resources transactions
Allegiance Telecom Inc.	Online Benefits	Human resources			Employee policies and benefits information provided via Internet
Bombay, Inc.	ProBusiness Services	Human resources			Payroll and payroll tax services
Border Chemicals and Plastics	Resource Partners	Human resources			Operation of PeopleSoft applications
Cole Managed Vision	CSC	Human resources		5 yrs (extension of 8-year contract)	Application development, claims processing and benefits set-up, and management
Core States	Genesys	Human resources			Payroll
Firstar Corp.	Fiserv	Human resources			Payroll, human resources, and benefits processing

(Continued)

Exhibit 1.2 BPO Transactions *(Continued)*

CUSTOMER	VENDOR	PROCESS CATEGORY	ESTIMATED CONTRACT VALUE IN U.S. DOLLARS (MILLIONS)	TERM IN YEARS	POINTS OF INTEREST
GreenPoint Financial Group	Fiserv	Human resources			Payroll, check production and distribution, and tax filing
Humana	PCS Health Systems Inc.	Human resources			Pharmacy benefits
Intellicell Corp.	Administaff, Inc.	Human resources			Administaff as a Professional Employer Organization (PEO) would be co-employer, offering 401(k), retirement plan, a comprehensive health plan, employee training programs
Lucas Varity plc		Human resources			Benefits plans for 6,500 employees
Kinkos	ProBusiness Services	Human resources			Payroll and payroll taxes
Ogelthorpe Power Corp.	Intellisource	Human resources			
PECO Energy Co.	IBM	Human resources		10	Administration and payroll
Samsung (North America)	ProBusiness	Human resources			Payroll and payroll tax
Somerset County Council	ITNET	Human resources	$8		
State of Florida	Unisys	Human resources			Management of health-care program (agreement terminated)
Ascend Communications	Icon Professional Services	Miscellaneous			Independent contractor compliance programs
American Express	REMITCO	Miscellaneous			Remittance processing
Boeing	Trigen Energy	Miscellaneous			Energy services for new factory in Alabama
British Government	Capita	Miscellaneous			Management of nursery voucher schemes; administration of written driving tests
Digital	EDS	Miscellaneous			Contract administration
DirecTV	MATRIXX	Miscellaneous			Telephone customer services and sales support, including equipment dealer referrals and programming set-up

(Continued)

Exhibit 1.2 BPO Transactions (*Continued*)

CUSTOMER	VENDOR	PROCESS CATEGORY	ESTIMATED CONTRACT VALUE IN U.S. DOLLARS (MILLIONS)	TERM IN YEARS	POINTS OF INTEREST
Equistar Chemical	Trigen-Cinergy Solutions	Miscellaneous			Energy services at Tuscola, IL plant
Flowers Industries	ServiceMaster	Miscellaneous			Food processing
Iomega Corp	Icon Professional Services	Miscellaneous			Independent contractor compliance programs
KPMG	Mailroom Management Services	Miscellaneous			Interoffice mail
Kraft	Duke Solutions	Miscellaneous			Natural gas management, transitional electric, efficiency and administrative services to 70 facilities in North America
Kraft	ServiceMaster	Miscellaneous			Food processing
Merrill Lynch (UK)	Pitney Bowes Management	Miscellaneous			Interoffice mail
Novell Inc.	Icon Professional Services	Miscellaneous			Independent contractor compliance programs
Oracle	Wackenhut Corporation	Miscellaneous	$2.5/year		Security personnel (130 personnel)
Planters Lifesavers	ServiceMaster	Miscellaneous			Food processing
United HealthCare	Corporate Transfer Service, Inc. and PHH Relocation	Miscellaneous			Employee relocation
US Dept of Energy	Duke Solutions	Miscellaneous			Energy efficiency services for federal facilities in the Southeast
Wachovia Bank of Winston-Salem	Strategic Resources Solutions	Miscellaneous			Management of energy use at 708 sites in North Carolina, South Carolina, and Georgia
Xerox Corp.	Ryder (Logistics Unit)	Miscellaneous			Delivery, set up, and training for copiers
Adidas America	Caliber Logistics, Inc.	Procurement/Logistics			Warehouse/procurement management
BBC	Energy Information Centre	Procurement/Logistics			Energy purchasing
British Petroleum	PricewaterhouseCoopers	Procurement/Logistics			
Deere & Co.	Ryder (Logistics Unit)	Procurement/Logistics			Storage and moving of parts; labeling and packaging of repair kits
Dow Chemical	Dixie Carriers (Division of Kirby Corp.)	Procurement/logistics			Barge fleet logistics

(Continued)

Exhibit 1.2 BPO Transactions (Continued)

CUSTOMER	VENDOR	PROCESS CATEGORY	ESTIMATED CONTRACT VALUE IN U.S. DOLLARS (MILLIONS)	TERM IN YEARS	POINTS OF INTEREST
Dow Chemicals	Menlo Logistics	Procurement/logistics			Inbound/outbound packaged goods transportation
Dow Chemicals	Alliance Logistics	Procurement/logistics			Dry bulk shipments
Ford Motor Company	Ryder (Logistics)	Procurement/logistics			Design and management of an integrated just-in-time supply-chain and transportation system for 20 manufacturing plants
Helix Health Inc.	CSC	Procurement/logistics	$70	10	Materials management (purchasing, inventory and distribution)
Hilton Hotels Corp. (Equipment Subsidiary)	EDS	Procurement/logistics		10	EDS took over management of supplies of linens and other goods; EDS manages oracle database, accounts receivable and general ledger applications supporting the process
National Semiconductor	Federal Express	Procurement/logistics			Logistics
Nike Inc.	Menlo Logistics	Procurement/logistics			Inflation of sports equipment; packaging
Ogelthorpe Power Corp.	Intellisource	Procurement/logistics			Purchasing
OxyChem	Mark VII	Procurement/logistics			Transportation
PROTON Bhd	Konsortium Perkapalan	Procurement/logistics			
Telstra Corp.	TNT Australia	Procurement/logistics			Control over warehousing and transportation functions
The Timken Co.	Logix Services	Procurement/logistics			Inventory management and logistics
The Toro Company	GATX Logistics	Procurement/logistics			Logistics management and systems integration services
United Technologies Corp.	IBM	Procurement/logistics			Procurement of indirect or "nonproduction" sales/goods; IBM to leverage own Lotus Notes

Exhibit 1.2 BPO Transactions (*Continued*)

CHAPTER 2

PLANNING STAGE

2.1 OUTSOURCING AS AN OPTION

(a) The Directive   With the cost of some noncore business processes amounting to between 7 and 11 percent of a company's revenues,[1] senior management is paying more attention to how individual processes are being handled, looking for new ways to cut costs and increase profitability and performance. Outsourcing is seen by senior management as a means for handling, either short or long term, a particular process and, in many cases, broader organizational needs. For example, the outsourcing vendor may be willing to pay the customer a much needed upfront lump-sum payment for assets that support the business process to be outsourced or outsourcing may provide the resources to implement new methodologies and/or technologies more rapidly than the customer would have been able to accomplish with its own in-house staff. It is no surprise, then, that in most cases the directive to consider outsourcing comes from senior management, particularly since middle- or lower-level management often views outsourcing as placing their jobs at risk.

The reasons for issuing the directive to consider outsourcing varies from customer to customer and may vary depending on whether it comes from senior management or management responsible for the business process. Senior management typically decides to evaluate outsourcing as part of:

- An organization-wide directive to outsource noncore business processes
- An effort to globalize/standardize business processes throughout the organization
- An organization-wide directive to downsize or cut costs
- The reorganization of a business department, often in response to a reengineering study
- The redirection of certain methodologies/technologies in an effort to remain competitive
- An effort to enhance public perception

Managers responsible for the business process, whose reasons for considering outsourcing are often more focused, typically target outsourcing as an option:

- As part of the reorganization of all or part of the business department
- As a means to cut business process costs

---

[1] Kiely, Thomas, "Business Processes: Consider Outsourcing," *Harvard Business Review* (May/June 1997) (quoting G2R, a leading outsourcing and information services research firm).

- As a means to focus more resources on business process strategy
- In an effort to enhance performance
- As part of the roll-out of new methodologies/technology
- In order to provide lacking expertise/experience

The reasons underlying a company's decision to evaluate outsourcing as an option will affect the process, timetable, and substance of the transaction. If, for example, senior management has decided to outsource noncore capabilities as part of an organization-wide downsizing initiative or the customer wishes to sign the contract by the end of the customer's fiscal year, the customer may spend limited resources on assessing the benefits/risks of outsourcing and move quickly to the request for proposal or vendor selection stage. In other instances, for example, where the go-ahead to consider outsourcing comes from management of the business process and the primary objective is to improve performance, there may be a more lengthy evaluation and negotiation process.

(b) Obtaining Management Support and Forming the Outsourcing Team   Once the decision is made to consider outsourcing all or part of a customer's business process, it is necessary to solicit the necessary support from the department of the business process being outsourced, from senior management and, in some instances, from the board. Support from within the particular business department and from senior management is critical to moving the process along, particularly since the customer will need to commit significant resources to carrying out the evaluation, proposal, and negotiation processes. These resources include financial resources for such expenses as travel, meeting rooms, overtime, and consultant/legal fees, as well as personnel resources (top managers who will likely work exclusively on this project for several months). Many customers overlook the necessity of obtaining board support. Since the total amounts to be expended in many outsourcing contracts can be substantial, the customer should consider whether the decision to outsource is subject to board approval prior to going forward with the evaluation process or, more likely, prior to signing a contract. Even if board approval is not necessary until later, it is often useful to get the board "on board" at an early stage so that any negative perceptions or reactions can be dealt with before too many resources are expended.

The next step is to select the customer's project leader. It is important that the project leader receives clear direction about what the customer's objectives are and the time frame for achieving these objectives, and the empowerment to carry out these directions and make decisions. The project leader typically organizes a team from:

- Within the particular department being outsourced
- One or all of the following departments: purchasing, finance, human resources, legal, audit, tax, risk management and other affected areas (e.g., mergers and acquisitions may get involved if there is an asset transfer)
- Outside consultants and lawyers

It is important to get all members of the project team involved at an early stage since some pieces of the transaction may require substantial lead time.

(c) Guidelines and Internal Evaluation   Once the outsourcing team is formed, the team should consider preparing guidelines for the project, including procedures relating to confidentiality and internal and external communications. It is prudent to implement a system for marking documents (e.g., proprietary and confidential, authorized access only). Many customers also set up separate working rooms for the team, with dedicated fax and telephone lines.

An essential step—which must be executed prior to performing preliminary due diligence—is for the team to establish its top 5 to 10 objectives for outsourcing. Senior management's reasons for issuing the directive to evaluate outsourcing should help shape the customer's objective for outsourcing. It is a common outsourcing myth that the main reason that companies or government entities outsource operations is to cut costs. While the potential for immediate capital and overall cost savings exists, it is not always realized, nor is it always the primary objective in pursuing outsourcing.

In addition to cost savings, other common objectives include:

- Concentrating resources on core capabilities
- Implementing a variable cost approach
- Obtaining an immediate cash infusion (typically associated with the transfer of assets to the vendor)
- Improving overall performance
- Improving efficiency
- Improving end user/client satisfaction
- Keeping apace of industry trends
- Providing access to new methodologies/technology
- Reducing risk
- Sharing risks
- Implementing tools for growth
- Standardizing diverse methodologies/technology
- Facilitating migration to new methodologies/technology
- Managing legacy methodologies/technology while the customer or the vendor implements new methodologies/technology
- Obtaining new or additional resources
- Providing flexibility to increase or decrease resources

Once the list of objectives is compiled by the outsourcing team, it is useful to submit the list to management at an early stage for its approval. This process enables the outsourcing team to evaluate whether its initial objectives were achieved when the final deal is presented to management.

The next step is for the outsourcing candidate to commence an internal evaluation process to determine whether outsourcing is desirable from a business, financial, technological, operational, regulatory, and legal perspective. Issues to consider as part of this initial due diligence include identifying the scope of services to be outsourced and whether there are any obstacles to outsourcing (e.g., corporate initiatives, acquisition, restructuring or divesture plans, restrictive relationships with third parties, regulations). In addition, the customer should determine whether there is any precedent for outsourcing within the organization and learn how employee, asset transfer, and other issues were dealt with in previous or contemporaneous transactions. The customer should also investigate whether there is any outsourcing within the customer's organization of or relating to the particular business process, who the vendors are, and the status of the relationship. Finally, the customer should consider how outsourcing of the particular business process will impact other areas within the organization. For example, will new methodologies or technology be introduced that are not compatible with, or capable of being integrated with, existing methodologies or technology within the organization?

In addition to the tasks discussed in the preceding paragraph, at an early stage the customer should initiate an investigation into whether any approvals, authorizations, notices, or other requirements are necessary pursuant to corporate ordinance, regulation, or law. In connection with such investigation, the customer should determine the steps necessary for compliance with any such approvals, authorizations, notices, or other requirements (e.g., notice to a government agency, board approval, parent approval). Subject to the customer's confidentiality commitment, due diligence that has proved very useful in this regard is for the customer to talk to other outsourcing customers to learn from their experience (and mistakes). As the outsourcing process proceeds, the customer may wish to consult with the preferred outsourcing vendor or vendors to discuss possible corporate, regulatory, or legal requirements applicable to the customer, as well as those applicable to the vendor that may impact or involve the customer.

Any customer deciding whether to outsource will need to outline the benefits and risks of outsourcing and assess whether the benefits outweigh the risks. An example of a typical benefit/risk analysis follows:

Benefits:
- Cost savings/benefits
- Greater ability to concentrate on core business
- Implementation of wide initiatives
- Sale of assets (moving assets off books, capital infusion)
- Greater resources to move to new environment/systems in a faster timeframe
- More/varied skills and resources
- Better access to new methodologies/technology
- Training expense reduction
- Greater flexibility

Risks:
- Loss of control
- Difficulty in managing costs
- Additional liability
- Difficulty bringing business process back in-house
- Reduced flexibility

(d) Preparing a Timetable   The period of time from which a customer decides to pursue the possibility of outsourcing until the actual outsourcing contract is signed may vary from two months to three years, depending on the customer's reasons for outsourcing, the customer's and the vendor's negotiating flexibility, and the complexity of the transaction. For example, the outsourcing team may have only a couple of months to select a vendor and negotiate and sign a contract if senior management decides that the contract must be signed by a specific date so that the announcement of the outsourcing transaction coincides with the announcement of a larger organizational restructuring (e.g., a public offering). On the other hand, there may be less time pressure in situations where the business department introduces the idea of outsourcing all or part of the business process and wishes to perform due diligence prior to escalating the idea to a senior-management level for approval. In more complex transactions (e.g., those involving several international sites), it may not be the customer that dictates the timeframe as much as regulatory and legal requirements (e.g., financial institutions may need to obtain the consent of banking authorities, transborder data flow restrictions may require the customer to obtain government or agency consent, local law may impose a notice period prior to transitioning employees). From the vendor's perspective, it is almost always desirable to "close the deal" as quickly as possible.

The length of the time period that a customer has to conclude an outsourcing transaction often dictates the process. A truncated timetable invariably means cutting corners with respect to due diligence, vendor selection, and negotiation. The customer should weigh the advantages of completing the transaction within a certain period against the loss of leverage and thoroughness that may result from the short period of time. While it is desirable to spend time defining requirements, performing due diligence, preparing a comprehensive request for proposal and negotiating the transaction, there are advantages to moving the process along as expeditiously as possible, most notably that the process uses a significant amount of personnel and may involve incurring significant expenses (e.g., travel, consultants, lawyers). In addition, some customers have found that a drawn out process may be particularly damaging to employee morale. Timing is often used to obtain concessions from the party under time constraints. The vendor, for example, may wish to complete the transaction by the end of the fiscal year, and the customer may use this to its advantage if it does not have similar time constraints.

Once the customer has determined, at least generally, the time that it wishes to commit to due diligence and negotiation, it is useful to prepare a timetable of key dates relating to the outsourcing process. What is considered key will depend upon the scope of the transaction, whether the customer is putting the transaction out to bid, and whether there are regulatory restrictions. A list of key dates to keep in mind when developing the outsourcing timetable are included in Exhibit 2.1. This list is by no means exhaustive and will vary depending on the parties to the transaction, the types and scope of services being outsourced, and the requirements of the business deal. For example, time-sensitive regulatory requirements may vary for transactions involving financial institutions as opposed to retail companies or manufacturers; among asset management, benefit administration, and procurement transactions; and involving employee or asset transfers. In addition, not all of the items on the list provided in Exhibit 2.1 may be applicable to a particular transaction. For example, a customer may have advance knowledge of the vendor community or a preferred vendor and, therefore, may forego the RFI process.

ISSUE	RESPONSIBILITY	TIME FRAME
1. Select and form internal outsourcing team		
2. Establish outsourcing objectives		
3. Obtain management support		
4. Determine internal communication strategy		
5. Develop and issue RFI (if applicable)		
6. Review and evaluate RFI responses (if applicable)		
7. Develop and issue RFP		
8. Review and evaluate proposals relationship structure Definition of any teaming relationships Pricing structure Scope of services New initatives		
9. Select preferred vendor(s)		
10. Develop negotiation strategy		
11. Customer due diligence Financial Legal Regulatory Audit Tax Data-related issues Employee-related issues Site/local issues Intercompany issues		

(Continued)

Exhibit 2.1   Draft Timeline

ISSUE	RESPONSIBILITY	TIME FRAME
12. Vendor due diligence		
Pricing structure		
Scope of services		
Legal		
Regulatory		
Tax		
Data-related issues		
Employee-related issues		
Local issues		
13. Term Sheet		
Prepare term sheet		
Negotiate term sheet		
Identify key issues		
14. Service Contract(s)		
Determine contract(s) structure		
Determine parties to each contract		
Prepare contract(s)		
Negotiate contract(s)		
Identify key issues		
15. Service level agreements		
Establish service levels		
Negotiate SLAs		
16. Exhibits		
Determine applicable exhibits to contract(s)		
Delegate responsibility for each exhibit		
Legal review		
17. Employee-related issues		
Develop transition plan		
Make offers to employees		
Employee acceptance date (for each location)		
Employee start date (for each location)		
18. Approvals/notices		
Corporate approvals/notices		
Regulatory approvals/notices		
Local approvals/notices		
19. Sign contract(s)		
20. Press release (if applicable)		
21. Asset transfer (for each location) (if applicable)		
22. Notify third-party vendors (if applicable)		
23. Contract commencement date		

Exhibit 2.1　Draft Timeline (*Continued*)

(e) Internal Communications　An important issue to consider early in the planning process is how employee/internal communications will be handled. Customers typically follow one of the following three general approaches.

1. Wait until the deal is ready to be signed before telling employees
2. Tell the employees that outsourcing is being considered and that no other information is available until contract negotiations are well under way
3. Be candid with employees and communicate all steps of the outsourcing process

Wait until There Is a Deal

Pros:

- Negotiating position is not compromised by employee reactions/demands
- Negotiations are not strained by fear that employees will resign during negotiations (particularly if all employees are not being transferred and severance is not an incentive to stay)
- Less risk of leakage to the press
- Avoid false alarm—if decide not to outsource

Cons:

- Breeds distrust among general employee population
- Employees may claim that they were not treated fairly
- Allows employees little opportunity to evaluate options

On a Need-to-Know Basis

Pros:

- Breeds trust with employees
- Likelihood that employees will not leave until they know what the situation is
- Mitigates claims from employees that they were not adequately informed

Cons:

- Risk that employees will leave
- Employees may claim that they were kept in the dark
- Incomplete disclosure may result in unfounded rumors
- Possible loss of negotiation leverage since it may be difficult not to outsource once announcements are made

Be Upfront from the Start

Pros:

- Breeds trust/loyalty with employees
- Reduces risk of claims that employees were kept in the dark
- Often helps in the negotiation process to learn what employee concerns are

Cons:

- Risk that employees will resign (particularly those who will not be transferred to the vendor)
- Negotiation process may be driven by employee reactions/demands
- Poor employee morale may result in pressure to close the deal

Once a customer has chosen its approach, it will need to prepare a communication strategy. The strategy may differ and become more complicated for multisite and international transactions. The customer should ensure that all employees receive the same information at as close to the same time as possible. This typically involves close communication with all sites and prepping prior to employee communications. A more detailed discussion of employee transfer issues is set forth in Chapter 7.

2.2 DEFINING THE SCOPE OF THE TRANSACTION

(a) Defining the General Scope   For some customers, it is easy to define the general functions within the business process that will be outsourced. Part of the outsourcing directive, for example, may be to outsource all of the business process functions except for strategic planning. Other customers are not sure which business process functions to outsource, mostly because they are not sure what the vendor can deliver and how much it will cost. If a customer is not sure what to outsource, it can be beneficial to be over-inclusive of what is to be outsourced and to include a requirement that the vendor "unbundle," or provide separate pricing for, certain functions.

In addition to defining what business process functions are in scope, many customers have a difficult time determining which sites will be in scope. Is just one site being outsourced or are all sites to be outsourced? Will the deal be just the United States or will it be global? Will particular countries be out of scope? Many customers—particularly larger customers with geographically dispersed locations—spend a great deal of time assessing which sites should be outsourced and which should either stay in-house or be part of a separate transaction. The decision about whether certain sites should be included in scope is in some instances guided by local law requirements. For example, if a state or country has prohibitively high services taxes or restrictive laws relating to employee transfers, the customer may decide not to outsource services provided to or from that site or country. Another factor that affects which sites or countries are in scope is the customer's management structure. If a customer has a decentralized structure, it is often difficult to get a consensus about which sites should be outsourced. Managers often have conflicting ideas about whether outsourcing is the right solution for all sites. An option for customers who are hesitant about outsourcing is to first enter into a proof-of-concept phase, where a few sites are outsourced with the understanding that if the trial period is successful, other sites will follow.

Determining where the services will be provided will aid in assessing the complexity of the transaction—and often the cost (and consequences). Even if the deal is United States only, questions are raised regarding state and employment law issues. If foreign locations are to be included, more lead time will be necessary to assess the requirements for local approvals, authorizations, and notices. It can be time consuming and costly to coordinate with these foreign locations. One thing to keep in mind is that international transactions often require local counsel and in some instances local consultants. The outsourcing team will need to be expanded to include representatives from the various local sites.

Other issues to consider when starting to define the scope of the transaction include:

- Are any other entities currently being provided services? Will they be in scope?
- Who are the users? Employees? Customers? Suppliers? Independent consultants?
- Are any existing outsourcing or subcontracting arrangements in effect that cover in scope services? Are there costs associated with terminating or transferring these relationships?
- Will assets be transferred to the vendor?
- Will employees be transferred to the vendor?
- Consider alternative structures such as forming a joint venture, spinning the business process off into a separate entity.

Just as important as defining which services are to be outsourced is defining which services the customer wishes to keep in-house. The scope of retained responsibilities may vary from function to function with respect to financial, administrative, and operational responsibilities. For example, the vendor may assume responsibility for managing third-party maintenance while the customer retains financial responsibility for the third-party maintenance contracts. Areas that are often "retained" in whole or in part by the customer are listed next. Obviously, these areas will vary depending on the business process being considered:

- Process control
- Strategical planning

- Asset acquisition
- Technology upgrades, replacements
- Provision of office space
- Business recovery
- Office-related services
- Payment of third-party invoices
- Off-site storage
- Print
- Microfiche
- Report distribution
- Data entry
- Telephone charges

(b) Understanding Your Existing Resources It is important for any customer wishing to outsource to have a strong understanding of the tasks that its staff, responsible for the business process functions to be outsourced, performs today. This is an important early step for a number of reasons:

1. It is difficult to define which services the customer wants the vendor to provide if it does not know what it is doing today.
2. It makes writing the request for proposal and service exhibits to the outsourcing agreement less overwhelming.
3. If the customer does not have a clear and comprehensive understanding of its current tasks, it loses much at the negotiating table, particularly if the vendor has done its due diligence. We have been involved in many situations where the vendor knows more about the customer's business process environment than the customer does. The greater understanding a party has of the business environment to be outsourced, the better such party's negotiating position will be.

In addition to understanding the current scope of services being provided by the customer, it is useful to understand the customer's strengths and weaknesses with respect to the performance of these services. Often, in fact, it is the knowledge of the customer's weaknesses that serves as a strong negotiating tool in ensuring that the vendor fills these weaknesses. This is in many cases why the customer is outsourcing! If the vendor understands the customer's weaknesses better than the customer, the customer is at a disadvantage at the negotiating table.

The following sections provide an overview of areas that are useful to understand prior to issuing the request for proposal.

(i) Relevant Budget. A useful starting point in determining what the business department's existing responsibilities are is a review of the budget for such business process. The budget is often what the vendor will use to show how it can perform the same services more efficiently and at a lower cost. It is important, then, to understand the budget and to be able to clearly define what is and what is not included.

(ii) Shadow Support. One thing the budget does not often reveal is the "shadow support" the business department provides to users or the shadow support the business department receives from other departments. If there are shadow organizations that provide business services that are not within the business process department, the outsourcing team should be aware of these people and consider whether these are services that the outsourcing vendor should be responsible for and, if so, whether these people should be transferred to the

vendor. It is helpful to understand all of the seemingly minor things that the business department is responsible for. For example, if the president of the customer receives special weekly reports, this should be either included in the list of services to be provided (or covered at least generally) or provided for by some other group. If the service is not included, the president may request his or her report, and the customer will have to pay extra for it if it is not an in-scope service or provide it through internal resources if possible.

(iii) Organizational Structure.   If the customer has not already prepared a list of in-scope personnel, it is useful to do this early in the process. This can be done by preparing an organization chart specifying the names, duties, and location of each of the employees and subcontractors performing business process functions. For example, the chart should specify how many people (managers, full-time employees, part-time employees, contractors) are responsible for each function.

(iv) Management Structure.   An area to pay particular attention to is the internal management structure. Does it work? Does it work efficiently? Outsourcing is a good time to get the management structure in line with the changing role of operational management to contract management.

(v) Inventories.   One area that is inevitably lacking (particularly with customers with numerous field sites) is an inventory of assets that the customer owns, leases, or licenses that are used in connection with the provision of business process services. If the customer understands what is out there, it will be easier to evaluate whether to transfer its assets or simply allow the outsourcing vendor to use the assets to provide the services. In addition, it is difficult to understand what the upgrade, replacement, and refresh responsibilities will be without an inventory of existing assets.

(vi) Service Levels.   Another topic to consider early on is service levels. What service levels does the customer measure today? What service levels does the customer want to measure that it does not measure today? What is the industry standard? Service levels are one of the most important aspects of the outsourcing agreement, yet often attention is not paid to these levels until late in the transaction. Typically, vendors will commit to what the customer is doing today or better, but what is it that the customer is doing today? If the customer does not know prior to entering into the outsourcing transaction or does not have historical data to analyze, the vendor will often take the position that it will measure the service levels over a period of time ranging from 30 to 180 days after the effective date of the agreement. The more the customer can get a foot up on service levels, the better service levels it will likely be able to negotiate.

(vii) Critical Services.   Another area that is often overlooked until too late is critical services. The customer is outsourcing a business process—which services within the business process does it really care about? Which services, if they are not provided for an hour, a couple of hours, a day, a week, would it cause serious damage to the customer (would it cause you to lose your job)? Customers often do not have a defined list of critical functions. If the customer has an understanding of its critical functions early on, it can negotiate more stringent remedies if these critical functions are not met. Defining a customer's critical functions is not always easy. In fact, in some instances, it may not be possible or may be subjective. What is critical to one employee or user may not be as critical to another.

(c) Developing A Long-Range Plan   Many customers find it useful to develop a long range plan prior to issuing an RFP. Where would the customer like to see its business process operations in the next three, five, and seven years? For example, does the customer wish to upgrade or standardize its methodologies or technology? The long-range plan should include a list of all of the projects that the customer foresees implementing in the next three, five, and seven years. What are the anticipated costs of these projects? Does the customer want these projects to be in-scope? Does the customer wish to obtain from the vendor a pool of resources to perform these projects or will each project be priced separately? Other aspects of the long-range plan should include upgrades and replacements, as well as any significant capital expenditures. The customer will need to consider which upgrades, replacements, and other capital expenditures are part of the business deal.

The customer will need to build into its analysis what the customer's business needs are currently and in the future—this includes new or divested sites and any anticipated expansion or downsizing. More often than not, the outsourcing team works in a vacuum, and part way into negotiations, someone will tell the team that some significant restructuring or organization-wide initiative will affect the transaction. If possible, the outsourcing team should be tapped into management—its own and often its parent's—to understand the direction the overall customer organization is going in.

Finally, the customer will need to evaluate the extent to which corporate initiatives in respect of other business processes may impact the outsourcing of this particular business process. For example, the customer would be better positioned if it was aware of a corporate initiative to move to a certain technological environment so that it can ensure that the vendor technology is compatible with such customer environment. Another example is where there is a mandate within the customer organization to comply with certain standard technology and the technology proposed by the vendor is not within the standard package.

2.3 SELECTING A GROUP OF POTENTIAL VENDORS

(a) Making the First Move   Once the customer has decided to move forward with assessing outsourcing as an option, the customer will need to identify the potential vendor or vendors that have the resources, capabilities, and requisite experience to provide the desired services. In some cases, the customer will not have to look far. Unless the decision to evaluate outsourcing has been kept confidential, the vendors will hear through the grapevine, through an existing relationship with the customer, or through the vendor's marketing efforts that the customer is considering outsourcing. The organization may already be targeted as a potential outsourcing customer. Even if the customer has an existing relationship with the vendor and thinks that in the long run this vendor is the right match for the customer, the customer should seriously consider performing at least minimal due diligence to see who else can provide similar services. Such due diligence enables the outsourcing team to demonstrate that it has evaluated all of its alternatives with respect to the chosen vendor. Government agencies, government contractors, and publicly held companies should keep in mind that they may be required to look at more than one vendor pursuant to government or security regulations.

Some customers have an idea about whom to talk to, some do not know who is out there (this is particularly true for international outsourcing deals—U.S.-based business departments typically do not have reason to be familiar with vendors in foreign markets). If the customer has an idea of whom to talk to—or if the customer knows the vendors that it wants to target—it is useful to draw up a long list, then, after doing due diligence on the vendors, shortening this list to the target vendors (typically between three and eight vendors). If the customer is not familiar with all of the potential vendors, the customer may wish to:

- Obtain vendor information from industry reports/surveys
- Look at industry publications
- Talk to other outsourcing customers

(b) Vendor Experience and Resources   The next step is to commence due diligence on the pool of vendors that the customer is targeting. Due diligence may include:

- Issuing a request for information (RFI)
- Talking to outsourcing clients
- Visiting outsourcing clients' sites
- Visiting vendor sites
- Checking customer's previous experience with vendor
- Performing a newspaper search for recent articles
- Checking litigation involving vendor
- Obtaining annual reports
- Obtaining industry surveys/reports

During due diligence, the customer is able to begin to sense which vendors have the resources and experience to provide the desired services. Useful questions to ask during due diligence either on a formal basis (e.g., through a written RFI) or an informal basis (e.g., during a telephone interview) include:

Vendor reputation. What is the vendor's reputation in your industry? What is the vendor's reputation in each of the countries where the customer wishes to outsource? Are there any conflicts or problems? Will the vendor's reputation or culture fit in with the customer's reputation or culture?

Vendor history. What is the vendor's history? How long has it been in business? What has its market share been during the period that it has been in business? Have there been any unusual peaks or valleys? Has the vendor been in any significant or relevant disputes or litigations?

Financial security. Is the vendor financially secure? What is the vendor's market share? Has the vendor acquired/divested entities recently? Ask for a copy of the most recent financial statements, annual report. Are there any pending or threatened claims that could affect the vendor's financial standing?

Organization. How is the vendor organized? By industry? By value of contract? Is there one international outsourcing entity or is there a web of local entities that work together?

Resource distribution. Where are the vendor's main service centers? Where are the vendor's employees located? Does the vendor have resources in the locations that your organization requires them? What are the extent of these resources (e.g., does the vendor really have an office in Singapore)?

Experience—customer environment. Does the vendor have experience with your current/future environment? Does the vendor have the capabilities to provide other services (e.g., reengineering)? Ask for examples and references.

Experience—industry. Does the vendor have experience dealing with customers in your particular industry? Ask for examples and references.

Employee transition. What is the vendor's experience transitioning employees? How many transitions has the vendor done? In what states/countries? Has the vendor ever been sued in connection with a transition?

Roll-out. What is the vendor's experience with implementing new methodologies/technology?

Customer base/references. Ask for references and contact names.

Subcontractors/partners. Does the vendor typically partner with another entity to provide certain services? Who? What is the relationship with the partner?

(c) The RFI   If a customer does not have easy access to information regarding certain vendors that it is interested in or the customer is particularly concerned about documenting all phases of the selection process, one approach is to conduct a formal request for information (RFI) process. RFIs have proven to be particularly useful to customers who want to outsource overseas who do not know much about potential overseas vendors and customers who are not necessarily interested in doing business with one of the top outsourcers. However, customers who have targeted vendors or are dealing with an industry with which they are very familiar typically feel that issuing an RFI delays the selection process. Much of the information requested in the RFI could be requested in the customer's RFP. In addition, some customers feel that vendors will not answer the questions other than by providing promotional materials.

The RFI is typically issued by the customer on a confidential basis or by the customer's consultant without direct reference to the customer. The main reasons for keeping the identity of the customer confidential are to minimize disclosure to employees, consultants, and the public (particularly shareholders) prior to making any formal decision as to whether outsourcing is a viable option and unwanted marketing or sales calls. An example of a generic RFI is set forth in Appendix 2.4. Any RFI will need to be tailored to the organization's particular outsourcing requirements.

(d) Narrowing the Vendor Group Most customers choose to narrow to between three and eight the group of vendors the customer will seriously consider or, if the customer will be issuing an RFP, to which the RFP will be distributed. The screening process typically involves taking the long list of vendors developed during initial due diligence and determining which among the top vendors meets the customer's requirements. As part of the screening process, it may be a usual exercise to distribute to the outsourcing team (and members of management if appropriate) a list of the vendors, a list of criteria on which to judge the vendors, and a system pursuant to which the vendors can be ranked for each of the criteria. The results of the team's evaluations can then be compiled and used to select the top three to eight vendors. Sample criteria and evaluation models are set forth in Appendix 3.1.

2.4 REQUEST FOR PROPOSAL

(a) Single Bid vs. Multiple Bids In some cases, customers decide early in the process that they are going to issue the RFP to only one vendor. While this is generally not the recommended approach, it may make sense in situations where:

- The customer has a history with one particular vendor who is familiar with the customer's organization
- The customer is under considerable and real pressures to get the deal done

There are, however, significant disadvantages to requesting a bid from only one vendor. The most obvious is that the customer forfeits substantial negotiating leverage. Where else can the customer turn? Other disadvantages may include:

- Impact on pricing and service level commitments because the bid is not competitive
- No comparative data or pricing
- The vendor may be less flexible
- Sending a negative message to other vendors (why bid on other projects if they do not have a chance?)

For some outsourcing candidates, single bidding is not an option.

- Government contractors may be required to go out to competitive bid in order to comply with federal acquisitions regulations.
- Government entities are usually required to go out to competitive bid.
- In some cases, publicly held companies are required to obtain competitive bids (may be true where there is a substantial expenditure or it is necessary to show that the contract is competitive for corporate audit purposes).

For most customers, requesting multiple bids is the preferred approach because it:

- Adds to project legitimacy
- Demonstrates that due diligence was performed
- May lead to competitive pricing or service levels
- Enables the customer to use the possibility of other interested vendors as a negotiating tool
- Provides access to alternative solutions

(b) Single Vendor vs. Multiple Vendors   Prior to issuing an RFP the outsourcing customer should determine whether it wishes to request bids from single vendors for all of the services (i.e., single source outsourcing) or bids from different vendors for different areas of the services (i.e., multisourcing). There are significant differences between "unisourcing" and multisourcing. The most compelling difference is that they require different internal management structures. Multisourcing requires a broader internal management equipped to manage several vendors at a time. In addition, there are liability issues: unisourcing allows the customer to look to one party for performance, while multisourcing may allow a vendor to look to the other vendors for responsibility.

There are also cost benefits and risks associated with the two approaches. Bundling services together may allow the vendor to quote a better overall price for the services. On the other hand, if the vendor is not an expert in a particular area—and therefore has to build the necessary infrastructure or hire a subcontractor—it may be more cost effective for the customer to contract directly with the subcontracting organization.

(c) Preparing the RFP   Most customers wish to issue a formal RFP outlining the customer's objectives in outsourcing and detailing the scope of services to be outsourced. Preparing the RFP is useful not only in obtaining vendor responses but in forcing the customer's internal team to formally establish and document its objectives, business requirements, and scope of services. The content of the outsourcing RFP varies greatly from customer to customer. The following checklist shows some common RFP topics. A sample RFP is provided in Appendix 2.5

Introduction
1. *Cover Letter.* Include a general cover letter outlining your intentions. Note which provisions are binding upon the vendor (e.g., confidentiality, response requirements). Attach an Intent to Bid form and ask the vendor to fill in the form within a week or so. This will give you early warning signs as to how many vendors will be bidding and whether there are any vendors who will "no bid" the deal.
2. *RFP Format.* Identify on the cover sheet what the document is meant to cover. Include a general confidentiality provision. Number the RFPs being distributed and fill in to whom the RFP is distributed. Include a table of contents and a list of appendices.
3. *Objectives and Overview.* Describe in general terms the functions that the customer wishes to outsource. Describe what the customer's goals and objectives are (cost savings, enhanced performance, new environment).
4. *Proposal Submission Date.* Note the date the proposal is due.
5. *How to Respond.* Describe how the vendor should respond (e.g., number of copies, copy on a disk—be sure to note disk requirements). Who should responses be sent to? Does the customer require sealed envelopes, no taxes?
6. *Proposal Format.* Describe the format the proposal should follow. It is useful when evaluating the proposals that all proposals follow the same format.
7. *Customer Contacts.* Note whom the vendor may contact for which areas.
8. *Communications.* Outline how communications with the customer should be handled (e.g., in writing only, by phone).

9. *Clarifications.* Describe how questions or clarifications should be handled.
10. *Vendor Presentations.* Include a provision either requiring or giving you the option to require that the vendor make a presentation at the customer's site.
11. *Confidentiality.* This provision may prove to be <u>very important</u>. Include a detailed confidentiality provision. You may even wish to require the vendor to sign a confidentiality agreement prior to disseminating the RFPs.
12. *Ownership.* Note that the customer will retain ownership of all of its data and that the vendor must return all customer data upon request. The customer may wish to identify who owns the proposal—or at least specify that the customer has the right to use any materials in the proposal.
13. *Scope of Proposal.* Note that the vendor's proposal should be as comprehensive as possible and reflect the vendor's best bid. If the vendor will not be bidding on some or all of the services, this should be noted up front.
14. *Multivendor Proposals.* If the vendor is partnering or plans to subcontract any portion of the services, this should be specified. The vendor should describe the services to be provided by the other party, the role of the other party in the outsourcing relationship, and the relationship between the responding vendor and the other party.
15. *Time Table.* Outline the key dates in the RFP/proposal process.
16. *Firm Offer.* Note that all offers should be firm for a period of time (e.g., 60–180 days).
17. *No Obligation.* Note that the customer is under no obligation to enter into an agreement with any vendor.
18. *Right to Negotiate with Other Parties.* Include a sentence reserving the right to negotiate with other parties.
19. *Costs/Expenses.* The vendor is typically responsible for paying all of its own costs and expenses incurred prior to contract signing.

Vendor Background Information
20. *General Information.* Ask for general background information (e.g., number of employees, locations).
21. *Industry Information.* What is the vendor's experience in the customer's industry?
22. *Financial Information.* Ask for information regarding the vendor's financial status, annual revenue, and position in the industry. Ask for copies of vendor annual quarterly reports and financial statements.
23. *Organization.* How is the vendor organized? What is the management structure?
24. *Resources.* How are the vendor's resources dispersed? Where are they located?
25. *Customer Base/References.* Ask for a summary of the vendor's customer base and at least three references.
26. *Partners/Subcontractors.* Ask for the same information for any partners/subcontractors.

Customer Background Information
27. *General Description of Customer.* Provide general background information—type of business, size, locations.
28. *Description of Existing Services.* Describe existing services to be outsourced (e.g., functions, locations).
29. *Description of Short- and Long-Term Goals.* Describe where the customer would like to be in the future (e.g., 3, 5, 10 years).

Services to Be Provided
30. *Services.* Provide a description of existing services and the services that the vendor will be required to provide.

31. *Locations.* List affected locations or entities.
32. *Transition.* Ask for a description of the plan pursuant to which the vendor will assume responsibility for the customer's business process functions. Require the vendor to identify any hurdles to outsourcing (e.g., regulatory approvals, notices).
33. *Migration.* Ask for a description of the plan pursuant to which the vendor will migrate functions to vendor locations and methodologies/technology (if applicable).
34. *New Environments.* Describe new environments. Ask vendor to describe proposed solution and implementation strategy.
35. *Projects.* Describe any projects that the vendor will be required to undertake.
36. *Services Not Provided.* Ask the vendor to list any services that it expressly will not be providing. In addition, ask the vendor to list those services that it expects the customer to provide.

Performance

37. *Service Levels.* Describe current service level measurements (if available). Specify service levels that the vendor will be required to meet.
38. *Liquidated Damages.* Require vendor to indicate how liquidated damages will be applied in the event that the vendor does not achieve service level commitments.
39. *Root Cause Analysis.* Require vendor to perform a root cause analysis for any service failures.
40. *Reports.* Describe reporting requirements with respect to service level.
41. *Benchmarking.* Describe benchmarking procedures.
42. *Customer Satisfaction Surveys.* How will vendor implement customer satisfaction surveys?

Management and Control

43. *Management Procedures.* Ask the vendor to describe.
44. *Change Control.* How will change be implemented?

Employee Issues

45. *Transfer of Employees.* Will any employees be made offers by the vendor?
46. *Offers.* What compensation or benefits will offers include? The customer should clearly specify any desired employment terms (see Chapter 7).
47. *Transition Plan.* How will the vendor transition the employees?
48. *Employment Agreement.* Ask for a copy of any employment agreement that transferred employees will be asked to sign.

Project Staff

49. *Project Executive.* There is typically a requirement that the vendor provide the name and qualifications of the initial project executive. The customer should be provided the opportunity to meet and interview the candidate. The customer should also reserve approval rights over all project executive appointments. The vendor may be prohibited from "churning" project executives (e.g., specify minimum duration of appointment).
50. *Key Employees.* Similar to the section on project executives, there is typically a requirement that the vendor provide the name and qualifications of any key employees in addition to the project executive. This usually includes the project executive's direct reports as well as employees key to certain projects. The customer should be provided the opportunity to meet and interview the candidates. The customer should reserve approval rights over all key employee appointments. The vendor should also be prohibited from churning key employees (e.g., specify minimum duration of appointment).
51. *Organization.* Ask the vendor to provide an organizational chart.

Pricing

52. *Pricing.* The customer may wish to include its budget. (Note: Some customers take the position that they do not want to provide their pricing information until they have chosen a preferred vendor.)

53. *Base Case.* Ask the vendor to provide its best base case figures. The vendor should clearly specify what is included and what is not.

54. *Unbundle.* Ask the vendor to provide separate pricing for functions or projects (if desirable).

55. *Volumes.* How will changes in volume affect the price?

56. *Growth.* Is any growth built into the price?

57. *Methodologies/Hardware/Software.* What is included and excluded?

58. *Baseline Adjustments.* How will adjustments be handled? What are the customer's requirements?

59. *Incremental Fees.* Describe the mechanism pursuant to which the vendor will increase or decrease services. In some cases, rates should be provided on an hourly, weekly, and monthly case.

60. *Additional Services.* How will additional services be priced?

61. *Significant Changes.* Note that significant changes in business requirements should trigger renegotiation or changes to pricing structure.

62. *COLA.* How will cost-of-living adjustments be handled?

63. *Currency.* What currency will payments be made in? Who bears the currency risk?

64. *Taxes.* Who will be responsible for services and other taxes?

65. *New/Divested Entities.* How will new or divested entities be handled?

66. *Invoicing.* Describe desired timing for invoice payment. In addition describe invoice detail.

Termination

67. *Termination.* Specify circumstances that may trigger termination, for example:
    - Convenience
    - Cause
    - Failure to provide critical services
    - Change of control

68. *Termination Assistance.* What assistance will the vendor provide upon termination?

69. *Exit Rights.* What rights will the parties have upon expiration or termination (e.g., with respect to methodologies, technology, assets, third-party service contracts)?

Contract Terms

70. *Intellectual Property.* What will each party's rights be with respect to customer proprietary intellectual property, vendor proprietary intellectual property, and third-party intellectual property?

71. *Required Consents.* Who will be responsible for paying for or obtaining third-party consents?

72. *Insurance.* What are the customer's insurance requirements?

Appendices

73. *Reference Exhibits.* In many cases, the customer will already have prepared a large amount of the ancillary information typically attached to the RFP (e.g., inventory lists, service levels).

Terms and Conditions

74. *Terms and Conditions.* Consider attaching a general outline of terms and conditions to the RFP. (An example of a term sheet is provided in Appendix 4.2.)

CHAPTER **3**

SELECTING THE VENDOR

3.1 EVALUATING THE PROPOSALS

Once final proposals are received from the vendors, the outsourcing team will need to take some time to review each of the them and evaluate which vendor or vendors are best suited to provide the desired services. The time period allotted for proposal review and evaluation typically ranges from two to eight weeks. The structure and scope of the vendor evaluation process will vary depending on the customer's approach, the number of vendors being evaluated, time constraints and audit and report requirements. Common steps include:

- Selecting key evaluation criteria
- Identifying who will be asked to participate in the ranking of vendors
- Establishing a scoring system
- Weighting the key criteria
- Implementing final sign-off procedures

By the end of the evaluation period, the customer should have identified a preferred vendor or vendors (depending upon whether the customer elects to negotiate with one or more vendors).

Evaluation Criteria

To facilitate the evaluation process, it is helpful to prepare a list of key criteria on which to judge the vendors and their proposals. The items included on this list should reflect the customer's list of objectives for outsourcing. For example, if one of the customer's main objectives for outsourcing is to cut costs, then the vendors' financial proposals will likely be a key criteria. Similarly, if a key objective for outsourcing is to move the customer to a new environment, then the vendors' proposed solutions will likely be considered key. The types of criteria that a customer considers key will vary depending on the scope, value, and complexity of the proposed outsourcing transaction. A customer wishing to outsource services in the United States will have different (and likely fewer) criteria than a customer wishing to outsource in multiple countries. Examples of key criteria include:

- The Proposed Solution
    Methodologies
    Technology (hardware/software/network)

    Configuration
    Committed resources
    Innovativeness
    Flexibility
    Fit with customer's environment/organization
    Willingness to share risk

- Ability to Deliver Services
  Experience/skill levels of staff
  Methodologies
  Technology (hardware/software/network)
  Vendor reputation
  Vendor experience
  Proposed implementation schedules
  Physical security
  Data security
  Disaster recovery/business continuation

- Ability to Implement New Methodologies or Technology
  Technical resources/ability
  Access to new methodologies or technology
  Flexibility
  Innovativeness
  Open methodologies or technology vs. proprietary methodologies or technology
  Willingness to use third-party products
  Implementation schedules
  Remedies for failing to meet schedules

- Ability to Meet Performance Standards
  Methodology
  Proposed service levels
  Remedies for failing to meet service levels
  Benchmarking services
  Benchmarking service levels

- Value-Added Services
  Profit sharing
  Incentive mechanisms
  Access to new methodologies or technology
  Cross-marketing

- Financial Proposal
  Base pricing
  Variable pricing
  Cost savings
  Budget comparison
  Ability to increase or decrease services
  Cost-of-living adjustments
  Taxes
  Payment schedule
  Expenses

- Vendor Reputation/Financial Standing
  Financial stability
  Quality of personnel
  Vendor culture
  Prior or existing customer relationships
  Vendor presence in customer locations

- Vendor Experience
  Outsourcing experience
  Experience in industry
  References
  Number of clients
  Experience in relevant Locations

- Vendor Flexibility
  Adjustment of services
  Adjustment of fees
  Adjustment of service levels
  Ability to add or take away entities
  Ability to terminate early
  Ability to Terminate in Part

- Keeping Abreast of Industry Developments
  Hardware
  Software
  Network
  Methodologies
  Processes
  Tools
  Regulations
  Taxes

- Terms and Conditions
  Proprietary rights
  Third-party consents
  Indemnities
  Insurance
  Rights to terminate
  Rights upon termination
  Audit rights
  Damages

- Human Resources
  Number of employees to be transitioned
  Salary
  Health benefits
  Deductibles/Co-payment
  Bonuses
  Savings plans
  Retirement plans
  Severance
  Preemployment screening
  Employment agreement

The Respondents

Once the evaluation criteria are agreed upon by the outsourcing team, the customer should rank the vendors based on their fulfillment of the criteria. This can be done formally or informally. To benefit from the judgment of each member of the outsourcing team, many customers implement a voting system allowing each team member to submit his or her individual assessment of the proposals and vendors. In many cases, the group of people participating in the evaluation process extends beyond the outsourcing team and may include other key players, such as the CIO and members of senior management. Certain members of the outsourcing team may be asked only to submit evaluations on certain criteria (e.g., human resources may be asked only to evaluate the human resources piece of the proposal, while other members of the outsourcing team—e.g., outside consultants—may not be asked to participate in the evaluation process at all). It is useful for audit and reporting purposes for the customer to keep or ask the respondents to keep any documentation or data used to support the respondents' assessments.

Scoring

Next, a scoring system should be established. Each of the criteria should be assigned a score ranging from poor to outstanding. A common (and easy to tally) scoring system is to rank the vendors in each category from 1 to 10, where 1 = poor, 5 = acceptable, and 10 = outstanding.

Weighting the Criteria

Not all evaluation criteria may be of equal importance. For example, the technical solution and human resources may each be considered key criteria, while greater importance may be placed on one rather than the other depending on the transaction. Customers engaging in more formal (or structured) evaluation processes should consider weighting each of the criteria to reflect the importance given to each. A common approach for weighting the criteria is to assign a weight or percentage to each general category, with the total of all of the weights equaling 100 percent (see Exhibit 3.1). Some customers assign weights to subcategories of the general categories in order to allow for a more detailed analysis. Again, weights or percentages are assigned to each subcategory, with the total of all of the weights equaling 100 percent (see Exhibit 3.2). The total weighted score of the subcategories should then be inserted as the raw score for the general category on Exhibit 3.1.

Tallying the Ballots

After the evaluation ballots have been filled out and returned to the outsourcing team leader or his or her designee, the results should be tallied (see Exhibit 3.3). Although the customer typically chooses to keep the individual ballots confidential, the tally of all of the ballots is usually distributed to the outsourcing team and senior management.

Criteria	Weight	Raw Score	Score	Weighted
Proposed solutions	25%			
Ability to deliver services	25%			
Financial proposal	25%			
Terms and conditions	5%			
Human resources	20%			
Total	100%			

Exhibit 3.1   General Categories Weight Assignment

Financial Proposal	Weight	Raw Score	Score	Weighted
Base pricing	25%			
Variable pricing	15%			
Overall cost savings	10%			
Ability to increase/				
decrease services	20%			
Cost-of-living adjustments	10%			
Taxes	10%			
Payment schedule	5%			
Expenses	5%			
Total	100%			

Exhibit 3.2   Subcategories Weight Assignment

Final Selection Process

Once the ballots have been tallied, the outsourcing team should take a final look at the top vendor or vendors. This can be done in a number of ways:

- An informal sign-off from the outsourcing team
- An informal sign-off from senior management
- A formal approval vote by the outsourcing team and/or senior management
- A formal letter of approval from senior management

Some customers go so far as to have respondents who disagree with the top vendor or vendors to note the reasons for such disagreement.

3.2 NOTIFYING THE PREFERRED VENDOR(S)

(a) Making the Announcement   The manner in which the preferred vendor or vendors are to be notified should be discussed by the outsourcing team and senior management. Depending on the size of the proposed transaction, a member of the customer's senior management may wish to contact a member of the vendor's senior management and advise him or her of the decision. In other cases, the outsourcing team leader will notify the lead contact person for the vendor or vendors of the decision. Issues for the customer to keep in mind when making the announcement include:

- Reserve the right to negotiate with other vendors
- Refrain from making any promises or representations regarding entering into a definitive agreement
- Identify key issues that must be resolved (e.g., the price must come down a certain percentage)
- Emphasize that all negotiations and communications are confidential
- Note that the vendor should not make statements to customer employees or the press without the customer's consent
- Obtain a commitment that the vendor will provide a top negotiating team that is empowered to make decisions
- Discuss the proposed schedule

(b) Commitment and Costs   The preferred vendor or vendors typically will need to (or be asked to) increase the number of personnel working on the potential deal. Such personnel may include:

- A senior manager empowered to make decisions
- Marketing representatives
- Proposed project executive(s)

VENDOR A

Ballot 1

Criteria	Weight	Score
Proposed solutions	25%	5
Ability to deliver services	25%	8
Financial proposal	25%	6
Terms and conditions	5%	6
Human resources	20%	6
	100%	

Ballot 2

Criteria	Weight	Score
Proposed solutions	25%	10
Ability to deliver services	25%	9
Financial proposal	25%	9
Terms and conditions	5%	8
Human resources	20%	8
	100%	

Ballot 3

Criteria	Weight	Score
Proposed solutions	25%	7
Ability to deliver services	25%	7
Financial proposal	25%	5
Terms and conditions	5%	5
Human resources	20%	7
	100%	

VENDOR B

Ballot 1

Criteria	Weight	Score
Proposed solutions	25%	6
Ability to deliver services	25%	9
Financial proposal	25%	7
Terms and conditions	5%	6
Human resources	20%	8
	100%	

Ballot 2

Criteria	Weight	Score
Proposed solutions	25%	10
Ability to deliver services	25%	9
Financial proposal	25%	9
Terms and conditions	5%	8
Human resources	20%	8
	100%	

Ballot 3

Criteria	Weight	Score
Proposed solutions	25%	7
Ability to deliver services	25%	9
Financial proposal	25%	9
Terms and conditions	5%	8
Human resources	20%	8
	100%	

VENDOR C

Ballot 1

Criteria	Weight	Score
Proposed solutions	25%	4
Ability to deliver services	25%	4
Financial proposal	25%	4
Terms and conditions	5%	5
Human resources	20%	5
	100%	

Ballot 2

Criteria	Weight	Score
Proposed solutions	25%	6
Ability to deliver services	25%	5
Financial proposal	25%	5
Terms and conditions	5%	5
Human resources	20%	5
	100%	

Ballot 3

Criteria	Weight	Score
Proposed solutions	25%	5
Ability to deliver services	25%	4
Financial proposal	25%	4
Terms and conditions	5%	4
Human resources	20%	5
	100%	

TALLY Number of Respondents: 3 — Best possible Score: 30

Vendor A

Criteria	Weight	Score	Value
Proposed solutions	25%	22	5.5
Ability to deliver	25%	24	6
Financial proposal	25%	20	5
Terms and conditions	5%	19	.95
Human resources	20%	21	4.2
	100%		21.65

Vendor B

Criteria	Weight	Score	Value
Proposed solutions	25%	23	5.75
Ability to deliver	25%	27	6.75
Financial proposal	25%	25	6.25
Terms and conditions	5%	22	1.1
Human resources	20%	24	4.8
	100%		24.65

Vendor C

Criteria	Weight	Score	Value
Proposed solutions	25%	15	3.75
Ability to deliver	25%	13	3.25
Financial proposal	25%	13	3.25
Terms and conditions	5%	14	.7
Human resources	20%	15	3
	100%		13.95

Exhibit 3.3 Sample Ranking

- Business process experts
- Methodology or technology experts
- Tax expert(s)
- A dedicated human resources representative
- Legal counsel
- Industry experts (e.g., retail consultant)
- Local representatives, counsel (for international deals)
- Temporary staff (if customer staff is at critically low levels)
- Due diligence team
- Contract administrators

This commitment may also include increasing nonpersonnel resources (e.g., access to certain technologies, temporary loan of equipment, travel expenditures). The customer will likely also need to step up its commitment of personnel and resources to keep up with the team put together by the vendor(s).

With the increase in personnel and resources committed by the customer and the vendor(s), there should be at least an understanding between the customer and the vendor(s) as to how costs and expenses will be allocated. Typically, the customer and the vendor(s) each bear their own costs and expenses. In some cases, however, the customer may agree to pay for some or all of a vendor's expenses (e.g., cost of temporary staff provided to the customer in the event a definitive agreement is not entered into with the vendor or certain travel expenses).

(c) Letters of Intent   The preferred vendor may push for the customer to enter into a letter of intent with the vendor which, at a minimum, sets out the general objectives of the parties. Vendors typically want to include a provision in the letter of intent that provides that the customer will enter into exclusive negotiations with the vendor for a certain number of days. Other common provisions include allocating costs and expenses, indemnifications for representations made to customer employees, and restatement of the parties' confidentiality obligations.

Letters of intent are usually not appropriate if the customer is negotiating with two or more vendors simultaneously. Obviously the customer could not commit to an exclusivity arrangement if it intends to negotiate with more than one vendor at a time. Most customers resist signing anything with the indicia that there is a commitment between the parties prior to the signing of the definitive agreement. In cases where the customers have agreed to sign a letter of intent, it is because they have been relatively confident that they would ultimately sign a definitive agreement with the vendor. Examples of letters of intent are set forth in Appendices 3.2 and 3.3.

(d) Communication Strategy   Once the customer has selected the preferred vendor or vendors, the customer will need to decide whether to make an internal announcement to employees and/or a formal announcement to the press. A customer's decision to announce the selection of a preferred vendor will depend largely on whether it has chosen one or multiple vendors with whom to continue negotiations. If the customer has decided to engage in simultaneous negotiations with several vendors, it is unlikely that the customer (or the vendors) will wish to announce this strategy.

If one vendor is selected, the decision to announce the selection of a preferred vendor often depends upon the customer's communication strategy with its employees. Announcing the selection to customer employees often leads to a leak to the press. Many customers who choose to announce the selection of a preferred vendor to employees simultaneously issue a press release. Customers who elect not to make an announcement to employees or to the press at the preferred vendor selection phase typically do so because they feel that they may forfeit negotiating power, lose the interest of other vendors, cause unwarranted public speculation or, possibly, impact public perception (including stock prices).

CHAPTER 4

NEGOTIATIONS: STRATEGY AND PROCESS

4.1 FORGING THE LEGAL RELATIONSHIP

Neither party in an outsourcing negotiation is likely to be able to obtain whatever it has determined to be the optimal contract because a negotiation is by definition a process of give and take. The customer and the vendor may, however, endeavor to obtain a *fair* contract that will anticipate the likely occurrences over the term and establish an executable mechanism for resolving disputes and adding additional work. For both sides to accomplish this goal, each must first evaluate the basic risks and rewards with respect to the transaction.

The initial step in a risk/reward evaluation is for each party to determine precisely why it wishes to enter into the outsourcing arrangement. Most parties are able to develop a list of three to five key objectives, and these objectives become the foundation from which negotiations begin. All too often, however, defining objectives is the only formal strategy that the customer applies during negotiations. As a result, the customer is often at a disadvantage during negotiations because the vendor is at least presumably experienced in negotiating outsourcing agreements and more familiar with the ebb and flow of the negotiations process. The principal cause of this power imbalance is that the typical customer does not view negotiating the contract as part of the outsourcing process. Instead, he or she merely regards the contract as a necessary evil. The typical vendor, on the other hand, regards the contract as the final stage in the sales cycle, and its representatives are schooled on how best to close the deal while at the same time protecting the vendor to the greatest extent possible given the value of the transaction.

Forging the legal relationship between the parties is all too often regarded as an administrative task. Although it is true that lawyers often plan the divorce before the marriage is consummated, it is equally true that too many businesspeople take the wedding vows without reading the prenuptial agreement. The contract must be regarded as part of the outsourcing process—perhaps not the most important part but a significant part. Accordingly, the representatives of both parties should be well versed in the various subject matters that are dealt with in a BPO agreement (e.g., human resources, tax, insurance). This will allow the parties to avoid unnecessary conflicts over issues with little or no practical effect on the project.

At this point, a brief examination of the contract's role is in order. A contract is a sword or shield to be used in the event of a dispute between the parties. This ultimate purpose should be kept in mind during the negotiation and the preparation of the agreement. It can be safely assumed that most business people desire to live up to their obligations and that most of them substantially do so. The contract, then, must address the various matters that are to be accomplished and must focus responsibility on the party whose obligation it is to accomplish each one. Most disputes arise when the parties have failed to consider some potential problem and have neglected to specify in the contract who will be responsible.

Finally, this chapter is not intended as a text on negotiation, but instead is intended to highlight some of the issues that the parties should consider as part of negotiations. This discussion is not an argument for tough contracts; it is a plea for well-thought-out, clearly articulated, and detailed contracts. If the duties, obligations, and expectations of each party are expressed, negotiated, agreed to (with an understanding of their implications), and clearly set forth in a written agreement, the chances that both parties will be satisfied with the contract are increased immensely.

4.2 NEGOTIATING PROCESS

Steps in the negotiation process that both the customer and the vendor may wish to consider when developing their negotiation strategy are:

Understand negotiating position. The strategy employed by both customers and vendors when negotiating a BPO agreement is largely determined by three basic factors: (1) the underlying objectives of each of the parties, (2) the scope of services being outsourced, and (3) the relative bargaining positions of the parties. The underlying objectives of the customer and the vendor in an outsourcing transaction are often divergent. On one hand, common customer objectives are to reduce costs, gain a competitive advantage in its industry, provide greater flexibility and variability to its users or customers, or (as is typically the case) some combination of these and other factors. A BPO transaction that is essentially a financing arrangement in which cost reduction is the customer's primary goal will likely be a different type of contract in substance and form than one in which the quality of the services, as opposed to their cost, is the customer's main concern. On the other hand, common vendor objectives are to provide services that are cost effective to the customer while at the same time enhancing vendor profitability and increasing the vendor's market share and market exposure. The scope of the outsourcing transaction (the second factor) is driven by the customer's business requirements and will, in many instances, impact a party's position regarding certain legal terms. If, for example, the outsourcing arrangement includes a significant amount of project work, the contract must take into consideration different elements (e.g., implementation schedules, liquidated damages for delays) than if it were a straight, ongoing services deal. The third factor, the bargaining position of the parties, is typically driven by the dollar value of the transaction, the urgency of the customer to enter into the transaction (e.g., by fiscal year end), the exposure that the transaction offers to the vendor (e.g., entry into a new industry or market), the dominance of the vendor in the market (e.g., are there any competing products/services?) and the desire of the vendor to do business with the customer (e.g., is the customer a financially stable organization with opportunities for repeat business?).

Establish objectives. As discussed earlier, the parties' reasons for entering into the outsourcing transaction largely determine the substance and form of the transaction. The process by which a party prioritizes its goals is the most basic step in any negotiation. This list must be reviewed and updated throughout the negotiation since issues that will affect the priority and content given to key objectives may arise.

Define scope. The subject matter of the contract is, of course, determined by the scope of the transaction, that is, the services and processes that the customer will outsource to the vendor. Defining the scope of the transaction is typically a mutual process, requiring input and direction from both parties. The customer typically takes the first crack at defining the scope of the transaction in the RFP, or, if there is no RFP, in its requirements definition. The scope of the tranaction is further defined by the vendor in its response to the customer and will continue to take shape during negotiations and contract drafting. The scope of the transaction and the extent of each parties' responsibilities will, in many cases, impact the parties' position with respect to certain issues.

Determine value attributed by other party. It is important to understand what the value of the contract is to the other party as a means of gauging how much such party will be willing to concede. This value may not only be economic. In addition to revenue (and, most notably, profits), a party must consider the public relations value of the contract. From the customer's perspective, this may include favorable reaction from consumers (e.g., the customer will now be able to focus on its core competencies) and from the stock market. From the vendor's perspective, the public relations value may include entry into a new industry, the breakthrough in establishing even a small relationship with the particular customer, or the prestige associated with the customer's name. Even though the economic value of a contract usually predominates, each party should attempt to forecast what the total value of this contract might be to the other party. In addition to the direct value of the contract, which is partly determined on the basis of the profits it can generate, other values to the vendor can be quantified. It is clear, for example, that a successful vendor will have a significant probability of selling additional services during the life of the contract. This means that the probability of future profits can and should be assessed.

There is also a psychological and financial impact associated with *not* finalizing the contract. Each party has made an investment in the process. The customer has invested significant time and resources and, in many instances, political capital in introducing, evaluating, and negotiating the potential outsourcing arrangement. The vendor often incurs expenses as high as $250,000 to $1,000,000 in connection with marketing its services, developing the proposal, and entertaining the customer. This investment is lost if the contract is not obtained.

There is also a psychological loss, which is the converse of the public relations benefit of obtaining the contract. From the customer's perspective, this may include the internal perception of not being able to close the deal. If information regarding the outsourcing has been communicated to employees or the public, it may include having to announce that an agreement was not reached. From the vendor's perspective, the absolute value of the loss can be important; allowing another vendor to enter a new market or obtain a new client can be equally important. All of these factors, economic and psychological, should be analyzed for negotiating purposes.

Clearly the negotiation will fail if a party's negotiating team demands more than the value of the contract or more than the losses associated with not obtaining it. Thus the negotiating team should carefully balance demands with value and recognize what is available to be negotiated.

Define roles. Each party must determine the role it intends to take during the negotiation. Will it control the process by drafting the agreements, setting the timetable for the negotiations, and dictating the content of the meetings, or will it allow the other party to perform these tasks? In an ideal situation, a framework for the negotiations is established mutually, but as a practical matter, one party must lead and the other party follow. If the customer determines that it will lead the transaction, it must have the internal strength and support to take such a position since the vendor is typically poised to dominate the negotiating process (and armed with the ammunition that this is what it does).

Find a lawyer. Although many businesspeople prefer not to involve lawyers in a project until it is absolutely necessary (and while it may seem to be in the authors' parochial interests to say so), it is advisable to choose a lawyer early in the selection process and to have that lawyer assess the legal risks associated with the legal relationship. For the customer, if its organization has a corporate counsel's office, an effort should be made to identify a lawyer there who has experience with contracts related to the business process being outsourced. If it is necessary to engage outside counsel, the customer should seek recommendations from other outsourcing customers and should ensure that the lawyer chosen has extensive experience in drafting and negotiating outsourcing agreements on behalf of customers. The vendor, on the other hand, is more likely to have an internal legal department or contract administration department experienced in negotiating outsourcing contracts. For particularly complex transactions or when additional legal resources are necessary, vendors may also choose to engage outside counsel. Engaging outside counsel has the added advantage of allowing the businesspeople to distance themselves from counsel should negotiations become adversarial (e.g., the lawyers are not part of our organization, but they are the experts, and we have to listen to them). Once a lawyer is chosen, the party should clearly identify the lawyer's responsibilities and should decide the best method of involving the lawyer in the negotiation process.

Identify the lead negotiator. Each party must determine which roles each individual on the negotiation team will play. Will a businessperson take a lead role in raising and framing issues, or will attorneys take on that responsibility? The negotiation of any contract is inherently an adversarial process because of the competing interests of the parties. This does not, however, mean that every contract negotiation should be adversarial. Despite the a party's best intentions, however, their lead negotiator will at some point be regarded as hostile by the other party. This feeling, in turn, could carry over to the postcontract period and make the relationship between vendor and customer difficult. For this reason, many parties appoint counsel as the lead negotiator. Lawyers are familiar with the role of articulating positions and are less inclined to respond emotionally to the other party's counterproposals. Similarly, having the lawyer serve as the lead negotiator establishes a distance between the positions advocated by the lawyer and those of the businesspeople, and enables the businesspeople to play the role of problem solver. Before placing this responsibility on the lawyer, however, the businesspeople should make certain that the lawyer fully understands their position on the legal issues and that the lawyer is willing to defer to the businesspeople's judgment at the appropriate time.

Identify drafting responsibility. Most vendors are accustomed to dominating the negotiation process and are reluctant to disturb the protective blanket of their standard form. The customer should make it apparent to the vendor early in the selection process if it will not accept the vendor's form contract and that it has certain contract terms that must be included in any agreement between the parties. If the customer allows the vendor to believe that this will be an ordinary negotiation process until the vendor delivers signed copies of its standard form, the resulting disturbance in the business relationship may not be worth any improvement in the legal relationship. The customer should be careful not to be confrontational in suggesting changes or demanding additional protection. Vendors are generally more inclined to accept modifications than concessions. Although clarifying the legal relationship between the parties is useful and sometimes essential, the parties should never lose sight of the fact that both parties must be willing to cooperate after the contract is signed. If the negotiation has dampened a party's enthusiasm, the real objective of the contract (e.g., the successful implementation of a new environment) will not be achieved regardless of how well crafted the contract is.

One of the fundamental truths of the outsourcing industry is that no matter which side prepares the first draft of the term sheet or the agreement, it will invariably be deemed inadequate by the other side. This suggests that counsel be involved as soon as possible. Ideally, this should take place during the RFP and proposal stage so that counsel from both sides may review any underlying legal issues and become familiar with the transaction. A vendor's willingness to be reasonable in its legal relationship with the customer should be a significant (although not determinative) factor in the vendor selection process just as the customer's willingness to accept reasonable risks will determine whether it chooses to outsource.

Term sheet. One party often seeks to seize the initiative in the negotiation process by preparing a term sheet for delivery to the other party. The term sheet is a document that defines the parties' positions on the salient terms of the contract, This document can be used to inform the other party of a party's position or as a checklist for use in determining the content of the ultimate services contract.

From the customer's perspective, the term sheet ideally should be issued with the RFP and should require the vendor to note any objection to its terms in the vendor's proposal. This allows the customer to seize the high ground in determining the legal relationship between the parties by establishing the terms from which this relationship will evolve. Each proposal can then be evaluated in terms of the vendor's willingness to accept the basic contract terms. If the vendor does not issue a formal proposal, the customer may wish to use the term sheet as an outline from which to inform the vendor of the customer's expectations. The vendor, if presented with a term sheet by the customer as part of the RFP or vendor selection process, should review each legal term carefully. The vendor's willingness to accept certain legal terms should be built into its risk/reward analysis. The vendor's response to the term sheet (e.g., compliance, noncompliance) is often more an art than a science and should be reviewed by legal counsel.

The term sheet often becomes a vital document in the negotiation process because it provides a framework within which the parties can build a viable contract. There are, however, a number of other reasons for developing a comprehensive term sheet. The first and perhaps most important reason is that developing such a document forces the parties to consider the operational and legal issues associated with the project. Through the analytical process of selecting and framing the applicable clauses, the key elements of the project are reinforced and the parties will begin to become aware of the ramifications that a decision regarding one such element will have on another. This, in turn, allows the parties to consider most issues before they arise during the negotiation of the definitive contract terms. In addition, the term sheet may set the framework of the transaction from the viewpoint of the drafting party and psychologically require the other party to tailor its needs to fit within that framework. The term sheet also provides early insight into a party's position and can help identify weaknesses that need to be addressed.

If the term sheet is included by the customer in the RFP or used as part of the vendor selection process, the position of other vendors included in the selection process but not selected is also helpful in the negotiation and is obtained through the term sheet. Thus, if the customer knows that one vendor is willing to concede a specific issue, this information can be used in the actual negotiating sessions to induce another vendor to concede that point. The term sheet, when issued to all vendors involved in the process, will serve to provide valuable input to the negotiator. The customer may wish to rank the vendors on their willingness to negotiate. This ranking may be added to the selection process criteria matrix in order to determine which vendor is most willing to negotiate.

4.3 EXPOSURE ANALYSIS

To further assess the impact of a contract—or the impact of not having coverage in areas where protection is desirable—a brief analysis of exposure can be made in recognition of the risk on an area-by-area basis. The first step in this analysis is to divide the contract terms into categories of importance for both the customer and the vendor. These categories could be identified as follows:

- Key contract terms
- Significant contract terms
- Minor contract terms
- Terms with no quantifiable impact

An alternative approach is to classify terms by the degree of risk associated with each term for both the customer and the vendor. In a typical outsourcing contract, this might result in the following:

- A risk of $0 to $500,000
- A risk of $500,000 to $5,000,000
- A risk of more than $5,000,000

It is important to evaluate both your risk as well as the other party's risk. An analysis of the other party's risk will provide valuable insight into where there is potential for give and take.

This is a mechanistic method of assessing the exposure of a contract, and it may not be specific enough or it may be too specific in certain areas. It is only a tool used to assess the contract and to identify areas where it can be improved. It should never be used as the sole basis for negotiation, since common sense obviously will override the purely numerical conclusions provided by this technique. However, the technique is useful in providing insight into a party's responsiveness and willingness to negotiate.

4.4 PEOPLE NEGOTIATE, NOT COMPANIES

In attempting to understand the position of the other side in the negotiation, the personality of the individuals concerned should also be considered. In addition to a checklist of value items that the negotiator prepares, he or she should also prepare a short biographical sketch of the individuals who will be participating on the opposing side. Each sketch should include the background of the individual, his or her current position, and personality traits. Traits such as quickness to anger or willingness to compromise should be identified where possible to ensure that the negotiating team has a realistic understanding of the participants' personalities and can appeal to the characteristics most likely to result in negotiating advantages to the customer.

Often, negotiations are performed by individuals who have a personal interest in the negotiation process. For the lead businessperson on the customer's side, this may be one of the most significant transactions that he or she has worked on. It could be a defining point in his or her career. This person will likely have competing interests of wanting to show that he or she got a good deal and wanting to show that he or she can close the deal. The interests of the technical personnel appointed by the customer will differ depending upon whether the individual is being retained by the customer or being transferred to the vendor. Because there is no other choice, the customer may appoint individuals to the outsourcing team who themselves will be outsourced. These people will have competing interests of wanting to do a good job and of making a good impression on their new employer—the outsourcing vendor.

To the vendor's salesperson, the contract being negotiated may be the most significant opportunity of the year (or, indeed, a career). It may mean a large commission or a promotion. The salesperson as an individual has a great deal more to gain or lose from the contract than the vendor. Accordingly, the salesperson is likely to be most oriented toward negotiating a contract favorable to the customer, since the salesperson is interested in obtaining the business at almost any cost. The salesperson will likely get his or her commission regardless of the concessions the vendor makes in the contract. The salesperson is, in most cases, often least able to commit the vendor to any significant concessions. Yet by knowing the vendor's internal organization, he or she can often facilitate compromise. Next in line in terms of interest in finalizing the contract is typically the vendor's account manager (e.g., the individual who will administer the contract). In many cases, this individual receives some commission, and in all cases, account managers are held responsible for meeting the quota for their business unit. Thus, the vendor's account manager is equally interested in being awarded the contract. This level of management is responsible for a budget, and must maintain its total concessions with customers within a specified fraction of the total sales of the business unit.

4.5 NEGOTIATING STRATEGY

As noted in Section 4.1, although this is not a text on negotiating strategy, some points will be mentioned to assist the parties in carrying out the negotiating process in a reasonable manner.

Although it may seem obvious, customers constantly need to be reminded that it is not desirable or productive to present the other side with an overwhelming series of requests at the beginning of the negotiations. If the vendor has already received the term sheet and has responded to it, the vendor is aware of the customer's legal concerns, which may be fairly different from the terms of the vendor's standard contract. The vendor, therefore, has already been placed on guard. Further demands might create a difficult situation in which the vendor might decide to walk out rather than deal with a massive problem in the contract. If the vendor has made it to the negotiating table in spite of having seen the term sheet, then the vendor is prepared to negotiate and compromise. Accordingly, it is not desirable to overwhelm the vendor at the initial negotiating session. Clauses should be grouped into categories so all the major ones are not discussed at the beginning. For this reason, it is beneficial to discuss the sequence of clauses prior to the start of the negotiation. Many vendors will attempt to engage the customer in a line-by-line review and discussion of the agreement at the onset of negotiations. This is a decidedly unproductive approach as the participants' attention span undoubtedly declines as the "death march" proceeds through the contract. A line-by-line analysis of the agreement is best postponed until the major issues have been resolved and, as a threshold matter, should be conducted by the lawyers off-line until the issues that arise from this discussion can be distilled to a manageable number.

A negotiating session will have a varying number of phases. Difficult periods of argument and acrimony should be alternated with periods of attention to clauses or agreements that are considered reasonable by both parties so that there is the opportunity to establish a friendly relationship during the negotiation. Alternating these periods in a regular manner ensures that neither party walks out of the negotiation without just cause.

Similarly, a negotiating session, of necessity, is a process of give and take. These trade-offs should be used very carefully. When a party is prepared to accede to a request from the other party or realizes that there is no choice but to accede because the other party is intractable on a point, then the trade-off capability should be used. At that point, the negotiator might go back to a clause that had been suspended because no agreement has been reached and indicate that he or she will accede to the point in question if the other party will agree to accede to the preceding point.

If it is impossible to reach an agreement on a particular issue, the parties should be prepared to drop that issue and suspend it until the next session. It is possible that in subsequent discussions the issue might become irrelevant, or a resolution or alternative may be found if time passes. In the next negotiating session the negotiator should determine whether either party is prepared to move from the position taken earlier. Resuscitation of these issues might take place as part of a trade-off or a give-up of another issue.

It is desirable to always have a fall-back position for each issue under discussion and for the negotiation as a whole. A fall-back position for a specific clause might simply be a softening of that clause or preparedness to accept an inferior position. This can be brought out when a party is unprepared to accept the clause as written. If the party offers an alternative, then the fall-back position can be tried if it is better than the offered alternative or if it can be made to appear as a reasonable option.

In addition to the fall-back in each clause, the customer may wish to have an overall fall-back position. The customer should remember that the vendors were selected on the basis of the commitments they were prepared to make either in the proposal or as a result of separate discussions. If the prime vendor becomes unwilling to make such commitments in a written contract, then the selection of this vendor might have been an error in the first place, and the second-ranked vendor would be the better choice. If at any time the vendor declines its previous commitments or if the negotiating position of the vendor is so intractable as to render a potential contract meaningless, it may be desirable to actually switch the negotiation to the second-ranked vendor. The authority and the knowledge that it is possible to shift to another vendor will make the negotiator more effective, even if this option is never exercised. The vendor, on the other hand, will want to limit the customer's ability to shift negotiations to another vendor. In order to do so, the vendor may wish to establish up front that negotiations will be exclusive at least for a stated period of time.

Finally, there may be occasions during the negotiation when it is better to stop all further discussion rather than generate further acrimony. If the negotiations have broken down or if there is considerable disagreement and no apparent resolution is in sight, there should be some exit opportunities during which the situation can be reconsidered. At this point, the customer and the vendor personnel should separate and perhaps discuss among themselves the approaches to be taken. It is at this point, for example, that the business-people might convince the negotiator to soften his or her position. Thus, opportunities to break and separate for dinner, for coffee, or just to regroup are desirable in any negotiating session.

CHAPTER 5

BUSINESS PROCESS OUTSOURCING CONTRACT

5.1 OVERVIEW

The most common form of BPO contract involves the transfer of control and ownership of all or part of a customer's business process operations to an outsourcing vendor. In return, the customer agrees to compensate the vendor according to a negotiated fee schedule. The transfer of business process operations to the vendor[1] typically includes some or all of the following:

1. The transfer to the vendor of customer assets used to manage and facilitate the business process (e.g., facilities and office equipment used by the business process department) and other related tangible assets
2. The assignment or license to the vendor of proprietary methodologies and/or technology used by the customer in connection with its business process operations
3. The assignment or sublicense to the vendor of any third-party methodologies and/or technologies previously used by the customer in connection with its business process operations
4. The transfer to the vendor of all or a significant portion of the customer employees previously involved in providing business process services to the customer's organization

Thereafter, the vendor assumes responsibility for operating and managing the customer's business process operations and providing the business process services previously provided by the employees and consultants of the customer (except for certain responsibilities specifically retained by the customer, e.g., strategic control).

Given the wide variety of business issues and the many different legal disciplines involved in even the simplest form of outsourcing transaction, it should come as no surprise that one of the most difficult, if not the most difficult, stages of an outsourcing transaction is drafting and negotiating the contract. To an attorney familiar with general corporate

---

[1] In BPO transactions where the vendor is teaming with other service providers or subcontracting a major piece of the services, transfers, assignments, licenses, and sublicenses described in the following list may be to the vendor's teaming partner or subcontractor.

practice, an outsourcing agreement may resemble a hybrid asset purchase and sale agreement and sale/leaseback agreement, in that there is typically a sale of assets or transfer of operations, a transfer of employees, and a lease back to the customer of the business process services that were divested. In an increasing number of BPO transactions, the basic structure of the deal resembles a project finance arrangement. Add to this the fact that an outsourcing contract is essentially a services agreement, and one can see how the BPO contract may be more than a hundred pages long.

While it may seem daunting, drafting and negotiating a BPO contract can be distilled into five basic issues that must be considered and addressed by the parties:

1. What is it?
2. Who does it?
3. Who owns it?
4. How much is paid for it?
5. What happens if it is not done?

If, at the end of the contract negotiation process, the parties are confident that these five issues have been fairly and comprehensively addressed, it is likely that the relationship between the parties will survive the inevitable day-to-day disputes that arise in complex contractual relationships and, hopefully, flourish as methodologies and technology advance.

It is important to note at this point that a fair contract is not one that is necessarily ideal from either party's perspective. As discussed in Chapter 4, a negotiation with respect to an outsourcing arrangement is not one that either party should seek to win. A fair contract may well be one that requires both parties to perform in a way that will not result in optimal economic performance (as each party may define it). Similarly, there is no bright line for determining when a contract is sufficiently comprehensive, because comprehensiveness is in the eye of the beholder. A contract that might be deemed comprehensive for one organization could, in the eyes of another organization, be deemed insufficiently detailed to allow the customer to realize the anticipated benefits.

In any event, the threshold concern in addressing the five basic issues set forth earlier is to determine what the "it" is. From the vendor's perspective, the "it" is a sufficient level of detail so that the vendor is not required to perform services it did not anticipate in its cost models (or, perhaps more important, services it did anticipate at service levels it did not account for in its cost models) and for the customer to receive the services it anticipated receiving when it made the decision to enter into the agreement. With respect to the customer's employees who are being transitioned to the vendor, the "it" is to adequately address the terms under which such employees will be hired and fired (e.g., to define the benefits the employees will be receiving).

As with any contract, the contracting party must identify and evaluate the fundamental risks and anticipated benefits associated with the transaction before negotiations begin. As discussed in Chapter 4, the key risk and reward factors must serve as the basis for any negotiation strategy (regardless of which side of the transaction you represent) and should be reviewed and updated as the negotiations proceed.

5.2 USE OF ATTORNEYS

One virtually unavoidable consequence of entering into an outsourcing transaction is that the customer will need the services of an attorney, whether corporate or outside counsel. Most vendors make extensive use of corporate (and to some extent outside) counsel, as well as "contract professionals" who often function in the role that an attorney would typically fill. In addition, many companies have rules requiring the involvement of an attorney with respect to any contract for more than a specified amount of money. In many instances, it is simply the complexity of the vendor's standard form or the obvious attempts by the vendor to limit its liability and disclaim all forms of warranties that leads the customer to seek legal advice.

Regardless of whether the attorney involved is a conscript or a volunteer, he or she is all too often used in an inappropriate manner. Business professionals who would never consider entering into a new project without clear-cut objectives, a timetable for development, and contingency plans in the event the project fails will assume that the attorney involved will be able to accurately capture in detail that which is often reflected by only the barest of writings. Perhaps the best advice to give to a business professional with respect to the proper use of counsel in an outsourcing transaction is to view the attorney as one would view a project leader who has been asked to draft a project plan that will consider the various contingencies that may arise over the long term (perhaps as long as 10 years), accurately reflect the hundreds of obligations that the parties need to perform, and make specific provision for what happens in the event that none of the foregoing happens—and to do all of this as soon as possible. Just as the success of the project leader in this example would be largely contingent on the input he or she was given, even the most obstreperous and recalcitrant attorney can be effectively managed by his or her client—and provide value—if the client takes the time to consider what information the attorney will need to perform his or her tasks, periodically monitors these tasks to assure that they are being handled in an efficient and effective manner, and perhaps most important, realizes that a deal that has taken several months to forge cannot usually be codified overnight.

In addition to drafting and assisting in the negotiating of the agreement, an attorney can be useful as a lightning rod around which difficult issues can be discussed. An outsourcing agreement is at its essence a service agreement, and it is important that the individuals who will be involved on an ongoing basis in providing and receiving the services develop a candid but professional relationship during the negotiations. As was discussed in Chapter 4, conflict is inevitable during any negotiations, and, while this does not necessarily mean that the negotiations have to be adversarial, discussions often become heated. The focus of these conflicts should be primarily the parties' legal representatives, not the parties themselves. This will allow each side to articulate its perspective openly without personalizing the discussion. The resolution of most difficult issues is often left to businesspeople, but attorneys should be responsible for framing the issue and, ideally, for proposing alternative solutions.

5.3 KEY CONTRACT ISSUES

This section provides a general discussion of certain key clauses that are typically included in (or at least considered when drafting) the BPO contract. The content, and in some instances the applicability, of many of the clauses discussed in this section will vary depending on the type of business process being outsourced (e.g., the audit clause in a contract for accounting services will require different language than the audit clause in a contract for procurement services), the scope and duration of the transaction, the overall contract value and the critical nature of the services (i.e., critical versus noncritical services). While this section is intended to provide some guidance for structuring and negotiating the BPO contract, it is not intended to be an exhaustive discussion of all of the possible contract issues that may arise. Parties negotiating a BPO contract also should be mindful that the enforceability and applicability of certain contract provisions (e.g., liability, disclaimers, liquidated damages, noncompetition, transfer of employees, nonsolicitation) may depend on the law governing the contract. These may be state or county laws and may differ even among the transaction documents for deals that involve multiple agreements, such as international and possibly multisite deals. Accordingly, legal and other counsel as appropriate (e.g., regulatory, audit) should be consulted prior to entering into any BPO contract.

Ideally, such counsel should be part of the team considering outsourcing and responsible for negotiating the transaction in order to assist the relevant party in fleshing out any particularly troublesome legal issues as early as possible.

In addition to the discussion of key contract issues set forth in the following list, the reader may find useful the checklists for the BPO agreement set forth in Appendices 5.1–5.5.

(a) Structure of the BPO Agreement   One of the first issues confronting legal counsel in the outsourcing process is how to structure the BPO contract. For a single-country transaction covering the ongoing provision of existing business process services only, a single services agreement setting out each party's responsibilities, obligations, and possible liabilities may be appropriate. However, for more complex transactions, the parties may wish to consider different contract structures. For example, multiple agreements may be necessary to document transactions that include some type of strategic alliance, such as a joint venture, joint marketing, or gainsharing agreement. For multicountry or even multisite transactions, the parties may wish to enter into a master agreement that sets out the general terms and conditions governing the overall provision of services, together with separate country or site agreements setting out the country- or site-specific services as well as any legal or regulatory provisions unique to the country or site. For transactions that include the provision of ongoing services as well as other related services (e.g., business process reengineering, development, or change management), multiple agreements may be appropriate to effectively capture the various components of the business deal. In transactions that involve multiple agreements, the parties will need to determine the interrelationships of the various agreements, such as duration of term, cross-termination, and set off of payments.

Other issues that may drive how a particular outsourcing arrangement is structured include (1) the relationship between the various entities receiving/delivering the services, (i.e., is the contracting entity for each of the parties able to bind each of the entities that will receive/deliver the services or must each of the recipient/delivering entities formally agree to be bound by the terms of the BPO contract), (2) cost allocation requirements internal to the customer (e.g., chargebacks), and (3) tax, currency, or other pricing requirements that would necessitate separate country or site agreements (particularly relevant in international transactions). The factors determining the structure of a particular BPO transaction will be shaped largely by the scope and geographic reach of the business deal.

(b) Scope of Services   One of the most important parts of every BPO contract is the description of the services that will be provided by the vendor. This is often the most difficult part of the agreement to draft since a list of the services currently being provided by the in-house staff typically does not exist and is very time consuming to create. The services are typically described in an exhibit or schedule (or a series of exhibits or schedules) to the agreement, which can vary from a broad statement of the services to be provided to a detailed specification of each service to be provided. As part of the effort to codify the services to the greatest extent possible, customers often hire a consultant familiar with BPO transactions to develop a list of the services and the service levels historically provided by the in-house personnel. When creating this list of the services to be provided by the vendor, the customer should be sure to include any ancillary services (e.g., consulting, training, storage, reporting) it will also require.

(c) Term   The term of the BPO agreement may run from as few as 1 to as many as 10 years, with renewal options. The duration of the contract term typically depends on the customer's objectives in outsourcing, the scope of services being outsourced, whether employees are being transitioned and/or assets are being transferred, the ramp-up costs incurred by the vendor, and the pricing structure offered to the customer. Many vendors favor evergreen contracts in which the agreement remains in effect until terminated by a party for cause or upon a specified period of notice, but key provisions such as price are periodically adjusted. Many customers, however, are seeking shorter terms of one to five years in order to retain greater flexibility with respect to their business process operations.

In addition, a large number of BPO arrangements involve the provision of BPO services as well as other project-related services, such as business reengineering, consulting, or change management services. The agreements documenting these types of arrangements, in some instances, have been divided into two phases—the project phase followed by the BPO phase—with the option to terminate or reevaluate the agreement after the end of the first phase. In other instances, however, there is an overlap in the time period during which project services are provided and the time period during which BPO services are provided, which makes a multiphase approach less appropriate.

(d) Transition   The parties should have a clear understanding, typically set out in a detailed transition plan, as to how operations, assets and employees will be transitioned to the vendor. Depending on the type of operations to be transitioned to the vendor, the parties may want to consider including testing requirements in the agreement, as well as the operation of parallel operating environments for a specified period of time. In order to reduce customer dissatisfaction in the early phases of the outsourcing relationship it is useful for the parties to have an understanding as to the levels of service to be delivered to the customer during transition.

(e) Integration   A critical, although often overlooked, issue is how the provision of BPO services (including the introduction of new methodologies and/or technology) will be integrated into the customer's organization. For example, if the information technology (IT) department has established a standardized environment (often after much difficulty), the parties should evaluate whether the new methodologies and/or technology to be introduced by the BPO vendor are compatible. The parties will also need to discuss how IT-related failures are to be handled (e.g., through the IT help desk or a business process help desk).

To flesh out any integration issues, it is important that the customer, and perhaps the vendor if there is a due diligence period, contact representatives from other business departments within the customer organization that may be impacted by the outsourcing arrangement.

(f) Measuring Performance   A brief overview of some of the key issues involving performance follows. A more detailed discussion of how the parties may measure performance under the BPO contract is provided in Chapter 6.

Service levels. As discussed in Chapter 6, customers and most vendors view service levels as useful measures of ongoing performance. Areas that are commonly measured to assess the level of service provided to the customer include response times, delivery requirements, reporting requirements, customer satisfaction, and guaranteed savings or cost reductions. The types of service levels measured and monitored under a BPO transaction typically depend on the type of business process outsourced (e.g., tax compliance outsourcing may focus on reporting requirements and the ability of the vendor to reduce taxes while asset and property management outsourcing may focus on help desk responsiveness and customer satisfaction) and which services the customer considers important to its overall business operations. There are a number of different approaches for documenting and monitoring service levels. Although the preferable approach is to document the existing service levels achieved by the customer's business process group prior to sending out the RFP or at least prior to contract signing, an increasing number of customers seek to streamline the process by entering into agreements in which service levels will be established by the joint efforts of the parties after the contract has been signed. Accordingly, a large number of BPO agreements establish or include a methodology for establishing the service levels to be met by the vendor. While most vendors agree to establish service levels and report ongoing adherence to service levels, a topic that is a bit more contentious is the consequence if service levels are not achieved. Most customers wish to tie some type of liquidated damage (see the discussion of liquidated damages later in this chapter) or credit to the vendor's nonperformance. The amount and schedule for paying any liquidated damage or credit varies from deal to deal and is typically driven by the overall value of the transaction, the potential damage if there is nonperformance, and the negotiation leverage of the customer.

Customer satisfaction. A key reason for the customer to enter into a BPO transaction is to improve user and/or management satisfaction. Increasingly, customers include a requirement that the vendor or a third party perform regular satisfaction surveys, often with an obligation to improve survey results on a periodic basis. In instances where the parties agree to include a mechanism for measuring customer satisfaction in the BPO contract, the parties typically negotiate the content of the satisfaction survey as well as the group of individuals to be surveyed.

Benchmarking. Depending on the scope and duration of the BPO arrangement, the parties may wish to consider including in the BPO contract a mechanism for benchmarking the customer's services and pricing against others in the industry. As discussed further in Chapter 6, if the parties agree to benchmark services and/or pricing, they will need to negotiate the scope of the benchmark (e.g., overall versus individual services), the pool of organizations that will be benchmarked, and the benchmarker.

Gainsharing. As outsourcing customers become more sophisticated and the BPO market matures, more customers—and often vendors—are looking for ways to share in gains generated by the outsourcing relationship. Accordingly, the concept of gainsharing is receiving a significant amount of attention in the outsourcing industry. Examples of gainsharing mechanisms include payment to the vendor of an incentive based on customer profits, providing options to the customer, and the payment to the vendor of an incentive based on actual savings generated by the vendor. A more detailed discussion of gainsharing is set forth in Chapter 6.

(g) Year 2000 Compliance   The parties to any BPO transaction should consider the extent, if any, of the vendor's responsibility to provide year 2000 compliance services. In this regard, the customer and the vendor will need to explore their respective obligations to provide year 2000 compliance services in respect of:

1. The customer's existing proprietary and third party methodologies/technology
2. The vendor's proprietary methodologies/technology
3. The vendor's third party methodologies/technology
4. Modifications and enhancements to the customer's proprietary and third party methodologies/technology
5. Newly acquired methodologies, technology, and developments

In the event the vendor assumes responsibility for any year 2000 compliance services, the parties will need to negotiate appropriate representations and warranties relating to such services, as well as the vendor's liability (or disclaimer of liability) in the event of noncompliance.

(h) Euro Compliance   A topic that is receiving less attention than year 2000 compliance but which may cause just as many problems for customers and vendors is the conversion to a single European currency (the Euro). The question that arises for customers and vendors is whether the methodologies and technology used by the customer in connection with its business process or used, developed, or acquired by the vendor in connection with the provision of BPO services are or will be able to convert relevant financial and other data to account for use of the Euro and then read and process data using the Euro. It is also important to note that during the 1999–2002 transition period, methodologies or technology may be needed to read and process data in both national currencies and the Euro.

In negotiating the BPO contract, the parties should consider the impact, if any, of the introduction of the Euro. Obviously, the issue is more relevant for companies with European operations or those that do business in Europe (keeping in mind that electronic transactions and transactions over the Internet broaden the geographical activities of many companies). A brief discussion of several contract issues relating to Euro compliance for the customer and the vendor to consider when negotiating the BPO contract follows:

Scope of services. What are each party's responsibilities regarding ensuring that the customer, vendor, and third-party methodologies/technology are Euro compliant? Does the vendor have any development or maintenance responsibilities with respect to existing or new methodologies or technology?

Representations/warranties. Will the vendor represent that its methodologies or technology, certain third-party methodologies or technology and/or new developments are Euro compliant? What is the scope of the representation? (The vendor may wish to cover Euro compliance in an agreement separate from the BPO contract.)

Disclaimers. The vendor should consider including any express disclaimers of liability with respect to Euro compliance, particularly since there is some dispute as to whether year 2000 (and therefore likely Euro compliance) is covered by an implied warranty.

Limitation of liability. The customer and the vendor should consider whether any limitations or exculpations from liability are appropriate and, similarly, whether there are any indemnification issues. For example, should the customer be indemnified for failures or errors caused by third-party methodologies or technology?

Insurance. Finally, the parties should consider whether any special insurance should (or can) be obtained in the event of a failure or error. In addition, the parties may wish to investigate whether any failures or error would be covered by existing customer and/or vendor insurance.

Both the customer and the vendor should ensure that the BPO contract provides adequate protections regarding the use of the Euro and each party's responsibility and liability in the event the relevant methodologies/technology does not convert, read and/or process data correctly using the Euro or there are systems or business failures or errors due to the inability to convert, read, and/or process data using the Euro.

(i) Transfer of Employees   If the BPO arrangement between the customer and the vendor contemplates that the customer will terminate some or all of its business process employees in the hope or with the express requirement that the vendor will hire these employees to provide services to the customer, the BPO contract should expressly state the nature of the vendor's obligations with respect to these employees. Any transaction of this sort is replete with employment and labor law issues, most notably those involving pension plans, severance payments, termination notice requirements, union rights, and wrongful termination.

The manner in which the termination of the customer's business process employees and the subsequent hiring of such employees by the vendor is handled can determine the success of the customer's decision to outsource. Regardless of how this transfer of employees will be structured, the customer and the vendor must cooperate to ensure that the rights of the customer's employees are not violated by the contract or subsequent conduct of the parties. In light of the potential for such suits, however, the customer should have the BPO contract reviewed by an attorney familiar with labor and employment issues before entering into any outsourcing arrangement to ensure that the contract does not, on its face, violate any local, state, federal, or country laws.

It is in both parties' interests to be as detailed as possible in the contract with respect to their obligations to the customer's former employees. In this regard, the BPO contract typically provides for a transition period during which the customer will provide notice to and terminate employees who will no longer be required to provide business process services. As these employees are terminated, the vendor then offers employment to the individuals it intends to hire. Transition periods may run from three to six months. Another important aspect of the transfer of employees from the customer to the vendor is that the customer's relationship with the vendor may not continue indefinitely. For this reason, the customer may wish to retain certain key employees familiar with its business process operations and requirements to ensure that any migration to another vendor will be adequately supported. Similarly, the customer may wish to expressly retain the right to solicit certain vendor personnel, most notably those who previously worked for the customer, upon expiration or termination of the BPO contract. A more detailed discussion of employee transfer issues is set forth in Chapter 7.

(j) Staffing   Each party typically appoints one individual to manage the BPO contract and the overall provision and receipt of services. The vendor's representative will play an important role in the customer's organization and will interface with the customer's senior management, so the customer usually wishes to have the right to interview and approve such individual prior to appointment. Other possible restrictions on the vendor's representative include requirements that a particular individual remain on the account for a period of time and that this person will be dedicated to the customer's account on a full-time basis. Similar provisions often apply to other employees of the vendor that the parties consider key to the BPO relationship.

(k) Transfer of Assets   Many BPO arrangements include the transfer of all or some of the assets and/or facilities used to provide the business process services or facilitate business process operations. This transfer is often a critical part of the business deal since it may enable the customer to move assets or facilities off of its books and, in some instances, receive a much needed cash infusion or lump sum payment. In cases where there is an asset or facility transfer, the parties will need to negotiate a purchase and sale agreement (which is typically attached to the BPO contract as an exhibit).

(l) Management and Control   The parties will need to discuss how the procedures for managing and performing the services will be handled. In many cases, the BPO contract will require the vendor to develop a management procedure manual, as well as a manual detailing the vendor's day-to-day procedures. In addition, the parties will need to discuss how changes to the scope of services, manner of delivery of services and service levels will be handled. Finally, as earlier discussed under "Integration," the parties should negotiate the vendor's obligation to comply with the customer's standards, methodologies, and architectures as they may be in effect from time to time during the term of the BPO contract.

(m) Customer Responsibilities   Just as important as developing a detailed description of services to be provided by the vendor (discussed earlier under "Scope of Services") is identifying the roles and responsibilities of the customer. The customer typically wishes to retain certain strategic responsibility (see Section 5.4), which should be clearly set out in the BPO contract. In addition, the customer may be obligated to provide or make available certain services or assets, such as desktops, supplies, space, parking, and telephone services, as part of the business deal.

(n) Intellectual Property   Since the outsourcing of a customer's business process typically involves the access to and the use or development of valuable intellectual property, issues relating to intellectual property envelop the BPO transaction. A discussion of several of these issues follows:

Ownership rights. As a general matter, the BPO contract should include provisions with respect to the ownership of, and each party's right to use, any intellectual property assigned or licensed to the vendor or used by the vendor in providing services to the customer. Examples of the types of intellectual property that may be addressed in the BPO contract include:

- Methodologies
- Tools
- Software
- Firmware
- Patents
- Inventions
- Improvements that are used or developed in connection with the provision of the BPO services
- Related documentation
- Residual knowledge
- Trademarks

Different ownership and use rights may apply to items that are customer proprietary, leased or licensed by the customer from a third party, vendor proprietary, leased or licensed by the vendor from a third party, and newly developed or acquired. Ownership and use rights with respect to third-party intellectual property and vendor intellectual property are highlighted next.

Third-party IP. In a typical outsourcing agreement the customer assigns or licenses to the vendor its proprietary intellectual property that is used in connection with the services and assigns or sublicenses to the vendor any third-party intellectual property that is used in connection with the services. Prior to effecting any such assignment, license, or sublicense of intellectual property, the customer should determine whether it actually owns all of the rights in the intellectual property to be assigned or licensed or its agreements with the third-party licensors permit an assignment of the customer's license or sublicense. In most cases, the customer's agreement with a third-party licensor will expressly prohibit any assignment of the license or grant of a sublicense or will require that the licensor consent to any such assignment or sublicense or may prohibit use of, or access to, the intellectual property by a third party or to provide services to a third party. If the customer effects the assignment, grants the sublicense, or provides access in violation of its agreement with the third-party licensor, the customer runs the risk that the third-party licensor will obtain an injunction preventing the vendor and the customer from using the intellectual property, which could prevent the vendor from providing the services. In addition, the customer (and, perhaps, the vendor) could be liable for damages to the third-party licensor.

It is prudent, therefore, for the customer and the vendor to expressly state in the agreement which party is responsible for obtaining any required consents in respect of third-party intellectual property (or other proprietary material that may be transferred or licensed pursuant to the agreement) and specify which party will be responsible for paying any additional transfer, access, or license fees that may be imposed by the third party. In many cases, the additional transfer, access, or license fees are significant enough that the failure to allocate how such fees will be paid (e.g., split equally by the parties) can materially reduce the anticipated cost savings.

Many vendors advocate simply proceeding with the transaction as contemplated and providing notice of or soliciting a consent to the assignment or sublicense to the relevant third parties after the agreement is signed. The logic underlying this approach is that a third party will be more likely to impose an unreasonable transfer or license fee if it knows that the outsourcing transaction cannot be implemented until the transfer fee or license fee is paid. While this strategy is often successful, the customer should, at the very least, identify any third parties to whom notice should be sent and from whom consent is necessary, and include any anticipated transfer fees in its economic analysis of the transaction.

Vendor IP. The customer should also determine whether the vendor intends to convert the customer to intellectual property that is different than that used by the customer. If this is the case or if such a possibility exists the customer may wish to retain the right to disapprove of the vendor's selection of intellectual property as a means of retaining control over the services the customer receives. Finally, if the customer is assigning (as opposed to licensing) any proprietary intellectual property to the vendor, it may wish to take back a perpetual license to use the intellectual property in the event the outsourcing agreement expires or is terminated. One of the more controversial aspects of an outsourcing arrangement relates to the use of any vendor's proprietary intellectual property or vendor-licensed third-party intellectual property by the customer after the expiration or termination of the agreement. In many instances, without the right to continue to use the vendor's intellectual property, the customer runs the risk that the agreement will terminate without it having the right to continue its operations the day after the termination. The customer, therefore, may wish to include in the BPO contract an express right for it or its agent (such as another outsourcing vendor) to operate the vendor's intellectual property in the event of the expiration or termination of the agreement. As a result, many BPO contracts contain the salient provisions of an intellectual property license agreement as well. Another common approach is to incorporate a separate license agreement by reference into the outsourcing agreement. In any event, the customer may wish to ensure that the license granted to it will survive the termination of the agreement for any *reason.* The parties should carefully consider the terms of the license offered by the vendor before finalizing the BPO contract. For example, will the customer be obligated to pay for any transfer or access fees that may arise as a result of the expiration or termination of the underlying outsourcing agreement? A provision requiring a subsequent outsourcing vendor to sign the original vendor's standard form confidentiality agreement may well prevent the customer from entering into any subsequent outsourcing agreements because the terms of these confidentiality agreements are typically onerous. The scope of the license and any restriction placed upon the third-party maintenance of the intellectual property must also be considered. In addition, the customer should consider whether any of the vendor intellectual property (e.g., source code) should be placed in escrow for the customer's benefit in the event of the vendor's bankruptcy (or the bankruptcy of any of the vendor's licensors) or cessation of the vendor's business.

(o) Reports and Documentation   The BPO agreement typically specifies the types of reports that will be provided by the vendor to the customer, as well as the delivery times for each report. The parties should also discuss whether the vendor will provide any other documentation to the customer (e.g., manuals, user documentation) and, if so, which party owns such documentation.

(p) Ownership and Return of Data   From the customer's perspective, it is important that the BPO contract specify that the customer owns any data it submits to the vendor and has the right to recover, in a suitable form, a copy of all of its proprietary data upon termination or expiration of the agreement *for any reason.* Many standard form BPO contracts provide only that the customer's data will be returned upon expiration, as opposed to termination, of the agreement and do not specify the form that the data must be returned in or the method of returning the data. This can result in the customer being unable to promptly retrieve its data should the agreement terminate as a result of the vendor's default or retrieve its data in a suitable form upon any other termination or expiration of the agreement. Similarly, the customer should be wary of a clause that states that the vendor will return the customer's data provided that the customer has fully performed its obligations under the agreement at that time. The vast majority of disputes that arise under outsourcing agreements relate to whether the services are being performed according to the specified service levels. In these circumstances, it is quite common for the customer to withhold payment of all or a portion of the specified fees as a means of gaining negotiating leverage over the vendor. Withholding of payments is typically in violation of the BPO contract, and a court might well find that the customer has not performed all of its obligations under the contract should the vendor invoke that clause as a means of forcing the customer to pay all outstanding amounts prior to returning the customer's data. In effect, the customer becomes a hostage to the vendor's refusal to return its data until the vendor is paid in full. The customer should also seek to limit its expense of recovering its data from the vendor and should require the vendor to delete all of the customer's data from the vendor's records upon expiration or termination of the agreement. Finally, the BPO contract should protect the customer against the risk of the vendor withholding the customer's data in the event of a dispute between the parties by periodically requiring the vendor to provide a copy of such data to the customer or a third-party escrow agent.

(q) Confidential Information   The customer should assume that in any outsourcing transaction, the vendor will have access to some or all of the following information and data:

- Customer proprietary know-how, methodologies, and technology
- Lists of customers and prospective customers
- Internal financial data and projections
- Strategic plans
- New product development data
- Market surveys and analyses
- Research pricing, marketing, and inventory data and projections

The potential injury to the customer or to others who may make claims against the customer, by reason of the theft, misuse, misappropriation, or disclosure of information in the customer's possession, cannot be overstated.

For example, the customer may also have assembled a variety of information to which fiduciary obligations attach:

- Personal data concerning employees
- Reports received from franchises or licensees
- Confidential information concerning customers

Similarly, the customer will undoubtedly have access to certain vendor information and data that the vendor considers confidential. Such data and information may include:

- Vendor proprietary know-how, methodologies, and technology
- Strategic plans

- New product development data
- Operating procedures
- Pricing models

Accordingly, the confidentiality of each party's data and information should be protected by the BPO contract. The agreement must require each party and its agents to keep the other's proprietary data and information confidential and prohibit the use of such data and information for any purpose other than providing or receiving the services. The agreement should also give the parties the express right to obtain injunctive relief (see the discussion under "Injunctive Relief") to prevent the unauthorized disclosure of its confidential information.

The BPO contract may also include the following data-related provisions: a data security provision, a provision requiring the vendor to implement certain security measures in the event the vendor provides services to the customer's competitors at the same facility or using the same resources, and a provision outlining how attorney–client privileged documents should be handled.

(r) Business Recovery The customer should consider which obligations the vendor will assume with respect to business recovery in the event of a disaster or *force majeure* event (i.e., an event outside the vendor's control). For example, will the vendor be required to maintain a "hotsite" where services can be provided from until services can be restored at the regular service location? Will the vendor be required to interface with certain other vendors in the event of a disaster or follow certain escalation procedures? In addition, the customer may wish to consider limiting the duration of any interruption of the services by providing that the customer can terminate the agreement without liability or obtain services from a third party should the services be interrupted for more than a specified period of time. Finally, the contract should specify what priority will be given to the customer's services in the event of a disaster that affects more than one of the vendor's customers and may require the vendor to restore the customer's critical services within a specified period of time.

(s) Pricing/Fees A discussion of pricing/fee structures typically implemented in BPO arrangements is set forth in Section 5.5.

(t) Payments The parties will have to negotiate when invoices will be paid (e.g., in arrears, in advance) in which manner (e.g., wire transfer), and in what currency. Most vendors propose that payments be made in advance of the services being provided. Since the customer will lose the "cost of money" if payments are made in advance, the customer typically wishes to pay net 15 to 45 days. The customer's position may depend on its current payment practices with other vendors.

With respect to disputed amounts, the parties may wish to consider including a provision that allows the customer to withhold disputed amounts with an obligation to pay amounts in dispute exceeding a certain threshold into escrow. It is very important to the customer to include language that requires the vendor to continue to perform in the event of a fee dispute.

(u) Taxes The parties should research the extent of the tax liability that will be imposed in connection with the BPO contract and any supplemental agreements prior to entering into any BPO arrangement and determine how any such liability will be allocated between them. The allocation of tax is becoming an increasingly controversial subject in outsourcing agreements since many states and countries impose a tax on services.

(v) Dealing with Business Variability No customer's business remains static over the term of the BPO contract (particularly when the term is as long as 10 years). Therefore, it is important that the parties consider during contract negotiations possible changes in the customer's (and the vendor's) business over the term of the BPO contract and include provisions in the outsourcing agreement that allows for business variability. Examples of provisions that deal with business variability include:

Additional and reduced resource charges. The BPO contract typically includes rates at which the customer may receive additional resources or services, as well as rates by which the baseline fee will be reduced if lesser resources or services are used. The rates may vary depending on the amount of resource needed and the amount of notice given. *Renegotiation trigger.* The BPO contract may include a renegotiation right if the customer's demand for services increases or decreases above or below a certain level. An example of such a provision is:

> In the event that Customer's use of the Services increases or decreases more than [***] percent [in the aggregate] [per Service], Customer and Vendor shall negotiate and implement an appropriate adjustment to the Fees. In the event Customer and Vendor cannot agree on the adjustment to the Fees required by this Section, such disagreement shall be submitted to dispute resolution.

Termination right. The BPO contract may include a partial or full termination right if the customer's demand for services decreases below a certain level. Such a termination right may be tied to a termination fee.

(w) Audit

Services. The customer typically wishes to retain the right for its auditors and agents to audit the vendor's operations and records to ensure that the vendor is complying with its obligations under the BPO contract, as well as governmental rules and regulations. Such an audit may include the right to periodically inspect the vendor's premises. The parties will need to discuss each party's obligation in the event an audit reveals noncompliance with agreed on procedures, government rules, and regulations.

Fees. The customer should also have the right to audit the fees charged by the vendor. This right typically extends back for a reasonable period of time and the vendor is obligated to provide sufficiently detailed financial information to verify the charges under the BPO contract. Vendors are particularly sensitive, with good cause, about an audit provision that could potentially allow the customer to have access to the cost data with respect to the vendor's fees. It is unlikely that the customer has a legitimate need for this cost data and many customers simply choose to require that sufficiently detailed information be provided solely to verify the fees they have paid. In any event, the customer typically wishes to be able to recover the amount of any overcharges, plus interest from the date payment was made. Similarly, in most cases, the vendor may wish to be able to recover the amount of any undercharges.

(x) Representations and Warranties

Many agreements include extensive representation and warranty clauses. Most customers insist on warranties from the vendor to the effect that it will provide the services as specified in the agreement, it will accommodate a specified increase in the amount of the customer's use of the services, and any intellectual property provided by the vendor will not infringe upon the proprietary rights of any third party. Examples of other possible representations and warranties of the vendor are representations with respect to the vendor's financial viability, the number of vendor personnel that will be staffed on the project, and the vendor obtaining all necessary licenses and permits.

In an effort to reduce risk (and therefore liability exposure), the vendor also typically insists on certain representations and warranties from the customer. These representations and warranties may include that the customer is authorized to enter into the contract, the customer will pay any amounts due, including taxes, and any intellectual property provided by the customer will not infringe on the proprietary rights of a third party.

(y) Liability In the information technology (IT) marketplace, imposing some type of cap or limitation on direct and consequential damages has become the norm. Caps or limitations, however, are not always the practice in the BPO marketplace. In asset management transactions, for example, the parties may look to other custodial-type relationships for guidance on the grounds that such relationships are more analogous than IT outsourcing relationships. In contracts for custodial services, damages are often not capped or limited. The parties will need to consider each party's potential liability exposure, as well as the practice followed in service contracts for the particular business process being outsourced or similar business processes or functions.

(z) Liquidated Damages Damages cannot be awarded without proof of an economic loss. It is often difficult, if not impossible, however, for an aggrieved party to prove the dollar amount involved. The parties may agree to liquidated damages, an agreed-on monetary remedy, in instances where it is difficult to ascertain actual damages, for example, failure to meet project milestones or failure to meet certain service levels. In many outsourcing agreements, liquidated damages take the form of adjustments to the base fee under the agreement. For example, should the vendor fail to perform according to the service levels for a specified period of time, the liquidated damages to the customer might take the form of a credit against the next month's base fee.

Liquidated damage clauses are closely scrutinized since the law typically will refuse to enforce any provision it deems a penalty. A penalty, simply defined, is an agreed-on damage that bears no reasonable relation to the complained-of injury. As a result, liquidated damage provisions should attempt to establish a fair approximation of what actual damages would have been had the process of establishing actual damages been carried out. Thus, if the provision fixes an unreasonably large liquidated damage, it may be void as a penalty. The unreasonableness of a liquidated damages provision is judged as of the time the contract was entered into, as opposed to the time at which the damage arose. Although vendors typically resist including a liquidated damages clause in the agreement, a persistent customer can get the vendor to accept such a clause if the damages are reasonable and a cap is placed on the amount of such damages. Finally, it is important for the customer to realize that an enforceable liquidated damages provision may preclude a claim for actual damages for the complaint of breach of the agreement.

(aa) Termination The agreement should provide for a means by which each party may terminate the agreement upon the occurrence of certain events. It is critical that each party have the express right to terminate the agreement in the event of a material breach of the agreement by the other party. Agreements typically provide that, upon the failure of a party to perform any of its obligations under the agreement, the nonbreaching party may give the breaching party notice of such failure. The breaching party is then given a certain number of days to cure the breach. If the breaching party has not cured the breach within the specified period, the nonbreaching party may terminate the agreement. The agreement may limit any such cure period to a certain number of days (e.g., 30, 60, 90). When establishing a cure period, the customer should consider how long it can realistically wait for the vendor to cure a failure to provide a critical service. In many cases, a 24-hour period during which services are not being provided will cripple the customer's business. As a result, it is often necessary to establish different cure periods for different defaults.

In addition to termination for breach, the agreement may provide for termination upon the occurrence of other events (e.g., change in control of the customer's business, a *force majeure* event exceeding a certain number of days, failure to respond within a certain time period). Agreements with initial and renewal terms may typically be terminated upon a certain number of days' notice prior to the expiration of a term. Evergreen agreements are typically terminable by either party upon six months' to a year's notice.

Finally, most customers wish to include a right to terminate at any time for convenience. While such a right is typically granted to the customer, the vendor resists a broad termination for convenience provision. The parties need to negotiate the fees applicable in the event of an early termination.

(bb) Effect of Termination   Because of the critical nature of the services that the vendor is providing to the customer and the crucial nature of the data in the vendor's possession to the customer's business, BPO contracts frequently obligate the vendor to perform certain services after the termination or expiration of the contract. In this regard, the contract should require the vendor to provide post-termination services to support the customer's migration to another vendor or development of an internal business process organization for a specified period of time. This will also ensure that the vendor does not withhold performance as a means of gaining an advantage during a dispute as to whether the termination of the agreement was appropriate. Another important post-termination obligation of the vendor should be to return to the customer all of its data and information, together with any customer-owned methodologies, technology, and assets. The customer may also wish to require the vendor to cease using (and, perhaps, destroy) any of the customer's forms or stationery. Finally, the customer should consider whether it will continue to need use of any vendor methodologies, technology, and assets during the post-termination transition period after the termination or expiration of the BPO contract and, if so, include in the BPO contract a lease or license with respect to such methodologies, technology, and assets for the transition period.

(cc) Termination Assistance   The BPO contract typically requires the vendor to provide termination assistance services upon expiration or termination so that the customer is assured of an orderly transition of the services. These services should include the express right of the customer to receive the base services for some reasonable period of time after the expiration or termination date, together with any other services that might be reasonably requested by a customer in connection with the transition of the services to another outsourcing vendor or back to the customer. Many contracts seek to limit the amount and types of charges the vendor can impose with respect to these termination assistance services under the theory that an unfettered right to charge will lead to excess fees.

(dd) Dispute Resolution   Because operational disputes are an inevitable consequence of outsourcing arrangements, the BPO contract typically establishes an informal dispute resolution mechanism to deal with day-to-day operational disputes (e.g., processing priorities). Many BPO contracts provide for the formation of a management committee to administer such dispute resolution mechanisms. The management committee is typically comprised of both vendor and customer management personnel familiar with the arrangement between the parties and should be required to meet at specified times and in a specified location.

(ee) Indemnities   Most outsourcing contracts include a well-negotiated indemnification clause. Customers and vendors typically wish to be indemnified for human resource–related claims arising after (if the customer) or before (if the vendor) the commencement date of the BPO contract, certain property damage and personal injuries, certain security breaches, infringement claims based on the other party's intellectual property, and certain environmental claims.

(ff) International Issues   If the BPO transaction involves locations or services outside of the United States, additional legal issues may arise. Issues to consider include transborder data flow; data security; import/export controls; ownership of machines, software, methodologies, tools, and work product, audit requirements, methods of payment, currency risks, human resource issues, and taxes. A more detailed discussion of international issues is set forth in Chapter 9.

(gg) Assignment   An outsourcing agreement is analogous in many respects to a personal services agreement in that the customer has contracted for what it perceives are unique services from a particular source. Accordingly, the agreement typically provides that the vendor cannot assign the agreement to a third party without the customer's consent. At the least, this will prevent the vendor from assigning the agreement to a competitor of the customer. The vendor may request that the nonassignment obligations apply to the customer as well. The customer may, however, want to retain the right to assign the agreement under certain circumstances (e.g., merger or corporate reorganization) without the vendor's approval.

(hh) Governing Law and Venue   Virtually all standard form service contracts contain a provision setting forth the applicable law. In most instances, the vendor will assert that its corporate policy dictates the choice of governing law. Despite this assertion, the customer may insist on the governing law of its choice. For a contractual choice-of-law provision to be enforceable, the state's law chosen by the parties must bear a "reasonable relation" to the transaction involved. A court will not enforce a choice-of-law provision if the transaction has no relationship with a jurisdiction whose law is to apply.

While a choice-of-law provision may seem innocuous, it can have a substantial effect on the parties' rights. For example, some states hold that an inconspicuous provision limiting or excluding express and implied warranties is nevertheless enforceable as long as it was read and understood; other states' courts disagree and require a conspicuous (i.e., large type size) display. Thus, the application of a particular state's law may substantially affect the outcome of any dispute under the agreement.

(ii) Key Miscellaneous Provisions

Survival. Certain obligations of the parties, such as the indemnity and confidentiality obligations of each party, should survive any termination or expiration of the BPO contract. *Publicity.* Each of the parties may wish to limit the other's right to use its name in connection with advertising or marketing efforts.

No Solicitation.   It is common for a party, most frequently the vendor, to prohibit the other party from soliciting or hiring its employees. Such clauses typically restrict a party's right to solicit or hire an employee of the other party during the term of the BPO contract for a certain period after termination or expiration. As discussed earlier, the customer may wish to expressly retain the right to solicit and hire its former employees upon termination or expiration of the contract.

No Waiver.   Most outsourcing agreements contain a clause providing that the waiver of any breach is not a waiver of any subsequent breaches. Without the inclusion of specific contract terms, and sometimes even in the face of such provisions, the law has recognized that a party's conduct may modify his or her prior agreement. Where the conduct of the parties after signing the agreement clearly indicates that certain provisions were not given effect by the parties, courts will frequently treat such provisions as inoperative. Very often, waivers arise in law by reason of the inaction of a party. For example, an agreement may require the vendor to deliver a particular report every 24 hours. If over a period of months or years the actual delivery practice has been 72 hours, judges can be led to the conclusion that the time requirement set forth in the agreement was not really important and, in any event, was waived by the practice of the parties.

As has been stated, many service agreements require continuing performance over an extended time period. Inaction, even if occasioned by mere lack of attention on the part of a party, can have disastrous effects upon a clear and unequivocal agreement. Agreements generally provide that the only valid waiver is one reduced to writing and signed by the party to be charged with the waiver, that there will be no waiver implied by action or inaction, and that the waiver of a single breach shall not be deemed a waiver of any subsequent breach.

Injunctive Relief(ii) Key Miscellaneous Provisions.   There is a slightly more liberal attitude on the part of courts toward stopping or preventing people from doing things that might injure others. Injunctions often involve contractual elements known as restrictive covenants. Restrictive covenants are agreements, or portions of agreements, in which a party has contracted not to engage in a particular activity. Before a party can get an injunction, he or she must prove that the injury that will be sustained if the act is carried out cannot be adequately compensated for by money; that the party will be irreparably banned if the action is not prohibited; and that the party has no other remedy. For example, a person who sells a business and agrees not to solicit or do business with the existing customers of the business being sold will be enjoined from violating that agreement. The release of genuine trade secrets, in the face of an agreement not to do so, will conventionally be enjoined. If a particular methodology is developed by a consultant as a proprietary product for the customer, and if, in the face of a contractual prohibition, the consultant makes a copy of the relevant documentation and tries to sell that methodology to others, the courts will normally enjoin him or her from doing so. For restrictive covenants to be enforceable by injunction, they must be carefully drafted. Covenants that are overly broad, inadequately particularized, or unduly restrictive of free commerce will not be enforced by the judicial system. Restrictive covenants, when contracted for, are often of critical importance in a transaction and often involve matters in which monetary damages are inadequate. Accordingly, restrictive covenants should be drafted with great care.

5.4 REGAINING STRATEGIC CONTROL

One risk frequently identified when a customer is asked about the risks and benefits of outsourcing a business process is loss of control over the strategic direction of the business process. The outsourcing customer, however, does not necessarily have to turn over all control of the business process to the outsourcing vendor. In fact, the retention of strategic control by the customer is often key to a successful outsourcing relationship because it ensures that the customer has control over its business process direction, which is core to the customer's business even if the actual implementation of it may not be. This section will touch on some of the ways a customer can retain a degree of control without micromanaging the vendor.

(a) Technical Architecture and Product Standards   In an effort to retain control over the strategic direction of a business process, many customers wish to include in the BPO contract a provision stating that the customer is responsible for dictating and/or approving all technical architecture and product standards and that the vendor is required to comply with all existing *and future* standards dictated by the customer (possibly with the vendor's consultation). The cost of compliance with existing standards is typically included in the base fees. The cost of compliance with future standards may either be borne by the vendor as part of the base fees or borne by the customer to the extent that there are any incremental costs incurred by the vendor in connection with implementing any changes.

(b) Identifying Customer Responsibilities   It is important that the customer map out during the early stages of the BPO process which areas it considers strategic (e.g., the types of new methodologies or technology to be implemented) and what areas it considers operational (e.g., how the back office is run on a day-to-day basis). Examples of areas that customers may consider critical to their strategic direction include:

- Major changes in existing methodologies or technology (e.g., upgrades to existing hardware that will impact output or cost)
- Implementation of new methodologies or technology
- Changes to services
- Requirements for new projects
- Contract administration
- Internal liaison with corporate management

If an area is deemed strategic, and there are not overriding economic considerations, the customer should retain responsibility for that area either by maintaining that area in-house (e.g., some customers consider development of certain applications strategic and therefore wish to retain all or part of the development function in-house) or retaining control over that area (e.g., by having approval rights over how the function is carried out).

(c) In-House Capabilities   In many cases, the BPO contract includes provisions to allow the customer to retain strategic control of its business process operations, but the customer does not retain an adequate number of qualified personnel to manage the outsourcing relationship and exercise the terms of the BPO contract. The customer will need to weigh its need to manage the vendor and administer the contract against its desire to transfer as much responsibility to the vendor as possible. In a full-scale BPO transaction (i.e., where all functions of the particular business process are outsourced), the retained employees are typically managers and key technical personnel, such as:

- Project executive
- Project executive's direct reports
- Contract administrator
- Key operational and technical personnel (who understand and are able to manage and review day-to-day operations)

(d) Rights of Approval   The customer may wish to ensure that the BPO contract grants it adequate approval rights over strategic areas and functions. Examples of two key provisions are:

1. Except as may be necessary on an emergency basis to maintain the continuity of the Services, Vendor shall not, without Customer's consent, modify (1) the composition or the nature of the Services or (2) the manner in which the Services are provided or delivered if such modification or modifications would have an adverse effect on the business of Customer.
2. Except as may be approved by Customer, Vendor shall not make any changes or modifications to the Customer Intellectual Property, the Developed Intellectual

Property or the Vendor Intellectual Property (the "Intellectual Property") that would adversely alter the functionality of the Intellectual Property, degrade the performance of the Intellectual Property or materially affect the day-to-day operations of Customer's business.

(e) Vendor Concerns

Micromanagement. The vendor will likely object to any constraints on its ability to perform the services on the grounds that the customer should be concerned about output, not operations. The vendor may argue that to be able to provide the services at lower cost, it must have the freedom to control how operations are run. Why, for example, does the customer care about the methodologies or technology being used, if the output is not impacted? The answer, from the customer's prospective, is that the methodologies/technology being used may impact other costs and efficiency and cause integration and compatibility issues with other areas of the customer's organizations. While most customers agree that they should not micromanage the vendor, most also want to retain some control over the methodologies or technology being used.

Dedicated vs. shared environments. The vendor may take a different position on the amount of control retained by customer for dedicated and shared environments. The customer has an easier argument for retaining approval rights in a dedicated environment since other customers are not exercising similar approval rights.

Cost considerations. The vendor may argue that if the customer wants methodologies or technology that the vendor would not otherwise implement, then it will only implement these methodologies or technology at the customer's cost. Similarly, the vendor may argue that if the customer will not approve a change, the vendor is not liable for any problems caused by the failure to implement the change.

5.5 PRICING CONSIDERATIONS

The following discussion covers some of the possible pricing issues to consider when structuring the BPO transaction. This list is by no means exhaustive. Many customers and vendors are very creative in the ways that the fee schedules are engineered to address the needs and concerns of the parties.

(a) Pricing Structure

Fixed Fee. In fixed-fee deals, the customer pays a fixed (typically monthly) fee agreed upon during contract negotiation for the base services. The fixed fee may include all services within a particular business process or services up to a baseline (i.e., a specified number of help desk or customer service calls). It is of particular importance in fixed-fee deals to have a clear understanding of the scope and amount of services that are included. In most cases, the customer wishes to attach a detailed description of the base services. Any service not included in the description of base services or above a baseline will be considered an additional service and subject to an additional charge. A common problem in fixed-fee deals is that no matter how detailed the description of services, it does not (and likely cannot) account for all of the possible business changes that may occur.

Rate-Based Pricing. In deals with rate-based pricing, the customer and the vendor negotiate a set rate for a particular resource (e.g., maintenance hours, service calls, number of reports). The customer then pays for the amount of resource that it uses. Depending upon the amount of ramp-up resources needed to service the customer or the resources required to be held in reserve for the customer, the outsourcing deal may include a requirement that the customer purchase a minimum amount of services from the vendor. In addition, if the transaction involves more than one geographic location, the parties should consider whether there should be global rates or country-specific rates.

Fixed fee and rate-based pricing. A combination of fixed-fee and rate-based pricing is one of the most common types of pricing structures. Services that can be described in detail and quantified are subject to a fixed fee, and services that will likely increase and decrease over the term are subject to rate-based pricing.

Resource pool. In cases where the customer has not defined a project, the pricing may include a resource pool (e.g., a certain number of hours). The customer may then draw upon the resource pool during the term of the BPO contract, subject in some instances to certain restrictions (e.g., notice periods, limits on use of resources within a specified period).

Cost-plus pricing. In cost-plus pricing deals, the customer pays the vendor's cost plus overhead plus a specified profit. The parties negotiate which costs are allowable costs. Overhead is calculated according to a fixed formula, typically including such items as benefits, office space, and supplies. The profit varies from deal to deal, but typically ranges from 3 to 15 percent. Vendors typically resist cost-plus pricing on the grounds that they do not wish to disclose their costs. If the parties agree to cost-plus pricing, the customer should keep in mind that broad audit rights of all vendor costs are essential to monitoring whether the fees charged to the customer are accurate.

Percentage of asset cost value. Calculating the vendor's fees as a percentage of the cost of acquisition is a common pricing methodology in procurement outsourcing transactions (e.g., if a desk chair costs $100 and the percentage due the vendor is 5 percent of the asset cost, then the vendor would receive $5 per chair acquired on behalf of the customer). In other asset-based deals, such as asset management transactions, a possible pricing methodology may be to base the vendor's fees on the overall asset value (e.g., if the vendor will be managing $1 million of assets and the percentage due the vendor is 5 percent of the asset value, then the vendor would receive $50,000). Issues to consider when structuring a transaction using pricing based on the percentage of asset cost or value are at what point of time does acquisition occur (e.g., upon order, upon receipt) and how and at what point in time are assets valued (particularly with respect to financial products).

Time and materials. Time and materials pricing is typically used when the scope or potential duration of a project is not known or the specifications of a project cannot be defined. This type of pricing gives the customer the flexibility to start a project without knowing all of the variables. In some instances, the customer may elect to change from a time and materials contract to a fixed-fee contract after the project specifications are defined. The customer should ensure that the vendor is required to provide detailed back-up for all time logged in and materials purchased.

Pass-through expenses. The customer may wish to negotiate the pass through of certain expenses. The most typical examples are out-of-pocket expenses and travel. The vendor should be required to provide detailed back-up for pass-through expenses. The customer may even wish to consider having the vendor abide by the customer's internal expense policy, particularly with respect to travel expenses.

(b) Lump-Sum Payment for Assets   In outsourcing transactions where assets are being transferred from the customer to the vendor, the parties may negotiate a lump-sum payment to the customer due at contract signing. A lump-sum payment may provide the customer with a needed capital infusion or offset other transition costs.

(c) Spending Commitments   The customer may try to negotiate a lower price or a particular pricing structure (e.g., rate-based or cost-plus pricing) in exchange for a commitment that it will purchase all of its requirements from the vendor or that it will purchase a minimum amount of services from the vendor.

(d) Cost-of-Living Adjustments   The vendor will likely wish to reserve the right to periodically increase its fees at the end of each contract year to reflect the cost-of-living increase as reflected by an appropriate cost-of-living index. To avoid being confronted with an unreasonable increase in fees, the customer may wish to require that:

- A cap (e.g., an increase not to exceed the change in the Consumer Price Index for all Urban Consumers during the given year) be placed on any increase in fees
- Any cost of living increase apply only to inflation-sensitive pricing
- The cost of living adjustment does not apply until after the first or second year

(e) Other Pricing Considerations   In addition to the pricing considerations discussed earlier, the parties to the BPO transaction also need to consider how the items set forth in the following list will be handled and what, if any, impact these items will have on each party's pricing model. For example, the cost savings of a deal may change significantly if the customer will have responsibility for severance or redundancy payments to employees transferred to the vendor or if a 5 percent service tax will be added to all or a portion of the payments made to the vendor. Additional items that the parties should discuss when considering pricing include:

- Travel
- Out-of-pocket expenses
- Taxes
- Severance/redundancy payments
- Transition costs

5.6 ASSEMBLING THE TEAM

Because of the complex nature of the BPO transaction, it is useful for each party to assemble its team of experts as early in the transaction as possible. The team may include representatives from business, technical, finance, legal, audit, environmental, and human resources. If the transaction is international in scope, the team may need to be expanded to include local representatives from each of these categories.

CHAPTER 6

MEASURING PERFORMANCE

6.1 OVERVIEW

This chapter covers some of the mechanisms that customers and vendors may wish to consider including in the BPO contract to measure vendor performance. Measuring performance is an important part of the outsourcing arrangement because it allows the parties to assess the quality of service being delivered. In some instances, such mechanisms may be tied to a monetary charge for failure to perform in accordance with a certain level, an adjustment to services or fees for failure to perform in accordance with a certain level, or a monetary incentive if performance meets or exceeds a certain level. The mechanisms focused on in this chapter are the establishment and monitoring of service levels, benchmarking, and gainsharing.

6.2 SERVICE LEVELS

The information technology (IT) outsourcing marketplace in many respects rests upon a foundation of service levels in the outsourcing contract. During the early stages of the IT boom, the inclusion of service level commitments in the outsourcing contract was often resisted by the vendor and, accordingly, was the subject of much negotiation between the parties. If service levels were agreed to, it was often based on some commitment to establish the service levels at some date in the future (which in many instances never happened). As customers have grown more sophisticated and the marketplace matures, service level commitments are becoming the norm rather than the exception. Vendors, who once considered service levels as mechanisms used to hold their feet to the fire, are now taking a different approach.

The BPO marketplace has been following this trend as well. In the BPO market, users often want better, more efficient services (at lower costs) regardless of the terms of the outsourcing contract. Unlike IT, where the typical user is familiar with but not directly impacted by or responsible for the service levels specified in the contract, the users in a BPO deal are accustomed to seeing tangible results associated with the processes being outsourced. User perception, therefore, as to the level of service that they should be receiving is not always consistent with what the outsourcing contract requires the vendor to provide.

(a) Objectives for Using Service Levels   As discussed earlier, in many instances, both customers and vendors wish to include service level commitments in the outsourcing contract. Some common objectives for using service level commitments include:

Setting user expectations. It is important in any outsourcing transaction for the customer to not oversell the outsourcing deal. Users may view the proposed outsourcing as a means for obtaining better and more efficient services. While this is often the case, user expectations may exceed the services (and prices) agreed to under the contract. The customer may use the service level agreements to let users know what to expect. Many customers survey the users (or a core group of users) and ask them to buy in to the service level agreements before the service level agreements are negotiated with the vendor.

Setting management expectations. Just as important as setting user expectations is setting management expectations about the level of service to be provided by the outsourcing vendor. Setting management expectations is a key task for both the customer and the vendor. The vendor's first encounter with customer management is typically during the sales phase of the outsourcing transaction. In an effort to sell the deal, the vendor often uses general language, such as "best of breed" and "state of the art" when presenting the proposed deal to customer's management. Customer management often hears these terms and envisions better, more efficient services—and thinks that is what gets documented in the outsourcing contract. The BPO contract is much more specific and typically outlines the vendor's service level commitment in detail. It is important for both the customer and the vendor to level set management's expectations vis-à-vis the actual terms of the outsourcing contract.

Meeting end user requirements. In addition to setting end user and management expectations, service level agreements are often used to ensure that the outsourcing contract meets the end users' requirements. It is often good practice to survey the end users to determine their requirements and sort out what is required as opposed to what is a wish list item. Requirements may change once the end user understands the price associated with the better or enhanced service level. End user accountability for service level requirements and associated costs leads to fewer perception problems (as discussed earlier).

Monitoring performance. Both customers and vendors use service level agreements to monitor the vendor's performance. In most instances, the vendor is responsible under the outsourcing contract for providing to the customer performance reports that document whether the service level commitments are being met.

Demonstrating contract compliance or noncompliance. By monitoring service levels, the vendor is able to demonstrate its compliance (or noncompliance) with the terms of the outsourcing contract.

Targeting areas of needed improvement or overachievement. In addition to demonstrating vendor compliance or noncompliance with the contract terms, monitoring the service levels enables the customer and the vendor to see whether there are any areas that require improvement and, perhaps, the use of additional or enhanced resources. Similarly, the performance reports may reveal areas where the vendor is consistently exceeding the agreed-on service level. In these instances, the customer may wish to eliminate or reallocate resources.

(b) Establishing Service Levels While the parties may agree that the BPO contract should include service level commitments, discussions about the *actual* service level commitments to be used are often lengthy. The customer obviously wants the best service level commitments it can negotiate. However, the customer may not have service level agreements in place prior to the outsourcing or historical data necessary to validate the desired service levels. The vendor—who is often providing the services using equipment, methodologies, technology, and personnel inherited from the customer—only wants to commit to service levels that it knows it can meet (often with some buffer) using the resources at hand. Some common techniques used for establishing service levels include:

Existing service level agreements. More and more customers (but by no means all customers) have service level agreements in place prior to outsourcing. This enables the customer to include the service level agreements in the RFP, if there is one, or at least show the vendor the expected service level commitments so that it can make certain assumptions as it prices and allocates resources to the deal. Even if there are service level agreements in place, the vendor may wish to see performance reports documenting whether the customer actually met the service level commitments on a consistent basis. If the customer was not able to meet the service level commitments, the vendor may need to change, upgrade, or enhance the resources (such as equipment, methodologies, technology, and personnel) being used to be able to meet the service level commitments on a consistent basis going forward.

Historical data. If the customer has historical data that documents performance prior to the outsourcing, the customer and the vendor may be able to use such data to assess and establish service levels using the resources being transferred to the vendor. Again, the vendor may be willing to commit to better service levels by upgrading or enhancing the resources being used.

Benchmarking future performance. Often, the customer does not have historical data to document past performance. In these cases, the customer and vendor may agree to collect data and monitor performance during some representative period (e.g., the 180-day period after the commencement date). Such data will then be used to establish the service level commitments. Note that this method would not apply to time-sensitive service levels (e.g., tax filings, reporting) where the service level is tied to a specified date (see the discussions of customer requirements and business/regulatory requirements that follow).

Customer requirements. Another approach is to establish the service levels based on user requirements. While historical data or benchmarking may reveal on-time delivery 92 percent of the time, users may require on-time delivery 98 percent of the time. Therefore, the service level to be met by the vendor is 98 percent with the agreement that the vendor will upgrade or enhance resources as part of the base fees in order to be able to meet the 98 percent requirement.

Business/regulatory requirements. Service levels may also be driven by business or regulatory requirements. For example, the vendor may be responsible for generating reports that need to be filed with the tax authorities by a certain time or date. This deadline is likely to be met on a quarterly or annual basis. Arguably, the service level for this service should be 100 percent since, if the vendor misses the deadline, the customer may be penalized or fined.

Service levels during initial transition. As part of contract negotiations, the customer and the vendor should discuss the level of service to be delivered to the customer during the transition of services from the customer to the vendor. For example, the customer may wish to include in the outsourcing contract a commitment from the vendor that the service levels will not be degraded during the transition. The vendor, however, may wish to include a commitment to use reasonable efforts to meet service levels during the transition without making an outright commitment to do so.

(c) Service Level Agreements   The customer will need to decide the level of detail that it wishes to include in the service level agreement (SLAs). For example, will there be a general service level for response time for help desk calls or will there be more specific service levels for types of calls (e.g., priority 1, 2, and 3)? In most instances, customers have found the more specificity the better. Vendors, in turn, may commit to specific service levels with the understanding that they will only incur performance credits (see Section h) with respect to certain critical service levels.

(d) Excused Performance   Although most vendors agree to include service levels in the outsourcing contract, they also seek to limit their obligation to perform in accordance with the service levels in certain instances. For example, with respect to certain response-based service levels, the parties may agree to some scheduled or anticipated period during which services are unavailable. In addition, the vendor typically wishes to exculpate itself from liability to the extent that failure to meet a service level is due to customer's failure to perform its obligations or the failure of third-party equipment or resources that are not the responsibility of the vendor. The customer and the vendor should carefully review the instances for which the vendor is excused from meeting the service levels to ensure that they are not overly broad or too narrow in light of the services being provided.

(e) Innovative Service Levels   As the concept of service levels is becoming more common, customers and vendors are becoming more innovative about the types of service level commitments included in the outsourcing contract. Examples of innovative service levels include:

> *Customer satisfaction.* The vendor guarantees a certain percentage of positive customer satisfaction or the vendor guarantees a certain percentage of increase in customer satisfaction.
> *Productivity.* The vendor guarantees certain productivity improvements over a specified period.
> *Cost savings.* The vendor guarantees certain cost savings or reduced liability (particularly with respect to tax compliance services) over a specified period. These cost savings or reduction in liability may be tied to the vendor's ability to identify areas where services or operations can be reduced, eliminated, or consolidated.

(f) Reporting   To monitor the vendor's performance in accordance with the service levels, the vendor typically undertakes to implement performance monitoring tools that generate performance reports documenting vendor performance on a weekly, monthly, quarterly, and/or annual basis, depending on the service. The customer and the vendor typically discuss the content and breakdown of these reports during contract negotiations. It is important for the customer to review these reports on a regular basis to ensure that they are accurate and to document any service level failures on a consistent and ongoing basis.

(g) Adjustment of Service Levels   Service levels, like the underlying services themselves, typically do not remain static over the term of the contract. Therefore, the parties to the outsourcing contract may wish to consider including in the contract a mechanism for reviewing and adjusting service levels. Examples of these mechanisms include:

- An agreement for the management or advisory committee to meet once every calendar quarter to review the service levels in light of changes to services, methodologies, and technology as well as the customer's changing business needs and adjust them (and the fees if applicable) as necessary
- The adjustment of service levels based on the results of a benchmark conducted that shows the service levels are below industry standards
- A requirement that the vendor automatically adjust service levels to comply with certain business or regulatory requirements that are driven by external forces

(h) Remedies   Once the service levels have been agreed upon by the customer and the vendor, the next step (at least from the customer's perspective) is to discuss what happens if the vendor fails to meet the service levels. What is the customer's remedy? There are a variety of approaches for dealing with service level failures. The selected approach will depend upon a number of factors, including the types of services being provided (e.g., are they critical to the customer's business? are certain services more critical than others?), the degree of responsibility the vendor has for missed service levels (e.g., is the outsourcing vendor only one of multiple vendors responsible for a particular service?), and the value of the deal (e.g., how much revenue is the vendor willing to put at risk?). Remedies for service level failures include:

Root cause analysis. The outsourcing customer may wish to include a mechanism in the BPO contract that requires the vendor, upon the occurrence of a service level failure, to investigate the cause of the failure, remedy the failure, and provide assurances to the customer that the failure will not occur again. The vendor, although often willing to include some type of root cause obligation in the BPO contract, may wish to limit its obligation to perform root cause analyses to repeated failures (at least for noncritical failures). In addition, the vendor may wish to be absolved of responsibility (as well as the imposition of any performance credits) and compensated for the root cause analysis if the failure turns out to be the result of third-party services or resources not the responsibility of the vendor.

Performance credits. Most customers now wish to include a scheme by which the customer in effect receives a credit for reduced or failed performance. The performance credit scheme varies from transaction to transaction. In many instances, the customers and the vendors do not tie performance credits to every service level, but focus on certain critical service levels that would cause particular problems if they were missed. In addition, for service levels based on percentages (e.g., on-time delivery 98 percent of the time), the vendor's performance is often measured over a specified period (typically monthly) so that credits would only apply if the vendor failed to meet the service levels on the average during such measurement period. The amount of revenue at risk as performance credits is the subject of much negotiation. Examples include performance credits calculated as a percentage of the monthly fees, a fixed dollar amount, or as the amount of fines that the customer would incur for missed deadlines.

Performance bonuses. The vendor may argue that if the customer insists upon performance credits then it is only fair that the vendor be entitled to performance bonuses if it exceeds the service levels. Many customers welcome the opportunity for the vendor to overachieve and agree to put some amount into a bonus pool (which is typically netted out against the credit pool). Other customers reject such argument on the basis that they are comfortable with the service levels that they have agreed to and there is no additional value to the customer if the vendor overachieves (e.g., production is not enhanced or revenue increased).

Termination. A remedy in addition to or in lieu of performance credits is termination. If the vendor fails to meet the service levels (at least critical service levels or other service levels on a repeated basis), the customer may want the ability to terminate the vendor for breach. While this may be an implied right under the termination provisions in the BPO contract, many customers wish to add an explicit right to terminate upon the failure to meet certain service levels or if the performance credits exceed a certain amount over a specified period.

6.3 BENCHMARKING

It has become more common for customers to negotiate some type of benchmarking provision into the BPO contract. The general objective of a benchmarking provision is to provide a mechanism by which the parties periodically compare the services being provided and/or prices being charged against similar services being provided and/or prices being charged to a specified customer or industry group. While the effectiveness of benchmarking provisions is debatable, most customers feel that the inclusion of such a provision will at a minimum give the customer some leverage if the pricing, methodologies, technology, or service levels are significantly different than market standards. Vendors typically resist the inclusion of benchmarking provisions on the grounds that the comparative data is easily manipulated and the results are difficult to interpret.

(a) Scope of Benchmark   An overriding question that arises when considering the scope of a benchmarking provision is what will be benchmarked. Areas that may be benchmarked include:

- Total or aggregate cost
- Unit or element cost
- Types of methodologies or technology
- Manner of providing services
- Service levels

A related issue is the geographical scope of the benchmark. For example, will the benchmark assess whether the customer is receiving pricing as good as or better than other organizations in a particular country or region (e.g., organizations in the customer's industry in the United States) or will the benchmark assess whether the customer is receiving the best pricing offered to other organizations anywhere in the world? With respect to international transactions, the pricing structure may affect the scope of the benchmark. For example, if the customer pays one global rate for all resources, the benchmark will likely assess whether the customer is receiving the best global pricing. However, if the customer pays different rates on a country-by-country basis, the benchmark may assess whether the customer is receiving favorable rates on a country-by-country basis (rather than globally). An example of contract language dealing with the scope of the benchmark is:

> Customer and Vendor shall jointly implement the objective benchmarking measurement and comparison process described in Exhibit [* * *] in order to ensure that Vendor provides Customer with [unit pricing] [methodologies/technology] [service levels] equal to or greater than other organizations receiving similar services.

(b) Organizations Used for Comparison   The parties will need to select the peer organizations against which the costs, methodologies, technology, and/or service levels will be benchmarked. The group of organizations may include the following (and variations thereof):

- Organizations in the customer's industry generally
- Agreed-on competitors of the customer
- Organizations in the customer's industry that outsource similar services
- Other customers of the vendor generally
- Other customers of the vendor that are in the customer's industry
- Outsourcing customers generally
- Other outsourcing customers in the customer's industry in a particular geographic location (e.g., all retailers in the southeastern United States; all manufacturing companies in the United Kingdom)
- All outsourcing customers in the customer's industry worldwide

The customer and the vendor typically wish to identify peer organizations with as many characteristics similar to the customer's characteristics as possible, including:

- Similar types of services
- Similar volumes
- Similar services provided by an outsourcing vendor (rather than internally)
- Similar geographic location(s) (this is applicable if the scope of the benchmark is limited to a geographical or regional pool of organizations, rather than a worldwide pool of organizations)

The customer and the vendor may wish to agree on a method for level-setting organizations included in the benchmark that are not exact matches. For example, if the benchmark will assess whether the customer is receiving pricing as good as or better than prices received by other outsourcing customers in the customer's industry anywhere in the world, the benchmark may need to take into account market rates for personnel, inflation, and currency exchange rates. An example of a clause attempting to define the peer organizations to be included in the benchmark is:

> As part of the benchmarking process, the parties will identify the group of organizations against which the services and pricing provided to Customer will be measured ("Peer Organizations"). The parties will consider the following guidelines when identifying the Peer Organizations: [LIST; E.G., SIMILAR BUSINESS; SIMILAR SERVICES; SIMILAR VOLUMES]. The parties shall review in a timely manner the list of Peer Organizations prior to each implementation of the benchmarking process and, upon agreement of the parties, add and delete organizations from the list of Peer Organizations. If there is any disagreement between the parties as to the inclusion or exclusion of an organization as a Peer Organization, [Customer] [the benchmarker] [the Management Committee] shall make the final decision.

(c) The Benchmarker   The next question to be addressed when structuring a benchmarking process is who will perform the benchmark. There are a number of options to consider when deciding upon the benchmarker, including:

- An independent third party
- The customer's consultants (affiliated or nonaffiliated)
- The vendor's employees assigned to the outsourcing project
- The vendor's employees not assigned to the outsourcing project (to ensure the resources that should be dedicated to providing services and achieving service levels are not diverted to perform the benchmark)
- The vendor's consultants (affiliated or nonaffiliated)
- The vendor's employees or consultants initially, with disputes handled by an independent third party

The choice of who will conduct the benchmark typically depends on cost (it is expensive to have a third party conduct the benchmark) and the intended use of the benchmarking results (if the results are for informational purposes only, then having the customer or the vendor's in-house personnel perform the benchmark may be acceptable, but if the results will require the vendor to adjust the fees to be more in-line with other outsourcing customers or require the vendor to expend resources or capital, then an independent third party may be more appropriate). The customer may wish to reserve the right to have different organizations or resources conduct the benchmark for different types of services (e.g., for an accounting services transaction, one benchmarking organization may be better at benchmarking financial services while another is better at benchmarking the underlying systems used to provide the services). Many customers insist upon including the identity of the initial benchmarker or a list of acceptable benchmarkers in the BPO contract, thereby limiting the vendor's ability to delay the benchmarking process by disqualifying the customer-proposed benchmarkers. Some potential issues to consider when considering third-party benchmarkers include:

- Is the organization an independent entity (e.g., not affiliated with the customer or the vendor)?
- Is the organization a competitor of the customer?
- Does the organization have experience in conducting this type of benchmark for these particular services in this geographic area?
- What type of methodology does the organization use?
- Does the organization have satisfactory references?
- Does the organization have any potential conflict of interest?

As mentioned earlier, the potential costs of performing the benchmark may be expensive. The parties will need to discuss how the costs of the internal or third party resources used to perform the benchmarking are to be allocated. Cost allocation schemes may include:

- The vendor builds the cost of third-party or internal resources into its price
- The vendor charges the customer on a pass-through basis for the cost of the third-party benchmarker
- The vendor and the customer share the cost of the third-party benchmarker
- The vendor absorbs the cost of the benchmarker if it reveals that the vendor's prices, methodologies, technology, or services are not in line with industry standards

An example of a clause appointing the benchmarker is:

The benchmark shall be conducted by [* * *], or his or her replacement as provided in this Section (each, a "Benchmarker"). In the event (1) a Benchmarker is no longer providing the services necessary to conduct the benchmarking, (2) another individual or organization has a more appropriate benchmarking system or methodology as agreed by Customer and Vendor or (3) Customer and Vendor otherwise agree that the Benchmarker should be replaced, Customer and Vendor shall promptly replace such Benchmarker. The fees and expenses charged by the Benchmarker shall be paid by [Customer] [Vendor].

(d) The Process

Timing. Benchmarking may be conducted on a regular basis (e.g., annually, biannually, quarterly) or on an as-requested basis often with a cap on the number of requests made a year (e.g., upon request but not more than four times a year). Since benchmarking can be time consuming and expensive (particularly if a third party is engaged to perform the benchmarking), most customers and vendors wish to limit the amount of benchmarking that is required.

Underlying data. The benchmark will be based on data compiled by the parties or by an independent organization. The parties may wish to agree, either during negotiations or prior to the initial benchmark, upon the types and scope of underlying data to be used in the benchmarking process (e.g., data obtained from a company in a comparable position, from a group of companies, from an index, from a group of indices). The benchmarker will analyze the data and determine whether any assumptions need to be built into the analysis as well as whether the data should be leveled in any way (e.g., discounted).

The Results. The benchmarker will then take the data and assess whether the vendor's prices/methodologies/technology/services meet the benchmark requirements (e.g., in line with industry standards, best of breed). If the benchmarking results reveal that the vendor is not performing in accordance with the benchmark requirements, the vendor may then be required to:

Adjust the prices/methodologies/technology/services at the vendor's cost

Notify the customer of any necessary adjustment to the prices/methodologies/technology/services and allow the customer to assess whether it wishes to implement changes at the customer's cost

The vendor may try to contest the results on the grounds that the underlying data is flawed. The vendor may argue that the services being provided to the organizations studied are not the same as the services being provided to the customer or that the fees being charged to the customer are not in line with other organizations because they have been streamlined to allow for steady payments or have been engineered, for example, to reflect greater savings in the early years.

Reports. Both parties typically wish to receive copies of any benchmarking reports, as well as copies of the underlying data if such data is made available to the other party.

Dispute resolution. A major problem with benchmarking provisions is that it is difficult to construct a satisfactory dispute resolution mechanism. A common scenario is that the benchmarking results reveal that pricing is too high, the vendor disputes the results and then the parties are at an impasse with the only alternative being arbitration or litigation, which is typically undesirable for both parties. Some outsourcing agreements have tried to deal with this problem by making the interim findings of the benchmarker subject to review and discussion but making the final findings binding, or by building a mini-arbitration into the benchmarking provision with the arbitrator being an independent benchmarking company other than the company that performed the original benchmarking. Again, the decision of the arbitrator would be final and binding on the parties.

(e) Alternatives to Benchmarking

Most favored customer provision. In lieu of or in addition to a benchmarking provision, the customer may wish to include a most favored customer provision that requires the vendor to provide pricing, methodologies, or technology similar to or better than other similarly situated customers. The parties will need to negotiate what is intended by the term "similarly situated" (e.g., similar volumes, types of services in the aggregate/service categories).

Notification of new developments. One purpose of the benchmarking clause is to ensure that the customer is kept abreast of industry standards and trends. The customer may wish to include in the BPO contract a requirement that the vendor periodically update the customer as to new developments.

Right to competitively bid. Some customers have taken the position that the only effective way to "benchmark" is to reserve the right to competitively bid (and source) all or a portion of the services on a periodic basis. Most vendors resist such a provision since it may be difficult to segregate parts of the outsourcing contract (particularly if there has been some financial engineering), and since it may be possible that they may lose all or a portion of the BPO contract.

6.4 GAINSHARING

A favorite buzzword during negotiations of outsourcing transactions is "gainsharing." Customers are becoming insistent that the outsourcing deal include gainsharing arrangements, and vendors are agreeing to gainshare. What is meant by "gainsharing," however, is nebulous at best. On its face, the term means that the parties will share in the gain (interpreted as savings or revenue) realized by a party. Gainsharing has come to mean anything from simple cost-saving mechanisms included in the outsourcing contract (e.g., the vendor agrees to work with the customer to identify areas that can be eliminated or handled using fewer resources, without having a material impact on front-end services, and the parties will share in the savings to the customer) to options or warrants granted to the vendor in the customer (or granted to the customer in the vendor) and actual joint venture relationships (e.g., the parties will form a joint venture that will initially provide services to the customer and will ultimately provide similar services to other companies in the customer's industry).

The success of the implementation of gainsharing arrangements has been questionable. Often—at least early in the deal—the gainsharing provisions are overshadowed by transition and performance issues (e.g., if the customer is dissatisfied with the level of service that it is receiving, the implementation of a gainsharing arrangement such as co-marketing of a new product or application becomes a secondary concern). Other common problems include incentive payments or obligations becoming due at the same time a balloon payment is due under a financially engineered outsourcing deal, a change in customer management with the new management not able to understand why it is paying incentives to the vendor at all when services are not perceived as being satisfactory, and the gainsharing incentive is tied to customer or vendor revenue/profit that skyrockets in a particular year for reasons not related to the business process and, therefore, results in an unforeseen windfall to a party.

Exhibit 6.1 provides examples of several generic gainsharing arrangements. These arrangements are intended to be illustrative only. Gainsharing arrangements tend to be the subject of much negotiation and are, therefore, specifically tailored to the deal at hand. As with any business arrangement, gainsharing arrangements should be reviewed carefully by the parties from a business, legal, and tax perspective.

	GAINSHARING ARRANGEMENT	HOW IT WORKS	ISSUES TO CONSIDER
1.	• The vendor receives an incentive based on the actual savings against *budget* realized by the customer • The vendor receives an incentive based on the actual savings against *previous year's spending* realized by the customer	• The customer submits base budget or the previous year's spending to the vendor; the vendor commits to a certain percentage of savings over the portion of budget/spend outsourced • Savings commitment needs to be adjusted to reflect scope changes, volume changes, capacity changes, additional/fewer units, partial termination of services • Savings commitment does not pertain to retained portion of the budget/spend	• The vendor should require that budget/spend numbers reflect inflation • The parties will need to discuss which inflation indices apply • The customer may wish to require that budget is adjusted to reflect unanticipated changes resulting in windfall savings
2.	• The vendor commits to provide the services at prices that are comparable to the customer's peer organizations; the vendor receives an incentive for any savings below peer index	• The parties agree to benchmark services provided to comparable organizations • If the vendor can show savings against market rates, then the vendor receives an incentive	• The parties will need to negotiate who will perform the benchmarking (e.g., independent third party), what organizations will be surveyed and whether benchmark will apply to aggregate or unit services • Although vendors typically resist benchmarking provisions, this is an instance where benchmarking may be acceptable to the vendor
3.	• The vendor receives an incentive based on the amount of areas or projects that the vendor eliminates or reduces without cutting front-end services	• The incentive compensation is typically based only on the vendor's ideas that are actually implemented	• The vendor must have access to the customer's organization • The process should be clear and agreed to during contract negotiations (e.g., what services will be targeted; ideas are submitted to a committee then added to a database) • The customer may argue that the idea to eliminate certain services was not completely initiated by the vendor
4.	• The customer provides incentive compensation to the vendor for any business improvements delivered over the term through business process reengineering	• (Similar to item 3)	

(Continued)

Exhibit 6.1 Examples of Gainsharing Arrangements[1]

[1] © 1998 by John K. Halvey and Barbara Melby. All rights reserved. Reprinted with permission.

GAINSHARING ARRANGEMENT	HOW IT WORKS	ISSUES TO CONSIDER
5. • The customer commits to "respend" certain dollar amounts in services with the vendor to the extent vendor effectively eliminates/reduces services	• If the customer saves $_____, then the customer must respend a certain percentage of such savings within a specified time period	
6. • The vendor enters into a requirements contract with the customer	• If cost savings realized, then the customer must obtain certain types of services from the vendor only	
7. • The vendor commits to performance or productivity levels; if the vendor does not meet the specified levels, the vendor must give the customer a credit; if the vendor exceeds the levels, the vendor receives an incentive payment	• The parties need to agree to and set performance levels	• Most contracts include some type of performance charge if performance levels are not met; few include a bonus for overachievement on the basis that after a certain level, the customer is not benefited from the overachievement (e.g., 98% vs. 99% uptime)
8. • The vendor and the customer agree to share the risk or benefit of the implementation of new methodologies or technology	• The parties may share in implementation costs or the vendor may agree to spread the upfront costs over the term of the contract in return for the sharing in realized cost savings • The vendor agrees to liquidated damages in the event the roll-out is delayed due to the vendor's fault; the customer will compensate the vendor if the roll-out is delayed due to the customer's fault • If certain milestones are achieved (e.g., roll-out, achievement of requirements), the vendor receives an incentive payment	
9. • The vendor receives a bonus if the customer's [gross] [net] profits exceed a certain amount	• Partnership approach • Alternative to taking an equity interest and sharing in profits • Arguably more relevant when the vendor is investing up-front resources in the customer • The vendor is incented to make the customer more efficient/more marketable • Provision typically applicable on an annual basis	• The customer is often dissatisfied because there is no clear indication that the increased profits are directly linked to the business process services or improvements (as opposed to market or other business process improvements) • The vendor may become frustrated if the customer has unanticipated write-offs for the year that are not related to the business process • If profits are tied to annual report, financials may be subject to certain engineering

(Continued)

Exhibit 6.1   Examples of Gainsharing Arrangements *(Continued)*

	GAINSHARING ARRANGEMENT	HOW IT WORKS	ISSUES TO CONSIDER
10.	• The vendor receives a bonus if the customer's [gross] [net] revenues exceed a certain amount	• (Similar to item 9)	• The parties will need to discuss appropriate caps or thresholds
11.	• The vendor receives options/warrants in the customer in return for reduced fees	• Typically implemented when the customer is in financial trouble	
12.	• The customer receives options/warrants in the vendor as an incentive for entering into the outsourcing deal	• Typically implemented in large transactions or when the customer has significant negotiating leverage	
13.	• A party receives a seat on the board of directors of the other party		
14.	• The vendor has the right to use or market any newly developed methodology or technology with its other customers	• The vendor either owns the methodology or technology with a non-exclusive, limited license granted to the customer or the customer owns the methodology or technology with a license granted back to the vendor	• The vendor may provide a reduced development rate to the customer or commit additional resources/know-how to the development effort
15.	• The parties agree to market methodology or technology to third parties and share in the revenues	• Parties may enter into a co-marketing agreement where both parties market new products and share in any generated revenues or may form a joint venture or new entity to market the methodology or technology (see items 16 and 17 below)	
16.	• The parties form a joint venture or new entity to market methodologies, technology, or services to other companies in the customer's industry	• Formation of a joint venture or new entity	• Will the joint venture or new entity provide services back to the customer or will its sole purpose be to act as a vehicle to market methodologies, technology, or services to third parties? • What resources or capital will each party contribute? • How will equity or profits be allocated?
17.	• The parties form a join venture/new entity to develop, implement and market new methodologies/technology/services	• Formation of joint venture or new entity	• What resources or capital will each party contribute? • How will equity or profits be allocated?

Exhibit 6.1 Examples of Gainsharing Arrangements (*Continued*)

CHAPTER 7

HUMAN RESOURCES*

7.1 TRANSITIONING EMPLOYEES TO THE VENDOR

As part of the outsourcing arrangement, the outsourcing vendor may be required to make offers of employment to all or a substantial number of the employees of the outsourcing customer, who currently provide the business process services to be outsourced. The customer and the vendor will need to discuss and negotiate the number of employees to be offered employment with the vendor, the terms of the employment offers, the timing of the employee transition, the schedule for employee communications and, in some cases, procedures for dealing with precontract staffing problems (e.g., stay incentives, provision of temporary vendor personnel, etc.). The outcome of these discussions and negotiations will depend on a number of factors, including:

- The customer's outsourcing objectives (e.g., improvement of business process capabilities, cost savings, etc.)
- The services to be outsourced
- The service levels desired by the customer
- The ability of the vendor to be more efficient than customer in providing the services
- The need for the vendor to acquire business or technical knowledge of the customer
- Employee morale and expectations
- Customer precedent
- Comparability of customer and vendor compensation and benefits (e.g., salary levels, bonuses and other forms of incentive pay, benefits, severance)

The reduction in personnel costs occasioned by the transfer of employees to the vendor often accounts for a large percentage of the total direct cost savings anticipated by the outsourcing customer. While these savings may be significant, the customer considering outsourcing should be mindful of the associated business and legal issues. The costs and inconvenience associated with the administration and resolution of a mismanaged employee transition (e.g., litigation, arbitration, government proceedings, settlement) may

---

* Jane L. Hanson, an employment lawyer with Milbank, Tweed, Hadley & McCloy LLP, assisted in the preparation of this revised and updated Chapter 7.

prevent the customer from realizing many of the anticipated benefits of the outsourcing transaction.[1]

Personnel issues warrant particular consideration throughout the negotiation process. As noted in Chapter 2, human resources representatives from both the vendor and the customer should be included in the outsourcing teams as early as possible. The number of representatives will depend on the scope of the transaction and the number of sites or locations that will be transitioning employees (particularly if there are sites outside the United States) and may include legal counsel with employment law or human resources expertise. For the purposes of this chapter, human resources issues have been divided into five categories. The applicability and importance of each of these categories will vary from transaction to transaction. The categories are:

1. Due diligence (i.e., preliminary information gathering and analysis)
2. Terms and conditions of employment
3. Employee transitioning
4. Administrative and financial responsibilities
5. Contract-related issues (e.g., warranties, indemnities, rights upon termination)

7.2 DUE DILIGENCE

(a) Employees Affected by Transition Prior to sending out the RFP (or, if the customer does not intend to send out a RFP, at the early stages of the negotiation process with the outsourcing vendor), the customer's outsourcing team should determine how it wishes to structure the human resources part of the outsourcing transaction. This will involve first identifying which employees are in-scope or will be affected by the transaction (typically referred to in the outsourcing agreement as "in-scope employees" and/or "affected employees") and then determining whether all or only a portion of these employees should be transferred to the vendor's employment. Influencing this determination will be such factors as whether the customer wants the vendor to make the most cost-effective bid, with the option of hiring all or some of the in-scope employees, and whether there are some employees the customer wants to retain.

A useful exercise to get the process started is for the customer to prepare a list of all employees who currently provide business process services to be outsourced (including employees who may be transitioned to the vendor and those who may be laid off or retained by the customer; see Exhibit 7.1). When preparing this list, the customer typically includes employees who are included in the budget of the department or function to be outsourced.

---

[1] Articles and cases involving the transition of employees to an outsourcing vendor include:
- "Warning! Court Ruling: Companies that Don't Factor Staff in Outsourcing Deal Will Pay the Price," *Information Week,* December 20–27, 1993, p. 12.
- Halvey, John K. and Murphy, Barbara J., "Outsourcing and Bank Employees," *Bank Outsourcing Report,* September 15, 1992 (Vol. 1, No. 11).
- Complaint, *McMahon v. Eastman Kodak Company* (W.D.N.Y. February 25, 1992) (No. 92-6081-T) (11 former employees of Kodak brought an action for injunctive relief, actual damages, and $5 million in punitive damages against Kodak and its outsourcing vendor DEC alleging that Kodak discriminated against plaintiffs on the basis of age and breached its fiduciary duties to the plaintiffs under ERISA and that Kodak and DEC fraudulently induced the plaintiffs to agree to be hired by DEC).
- Employees from Nashville Electric Service (NES) filed suit against NES and outsourcing vendor Seltmann, Cobb and Bryant, Inc. seeking to enjoin outsourcing transaction from being implemented on the grounds that the transaction violated NES policies which stipulated that job transfers and layoffs must be based on seniority and performance.

EMPLOYEE NAME OR ID NUMBER	SITE/LOCATION	JOB TITLE OR DESCRIPTION	COMMENTS

Exhibit 7.1 Identifying In-Scope Employees[a]

[a] This exhibit, the other exhibits discussed later in this chapter, and most other human resources–related data and information compiled in connection with the outsourcing transaction contain sensitive information. To limit the disclosure of this information, the customer may wish to take the following protective measures:

- Designate one individual who will be responsible for preparing and revising the list
- Maintain a limited number of copies of the list—preferably one master
- Date each successive draft and identify it as "Strictly Confidential"
- Shred all prior drafts and copies of the list
- Notify the vendor(s) of these measures and require vendor compliance

In addition, the customer and the vendor should be careful not to include unnecessary information in these charts. For example, the charts should not contain information regarding any protected characteristic (e.g., sex, race, age (including date of birth), disability, etc.).

The customer should also consider employees who are not in the particular budget but provide shadow support.

Once the in-scope employees have been identified, the customer should make a preliminary assessment about which employees it wishes to retain (usually management-level employees and in some cases key employees with critical knowledge or expertise) and which employees more appropriately should be transitioned to the vendor or laid off. This assessment is often made in conjunction with the information contained in the vendor proposals and with direct vendor input. An example of a chart used to compile the employee information is set forth in Exhibit 7.2. The information contained in this exhibit should be updated throughout the course of the negotiations.

As the transaction progresses, the general information included in Exhibit 7.2 can be expanded on and separated into more specific charts relating to employees being transferred, retained and, if applicable, laid off (see Exhibits 7.3, 7.4, and 7.5). As with Exhibit 7.2, these charts should be updated throughout the course of the negotiations, particularly because the information in these charts is often used by the customer's financial analysts (or controllers) in assessing the cost benefits of the vendor's proposal and by the vendor's financial analysts in preparing pricing information.

(b) Compensation and Benefit Analysis   A standard requirement in most RFPs and vendor proposals is that the vendor offer customer employees who will be transitioned substantially equivalent or comparable compensation and benefits to those being provided by the customer. Failure of the vendor to provide equivalent or comparable compensation and benefits may also trigger rights under the customer's severance plan (i.e., a severance plan may provide that the customer will be responsible for severance if an employee is not offered employment with comparable or substantially equivalent compensation). For transactions involving countries outside the United States (particularly Europe) comparable compensation may also be a legal requirement. For example, in some countries if an employee is not transferred on substantially similar terms, he or she will be entitled to redundancy pay.

EMPLOYEE NAME OR ID NUMBER	SITE/LOCATION	JOB TITLE OR DESCRIPTION	TRANSFERRED (Y/N)	RETAINED (Y/N)	COMMENTS

Exhibit 7.2 Determining Employee Status[a]

[a]If employees are to be laid off, this chart should be revised to include a column for employees to be laid off.

Employee Name or ID Number	Site /Location	Job Title or Description	Salary	Bonus	Vacation	Overhead Costs (e.g., office, administrative, benefits)	Separation Costs Assumed by Vendor (e.g., severance, stay bonuses)[a]	Separation Costs Assumed by Customer (e.g., severance, stay bonuses)[a]	Comments

Exhibit 7.3 Transferred Employees

[a] Since it is often difficult to definitively assess separation costs, its may be useful to include a high and low number for evaluation purposes.

Employee Name or ID Number	Site/Location	Job Title or Description	Salary	Bonus	Vacation	Overhead Costs (e.g., office, administrative, benefits)	Comments

Exhibit 7.4 Retained Employees

Employee Name or ID Number	Site /Location	Job Title or Description	Salary	Bonus	Vacation	Overhead Costs (e.g., office, administrative, benefits)	Separation Costs Assumed by Vendor (e.g., severance, stay bonuses)[a]	Separation Costs Assumed by Customer (e.g., severance, stay bonuses)[a]	Comments

Exhibit 7.5 Laid Off Employees

[a] Since it is often difficult to definitively assess separation costs, its may be useful to include a high and low number for evaluation purposes.

Both the customer and the vendor will need to analyze the compensation and benefits being provided by the customer and to be provided by the vendor to assess comparability. To perform this assessment, the customer and the vendor must have access to each other's compensation and benefits plans, policies, and statistics. The timing for the exchange of this information varies from transaction to transaction. In some cases, the customer's RFP will include generic compensation and benefit information, with a request that the vendor's response include a compensation and benefits proposal and/or a comparison between the customer's and the vendor's compensation and benefits. If the customer is disinclined to disseminate personnel-related data in the RFP, it may require the vendor to describe its compensation and benefits proposal and at a later date disseminate its own information for a formal comparison.

The customer and the vendor should be careful to include *all* benefits in the comparability analysis. One of the most contentious benefits points for transitioned employees is whether the vendor will give them credit for their years of service with the customer when determining vesting, eligibility, and accrual rights with respect to certain benefits (particularly retirement and pension benefit plans, severance, vacation, savings plans, and stock options). In addition, seemingly minor benefits that are frequently ignored but which are typically "hot points" for the employees include fitness facilities, transportation discounts, store discounts, cafeteria access, and parking.[2]

(c) Review of Severance/Redundancy Plans and Policies A task that the customer *must* undertake early in the due diligence process is the review of its severance/redundancy plans and policies. The customer's potential severance/redundancy liability is important in assessing the total cost of the deal. Employees may be entitled to severance pursuant to a formal plan adopted by the customer and distributed to its employees or pursuant to an informal or unwritten policy or practice. When reviewing the plan or policy, the customer should identify the events that trigger severance/redundancy obligations to ensure that the customer has not inadvertently provided for severance/redundancy benefits to transitioned employees who do not lose their jobs or suffer a break in service as a result of the outsourcing transaction. While formal severance/redundancy plans often anticipate mergers, acquisitions, and asset sales, they frequently do not contemplate outsourcing. Unless the customer's plan is worded correctly, even the employees who are transferred to the vendor may be eligible for severance/redundancy payments. If the customer's plan or policy does not clearly exclude an outsourcing transaction from severance entitlement, an amendment is advisable. Moreover, to minimize the risk of claims being made by transitioned employees that they have relied to their detriment on their belief that severance benefits would be available, any necessary amendments should be made and communicated to the employees at the earliest point possible.[3]

---

[2] The case of *Vizcaino v. Microsoft Corp.*, 120 F.3d 1006 (9th Cir. 7/24/97) has caused some concern that outsourced employees could, depending on the circumstances of the particular transaction, be deemed to be the common law employees of the customer after they are transitioned to the vendor's employ. However, Judge O'Scannlain's statement in his partial concurrence and dissent, that "[a]ll agree that those freelancers who were converted into employees of outside employment agencies have no valid claim for participation in [the benefits plans] after the date of their conversion," suggests that this concern may not be warranted.

[3] For an example of how failure to amend a severance plan to specifically exclude outsourcing as a qualifying event can have unintended consequences, see *Carrol v. Blue Cross and Blue Shield of Massachusetts* 34 F.3d 1065 (1st Cir. 1994). Because the outsourcing customer's severance plan unambiguously excluded only internal transfers from its severance benefits provisions, the court held that the affected employees were entitled to severance from the customer even though they were hired by the vendor.

In addition to reviewing its own plan or policy, the customer will need to review the vendor's severance/redundancy plans and policies as a part of its compensation and benefits analysis. The vendor's policies often are not as generous as the customer's policies, and most vendors do not offer credit for years of service with the customer for severance/redundancy calculations. Many customers choose to negotiate enhanced severance/redundancy benefits for transitioned employees so that if an employee is discharged by the vendor within a certain number of months or years from the date of transition, he or she will receive supplemented severance/redundancy payments either comparable to what the employee would have received if he or she had remained in the customer's employ or a percentage of what he or she would have received. The customer may also consider restricting enhanced severance/redundancy to employees who are still assigned to the customer's account at the time of termination—which will depend largely on the vendor's staffing plans. The customer and the vendor will need to negotiate the administration of and financial responsibility for enhanced severance (e.g., the cost may be built into the base fees or the customer may reimburse the vendor on a pass-through basis).

Another part of due diligence will be to determine whether there are any statutory or regulatory requirements effecting severance/redundancy. While there is no general obligation to pay severance under federal law and the laws of most states, transitions outside of the United States may be subject to legal requirements of the applicable jurisdictions.

(d) Laws and Regulations   The customer and the vendor will need to determine whether there are federal, state or local laws, regulations, or rules governing the outsourcing transaction, such as notice requirements that must be complied with or special authorizations or consents that must be obtained in connection with the employee transition. Relevant United States statutes that should be reviewed include:

- The Worker Adjustment and Retraining Notification (WARN) Act of 1988
- The Employee Retirement Income Security Act (ERISA) of 1974
- Federal, state and local antidiscrimination and fair employment laws
- Federal and state banking regulations

Generally speaking, the WARN Act requires employers with 100 or more employees to give at least 60 days notice of a plant closing (including the closing of a facility or operating unit within a single site of employment) or a mass layoff. In the event of litigation, a persuasive argument can be made that WARN notice obligations are not triggered if all affected employees are transitioned to the vendor's employment or the requisite number of affected employees are not laid off. In other words, the mere fact of an outsourcing, without actual job loss, will not implicate the WARN Act. Support for this argument is found in the analogous provision of the WARN Act that deals with notice of a plant closing or mass layoff in the event of a sale of part or all of an employer's business. In any event, the circumstances of a particular outsourcing transaction must be examined to determine if a sufficient number of employees will lose their jobs to implicate the act. In addition, because of the absence of dispositive case law, as a protective measure many outsourcing customers will ensure that affected employees are given at least 60 days advance notice of an outsourcing transaction.

ERISA governs the rights of employees under such employee welfare benefits as severance and under employee pension benefits, many of which are discussed in the section on employee benefits later in this chapter. To the extent that an employee's status under the existing pension or welfare benefits of the customer is changed in the course of an outsourc-ing transaction, issues may arise under ERISA.[4]

If all affected employees are not going to be offered positions with the vendor, care must be taken to ensure that the process by which employees are selected for employment with the vendor do not violate federal, state, and local antidiscrimination and fair employment laws, such as the Civil Rights Act of 1964, the Age Discrimination Act of 1967, and the Americans with Disabilities Act of 1992. In addition, if the selection process is solely the responsibility of the vendor, the customer will want to ensure that the vendor accepts lia-bility for its choices and indemnifies the customer in the event of litigation by any employee of the customer who was not hired by the vendor.

In Europe, the Acquired Rights Directive and Work Council regulations typically include specific notice, authorization, and consent requirements that must be consulted if the out-sourcing transaction includes employees in Europe.

(e) Outplacement Services In connection with the employee transition, many (mostly larger) customers offer the employees who are to be laid off a variety of outplacement ser-vices. Such services may include:

- Job posting
- Resume preparation assistance
- Job search assistance
- Counseling
- Access to offices, telephones, computers for a certain period of time
- Extension of loans

The customer also should consider whether to seek the vendor's assistance, for example, by allowing the laid off employees to post for vendor jobs. Professional outplacement assis-tance can be useful in helping the laid off employees channel any negative feelings about their job loss into positive action.

(f) Due Diligence Checklist A list of issues for the customer's human resources team to consider follows. Many customers find it useful to involve the vendor in this process.

- Will any customer employees be hired by the vendor for a short period of time?
- Are any customer employees on an approved leave of absence from active employ-ment with the customer for reasons other than layoff (e.g., family or medical leave or disability leave)?
- Are any of the affected employees members of a union or subject to collective bar-gaining agreements?

---

[4] That the outsourcing customer must be concerned about the stringencies of ERISA was made clear in *Inter-Modal Rail Employees Association v. Atchison, Topeka and Santa Fe Railway Company,* 117 S.Ct. 1513 (1997), *remanded on remand,* 117 F.3d 1136 (9th Cir. 1997). In this case, the Supreme Court reminded us that Section 510 of ERISA permits a participant in a plan that is subject to ERISA (in this case, an out-sourced employee) to sue an employer who would discharge (outsource) him to interfere "with the attain-ment of any right to which such participant may become entitled under the plan." Here, the rights that the plaintiff alleged were lost were welfare benefits of a level provided by the employer but not the vendor. The lesson that *Inter-Modal* teaches is that ERISA allows employers great flexibility to amend pension and wel-fare benefits to reduce benefits costs, but if the employer reduces its workforce for the sole purpose of ac-complishing the same objective, the employer could be exposed to claims under ERISA Section 510.

- Will there be a freeze date for new hires?
- How long will the customer employees have to consider an offer of employment from the vendor (this period may be very short, e.g., 5 to 10 days)?
- Who will be making the offer of employment—the vendor or a subcontractor? What will the customer's relationship be with the subcontractor (particularly for liability purposes)?
- When will the employees commence employment with the vendor? Will all employees commence employment on the same day?
- Will there be any hiring requirements (e.g., background checks, credit checks, drug testing)?
- Will the vendor require the customer employees hired by the vendor to sign an employment or confidentiality agreement? If so, a copy of such agreement(s) should be obtained.
- Will the customer want any type of release from the transitioned employees?
- What will the starting salary be? How will bonuses that may have been earned during employment with the customer be handled (e.g., will the customer pay pro-rated bonuses immediately prior to the transition date)? Will there be any salary adjustments to compensate for bonuses or matching programs not provided by the vendor?
- When will the vendor start paying the customer employees hired by the vendor? (There may be some timing issues with respect to payroll administration.)
- Will performance reviews be given after the first 90 days of transition?
- What are the opportunities for promotion within the vendor?
- Will the vendor's offers of employment be for comparable positions?
- How will credit for the employees' service with the customer be handled for eligibility, vesting and benefit accruals under pension and/or welfare benefits provided by the vendor?
- How will the vendor deal with preexisting conditions limitations, if any, and waiting periods for entry into group health plans?
- Will any obligations under the customer's pension plan be transferred to the vendor's plan?
- Will employees lose valued early retirement benefits when they cease participation in the customer's pension plan?
- Are retiree medical benefits provided by customer? If so, how will retiree medical be handled by the vendor?
- How will profit sharing or savings plans be handled? Will participants' account balances be transferred or rolled over to vendor's plans? How will outstanding employee plan loans be handled?
- Will employee terminations result in a partial termination of customer's pension plan?
- How will payments toward medical "deductibles" in the current year be handled? How will co-payments be handled?
- How will claims for health care reimbursements from the customer's flexible spending arrangement be handled after the employees are transitioned?
- Are there any deferred compensation obligations to be addressed?
- What is the vendor's vacation policy? How will days accrued but unused before transition to the vendor be handled?
- Will vacation or designated holidays be prorated during the first year of the agreement?
- What are the vendor's holidays?
- What is the vendor's working day? Is it the same length as customer's working day?
- What is the vendor's dress code?
- Does the customer reimburse employees for tuition costs? If so, for any program of study or exclusively for work-related courses? How will reimbursement for courses commenced prior to the effective date but continuing after the effective date be handled?

- How will vehicles or personal computers provided by customer be handled?
- Are there any housing subsidies or loans? Are there any meal allowances?
- Does customer provide any miscellaneous benefits (e.g., fitness facility, employee discounts, parking)?
- Will the customer require access to any information regarding its employees for administrative purposes after their transfer to the vendor?
- Will the customer have any shut-down issues?
- How will severance or redundancy be handled? What are customer's potential severance or redundancy obligations?
- Will the customer or vendor provide any outplacement services to employees who are not offered employment with the vendor or whose employment is terminated shortly after transitioning?
- Relevant customer/vendor policies will need to be reviewed, including:
  - Human resources policies and procedures manuals
  - Employee handbooks
  - Equal employment opportunity (EEO) policies
  - Employment agreements with specific employees
  - Disciplinary/grievance procedures
  - Safety policies
  - Performance appraisal processes
  - Union/collective bargaining agreements
  - Recruiting and offer letters
  - Summary plan descriptions and plan documents of benefit plans

7.3 TERMS AND CONDITIONS OF EMPLOYMENT

(a) Request for Proposal   The terms and conditions pursuant to which the vendor will employ the customer's employees is often one of the most heavily negotiated provisions of the outsourcing contract. A useful negotiation tactic is for the customer to take a position in the RFP as to certain important terms and to ask the vendor what its position is with respect to terms concerning which the customer has not finalized its position or is not ready to take a position. This tactic forces the customer to perform substantial (necessary) due diligence at the RFP stage and allows the customer to use the vendors' responses to the human resources section of the RFP as part of the selection process. Model human resources terms that may be used as a guide when preparing the RFP are provided in Appendix 7.2. The parties will need to draw on information contained in the RFP, the vendor's proposal, and further due diligence performed as part of the negotiation process when drafting the human resources section of the outsourcing agreement.

(b) Drafting the Human Resources Terms   A checklist of issues that the parties should consider when drafting the human resources terms follows. In addition, an example of standard human resources contract section is provided in Appendix 7.3.

The Transitioning Process

Employees To Be Transitioned   The employees to whom offers will be made should be set forth in an exhibit to the agreement. This exhibit typically lists the employee name or identification number, the salary (adjusted for bonuses and matching benefits contributions), the date the employee started work with the customer, and the number of accrued but unused vacation days. The anticipated employment start date should be specified, with extensions for employees on disability leaves or other approved leaves of absence. Special provisions will need to be negotiated and included if there are union employees or employees subject to collective bargaining agreements.

Vendor vs. Subcontractor Hiring   In some cases, a subcontractor rather than the vendor will make offers of employment to certain employees. This is more likely to occur in international transactions in which the vendor does not have a presence in a particular country or in transactions where certain services will be provided by another entity (e.g., network services). The customer should require the vendor to disclose any proposed subcontractor hiring in its proposal. The customer will need to consider what relationship (if any) it wishes to have with the subcontractor. The customer may also wish to obtain an indemnity from the vendor for any claims resulting from the subcontractor's actions.

Hiring Requirements   Often vendors will make offers of employment contingent on the employees meeting certain preemployment screening requirements. Such requirements may include:

- Background check
- Credit check
- Reference check
- Drug screening

Some customers are able to successfully negotiate the vendor's acceptance of employees "As is" without any preemployment screening. The ability of the customer to get the vendor to waive preemployment screening may depend on the strength of the customer's own policies (e.g., if the customer engages in drug testing on a regular basis, the vendor may be more willing to waive drug testing).

SAMPLE CLAUSE: Vendor shall hire all Affected Employees who:

1. Are employed by Customer and have not been reassigned to an out-of-scope position within Customer as of the date the offer is made;
2. Accept the offer of employment from Vendor within [***] business days from the date the offer is made; and
3. If requested by Customer, sign a release substantially in the form set forth in *Schedule [***]* ((1) through (3) collectively, the "*Hiring Requirements*") (the Affected Employees hired by Vendor collectively, the "*Transitioned Employees;* each, a "*Transitioned Employee*").

Vendor shall make hiring decisions regarding the Affected Employees based on the Hiring Requirements. Vendor shall be solely responsible for making such hiring decisions, subject to the provisions of this Section.

Start Date   In most cases, the customer will prefer that the employees being transitioned to the vendor become vendor employees as of the date the vendor commences providing services. The vendor, however, may resist a start date on or close to the date the agreement is signed because it will need time to prepare for the transition (e.g., preemployment screening, interviews, etc.). The time period proposed by the vendor typically ranges from 30 to 90 days after the date the agreement is signed. In some instances, the parties may agree to allow the vendor to commence the transition process prior to the signing of the agreement. The customer, therefore, will need to begin to notify the employees to be transitioned of the proposed outsourcing transaction before the vendor takes any action. Any communications with the customer's employees prior to the signing of the agreement should be prefaced with a notice that all activity is contingent on the signing of an agreement with the vendor. If circumstances require the vendor to commence providing services before the transitioning process is complete, the parties may need to enter into a second agreement that will define the parties' respective obligations and liabilities during this interim period.

Base Salary   The agreement should specify the base salary to be offered each of the transitioned employees. The specified salary should include any adjustments for bonuses and other amounts agreed on by the parties to ensure compensation and benefit parity.

SAMPLE CLAUSE: Each offer of employment to an Affected Employee shall include an initial base salary of not less than the base salary that each such Affected Employee received from Customer as of the Agreement Date, with any adjustments thereto made by Customer in accordance with Customer's normal salary adjustment policies. The Affected Employees' base salaries as of the Agreement Date, **[plus the applicable adjustments]**, are set forth in *Schedule [***]*.

Positions   A concern of many employees, and therefore a critical factor in employee morale, is whether they will be offered employment in comparable positions. A manager may not wish to accept an offer of employment for a nonmanagement job even if the compensation and benefits are comparable. In addition, the customer's severance plan may provide that severance benefits will be payable if the employee is not offered a comparable position with comparable compensation.

SAMPLE CLAUSE: Vendor shall offer employment to each Affected Employee to perform job responsibilities that are substantially similar to the job responsibilities performed by the Affected Employee at Customer as of the Agreement Date.

Minimum Employment Period   When structuring the human resources portion of the transaction, the customer should consider whether it wishes the vendor to commit to employing certain of the transitioned employees for a certain period of time. Obtaining such a commitment from the vendor typically improves employee morale. The customer may also wish to require the vendor to keep certain transitioned employees assigned to its account for a period of time (e.g., for a minimum of 1 to 2 years, through the migration to the vendor or through the migration to a new platform/environment to be implemented by the vendor). In some instances, the vendor may suggest separating the employees into two classes: temporary employees (who will only be employed during a transition period) and regular employees (for whom the customer may wish to obtain a longer employment commitment from the vendor).

SAMPLE CLAUSE: Vendor shall not terminate any Transitioned Employee during the [***] [e.g., the first six months to a year] of his or her employment with Vendor, nor shall Vendor terminate any Critical Support Personnel in the first two years of their employment, except in either case for cause, as such term is defined or used by Vendor in its applicable policies, procedures and practices; *provided, however,* that all employment decisions regarding Transitioned Employees shall be the sole responsibility of Vendor.

Work Days/Hours   If the vendor's work days and work hours conflict with the customer's work days or hours, the customer may wish to consider including a provision requiring the vendor to allow the transitioned employees to follow the customer's work days and hours while on the customer's premises.

SAMPLE CLAUSE: The work days, including daily work hours and holidays, of the Transitioned Employees assigned to any Customer location shall be the same as the work hours in effect at that Customer location.

Performance Appraisals An issue that may be of concern to transitioned employees is when performance appraisals will be administered. This is of particular significance if appraisals are linked to salary increases and the employees are scheduled to receive performance reviews shortly after the agreement is signed.

Stay Incentives Often, the customer and the vendor wish to adopt measures to encourage certain employees to remain with the customer or vendor through a critical period. Examples of the types of employees to whom stay incentives are typically offered include:

- Employees who are to be laid off because the location that they service will be closed but whose services are necessary until the closing
- Critical support or other key employees either retained by the customer or transitioned to the vendor who are essential to the transition process or to a particular project
- Employees to be hired by the vendor on a short-term basis whose services are necessary for that term
- All employees who stay with the vendor through the transition to the vendor or migration to a new platform/environment

A discussion of the different types of stay incentives that may be used is provided in Appendix 7.1.

Replacements The parties will need to consider how jobs for employees not accepting offers from the vendors will be filled. Typically the vendor will be responsible for filling these positions at its expense.

SAMPLE CLAUSE: Vendor shall be responsible for filling the positions of any Affected Employees not hired at comparable skill levels by Vendor pursuant to this Article. Vendor shall be responsible for the salary and benefits for such replacements.

Vendor Employment Agreements The customer should ask whether the vendor will require the transitioned employees to sign an employment or confidentiality agreement as a condition of employment. If the vendor does require such an agreement, the customer should request a copy of the proposed agreement for its review and comment. Provisions that warrant particular consideration include noncompetition provisions, ownership provisions, and training provisions.

Dress Code If a vendor's dress code conflicts with the customer's dress code, the customer may wish to consider including a provision requiring the vendor to allow the transitioned employees to follow the customer's dress code while on the customer's premises.

Employee Benefits

General Benefits Provisions As a general matter, the customer will want to ensure that the transitioned employees will be eligible to participate in all employee benefit programs, plans, and policies maintained for the vendor's employees under the same terms and conditions that apply to the vendor's employees. This will require the vendor to take any actions that may be necessary, including adopting additional plans, amending existing vendor benefits plans, and contracting with insurance carriers to provide the required benefits to the transitioned employees.

Service Credits Of particular importance to employees who have been employed by the customer for a number of years is the extent to which the vendor will give them credit for their years of service with the customer for eligibility, participation, vesting, and accrual purposes for certain benefits (e.g., pension plans, vacation accrual, savings plans, severance).

SAMPLE CLAUSE: Except with respect to those benefit plans for which Transitioned Employees shall immediately vest pursuant to this Article, Transitioned Employees shall be eligible to participate in all of Vendor's welfare plans, including disability plan and retiree health plan and other such plans based on the Transitioned Employees' years of service with Customer.

Health Care Benefits The agreement should specify which health benefits the transitioned employees will be eligible for and when the employees will be eligible.

SAMPLE CLAUSE: Each Transitioned Employee shall be eligible as of his or her Start Date for enrollment in Vendor's health care plans, including [major medical, hospitalization, dental, vision, life insurance, short term and long term disability, pharmacy and personal accident coverage]. Vendor shall provide each Transitioned Employee with health care coverage so that on the Transitioned Employee's Start Date, he or she (and any family and any dependents who meet eligibility requirements) is (are) covered by such health care plans, and all pre-existing condition limitations, exclusionary provisions and waiting periods are waived with respect to the Transitioned Employee (and family and dependents). Vendor shall be responsible for all medical or health expenses incurred by the Transitioned Employees to the extent incurred on or after the Start Date.

Deductible/Co-payment Reimbursement Unless an employee's start date coincides with the beginning of a new plan year, the customer should consider including a provision in the agreement that gives the transitioned employee credit under the vendor's plans for deductibles and co-payments made during the existing plan year under the customer's plans.

Pension Plans Questions to ask with respect to pension benefits include: What are the vendor's pension benefits? Will the transitioned employees be immediately eligible for participation in vendor's plan? Will the transitioned employees immediately vest in the vendor's plan? In the customer's plan? If not, which employees are disadvantaged? Can the accrued benefits of transitioned employees under customer's plan be transferred to vendor's plan? Typically, the vendor will grant credit for years of service with the customer for vesting and eligibility purposes under the vendor's plans but not for benefit accrual purposes.

SAMPLE CLAUSE: [LANGUAGE DOES NOT CONTEMPLATE ASSET TRANSFERS BETWEEN PLANS] Vesting and eligibility under **[Vendor Defined Benefits Plan]** shall be determined by the Transitioned Employee's length of service with Customer and Vendor.

Savings Plans The customer and vendor will need to negotiate how, if at all, the vendor will deal with any savings plan benefits of the transitioned employees. In some instances, the vendor will agree to a trustee-to-trustee transfer of the benefits of transitioned employees into the vendor's plan. The ability and willingness of the vendor to accept a transfer of the transitioned employee's benefits will depend largely on the terms of the vendor's plan. (This is true of transfers of pension benefits as well.) Additional issues to consider include:

- If the customer's plan provides for matching contributions or other employer contributions, does the vendor's plan have similar features or, if not, will the transitioned employee receive other benefits of comparable value?
- Will the customer fully vest matching contributions of transitioned employees under its plan?
- How will transitioned employee plan loans be handled?

SAMPLE CLAUSE: [LANGUAGE IF BENEFITS OF CUSTOMER EMPLOYEES ARE TO BE TRANSFERRED INTO VENDOR'S PLANS] Customer and Vendor shall cooperate in effecting the transfer of certain assets and benefit liabilities from accounts of Transitioned Employees under the [Customer's Savings Plan] to accounts established for such Transitioned Employees under [Vendor's Savings Plan]. Vendor represents to Customer, and shall provide such evidence and information as Customer may reasonably request to confirm, that the [Vendor Savings Plan] is in full force and effect and meets all the applicable requirements for qualifications under the Internal Revenue Code.

Retiree Medical   If the customer provides retiree medical benefits, does the customer expect the vendor to assume responsibility for these benefits?

Vacation   Since vacation accrual is often calculated based on the employee's years of service, the customer may wish to require the vendor to give each transitioned employee credit for his or her years of service with the customer for the purpose of calculating vacation accruals with the vendor. The parties will also need to consider how accrued but unused vacation will be dealt with. Options include requiring the vendor to assume responsibility for the accrued vacation (at least for the calendar year in which the customer employees transition to the vendor's employ) or having the customer pay the employees for their accrued but unused vacation prior to transitioning.

SAMPLE CLAUSE: Vendor shall calculate time off for paid vacation [and sick leave] purposes for each Customer Employee using each Customer Employee's length of service with Customer and Vendor.

Severance/Redundancy   The customer will need to perform due diligence (see Section 7.2) to determine what its severance/redundancy obligations are under its plans and policies, as well as pursuant to any statutory or regulatory requirements. Even if the customer does not owe severance/redundancy payments to the transitioned employees as a result of the outsourcing transaction, the customer will need to consider whether and how severance/redundancy payments may be made for terminations occurring after the transition. The customer and the vendor will also need to negotiate the administration of and financial responsibility for enhanced severance.

Relocation Expenses   The customer's severance plan or policy may provide that a severance payment is due if the employee is not offered employment within a certain geographical distance from his or her current position. To avoid unanticipated severance liability, the customer should review its plan or policy and, if necessary, amend the plan or policy to eliminate or limit relocation as a severance triggering event or include language regarding location in the agreement. If the location of the job will not be in or near the employee's current position, the parties may also need to discuss how relocation expenses will be handled.

SAMPLE CLAUSE: The Transitioned Employee shall be offered a position as of the Start Date that is at the same location as the Transitioned Employee was employed by Customer prior to that time or at a location within a reasonable commuting distance from the Transitioned Employee's primary residence.

Tuition Reimbursement   If the customer provides tuition reimbursement to its employees, the parties may wish to clarify each of their responsibilities with respect to courses that have been approved for reimbursement prior to transitioning but for which reimbursement will not be due until after transitioning.

SAMPLE CLAUSE: Tuition in respect of any course work in which a Transitioned Employee is enrolled as of the Start Date and for which Customer has approved reimbursement shall be paid for by [Customer/Vendor] upon the Transitioned Employee's presentation of evidence of satisfactory completion thereof. Course work that has been previously approved for reimbursement, but which has not yet begun, shall be reimbursed by [Customer/ Vendor]. For purposes of this paragraph, "course work" does not mean a degree program, but only refers to a specific class during a particular term.

Miscellaneous Benefits   The customer should be certain that it has considered all of the benefits it offers to employees. This is particularly important in international transactions where a large portion of compensation is often provided in benefits.

SAMPLE CLAUSE: The vendor will be responsible for providing (as part of the base fees) equal or substantially comparable benefits to the benefits that the Affected Employees currently receive. This will be determined on a country-by-country basis and may include such benefits as [a car allowance and housing and meal allowances]. It is the general intent of Customer that the transition to Vendor will not result in any severance or redundancy obligations of Customer. [If any such obligations are triggered as a result of the transition, Vendor will be responsible for any severance/redundancy pay.]

7.4 TRANSITIONING EMPLOYEES FROM CUSTOMER TO VENDOR

(a) Transition Plan   The customer and the vendor will need to prepare a roll-out schedule for implementing the transition (or, if applicable, termination) of affected employees. General guidelines for communicating and transitioning are:

- Identify and orient customer/vendor transition teams
- Develop a communication/transition plan that deals with the concerns of senior management, management responsible for the business process to be outsourced, and employees to be retained, transitioned, and laid off at each site
- Develop a timetable for transition that includes the dates on which:
    - The customer will provide the vendor with the names of affected employees
    - The vendor will communicate with the affected employees to obtain biographical information and commence any screening procedures that may be used
    - Vendor will send letters offering employment to the affected employees who have satisfactorily completed the screening process (or transfer letters in certain countries outside of the United States)
    - Employees must accept employment offers (i.e., within a specified number of days from receipt of the offer)
    - Affected employees who have accepted the vendor's offer of employment will commence their employment
    - The customer will transition administrative responsibilities to the vendor (e.g., payroll and benefits)

- Address union/collective bargaining issues
- Conduct customer/vendor meetings with senior management, management responsible for the business process to be outsourced, and employees to be retained, transitioned and laid off at each site
- Ensure that all notification, authorization, and consent requirements have been complied with

(b) General Tips for Communicating with Employees   Because of the complex nature of outsourcing transactions, the time between when the first RFP is sent out and when the agreement is signed can span many months. During this time, it is difficult, if not impossible, to keep the fact of the outsourcing confidential. As employees begin to ask questions, controlling the flow of information will be essential. The following tips may be helpful in this process:

- Develop communication materials (in the appropriate languages), including employee handouts, employee bulletins, e-mail announcements, vendor materials, and questionnaires.
- All communications sent to customer employees by representatives of the customer or the vendor should be reviewed and approved by the customer in advance.
- A representative from the customer should attend all meetings with employees and keep a record of what is said to the employees and copies of all written materials that are disseminated. (The customer may want to consider taping such meetings.)
- If a question and answer hotline is set up, individuals answering the calls must be carefully trained, and a written record should be kept of the questions asked and answers given. If the individual answering the call is unsure of an answer, he or she must tell the caller that the answer needs to be verified before it is given. In no instance should the individual try to guess the answer.

7.5 HUMAN RESOURCES REPRESENTATIVES

The customer and the vendor should each appoint one (or more depending on the size of the transition) representative who will be responsible for the human resources aspects of the transition. These representatives should be assigned to the customer's site and not replaced or reassigned until the transition is complete. These individuals should be involved in the outsourcing process from the very beginning.

SAMPLE CLAUSE: The Vendor human resources representative(s) responsible for the transition of the Affected Employees from Customer to Vendor shall be [***] (the "*Vendor HR Representative(s)*"). The Customer human resources representative(s) responsible for the transition of the Affected Employees from Customer to Vendor shall be [***] (the "*Customer HR Representative(s)*"). The Customer and Vendor HR Representatives shall be located at [***]. Neither party shall replace or reassign its HR Representative until [***] months after the Start Date without the other's consent (except if such replacement is required by reason of death or disability). There shall be no additional charge for the services of Vendor's human resources team.

7.6 CONTRACT-RELATED ISSUES

In addition to the section or exhibit of the BPO contract that outlines the terms and conditions pursuant to which affected employees will transition to the vendor's employ, human resources–related issues typically are addressed in several of the general sections of the outsourcing contract. As discussed in the following sections, these general sections may include the representations and warranties, the indemnities, and rights upon termination.

(a) Representations and Warranties The customer is often asked to represent that there are no pending claims by the employees being transitioned. If there are claims, these claims are typically identified in an exhibit to the outsourcing agreement.

(b) Indemnities Each party should indemnify the other party against claims arising out of any representations made by the indemnifying party or its representatives to an affected/transitioned employee, alleged violations of federal, state, or local antidiscrimination and fair employment laws or regulations by the indemnifying party's employees and the employees of the party's agents and subcontractors, work-related injuries caused by the indemnifying party, and any claims by the [affected/transitioned] employees arising out of the employment relationship [for the customer add "before the start date"] [for the vendor add "after the start date"].

(c) Rights upon Termination of the Outsourcing Contract The customer should consider whether, upon the expiration or termination of the agreement with the vendor, the customer wants the right to solicit employees of the vendor. In addition, the customer may wish to restrict the vendor's ability to solicit certain employees of the customer.

CHAPTER 8

PROJECTS

8.1 MOVING FROM A TO C

Many customers view outsourcing as a means for implementing new methodologies and/or technology or standardizing existing methodologies and/or technology of a type and at a rate that they would not be able to implement using their current resources without incurring significant up-front asset acquisition, development, personnel, training, and other costs. If the customer transformed its business process environment on its own, the transformation typically would be implemented in three (or more) phases:

A. Identify new methodologies and/or technology, continue to operate existing methodologies and/or technology
B. Transitional phase during which old methodologies and/or technology are operated in some locations and new methodologies and/or technology in other locations (may include refresh or upgrade of old methodologies and/or technology before new methodologies and/or technology are implemented; typically staff is trained in new methodologies and/or technology at Step B and ramp up of staff and subcontractors is necessary)
C. Full roll out of new methodologies and/or technology

The customer is looking to the vendor to move from Step A to Step C at a more rapid, more cost effective rate. The vendor is often able to substantially reduce the duration of Step B due to its ability to provide additional, temporary resources trained in the new methodologies and/or technology and experienced in implementing comparable methodologies and/or technology, thereby allowing for a quicker implementation of the target methodologies and/or technology and reducing ramp up, transition, and training costs.

8.2 INTERNAL CONSIDERATIONS

Prior to implementing a major new project, the customer will need to consider a number of internal issues, ranging from defining business objectives and direction to assessing the need to realign the customer's organization to absorb change. A list of general issues for the outsourcing customer who plans to introduce significant change to its organization to consider are set forth below. The level of involvement of the outsourcing vendor in addressing and resolving the internal "business" issues varies from transaction to transaction. The customer may choose to engage a third-party consultant to provide objective assistance and direction.

Business Direction

Business direction/strategy. What strategic direction is the customer moving toward? Are the proposed methodologies and/or technology consistent with this direction? Will the implementation of the proposed methodologies and/or technology assist the customer in moving toward this direction? Is the proposed implementation schedule too rapid or too slow? What are other organizations in the customer's industry doing? Are the proposed methodologies and/or technology consistent/compatible with the methodologies and/or technology used in other areas of the customer's organization?

Business priorities. What are the customer's business priorities? How should these priorities be considered when planning the project? Should the roll-out schedule focus on a particular site or type of methodology/technology first? What sites, methodology, and technology are critical to the customer?

Project Definition

Identify objectives. What are the customer's goals in implementing the new methodologies and/or technology? What does the customer wish to achieve? How will the customer be able to assess whether its objectives are achieved?

Requirements. What are the customer's business requirements? Have all relevant users/sites been surveyed? Will certain requirements be standardized? What will the new methodologies and/or technology do? What will they not do? What is the impact on the customer (at all levels)?

Process design. How will the customer implement the new methodologies and/or technology? How will the project be managed? What is the responsibility structure? How will the different users be educated in the objectives/operation of the new methodologies and/or technology?

Prototype of future environment. What will the new environment look like? How will it work?

Implementation schedule. Identify priorities for roll out. Are all sites ready for roll out? Are the new methodologies and/or technology more critical at certain sites? Should one or two non-critical sites be used as "pilot" sites?

Risk Assessments

Risk/benefit assessment. Identify the risks of implementing the new methodologies and/or technology. How can the risks be reduced (e.g., parallel environments, testing labs, pilot phases)? Are there any integration/compatibility issues? Identify the benefits of implementing the new methodologies and/or technology. Are the benefits consistent with the customer's business direction/strategy? Are the benefits consistent with the project objectives/requirements?

Cost analysis. What is the overall cost of implementing the new methodologies and/or technology? Will ongoing business process costs be reduced as a result of implementing the new methodologies and/or technology? Will any nonbusiness process costs be reduced? Are the costs of the new methodologies and/or technology warranted by the business benefit achieved?

Worst case scenario. What is the worst thing that can happen during implementation? What is the most that the project could cost? How can the worst case/costs be minimized? How should the contract be drafted to protect the parties (e.g., liquidated damages for delays/failures, deferral of payment)?

Management/Organizational Issues

Project management. How will the project be managed by the customer internally? Who will be on the customer's project team? Does the customer have the resources/expertise to manage the project? Have all of the affected areas of the organization been consulted to provide input? Are outside consultants necessary?

Management commitment. Has the customer's senior management been made aware of the project? Has the customer's senior management given its support?

Assessment of organization's ability to absorb change. What aspects of the customer's business will change? What aspects of the customer's business will be affected? What parts of the customer's business will benefit? What parts will be disadvantaged? Are all users ready to absorb the change that will take place as a result of the new methodologies and/or technology? What type of training/communication is necessary? How will the change be handled?

Staffing/management re-organization. Will the new methodologies and/or technology create different/new staffing needs? Will any functions be reduced/done away with? Will personnel need to be reorganized? Will tasks need to be reprioritized or restructures? Will the existing management structure work in the new environment? Does this reorganization work with broader enterprise-wide reorganizations that are occurring simultaneously as part of a larger reorganization?

Organizational awareness. Who will be affected by the business process changes? By the larger enterprise-wide changes? Are all of the areas that will be affected by the change aware of the change? What types of plans should be put into place? How will organizational awareness be managed?

Communications (internal and external). The communication plan should provide for the following:

- Building sponsor and change agent commitment
- Communicating the customer's vision
- Developing high-level transition strategy
- Developing a communications plan
- Training change implementation personnel
- Implementing educational and development programs

8.3 PROJECT DEFINITION

With any new project, one of the most difficult tasks is defining the project requirements. The first step is to determine who will be responsible for preparing the project requirements. Will the customer, the vendor or an outside consultant be responsible for project definition? In the event that the customer turns over the task of defining the project to another party, it should consider retaining approval rights over all aspects of the requirements.

The next step is to determine the scope of the project requirements. How detailed should the project requirements be? The customer will need to weigh the benefits of being as detailed and specific as possible against the benefits of allowing room for flexibility and changing business needs. Detail and specificity will enable the customer to hold the vendor to fixed pricing and time tables, while general requirements will allow both parties room to reprioritize. Often the parties will agree to the development of two project plans—the initial project plan reflecting the customer's general business requirements (usually done at an early stage in the project development) and a later, or final, project plan developed after vendor due diligence to which the vendor will commit to specific deliverables and deadlines. Depending on the level of understanding of the customer's business requirements at the time of contract signing, the parties may include a detailed project plan as an appendix to the agreement or include an initial project plan, with an agreement to develop a more detailed project plan within a specified number of days after contract signing. (It is preferable from a contractual perspective to have detailed commitments in the contract; however, this is not always practical from a business perspective.)

Topics typically included in the project plan include:

- Detailed project specifications
- Project management
- Site surveys
- Site requirements
- Inspections
- Asset requirements (including third-party vendors)
- Configuration requirements
- Pilot/test labs
- Installation and implementation requirements
- Methodologies
- Change management
- Cutover requirements
- Testing requirements
- Acceptance requirements
- Milestones
- Deliverables
- Implementation schedules
- Incentives
- Training
- User communication
- Documentation
- Conversion requirements (data, technology, and equipment)
- Environmental requirements
- Operating requirements
- Disposal/relocation requirements
- Reports (including risk assessment)
- Meetings
- Permits/authorizations
- Clearances
- Resource commitments
- Quality plans
- Customer responsibilities

8.4 MAINTAINING MULTIPLE ENVIRONMENTS

A key resource that the customer is frequently looking to gain from the outsourcing vendor is the ability to "ramp up" with additional personnel and assets as may be necessary to implement new projects. Often customers will want the outsourcing vendor to perform all or some of the following tasks: maintenance of existing environments at each site, maintenance of parallel environments during transition, and implementation and/or maintenance of the new environment while discontinuing the old environment. For example, a customer engaging in a short-term outsourcing transaction may want the vendor to maintain its legacy environment, while the customer redirects its own resources to implement a new environment. This allows the customer to retain the knowledge base for the operation of future methodologies and/or technology without requiring additional hiring. Other customers agree to maintain existing environments while engaging the vendor to develop, implement, and maintain new methodologies and/or technology. The knowledge necessary to keep the old environments going is not lost in the transition, and the vendor is able to start anew with the implementation of new methodologies and/or technology.

Key issues to keep in mind during the transition:

Service levels. Will service levels be maintained during any or all phases of the implementation?

Resource commitments. What resources is the vendor committing to the implementation? Are there unlimited resources until project completion or are resources capped so that additional resources will be at an additional expense? Do the vendor's resources have the appropriate expertise?

Parallel environments. To what extent will the vendor operate parallel environments and for how long?

Recovery mechanisms. What mechanisms (in addition to parallel environments) will be in place to ensure limited disruption to the customer's business (e.g., data backup at a hotsite)? Is the implementation schedule realistic? How long before a business recovery plan is in place?

8.5 USING SUBCONTRACTORS

Frequently, if the vendor does not have all of the requisite resources or expertise to implement the proposed project or the customer or the vendor targets a third party vendor with particular expertise or a particular product, the vendor will engage a third-party vendor to provide all or part of the services. The third party may provide all or part of the resources necessary to implement the new methodologies and/or technology, such as equipment, software (often in the form of a mature applications system), methodologies (again, these are often methodologies that are mature or well tested), customization services, installation services, connectivity, and ongoing support. Third-party resources may be required in specific locations, for example, the outsourcing vendor may need to subcontract resources in South America to handle the customer's South American locations if it does not have a presence there.

Depending on the role of the subcontractor and how the pricing will be handled, the customer may want to be involved in the selection of (or at least have approval rights with respect to) the third party, as well as be involved in negotiations with the subcontractor. In any event, the customer should enter into an understanding with the vendor regarding the vendor's responsibility for the subcontractor. The degree to which the vendor will assume responsibility for the subcontractor often turns on which party recommended the subcontractor or whether the vendor supports the selection of the subcontractor. The customer typically wants the vendor to accept responsibility for the subcontractor on the basis that the vendor can contract directly with the subcontractor to protect itself in the event the subcontractor does not perform. The parties should also consider whether the liability provisions in the subcontracting agreement should mirror the liability provisions in the outsourcing agreement. The subcontractor would ideally be liable to the vendor for any damages for which the vendor is liable to the customer due to the subcontractor's performance or nonperformance.

Other key issues to consider when agreeing to allow the vendor to subcontract to a third party include:

Licenses/leases. If methodologies and/or technology provided or developed by the subcontractor will be licensed or leased (rather than transferred outright), the parties should consider which party should be the licensee/lessee of record to the license/lease agreement for the new methodologies and/or technology. The customer often wishes to be the licensee/lessee for several reasons. One reason is that, in the event the relationship between the customer and the outsourcing vendor goes sour, the customer has a direct relationship with the licensor/lessor and can presumably continue to use the methodologies and/or technology if it takes the business process operations back in-house. Second, at least with respect to software, if the licensor/lessor goes bankrupt, the customer may be able to exercise its rights under the Bankruptcy Code as licensee/lessee of the methodologies and/or technology (otherwise the customer would have to rely on the vendor to exercise these rights). If the customer is the licensee or lessee of the methodologies and/or technology, the customer should ensure that the license/lease allows the outsourcing vendor (and any other agent who requires access in connection with the operation of the customer's business) to have access to the methodologies and/or technology (including rights of modification and enhancement if appropriate). Finally, if the outsourcing vendor is the licensee/lessee, the parties should consider whether the license/lease with the subcontractor should include assignment rights that allow assignment to the customer or the customer's designee.

Ownership issues. The parties will need to consider who will own modifications and enhancements to any methodologies and/or technology used in connection with the project. This should include modifications and enhancements made by the customer, the vendor and the subcontractor.

Ongoing support. Is the vendor contracting with the subcontractor for ongoing support or maintenance? If so, does the vendor and/or the customer have the right and ability to provide support if the subcontractor goes out of business or otherwise fails to provide support?

Assignability. The customer should consider whether it should as part of the outsourcing agreement require the subcontracting agreement (as well as any license/lease as discussed in the first item in this list) to be assignable to the customer and/or its alternative service provider.

Pass-through warranties and indemnities. The customer may wish to ensure that all warranties and indemnities that are provided by the subcontractor are passed through to the customer, particularly warranties for "no charge" support.

8.6 KEY CONTRACT PROVISIONS

The following list provides a number of key provisions relating to the definition, development, and implementation of a project that both the customer and the vendor should consider when negotiating the BPO contract.

Project Definition

As noted in Section 8.3, one of the most difficult tasks in any project is defining and creating the project requirements. What is it that the customer wants the vendor to deliver? What are the customer's objectives? What are the design requirements? What are the specifications? What assets are necessary? What assets are included? What are the integration/compatibility requirements? What are the site and installation requirements? What are the deliverables? What documentation is required? What training is required? What are the uptime/response time requirements? What are the runtime requirements? Often the customer will engage the vendor to identify and understand the customer's existing environment, business objectives and desired environment and produce recommendations or a preliminary report prior to creating the project plan.

Project Plan

Once the project requirements are prepared (or often at the same time as the project requirements are being prepared), the parties should prepare the project plan. The project plan typically includes: project management, definition of specific vendor tasks with milestone and deliverable dates, implementation schedules, the creation of a test environment, roll out, identification of necessary assets, documentation, and training. (See Section 8.3 for a checklist of topics typically included in a project plan.) The final project plan should be as detailed as possible with input (or at a minimum) sign-off from the customer. The more definition that the parties can give to the project early on in the process the better off the customer will likely be.

Assumptions

The vendor typically wishes to include in the project plan certain assumptions on which costs, capacity, and delivery dates are based. Assumptions may include the number of users, number of sites, volume, existing assets, amount of training, and level of customer participation. If these assumptions are not accurate, the vendor may seek to be excused from responsibility or increase the cost of the project.

Customer Responsibilities

In addition to project assumptions, the vendor likely will want to include customer responsibilities in the project plan, that is, a description of customer tasks that must be performed in connection with the project. As with assumptions, the vendor may consider these responsibilities as releases from responsibility if the implementation schedule is delayed or interrupted due to the customer's failure to perform its responsibilities. From the customer's perspective, it is useful to clarify functions or responsibilities that will be retained (and not included in the fees), areas that it has approval rights over and its acceptance testing responsibilities.

Implementation Schedule

It is in the customer's interest to include a detailed implementation schedule in the project plan that commits the vendor to certain dates while allowing the customer the flexibility to reprioritize or delay roll-out schedules in the event a customer location is not ready. The dates may include dates for the implementation of a pilot site or sites, delivery dates, installation dates, cutover dates, dates by which the methodologies and/or technology must be accepted, and milestones, or key, dates. If the project is priced separately (i.e., not included in the base fees), the customer may wish to tie payments to certain key dates or deliverables. For critical projects, most customers wish to impose some type of monetary incentive or damage on the vendor if such dates are not met. (A discussion of incentives, together with examples of contract provisions, is provided under the heading "Incentives" later in this chapter.)

Right to Reprioritize or Delay

The customer will need to weigh its need to have the vendor commit to a tight implementation schedule with its desire to be able to reprioritize or delay resources during the course of the project. It is not uncommon for the customer to determine *after* the implementation schedule has been prepared that certain locations should be rolled out before others or that certain locations are not ready for (or cannot absorb) the proposed change within the specified time table. What if management has decided to change the business strategy in a way that would make the proposed methodology/technology impractical? What if the company is not ready to absorb change? What if management wants more definition with respect to the project before roll out? Depending on the potential for change from within the customer's organization, it is useful to build into the outsourcing contract the ability to "shift" or re-prioritize resources. Typically, the contract will include detailed change control procedures (or a mechanism for developing change control procedures) to be followed in the event of a change to methodologies and/or technologies or schedules. In addition, or in lieu of, these procedures, the parties may wish to include guidelines pursuant to which schedule changes will be handled. (A discussion of changes to project schedules and requirements is provided under "Change Orders" later in this chapter). The vendor may resist allowing the customer to shift resources if the vendor will be ramping up staff at different levels for part of the roll out. In addition, the vendor may look to the customer to compensate the vendor for additional costs incurred as a result of the reprioritization or delay. Such costs (e.g., actual, out-of-pocket costs, costs plus mark-up, a base rate) will be a central part of the negotiations. The customer may argue that there should not be any additional cost for reprioritization or delay since the vendor was aware of the possibility of such reprioritization or delay early on in the process and that the vendor (as an experienced, multicustomer vendor) should be able to shift its own resources to minimize costs. Often a key negotiating point for both parties is the length of the period that the customer has to give the vendor of a change or delay in order to avoid incremental costs. If the customer provides the vendor a reasonable period of notice, the vendor may be able to reorganize its staffing to minimize or eliminate additional costs. The vendor's willingness to implement a change at no cost may depend upon the impact of the reprioritization on the overall roll-out schedule. For example, if the reprioritization causes the entire schedule to be extended (causing the vendor to have to retain resources longer than anticipated), the vendor may argue that additional costs should apply. While the customer wants the flexibility to delay, it does not typically want the vendor to have the same flexibility. What happens if the vendor delays? At a minimum, the customer would look to the vendor to absorb any additional costs associated with the delay. In addition, many customers include "incentives" for the vendors to stay on schedule. (See the discussion of incentives later in this chapter.) An example of a contract clause that sets out the parties' responsibilities in the event of a delay in the implementation schedule by the customer, by the vendor, and by agreement of the parties is:

1. Upon at least [***] days' notice from the customer that the customer desires the vendor to extend or re-prioritize an Implementation Schedule by more than [***] days, or an Implementation Schedule is extended for more than [***] days as a result of delays materially caused by the customer [or a party other than the vendor or the vendor's subcontractors or agents] (as determined by the Management Committee), the vendor shall, as part of the Base Services, extend or reprioritize an Implementation Schedule as requested or required by the customer. The customer shall not be responsible for any incremental or additional costs to the vendor as a result of such extension or re-prioritization.

2. Upon less than [***] days' notice from the customer that the customer desires the vendor to extend or re-prioritize an Implementation Schedule by more than [***] days, or an Implementation Schedule is extended for more than [***] days as a result of delays materially caused by the customer [or a party other than the vendor or the vendor's subcontractors or agents] (as determined by the Management Committee), the vendor shall, as part of the Base Services, extend or reprioritize an Implementation Schedule as requested or required by the customer. The customer shall not be responsible for any incremental or additional costs to the vendor as a result of such extension or re-prioritization other than the costs of the incremental resources necessary at the rates set forth in *Exhibit [***]*.

3. In the event an Implementation Schedule is extended as a result of delays materially caused by the vendor or subcontractors or agents of the vendor, (i) the customer shall pay the Base Fees subject to the customer's deferral rights set forth in *Section [***]* and (ii) the vendor shall be responsible for the customer's direct costs that would have otherwise been reduced or eliminated if the migration had occurred as scheduled.

4. In the event customer and the vendor agree to extend the Implementation Schedule, customer and the vendor shall negotiate and implement an appropriate adjustment to the Base Fees.

5. Prior to commencing a project, the customer and the vendor shall agree upon the effect of an extension or re-prioritization of or delay in the applicable Implementation Schedules as a result of requests from or delays by customer, the vendor and their subcontractors and agents.

6. In the event an Implementation Schedule is extended, customer and the vendor shall each use commercially reasonable efforts to minimize incremental or additional costs to the other party.

Change Orders

As noted under "Rights to Reprioritize or Delay," the BPO contract typically includes detailed change control procedures (or a mechanism for developing change control procedures) to be followed in the event of a change to methodologies and/or technology or schedules. In addition to, or in lieu of, these procedures, the customer may wish to include guidelines pursuant to which methodology and/or technology changes will be handled. It is typical once a project is started for a party or both parties to identify more compatible methodologies and/or technology or for changing business needs to arise that warrant a change to the methodologies and/or technology set out in the project plan. While the customer wishes to retain the ability to make changes, the vendor will want to extend the implementation schedule or adjust the pricing to account for the change. The vendor may wish to freeze the date on which the customer can make changes to the requirements. Any changes after this date will result in significant additional fees (including equipment return charges and contract termination charges). Similarly, the customer will want to limit the vendor's ability to come back and make changes due to design or compatibility miscalculations and, therefore, run up additional time and materials or attempt to impose additional fees.

Right to Cancel

In most cases, neither party believes at the outset of the BPO arrangement that canceling a project is a viable option. However, as the project takes form and the customer organization continues to grow (or downsize), it is not uncommon for the customer to wish to terminate or cancel a project. This may be due to the fact that the new methodologies and/or technology when examined closer do not perform as expected, that such methodologies and/or technology are outdated, or that the customer no longer wishes to spend the necessary money, resources, and time on the project. Whatever the reason, the parties should consider when negotiating the BPO contract the impaction the contract (particularly price) if a project is terminated or canceled.

Installation

As part of the project, the vendor may be required to install equipment, technology, or other assets at a customer site or sites or, in cases where operations are being migrated to or consolidated at vendor locations, at a vendor site. For installations at a customer site, the customer may be required to prepare the site. If possible, it may be prudent for the customer to have the vendor inspect and approve such preparations prior to installation. An example of a standard installation provision is:

Prior to the delivery date, the installation site will be prepared by the customer, in accordance with the installation instructions set forth in the Project Plan. After delivery, the vendor shall install the equipment, software, and other assets described in the Project Plan and make such equipment, software, and other assets operational. Installation of equipment consists of uncrating and unpacking, connection to peripherals, the power source, communication, and other utilities and performing the vendor's standard diagnostic tests. Installation of software consists of loading the software onto the applicable equipment and performing the vendor's standard diagnostic tests. [ADD INSTALLATION REQUIREMENTS OF ANY OTHER ASSETS] The vendor shall provide the customer with a written installation report on the date such installation is completed (the "Installation Date"). If installation by the vendor is prevented by local law or union agreement, the vendor shall supervise the installation and be responsible for the costs of any third party and any other costs occasioned thereby. The customer shall not be responsible for the Installation Charges if the vendor supervises installation.

Risk of Loss

The vendor may wish to pass the risk of loss of assets purchased by the customer and to be used at a customer site to the customer upon delivery of the assets to a carrier. The customer, on the other hand, would favor risk of loss for such assets to pass to it upon installation at the customer's site or acceptance by the customer. Responsibility for risk of loss of leased assets used at a customer site may depend on the leasing arrangements, particularly whether the cost of insurance is included in the lease fees. Risk of loss of (customer and vendor) assets used at a vendor site typically rests with the vendor. An example of a risk of loss provision is:

Purchased Equipment
The customer shall be responsible for all risks of loss or damage to equipment being purchased [upon acceptance by the customer of the equipment] [after delivery to the carrier at the vendor's point of origin], except as may be caused by the vendor, its agents or subcontractors. *[If second alternative is chosen add:* The vendor shall provide the customer, [***] days prior to the shipment of the equipment, with a notice describing the date and time of shipment of the equipment and the carrier that will be used by the vendor for the shipment. Upon the customer's request, the vendor shall arrange for the equipment to be insured at the amounts and in accordance with the requirements described by the customer in its request. The customer shall be billed directly by the third-party carrier for any such insurance or reimburse the vendor on a pass-through for the costs of such insurance.] The customer's responsibility for risk of loss or damage to purchased equipment shall terminate upon the customer's return of the equipment to the vendor.

Leased Equipment
While leased equipment is in transit and in the possession of the customer, the vendor shall relieve the customer of responsibility for loss or damage to leased equipment from theft, fire and other casualty insured by customary forms of insurance. The repair or replacement of leased equipment damaged by the negligence of the customer, its employees, agents, or subcontractors, or by failure or fluctuation of the customer's electrical power and not covered by customary forms of insurance shall be charged to the customer in accordance with the vendor's then-current commercial list prices. The vendor shall be responsible for risk of loss or damage to leased equipment while in the vendor's possession or control.

Cut-Over/Parallel Environments

The customer and the vendor will need to negotiate when to cut over from the old environment to the new environment. When will the cut-over occur? During business hours? On a weekend? Will there be overtime charges? Which sites will cut over first? Last? For critical methodologies and/or technology, most customers require the vendor to operate parallel environments for a period of time before and after cut-over to ensure limited disruption to the customer services in the event of problems with the new methodologies and/or technology. For standardized environments, the customer may wish to have the vendor support nonstandardized methodologies and/or technology for a period of time after standardization with a cut-off date, thereby allowing time for transition and training.

Acceptance Testing

The project plan should specify the criteria for acceptance of project deliverables, as well as the scope and type of acceptance testing to be performed by the customer and by the vendor. An example of a provision for acceptance testing is:

> Upon completion [and installation] each Project Deliverable (as defined in the Project Plan), the vendor shall notify the customer that the Project Deliverable [has been properly installed and] is fully operational. After receipt of such notification, the customer and, if required, the vendor shall perform the acceptance tests described in the Project Plan (the "Acceptance Tests"). If the customer determines that the Project Deliverable fails to meet the acceptance criteria set forth in the Project Plan (the "Acceptance Criteria"), the customer shall (a) promptly notify the vendor of such failure and (b) specify the nature of the failure. Upon receipt of such notice, the vendor shall promptly make such repairs, adjustments, modifications or replacements as are necessary to cause the Project Deliverable to meet the Acceptance Criteria. Upon completion of such repairs, adjustments, modifications or replacements, the vendor shall demonstrate that the Project Deliverable meets the Acceptance Criteria. At such time as the Project Deliverable meets the Acceptance Criteria and operates in accordance with the applicable specifications for the period specified in the Project Plan, but in any event a minimum of [***] consecutive days, the customer shall issue a certificate of conformance and accept the System (the "Acceptance Date"). The Acceptance Tests shall not extend for more than the number of days specified in the Project Plan (the "Acceptance Test Period") unless otherwise extended by the customer.

Failure to Pass Acceptance Tests

The customer may wish to consider including in the BPO contract a provision specifying the remedies available to the customer in the event the project deliverable(s) fail(s) to pass the acceptance tests described in the Project Plan. Typically, the vendor is first subject to specified monetary damages in the event the project deliverable(s) fail(s) to pass the applicable acceptance tests (see the discussion under "Incentives"). If a project deliverable fails to meet the applicable acceptance tests beyond any agreed-on grace period, the customer may wish to have the right to one or all of the following: (1) the right to terminate the project and, depending upon the project, the BPO contract, (2) a refund of all, or prorated amount of, monies paid in respect of the project, and (3) the right to engage an alternate provider to complete the project at the vendor's cost or an amount equal to the difference between what the customer would have paid the vendor and the alternate provider's costs. An example of a provision relating to the failure to pass acceptance tests is:

> In the event the Acceptance Date (as defined in the clause under "Acceptance Testing") has not occurred prior to the expiration of the Acceptance Test Period (as defined in the clause under "Acceptance Testing"), the customer may, upon notice to the vendor, reject the Project Deliverable(s) and terminate the applicable Project [and this Agreement]. Upon termination of a Project Plan, (a) the vendor shall, upon the customer's request,

promptly (i) remove the Project Deliverable(s) from the customer's premises in such a manner as to minimize the disruption of the services being performed by the vendor and the customer's business and (ii) refund to the customer all payments it has received under the applicable Project Plan, plus interest at the rate of one percent per month from the date each such payment was made, and the customer shall not be obligated to make any further payments pursuant to such Project Plan and (b) the customer may procure an alternate source to implement the Project. In addition to any payment owed pursuant to this Section and Section [***] (provision dealing with liquidated damages for delays), the vendor shall be liable to the customer for the difference between (x) any commercially reasonable amount of the customer's payments to such alternate source associated with such implementation and (y) the payments that would have been owed to the vendor pursuant to this Agreement to complete the Project.

Incentives

A common contract provision is a clause whereby the customer provides an incentive for the vendor to implement the project on time. As a general matter, there are three basic types of incentives: (1) liquidated damages, (2) deferrals, and (3) retainages. Examples of each of these incentives are:

Liquidated Damages

The vendor acknowledges that the customer will suffer damages, the amounts of which are difficult to specify at this time, should the vendor fail to implement the Project in accordance with schedule set forth in the Project Plan. Accordingly, the vendor shall pay to the customer the following amounts as liquidated damages and not as a penalty if the vendor fails to meet the milestone dates set forth in the Project Plan:

(a) within [***] days of the milestone date (or such other date as may be agreed upon by the parties), $[***];

(b) within [***] days of the milestone date (or such other date as may be agreed upon by the parties), an additional $[***];

(c) within [***] days of the milestone date (or such other date as may be agreed upon by the parties), an amount equal to the difference, if any between $[***] and [***] percent of the total price of the applicable Project Plan.

If the vendor's payments to the customer equal or exceed $[***], the customer may (i) terminate this Agreement upon notice to the vendor and (ii) procure an alternate source to implement the Project. In addition to any payment owed pursuant to this Section, the vendor shall be liable to the customer for the difference between (x) any commercially reasonable amount of the customer's payments to such alternate source associated with such implementation and (y) the payments that would have been owed to the vendor pursuant to this Agreement to complete the Projects. The customer's right to terminate this Agreement shall be without the right to cure.

Deferrals

For each [***]-day period that the vendor fails to achieve any of the milestones specified in the Project Plan, the customer shall defer, upon the customer's election, an amount for each such milestone equal to the amounts specified in the Project Plan for the preceding month. The customer shall pay to the vendor (a) [***] percent of the deferred amount for a milestone if the milestone is achieved in [***] days from the scheduled milestone date, (b) [***] percent of the deferred amount if the milestone is achieved in [***] days from the scheduled milestone date, (c) [***] percent of the deferred amount if the milestone is achieved in [***] days from the scheduled milestone date and (d) [***] percent of the deferred amount if the milestone is achieved in [***] days from the scheduled milestone date. If the vendor fails to meet a milestone by more than [***] days, the customer may terminate this Agreement without a right to cure. The customer's deferral rights shall not limit the customer's right to recover other damages as incurred by the customer as a result of such failure.

Retainages

Within [***] days of the Acceptance Date for a deliverable required to be delivered for a specific milestone under the Project Plan, the customer shall pay to the vendor the amount specified in the Project Plan for such milestone, less a retainage of [***] percent.

Half of the accumulated retainage shall be paid to the vendor within [***] days of the Acceptance Date, with the balance of the retainage to be paid at the conclusion of the express warranty period.

The customer may withhold payment for deliverables until the Acceptance Date or, where a defect in a Deliverable arises, the defect is corrected and the vendor provides written notice of such correction to the customer. The vendor shall not be entitled to interest on retainage or payments due to the vendor's failure to meet the Acceptance Date or the vendor's failure to cure a defect or breach of warranty.

As an incentive for timely performance, the vendor's compensation under this Agreement and the Project Plan shall be reduced by $[***] for each [***] following a grace period ("Grace Period") of [***] weeks of delay in acceptance. The Grace Period will not be modified if the project duration is modified due to an expansion of retraction of the scope of the Project Plan. There shall be no reduction in compensation for a delay of less than [***], or for partial [***]. The aggregate reduction in compensation shall not exceed $[***].

Staffing

The project plan should describe the vendor's staffing commitment, which may vary depending on the type of payment scheme agreed on. For example, the business deal may be that the vendor will supply a certain number of person hours in connection with the project. If it takes longer, the parties will need to adjust the price. This is typically the arrangement when there is not much definition to the project and there is a likelihood of redefinition. Alternatively, the customer may negotiate a fixed-fee deal where the vendor must implement the new environment at an agreed-on price, in which case the staffing commitment is up to the vendor. There are also modified versions of the straight time and materials and fixed-fee deals. For example, the vendor may estimate a resource commitment. If after further project definition, incremental resources are necessary, the parties will share in the incremental cost or the customer will pay a reduced resource fee up to a cap. In addition to specifying the amount of resources the vendor will provide, the BPO contract should also require the vendor to commit qualified, trained staff. Similarly, if the vendor is required to provide specific expertise, this should be committed to in advance.

Project Management

As part of the staffing commitment made by the vendor, the vendor may propose and implement a management structure for the project, with an overall project manager, site managers, and key personnel approved by the customer. The vendor's management structure typically takes into account the customer's management structure to facilitate communication and cooperation between managers. In addition, many customers wish to impose restrictions on the vendor's ability to reassign and replace project managers and key personnel.

Progress Meetings and Reports

As part of the project plan, the customer and the vendor project teams should meet on a regular basis to discuss the progress of the project. Many customers appoint a member of their own project team to take minutes of the meeting. In addition, the parties should consider requiring written reports documenting the progress of the project. An example of a provision regarding project reports is:

> Upon the customer's request, the vendor shall submit to the customer written progress reports describing the status of the vendor's performance under the Project Plan, including the service performed, the products shipped and installed and the progress expected to be made during the period specified by the customer. The progress reports shall describe the vendor's activities by reference to the Delivery/Implementation Schedules and the manner in which the vendor intends to overcome past delays.

Hardware

In many projects, the vendor will be procuring equipment for the customer. Depending on the extent to which the project requirements are defined, the customer may wish to specify the particular type and quality of equipment in the project plan (reserving the right to substitute the specified equipment), include an amount in the base fee to be applied toward the purchase of equipment, or require the vendor to estimate the amount of the equipment and have the cost of the equipment passed through to the customer (in some cases, up to a cap). In addition, the customer may wish the vendor to warrant that the equipment described in the project plan (or a functional equivalent) is all the equipment necessary to implement the project and that the equipment is compatible with other aspects of the customer's environment. An example of a provision contemplating the purchase of equipment by the vendor for the customer is:

> The vendor shall arrange for the customer to purchase in the customer's name and at the lowest cost reasonably available at that time the equipment set forth in *Exhibit [***]* (or equivalent hardware approved by the customer), which equipment shall be made available to the vendor for its use in connection with the implementation and operation of the [New Environment]. The vendor shall (a) notify the customer of the lowest cost reasonably available at the time that the Project Plan is complete and (b) submit to the customer for payment on a pass-through basis the invoices in respect of such equipment to be purchased. In the event the actual total purchase price (including taxes) for the equipment set forth in *Exhibit [***]* is greater than the lesser of (i) the estimated total purchase price set forth in the vendor's notice and (ii) $[***], the vendor shall be responsible for, and shall reimburse the customer for, the amount by which the actual total purchase price is greater than the estimated total purchase price or $[***], as may be applicable.

Methodologies

Many projects included in BPO contracts involve the development and/or implementation of new methodologies. This development and/or implementation effort may be part of a greater business reengineering initiative, which is typically tied to the roll-out of new technology (e.g., new applications) as well. As with software (discussed next), the parties will need to consider the best available option: standard (off-the-shelf) methodologies or customized methodologies.

Software

The customer may require the vendor to procure third-party software, customize third-party software or the customer's own software, or develop new software as part of the project. An example of a provision pursuant to which the vendor customizes (and standardizes) the customer's existing applications and new third-party applications is:

> The System shall (a) include the features and functionality included in the customer's existing applications, (b) include the third-party applications software packages operated in connection with the existing applications as of the Effective Date, (c) include the enhanced functionality described in the Project Plan and (d) at a minimum, allow the customer to support the products and services that the customer offers as of the Effective Date without resorting to manual processing where customer has automated support as of the Effective Date. The customer shall retain the right to (i) substitute a third party software package for any included in the Existing Applications and (ii) redirect the vendor resources that would have been used in the development of that functionality in the System, that have not already been utilized for that purpose, towards interfacing such package with the rest of System. If customer exercises this right, (x) vendor shall, as part of the Base Services, provide to the customer a proposal describing the schedule, financial and operational impacts of the substitution (including that, if the resources used to interface a package with the rest of the System are less than the resources that would have been used on development of that functionality in the System, customer shall receive a credit for the unused resources against the Base Fees for the next month after the month in which such resources were not used) and (y) the customer and the vendor shall negotiate the appropriate adjustments to each party's performance and financial obligations under this Agreement that are impacted by such substitution. The System shall be designed to facilitate customer's implementation of new products and services enterprise-wide in a competitive timeframe. As part of the Base Services, the vendor shall design the [New Environment] in such a manner as to allow any new feature/function (package or development) to be available to all customer users of the [New Environment] within the industry standard timeframe as measured by benchmarking by the customer against its principal competitors at the time of the acceptance into production of the new feature/function by the customer.

Software and Data Conversion

An often hidden cost not accounted for by the parties as either a cost assumed by the vendor or retained by the customer is the cost of converting existing software for use in the new environment. Does any software need to be converted? Who will be responsible for the conversion? Who will be responsible for the cost? Similar to software conversion is the responsibility for ensuring that the customer's existing data can be used on the new systems. This may require data conversion via electronic means or in some instances even direct data input.

Documentation

The customer may wish to ensure that as part of the project deliverables that it will receive operating and user manuals, as well as detailed specifications. The documentation should follow agreed-on methodologies and formats and the parties should agree on the software used to develop the documentation. It is helpful to have the documentation delivered in paper, as well as in a designated electronic format. Some vendors distinguish between deliverable and nondeliverable documentation. Deliverable documentation includes manuals and reports. Nondeliverable documentation includes such items as notes, design specifications, and drawings. While nondeliverable documentation may not be tied to a milestone or delivery date, the customer may wish to request copies as they may prove important in the provision of future maintenance and support.

Training

An important part of the implementation of new methodologies and/or technology is the training provided to both customer operations staff and end users. The parties will need to negotiate whether training is in scope and if so the type of training to be provided. Issues to consider with respect to training include: Will training be on or off site? How may classes will be offered? Who will be the attendees? What will be the syllabus? What documentation will be provided? Will the training be direct to the end user or will the vendor train the trainer? What expenses are not included (travel, accommodations)? Will a test environment or lab be provided? What assets will be provided?

Payment

The parties will need to negotiate the pricing structure of the project. Although the customer may pay the project fees as part of the overall base fees, the payment structure for the project generally falls within one of five types:

1. Fixed fee
2. Time and materials with certain amount of resources built into fee
3. Cost plus
4. Certain amount of resources built into the base fees with a cap on incremental exposure
5. Fees based on an estimate and if required resources exceed estimate a sharing above the estimate

Warranties

There are a number of warranties that the customer may wish the vendor to make with respect to the project and the project deliverables, such as:

* A warranty that the project deliverables will perform in accordance with specifications
* A warranty that any new methodologies or technology will be compatible with the customer's existing methodologies and/or technology
* For purchased assets, a warranty that valid title is being transferred free and clear of all liens or encumbrances
* A warranty that the project deliverables do not and will not infringe on the rights of any third party

Indemnities

The parties typically negotiate certain indemnities relating to the project, including responsibility for:

* Subcontractor claims
* Actions of subcontractors
* Use by or sale to third parties/other vendor customers
* Infringement claims
* Time bombs/viruses
* Environmental claims

Proprietary Rights

There will be a number of ownership issues for the customer and the vendor to consider, including:

- Will equipment be leased to/owned by the customer?
- Will methodologies or technology be licensed/owned by the customer and, if so, what residual rights will the vendor have?
- Will documentation be licensed or owned by the customer?
- Will improvements, modifications, or enhancements be licensed/owned by the customer?

Ownership and right to use issues are often contentious. The customer ideally would want to own or have unlimited rights to use methodologies, technology, and documentation. The vendor, however, may try to limit the customer's use to a user-based, equipment-based, or site-based license. With respect to software, the parties will need to determine whether the license is for object code only or object code and source code. If source code is not provided, the customer may want the source code escrowed so that it will have access on the occurrence of certain events. The vendor may also attempt to impose restrictions on third-party use and access. The customer should determine the extent to which third parties (contractors, suppliers, customers) may require access to the methodologies or technology and ensure that the license is broad enough to permit such use. Finally, the parties should consider the extent of the customer's rights to use methodologies, technology, and documentation upon termination or expiration of the BPO contract. Will the methodology, technology, or documentation license be perpetual? Will the customer or another third-party service provider have the ability to maintain/enhance the methodologies and/or technology upon expiration or termination? Are the methodology, technology, or documentation licenses and equipment leases assignable?

Third-Party Licenses

The project plan should specify whether any third party methodologies and/or technology will be provided as a project deliverables. If so, the parties will need to consider how the third-party methodologies and/or technology are acquired and in whose name the methodologies and/or technology will be purchased or licensed. The answers to these issues may depend on whether the methodologies and/or technology are standard (or packaged) or customized. For standard methodologies and/or technology, the vendor may procure the methodologies and/or technology with the ownership or license lying with the customer. Alternatively, the customer may choose to let the vendor license the methodologies and/or technology in its name with the right to assign the license upon termination or expiration of the agreement. With respect to software, in light of certain rights of licensees under the Bankruptcy Code, the customer may wish to license the software in its name in order to have direct privity with the technology vendor. If the methodologies and/or technology are customized, the parties will need to negotiate with the third party whether the methodologies and/or technology will be licensed or owned by the customer. In many instances, the third party will be customizing existing (or standard or packaged) methodologies and/or technology for the customer. Who owns the modifications or enhancements? Furthermore, who owns modifications or enhancements made by customer, vendor, and third party after implementation?

Right to Compete

The methodologies and/or technology developed as part of the project may play a critical role in business reengineering efforts. The methodologies and/or technology themselves may give the customer a competitive edge. If the customer owns the methodologies and/or technology, the customer may wish to include a provision in the BPO contract prohibiting the vendor from providing similar services to certain competitors or from assigning the project staff to the account of a competitor. If the vendor owns the methodologies and/or technology and licenses them to the customer, the customer may wish to ensure the methodologies and/or technology are not licensed to customer's competitors, that similar services are not provided to competitors or that project staff is not assigned to the account of a competitor. The extent of the noncompetition provision will depend on the uniqueness of the methodologies and/or technology, the impact of the methodologies and/or technology on the customer's business and the cost of the methodologies and/or technology.

Marketing Arrangements

The customer may wish to consider some type of marketing engagement with the vendor pursuant to which the vendor markets the methodologies and/or technology developed for the customer to other customers and third parties with a royalty payable to the customer. An example of a marketing clause is:

> As between the parties and subject to the rights of any applicable third party licensors, all Developments shall be owned by the customer. In consideration of the payments made, vendor hereby assigns, and shall cause the vendor's subcontractors and agents to assign, to the customer all of its interests in and rights to the Developments. The customer hereby grants to the vendor a [nontransferable, nonexclusive] right to market and sublicense the Developments in accordance with this Section. The customer may, by giving the vendor timely notice thereof, restrict the vendor from licensing, marketing or otherwise making available any specific functionality of the Developments that customer reasonably determines provides customer with a competitive advantage in the marketplace. Except with respect to any such restricted functionality, vendor may license and market the Developments to third parties and, unless otherwise agreed by the parties, the vendor shall pay to the customer the following amounts:

> (a) [***] percent of any fees received by vendor from the sale or license by vendor of the Developments, or any derivative or component thereof, or if no separate fee or if only a nominal fee is charged by vendor in respect of such sale or license, [***] percent of the portion of the fees received by vendor that would under ordinary commercial practices be allocable to the Developments, or any derivative or component thereof;
> (b) [***] percent of any maintenance revenues received from third parties by vendor, with respect to the Developments or any derivative or component thereof; and
> (c) the fees described in (a) and (b) above in situations where vendor provides service bureau support to third parties using the Developments, or any derivative or component thereof.

> Within [***], the vendor shall, for up to a [***]-day period, participate in and fund a planning initiative to develop a comprehensive business plan for marketing the Developments.

Additional Units

The project plan typically identifies the specific locations to which the new methodologies and/or technology will be rolled out. The customer may wish to consider reserving the right to roll-out additional locations at agreed on rates during or after the planned project implementation.

CHAPTER **9**

INTERNATIONAL CONSIDERATIONS

9.1 INTERNATIONAL TRANSACTIONS

International BPO transactions are typically very complex. As the term suggests, international outsourcing involves the outsourcing of business process operations of a company or organization (often including subsidiaries and affiliates) at sites in multiple countries. The international aspects of these transactions significantly increase the scale and complexity of the transactions, due to the need to understand, coordinate, conduct due diligence in respect of, and negotiate the contractual terms relating to current and future local business, technical, and legal requirements. Coordinating managers, staff, human resources, and legal counsel in different geographical locations is a time-consuming and often frustrating exercise in understanding different corporate organizations, different (corporate and local) cultures and customs, and different work ethics, work techniques, and languages. Adding to the complexity, the international BPO transaction is in many cases part of a global initiative of the customer to consolidate geographically dispersed and distinct business process and resources throughout its company or organization, standardize methodologies, systems and information output across the company or organization, and/or provide enterprise-wide connectivity.

9.2 CONTRACT AND LEGAL ISSUES

This section will examine many of the contractual, legal, and regulatory issues that a company or organization wishing to outsource business processes on an international level will need to consider. The general topics covered in this section include:

- Preparing the contract
    a. Contract structure
    b. Defining the scope of services
    c. Identifying service locations
    d. The effective date
- Contract management and approval procedures
    a. Contract management
    b. Vendor management
    c. Approvals
    d. Uniform policies and procedures

- Transfer of employees
- Laws and regulations
    a. Industry specific regulations
    b. Transborder data flow
    c. Data regulation and import/export controls
    d. Relocation of service locations
    e. Third-party processing
    f. Changes in laws and regulations
- Audit requirements
- New environments
- Monitoring performance
    a Performance standards
    b. Benchmarking
- Pricing-related issues
    a. Pricing
    b. Adjusting baselines
    c. Currency risks
    d. Cost-of-living adjustments
    e. Taxes
    f. Asset sales
- Retained responsibilities
- Termination rights
- Continuation of services

The applicability of each of these topics to a particular deal will differ depending on the countries that are being dealt with and the type of the transaction. Furthermore, the topics discussed in this section are intended to illustrate some of the more common issues that arise in international transactions. This section is not intended to serve as an exhaustive discussion of all of the types of issues that may arise in a particular transaction. As with any BPO transaction, appropriate legal and other counsel should be consulted.

Preparing the Contract

Contract structure. An issue of particular interest to the legal team will be how to structure the contractual framework. Companies with multinational offices will need to determine whether to structure the agreement as a single service contract or as a master contract (containing terms applicable to all sites receiving services) with schedules of work for each of the sites receiving services. The structure of the international BPO contract (i.e., a single or multiple document structure) may be driven by tax, corporate compliance, and/or regulatory concerns.

Defining the scope of services. The first step in structuring any outsourcing transaction is to understand and define the scope of services to be provided to each of the in-scope sites. This task is, in many cases, more difficult than it seems, particularly if the customer does not have a centralized business department (with an existing definition of tasks across all relevant sites) or the customer is moving to a new environment and therefore it is difficult to clearly define what the scope of services will be at each site. The more that the parties are able to define the scope of services at an early stage, the more the parties will be able to flesh out any hidden services and costs and the more productive negotiations will be.

Identifying service locations. An issue to resolve early in discussions is *to which* customer locations will services be provided and *from which customer and vendor locations* will services be provided. This issue is of importance for several reasons, the first being that identifying the customer locations to receive services will help in defining the scope of service. Second, the customer may wish to have its business process operations based in a certain city or country and the vendor may not have the requisite resources or facilities in such location; and finally, the customer may need to obtain special local approvals or authorizations to allow the vendor to provide or relocate services at that location.

The effective date. An issue that is often overlooked but is very important for determining financial and employee management responsibility is identifying effective dates. "Effective date" typically refers to the date on which the vendor will assume control of the customer's operations. Such date may vary on a site-by-site basis. External or internal events may control when the effective date will be for a particular site (e.g., government or third-party vendor consents that must be obtained prior to vendor assumption of responsibility, site readiness for vendor management, terms of third-party vendor contracts, employee communications, other corporate initiatives).

Contract Management and Approval Procedures

Customer management. How will the customer manage each of the sites receiving services on a local level? How will the customer centrally manage each of the individual sites? To have a successful outsourcing contract it is necessary to put into place an effective management team on a local and global level. Frequently, as part of the outsourcing transaction, the customer wants to reorganize its existing management structure (often distinct local organizations with limited central management) into a strong, centralized management structure with local management forming part of, and reporting directly to, central (global) management. In conjunction with the outsourcing transaction, it will be necessary to develop:

- The customer's "internal" organizational structure after business operations are outsourced
- The vendor's organizational structure (which should mirror the customer's organization)
- A mechanism pursuant to which the two structures will interact (typically a management committee or committees)

Vendor management. An important part of the management process are the vendor's managers. The success of an outsourcing relationship is often dependent on the vendor's global and site project managers. It is helpful to both parties if the customer approves the vendor's managers prior to contract signing so that the managers can be part of the negotiations and become familiar with the transaction. The parties will need to negotiate qualification requirements and reassignment provisions pertaining to vendor project managers and other key personnel. In addition, a common solution in international transactions where the selected vendor does not have required expertise or resources in a certain location is for the vendor to subcontract part or all of its service obligations. Vendors typically resist customer approval of subcontracting relationships on the grounds that the customer should be concerned about the quality of services received, not how the services are delivered. Customers, on the other hand, often wish to have the vendor identify the names of any proposed subcontractors and the services that each subcontractor will be responsible for, while retaining the right to approve subcontractors for all or, at a minimum, certain critical, or core, services.

Approvals. To avoid confusion regarding who may grant approvals for particular tasks, it may be helpful to develop and implement an approval system (e.g., termination for failure to provide the critical services required approval from senior executives, certain changes may be approved by the site project manager). This system can be incorporated into the outsourcing contract or done through a separate procedures manual.

Uniform policies and procedures. An issue that is tied in many ways to management is the implementation and use of uniform policies and procedures at all sites. Examples of procedures that are often standardized include procedures relating to management, operations, change control, training, reports, invoicing, and dispute resolution. To the extent possible and practical, the contract should specify which party is required, as part of the outsourcing arrangement, to develop procedures manuals for use by the customer and the vendor.

Transfer of Employees

Typically one of the most complicated areas in international outsourcing transactions is the transfer of employees to the vendor. Local law requirements are often very rigid and may vary significantly from country to country. It typically takes several months to compile the necessary employee information, conduct a comprehensive comparison of benefits and implement the transition (including allowing time for termination/transfer notices, offers, and a period for acceptance). The first step in determining employee-related issues is to identify those employees who will be transitioned and the countries in which these employees are employed. This is often not as easy a task as it may seem since by identifying the employees to be transitioned the parties are in effect defining the scope of the services to be outsourced. Once the outsourcing customer's list of affected employees is compiled, the parties may determine that for certain countries where there are only a few employees to be transitioned and where the employee laws are very stringent that it is easier for the customer to retain or lay off these employees than transfer them to the vendor.

Other areas to consider in connection with the transfer of employees are:

- Will the employees be transferred to the vendor or a subcontractor? It is not uncommon for an outsourcing vendor to propose for those countries where it does not have a presence that a subcontractor hire the customer's employees in those countries. In addition, some outsourcers do not have an international contracting entity, so instead of having one company perform the services, they have a corporate affiliate in each of the countries act as the subcontractor to provide the services. If not managed properly, this may result in the less-than seamless provision of services.
- A task that will require significant involvement from the human resources department is the evaluation of whether the customer's and the vendor's benefits are comparable in each of the affected countries. This comparison is necessary to ensure that severance/redundancy obligations are not triggered. As a result, benefits packages may have to be developed on a country-by-country basis.

In deals involving the transfer of employees in Europe, a significant amount of time is typically devoted to understanding and complying with the European Commission's Acquired Rights Directive. The Acquired Rights Directive provides for the protection of employees in the event of a change in employer by ensuring that the employee's rights under the previous employment contract are safeguarded. The directive allows employees to work for the transferee on the same employment terms as those existing with the transferor as of the date of transfer. Although there is some debate as to whether an outsourcing transaction constitutes a transfer for the purposes of the Acquired Rights Directive, the European Court of Justice (ECJ) tends to interpret the directive's concept of legal transfer liberally.

If the customer provides cars or meal allowances—which are common in European countries—the customer and the vendor must ensure that the vendor will provide the same or comparable benefits after the transfer is effective to avoid triggering redundancy payments. The parties must evaluate all of the customer's benefits (from medical benefits and health clubs to housing subsidies). In many countries where taxes are high, companies compensate the employees with in-kind benefits, such as child care, health, cars, housing. The parties will need to determine the extent to which these benefits will be provided to the employees once they are transitioned to the vendor and at what cost. Negotiations typically focus on *who* bears the costs of providing the benefits. The parties will also need to discuss how long the benefits will be available—since there is an argument that, if the benefits are materially reduced soon after the transfer is effected, then the employees were not transferred on comparable terms. Finally, an important issue to discuss with the human resources team is the employee communication plan—how and when will information be communicated to the affected employees—keeping in mind the possibility that the migration of duties to the vendor may be contingent on obtaining regulatory approvals.

Laws and Regulations

Industry-specific regulations. This category is particularly relevant to financial institutions and other heavily regulated industries. Four preliminary questions to ask when performing due diligence are:

1. What regulatory authorities are called into question? For example, if the customer is a bank, the parties will need to look at federal, state, and local banking authorities.
2. If the customer is regulated, are there regulations specific to the business process operations?
3. Do the regulations apply in this case?
4. What actions—usually in the form of notice requirements or approvals—are necessary precontract and postcontract signing? The issues addressed in this last bullet point are typically divided into conditions precedent and conditions subsequent. Making this distinction allows the parties to prioritize action items.

It is important to identify and understand the regulations that apply to the transaction early on. The requirements that are most daunting—and which could potentially change the time frame and scope of the deal—are those that require the customer or the vendor to obtain the permission of governmental or regulatory authorities. For larger transactions dealing with several countries, it is helpful, as part of due diligence, to divide the countries into four categories:

1. Countries where approval from a regulatory agency is necessary prior to the vendor taking over business process operations
2. Countries where approval from a regulatory agency is necessary prior to migrating business process operations to a vendor site
3. Countries where notice—either formal or informal—is necessary: This category can be further divided into two subcategories in order to reflect whether notice is required prior to the vendor taking over business process operations or whether notice can be given afterward
4. The fourth category is for those countries where no action is necessary.

This due diligence is important to do at an early stage of the transaction since getting input from the numerous local counsels as to the applicable laws and regulations, then getting approval from, for example, the Bank of England, can take a significant period of time. And if approval is not to be received, it is better for everyone to learn this as early as possible. The transfer of customer employees to the vendor and assumption of operational and financial responsibility may have to be delayed until necessary approvals are obtained. If authorities are not cooperative, the timing of the entire transaction can be thrown off. Most important is that the pricing may change if the customer has to retain certain assets and responsibilities for a longer period of time than contemplated while at the same time the vendor is ramping up for transitioning employees, migrating service locations and rolling out new developments. Particular concern typically revolves around communications to the employees—it may not look good from a human resources perspective if the customer is not able to convey to the employees a definitive date for transition or, worse yet, has to change the date it had communicated. In some cases, it could be more than a communications problem—there may be legal notice requirements that needed to be complied with that are contingent on the date the vendor takes over operations.

In addition to industry regulators, the outsourcing customer who acts as a government contractor should investigate whether there are any government regulations affecting the outsourcing of the business process. The government may wish to approve the outsourcer or, in some cases, ensure that there has been an arms-length transaction.

Once the parties have determined the impact of industry-specific regulations on the transaction, the parties should consider what will happen if certain conditions precedent do not occur. This is typically done by requiring the outsourcing vendor to implement necessary workarounds with as little impact on the outsourcing customer's business as possible. For example, common workarounds include continuing to run the customer's business process operations out of the customer's facility and running the business process operations out of a location acceptable to the regulatory authority. Perhaps just as important as identifying a suitable workaround is for the parties to negotiate which party will be responsible for the costs associated with the workaround.

Transborder data flow. Most countries impose some restriction on transborder data flow. This issue may not be significant if the customer already processes its data in another country, since the customer likely will already have obtained permission for data flow. If, however, the outsourcing transaction contemplates a different flow of data—through a new country or with a data center at a different location—the customer, and possibly the vendor, may have to reapply for permission.

Data regulation. The customer's obligations with respect to protection of client's data will vary from country to country. For example, some countries require the customer to obtain government consent prior to giving third parties access to client data. Some countries require certain minimal security measures (e.g., the use of access code, security software). Other countries require or prohibit encryption. Many countries require a testing environment that does not use production data. Data protection requirements may be industry specific. For example, financial institutions may have to obtain the consent of each of its customers prior to allowing a third party to process customer data. This requirement may be met by simply putting a notice on the customer's next statement, negative consent, or affirmative consent depending on the country. Some countries prohibit all third-party access to certain types of data.

Import/export controls. Many countries restrict, and impose duties on, the import/export of data and technology. The United States for example has restrictions on which type of technology can be imported/exported from the country. Many countries—including the United States—find it difficult to value data and technology. Often duties are imposed on the media on which the data and technology is carried. Because of the potentially high value of certain data and technology, countries are searching for a way to tax the import and export of technology. The applicability and scope of such restrictions should be assessed on a country-by-country basis.

Relocation of service locations. Many countries may require the customer to obtain government consent or notify the government prior to relocating a service location outside that country's borders. Other countries may expressly require the customer to maintain a service location in that country.

Third-party processing. In addition to permission or notice requirements relating to the relocation of a service location—some country's require the customer to obtain consent prior to allowing a third party to process data—this may be a general requirement or a requirement based on specific industries. Third party processing of data may not be relevant to all BPO transactions, particularly BPO transactions that do not have a systems piece (e.g., real estate management).

Changes in laws and regulations. The final issue relating to legal and regulatory concerns is how to go forward into the future with the outsourcing relationship. Laws and regulations will undoubtedly change over the term of the contract, and the contract should be drafted to deal with these changes. To the extent possible, the contract should deal with how changes in laws and regulations will be handled, as well as who will bear the costs of implementing such changes. In addition, the parties will need to determine responsibility for making changes required by external/internal auditors. If certain services or activities are prohibited or impeded due to a change in law, the contract should attempt to provide for suitable workarounds.

Ownership issues. Issues relating to the ownership of developed and newly acquired work product may be complex depending on the applicable local law. For example, the definition of a work made for hire will likely differ in the United Kingdom and India. In addition, customers who perform a good deal of government contracting work or who are government entities will need to identify and understand the regulations applicable to software and technical data ownership to ensure that the ownership provisions of the contract are effective.

Audit Requirements

The internal and external audit requirements of each affected site will need to be assessed and addressed in the contract. Banks, in particular, have a wide range of external and internal auditors, all of whose requirements must be met. The regulations applicable to the particular industry may require the customer to incorporate into the outsourcing agreement some minimum audit rights.

New Environments

Many outsourcing transactions serve as the platform pursuant to which the customer will move from one environment to another environment—or in many instances from a number of different environments to a standardized environment. The parties will need to consider how the roll out to each of the individual sites should be handled. What are the local requirements for the roll-out? Are the acceptance criteria the same for each site? What is the roll out schedule? What if the schedule is changed or delayed? What are the penalties for failing to meet the schedules on a site-by-site and a global basis?

Monitoring Performance

Performance standards. Global and site-specific performance standards should be specified in the contract. The mechanism for measuring performance on a global and site-by-site basis, as well as the damages applicable if performance standards are not met, should also be addressed in the contract.

Benchmarking. It is becoming more and more typical for the parties to include as part of the outsourcing contract a mechanism pursuant to which the pricing, methodologies, technology, and services provided by the vendor is benchmarked against pricing, methodologies, technology, and services provided to other vendor customers, as well as other companies in the customer's industry. If the parties agree to benchmark, other issues to consider are whether benchmarking should be performed on a global/per site basis, the allocation of the costs of the benchmarker, and the procedures for implementing improvements.

Technology review. Outsourcing contracts typically require the vendor to keep the customer abreast of new methodologies/technology and changes in methodologies/technology. As with benchmarking, the customer will need to consider whether any such methodology/technology review should be performed on a global/per site basis.

Pricing-Related Issues

Pricing. Some issues to consider with respect to pricing include:

- In some cases, the structure of the contract may effect the pricing. For example, pricing may be more favorable if the customer commits in the outsourcing contract to include a certain number of sites in scope rather than having a master agreement with an option for the customer to add sites.
- The parties may wish to evaluate the customer's budget for each of the affected locations when developing the fee structure.
- When negotiating price, the parties should discuss appropriate mechanisms for adjusting the price in the event of increases and decreases in services. This mechanism will likely vary on a site-by-site basis (since, for example, the cost of providing services in the United Kingdom is likely more than the cost in India).
- The base fees typically include a baseline of services with the customer paying incremental fees for services above and below the baselines. To reflect substantial changes in the customer's use of the services over the term (e.g., $\pm$ 20 percent), many customers wish to include in the outsourcing agreements a mechanism pursuant to which baselines can be adjusted on a periodic basis. The parties would need to determine whether any such baselines will be set on a global or a site-by-site basis and, similarly, whether adjustments will be made globally on a site-by-site basis.
- The vendor should be required to segregate its fees for each site receiving services (this is particularly important when assessing tax liability).

Currency risks. The contract should provide for when, where, and in what currency payments will be made. The currency or currencies in which payments are to be made is typically the subject of much discussion since one of the parties will always be bearing the risk of fluctuating exchange rates.

Cost of living adjustments. The applicability of COLA, if any, will likely vary from country to country. The parties will need to determine how inflation-sensitive countries are to be handled.

Taxes. The potential tax liability imposed in connection with outsourcing transactions may be substantial. The customer should work with the vendor to determine the potential tax exposure. The parties may wish to consider allocating responsibility for taxes (sales, use, service, VAT) on a country-by-country basis.

Asset sales. Many outsourcing transactions involve the sale of all or some of the customer's assets to the vendor in exchange for a lump sum payment or a reduction in annual fees. If assets are being sold or transferred by the customer to the vendor, the customer typically inventories on a site-by-site basis those assets being transferred. In addition, the parties will need to assess the most favorable means (from a tax and regulatory perspective) of transferring such assets on a site-by-site basis.

Retained Responsibilities

The parties will need to determine which assets the customer will retain managerial, administrative, operational, and/or financial responsibility for on a global/site basis. If the vendor assumes financial responsibility for assets retained by the customer, the parties will need to determine how, by whom and in which currency invoices will be paid.

Termination

Just as important as planning a smooth transition of business process operations to the vendor is safeguarding oneself in the event the relationship does not work out. There are a number of different types of possible terminations—termination for convenience, termination for change of control of vendor/customer, termination for cause, termination for failing to provide critical services, termination for failing to meet service levels, and termination for failing to restore services in the event of a disaster or a *force majeure* event. The parties will need to focus particular attention on how global/site terminations will be handled. With respect to multisite transactions, "cross-termination" rights (e.g., what is the effect on the master contract as individual sites are terminated) will need to be spelled out. In addition to negotiating the rights of the parties to terminate, the parties will need to negotiate the applicable fees (if any) for global/site terminations and the manner and currency in which such fees are payable.

Continuation of Services

An issue critical to any outsourcing transaction is how and when critical functions will be restored at each site in the event of a disaster or *force majeure* event. What is the minimum amount of service that the customer can live with on a site-by-site basis and on a global basis? With respect to disasters, the parties will need to determine whether business recovery is in scope. Depending on the contract scope, the parties may need to discuss developing and implementing business recovery plans for each of the sites—and possibly a global escalation plan if more than one site is affected. With respect to *force majeure,* the parties should examine closely the definition of a *force majeure* event. Are all of the possibilities for a particular country included? Is there anything that should be excluded? Is a disaster at one site a *force majeure* event at another site?

CHAPTER 10

THE EXHIBITS AND ANCILLARY AGREEMENTS

10.1 A CRITICAL PART OF THE BPO CONTRACT

While the BPO contract provides the general framework under which services are to be provided by the vendor and the remedies if obligations are not performed, it is in the exhibits to the BPO contract that the particular services to be provided are described, assets, methodologies, and technology are identified, service levels are specified, base and incremental pricing is provided, and the scope and implementation of new projects are detailed. Many of the hidden costs in outsourcing transactions can be found in the data and information contained in—or more likely, omitted from—the exhibits.

(a) What Should Be Included in the Exhibits? There are three general approaches regarding what should be included in the exhibits:

1. Be as detailed as possible with respect to the services to be provided, projects to be implemented, and assets and users covered
2. Be as detailed as possible, but leave areas where due diligence is necessary until after contract signing
3. Be as general as possible (e.g., the vendor will provide the services provided prior to the agreement date by the applicable business process department) on the grounds that too much detail could be detrimental since a party could argue that if it is not listed, then it is not covered

Obviously, there are benefits and risks to all three approaches for both the customer and the vendor. To the extent that the data is available and time allows, the more detailed the parties can be with respect to each of the exhibits, the more likely the parties will identify open issues and be able to reach an understanding as to such issues *prior* to contract signing. In reality, the parties usually come out somewhere between being too detailed and too general.

(b) Don't Leave the Exhibits until the End! Too often the parties focus primarily on the contract and leave the exhibits until the end. In many cases, the vendor will produce its own version of the exhibits and the customer will not focus on the work product at all or until there is little room left for negotiation. Regardless of who prepares the exhibits, once they are reviewed, the other party will usually determine that, to some degree, the exhibits do not reflect the business deal as the customer understands it, do not cover the scope of services that the customer believes it is receiving, and conflict with what is in the contract. A checklist of general issues to think about with respect to the exhibits is:

- What types of lists or inventories should be attached as exhibits? (Begin a checklist early in the process and delegate preparation to different groups if possible, particularly with respect to inventory lists.)
- Have you read all of the exhibits? (Often, important information regarding services and pricing may turn up in seemingly innocuous exhibits, such as reports or inventory lists.)
- Have the relevant subgroups reviewed exhibits dealing with their particular areas of expertise?
- Do the exhibits reflect the business deal?
- Are the contents of the exhibits as complete as possible?
- Do the exhibits cover all of the things that the contract says they should? (It is often helpful to do a search for the exhibits in the contract and prepare a cross-reference checklist.)
- What is missing from the exhibits that could mean add-on costs later (e.g., upgrades, replacement equipment, additional equipment, additional capacity, additional users, shadow support services that are provided today)?
- Are the contents of the exhibits negotiable? Have the contents of the exhibits been negotiated?

(c) Delegate Responsibility The exhibits should be read with as much (or more) attention by the outsourcing team as the contract. In some instances, it may make sense to delegate responsibility for the review of different exhibits to a subteam. For example, the exhibit describing customer service could be delegated to the customer/vendor service manager, the exhibit describing security services could be delegated to a subteam consisting of data control and audit, and the employee transfer exhibits to the human resources representative. After the subteams have reviewed and approved the exhibits, each of the exhibits should be reviewed by other members of the outsourcing team to ensure consistency with both the other exhibits and the contract.

(d) Business and Legal Reviews A common myth is that the contract is for the legal team and the exhibits are for the business team. Both teams need to be involved in the preparation and negotiation of both the contract *and* the exhibits. As much as the parties try to restrict legal issues to the contract and business issues to the exhibits, they always overlap.

10.2 EXHIBIT LISTINGS

The types, number, and scope of the exhibits to be attached to the BPO contract will vary depending on the scope, location, and value of the services to be outsourced and the time frame in which the contract is to be negotiated. For example, the exhibits for an accounting services transaction (which would include more detail regarding financial procedures, reports, and audit requirements) will be different than the exhibits for a deal outsourcing the human resources department (which would focus more on benefits, company policies, and employee groups).

While the content of the exhibits are tailored to the requirements of each deal, several general categories of exhibits included in almost all BPO deals (e.g., description of services, service levels, pricing, termination assistance). In some deals, the parties combine information and data in one exhibit (e.g., the description of services to be provided) that may be broken out into four or five exhibits in other deals (e.g., general services, customer service, security services, maintenance services, training). A list of possible exhibits to the outsourcing contract is set forth in Exhibit 10.1 (in alphabetical order). This list is intended to

Exhibit Name	Description
Ancillary Agreements	Copy of any ancillary agreements, e.g., escrow agreement, asset transfer or purchase agreement
Architecture and Product Standards	Description of the technical architecture and product standards used by customer as of the contract date that vendor must comply with (customer may reserve right to change standards)
Business Recovery Services	Description of business continuation plan and services to be provided by vendor
Change Control Procedures	Since the procedures are often developed within 30 to 180 days after the contract date, an example of the form of procedures or the table of contents of the procedures may be attached
Confidentiality Agreement	If the BPO contract requires vendor employees, vendor subcontractors, customer auditors, or customer third-party vendors to sign a confidentiality agreement, a copy of the agreement to be signed is typically attached
Critical Services	List of services considered critical to customer's business (if these services are not performed, customer may have certain remedies, e.g., liquidated damages, expedited termination)
Customer Assets (Leased and Owned)	Inventory of customer assets that will be transferred to vendor or which vendor will manage, operate, maintain, have financial responsibility for, and/or otherwise need access to
Customer Competitors	List of customer competitors that vendor is restricted in providing services to under the agreement or if vendor merges with/purchases/is purchased by any such competitors, customer may terminate the BPO contract
Customer Employees	List of employees to whom vendor will be making offers of employment; may be prudent to reference employees by social security number rather than name for confidentiality purposes; be mindful of not including any information that may be discrimination (e.g., age, sex, race, health condition)
Customer Facilities	List of customer facilities that will be transferred to vendor or which vendor will manage, operate, maintain, have financial responsibility for, and/or otherwise need access to
Customer Proprietary Methodologies/Technology	Inventory of customer proprietary methodologies/technology that will be transferred to vendor or which vendor will manage, operate, maintain, have financial responsibility for, and/or otherwise need access to
Customer Third Party Methodologies/Technology	Inventory of customer third-party methodologies/technology that will be transferred to vendor or which vendor will manage, operate, maintain, have financial responsibility for, and/or otherwise need access to
Customer Satisfaction Survey	Example of customer satisfaction survey to be distributed within the customer organization
Customer Service/Help Desk	Detailed description of customer services (or help desk services) to be provided by vendor, including levels of services, volume of service, escalation procedures
Description of Services	Typically a detailed description of the services to be provided by vendor; typically tracks all of the services provided today by the affected group of employees as well as any supplemental services agreed upon by the parties or additional services to be provided in a new environment; in some instances, certain services are broken out and described in other exhibits (e.g., implementation of new projects, training)
Employee Plans	Copy of any customer or vendor plans that are relevant for determining financial or administrative responsibility between the parties (e.g., profit sharing, severance, savings, pension); it is useful to attach the plans if there may be a dispute over which plan (or version of the plan) the parties are referring to in the agreement

(Continued)

Exhibit 10.1 Examples of Exhibits to Outsourcing Contract

Exhibit Name	Description
Employee Release	Form release to be signed by employee when accepting employment with vendor (may not be required for all locations; may vary from location to location)
Employee Transition Procedures	Description of how vendor will transition the employees, including employee communications, offers, acceptance periods, start dates
Expense Policy and Procedures	Copy of expense policies (either customer or vendor policies depending upon whose policies vendor is required to follow under the BPO contract when providing services for which customer pays expenses)
Fees	• Detail of fees payable to vendor for the services • Detail of additional fees payable to vendor for services above baselines (hourly, daily, weekly, monthly, with/without notice) • Detail of reduction in fees for services below baselines
Guarantee	Copy of guarantee to be signed by the parent or subsidiary of vendor or customer
Human Resource Claims	List of any pending or threatened claims against the customer by the affected employees
Invoice Detail	List of information to be included in vendor invoices; example of an invoice
Key Employee Listing	List of employees considered key to the outsourcing transactions and whose appointment/replacement is subject to certain approvals rights/restrictions under the BPO contract
Life Cycle	Description of system life cycle to be followed by vendor when developing new systems or methodologies
Liquidated Damages for Failing to Meet Service Levels	Description of how liquidated damages for failing to meet service levels are applied and the amounts payable by vendor
Long Range Plan	Description of customer long-term plan, including budgeted asset, service, and miscellaneous costs
Maintenance Terms	Description of maintenance services to be provided by vendor
Management Procedures Manual	Since the procedures are typically developed within 30 to 180 days after the contract date, an example of the form of procedures or the table of contents of the procedures may be attached
Master Lease Agreement	Copy of master lease agreement to be signed between customer and vendor for equipment/facilities to be procured by vendor under the BPO contract
Migration Plan	Description of how vendor will manage the migration of services from a customer to a vendor site
New Environment	Description of new environment to be implemented by vendor, including services or assets to be provided, implementation schedules, remedies for failing to meet schedule
New Services Schedule	Example of work order to be used when engaging vendor to provide out of scope services
New Services Fees	List of fees payable to vendor for out of scope services (e.g., time and materials rates)
Organizational Structure	Chart of vendor-proposed account organizational structure (typically covers top tiers of structure)
Performance Reporting Requirements	Description of performance reports to be provided by vendor
Price List	List (or catalog) of price for different assets that customer may request vendor to procure on customer's behalf
Project Staff Profile	Headcount/description of personnel to be providing services
Projects	Description of projects to be implemented by vendor, including services/assets to be provided, implementation schedules, remedies for failing to meet schedule
Security Services	Description of data and/or physical security services to be provided by vendor

(Continued)

Exhibit 10.1   Examples of Exhibits to Outsourcing Contract *(Continued)*

Exhibit Name	Description
Service Levels	List of service levels that must be met by vendor
Service Locations	List of customer sites and vendor service locations
Standardized Environment	Description of standardized environment that customer must comply with
Subcontractor Agreements	Copies of any agreements directly between customer and vendor subcontractor
Subcontractors	List of subcontractors that customer has approved for use by vendor, together with list of services to be provided
Supporting Data	Compilation of background data distributed by customer and vendor, e.g., RFP, proposal, addenda to proposal, other notes and memoranda
Termination Assistance Services	Description of termination assistance services to be provided by vendor for a period prior to and after effective date of termination/expiration
Termination Fees	List of fees payable by customer upon termination of the BPO contract for certain reasons (typically for convenience); list may include only fixed fees or fixed and variable fees
Third-Party Contracts	• List of third-party contracts that will be transferred to vendor • List of third-party contracts for which vendor will assume managerial, administrative, and/or financial responsibility
Training	Description of training to be provided by vendor, e.g., end-user, operational, train the trainer
Transition Plan	Description of how vendor will transition managerial, administrative and operational responsibility for the business process services from customer to vendor
Vacation Summary	Summary of: • Vacation days available to each of the affected employees for the remainder of the calendar year • Amount of vacation days to be bought out by customer or vendor
Value-Added Services	Description of any value-added services to be provided by vendor, e.g., cross-marketing opportunities, shared benefits
Vendor Employment Agreement	Copy of employment agreement to be signed by employees accepting offers of employment with vendor
Vendor Proprietary Methodologies or Technology	Inventory of vendor proprietary methodologies/technology that will be used by vendor to provide the services
Vendor Third-Party Methodologies or Technology	Inventory of vendor third-party methodologies or technology that will be used by vendor to provide the services

Exhibit 10.1   Examples of Exhibits to Outsourcing Contract (*Continued*)

be illustrative of the types of exhibits that may be attached to the BPO contract. It is not intended to be an exhaustive listing. The actual exhibits to the BPO contract at issue will depend on a number of issues, including the scope of the transaction, the value of the transaction, and available data and information.

10.3 CHECKLISTS FOR THE EXHIBITS

As mentioned in Section 10.2, what is included in the exhibits depends largely on the business deal and the customer's approach with respect to the exhibits. Set forth in Exhibit 10.2 are several checklists for exhibits that are often attached to the BPO contract regardless of the type of process.

PROCUREMENT

- Acquisition
    - Acquisition Services/Assistance
    - Acquisition and Approval Process
    - Track and Report Order Status
    - Delivery/Shipping
- Installation
    - Moves, Adds, and Changes
    - Delivery Process
    - Installation
        - Office
        - Remote
        - Field
    - System Set Up Requirements
    - Testing
    - Removal of Packaging Materials
- Asset Management
    - Inventory
    - Tagging Assets
    - Loading of Databases
    - Track Move, Adds, and Changes
    - Ensure Contract Compliance
    - Register, Verify, Track Warranties
- Technology Disposal
    - Resale assistance
    - Reuse procedures

CUSTOMER SERVICE/HELP DESK

- Location
- Centralized vs. Dispersed
- Levels of Support (Level 1, 2, 3)
- Receive, Log and Track Calls
- Call Tracking System
- Toll Free Number
- Languages Spoken at Help Desk
- Support Standard/Nonstandard Environment
- Hours of Operation
- Change Management
- Root Cause Analysis
- Remote Site (Store) Support
- Support Roll Out of New Environment
- Coordinate with Third-Party Vendors
- Escalation Procedures
- Administration Support
- Coordinate Equipment/Parts Distribution
    - Issue Supplies
    - File Transfers
    - Control File
    - Inventory Control
    - Polling
    - Asset Management
    - Warranty Management
    - Services Management
- Reporting
    - Number of Calls Received
    - Number of Calls Answered
    - Response Time
    - Priority of Calls Received

(Continued)

Exhibit 10.2   Checklist for Exhibits to the BPO Contract

PROJECTS

- Procedures for Requesting/Receiving Proposals
- Project Procedures
    Submit Project Request
    Prepare Proposal
    Develop Plan
    Design
    Documentation
    Testing
    Acceptance
    Implementation
    Support
- Prioritize Projects
- Training
- Quality Assurance
- Services
    Upgrades
    New Releases
    Enhancements
    Government/Regulatory Changes
    Training
    Reporting

IT-RELATED SERVICES

- Software
    Requirements
    Procurement
    Acceptance Testing
    Maintenance
    Upgrades
    New Releases
    Enhancements
    Replacements
    Additional Software
    System Monitoring
    Performance Tuning (Systems/Applications)
    Problem Resolution
    Backup/Recovery
    Vendor/Subcontractor Performance
    Reporting
- Data Transmission
- Current/Future Methods of Data Transmission
- Financial Responsibility for Data Transmission
- Management/Financial Responsibility for Contracts with Third Parties (e.g., subscriber agreements)?
- Technology Selection
    Technology Standards
    Corporate/Site Specific Guidelines
    Catalog for Standard Products and Services
    Configuration and Design Assistance
    Compatibility Assurance
    Design Assistance
    Evaluation Lab
    Deployment Strategy
- Operations
    Operate System
    Tape Management
    Data Entry
    File Services

(Continued)

Exhibit 10.2   Checklist for Exhibits to the BPO Contract *(Continued)*

IT-RELATED SERVICES (*Continued*)

- Operations (*Continued*)
  - Print & Microfiche
  - Print Distribution
  - Backup/Recovery
  - Test Environments
  - Documentation of Operation Procedures
  - Production Control
    - Operate/Monitor Systems Console
    - Manage Schedules
    - Implement Automated Scheduling
    - Batch Management
    - Report Balancing
    - Special Forms Inventory
  - Hardware Planning, Planning, and Installation
    - Upgrades
    - Replacements
    - Additional Equipment
  - Systems Management
    - Capacity Management
    - Performance Management
    - Change Management
    - Problem Management
    - Recovery Management
    - Configuration Management
    - Inventory Management
  - Facilities
  - Quality Assurance
- Maintenance
  - Preventative Maintenance
  - Problem Management/Resolution/Escalation
  - Identify, Track, Report, and Initiate
  - Resolution of Problems
  - Interface with Hardware/Software vendors
  - Inventory of Replacement Parts
  - Repair Service—On-Site/Carry-In
  - Upgrades
  - New Releases

BUSINESS RECOVERY SERVICES

- Customer's Current Business Recovery Plan
- Will Customer's Current Plan Be Terminated?
- Location of Vendor Hotsite
- Hotsite Configuration
- Customer Priority at Vendor Hotsite?
- Response/Recovery Times
- Scope of Vendor Services
- Notification Procedures
- List of Customer/Vendor Contacts
- Identify/Prioritize Critical Services
- Escalation Procedures
- Periodic Testing of Plan
- Allow for Growth

DATA SECURITY SERVICES

- Controls to Detect and Report Intentional or Accidental Invalid Data Access Attempts
- Installation, Maintenance, Upgrade of Existing/New Data Access Control Software
- Protect Application Resources via the Access Control Software
- Protect End User Data via Access Control Software
- Security Procedures Manual
- Establish, Change, Deactivate, and Remove Log-On IDs
- Review, Approve and Grant Request for Privileged User Authorities

(*Continued*)

Exhibit 10.2   Checklist for Exhibits to the BPO Contract (*Continued*)

DATA SECURITY SERVICES (*Continued*)

- Notify Data Owners and Customer of Invalid Data Access Attempts
- Emergency Security Requests
- Controls for Printed Output from Unauthorized Access while under Vendor Control
- Knowledge of Latest Concepts/Techniques Associated with System and Data Security
- Storage and Security for Portable Media

PHYSICAL SITE SECURITY

- Security Personnel
- Monitoring Devices
    Placement
    Maintenance
    Upgrades
- Help Desk
- Controls to Detect and Report Intentional or Accidental Unauthorized Access Attempts
- Installation, Maintenance, Upgrade of Existing/New Access Control Technology
- Security Procedures Manual
- Establish, Change, Deactivate, and Remove Access I.D.'s
- Notify Owners and Customer of Invalid Facility Access Attempts
- Emergency Security Requests
- Controls for Printed Output from Unauthorized Access while under Vendor Control
- Knowledge of Latest Concepts/Techniques Associated with Physical Security
- Storage and Security for Portable Media

Exhibit 10.2   Checklist for Exhibits to the BPO Contract (*Continued*)

10.4 ANCILLARY AGREEMENTS

Often in a BPO transaction, a number of ancillary agreements are entered into as part of or in conjunction with the main services contract. The particular types of ancillary agreements entered into in connection with the overall BPO transaction is driven by the business deal at hand and, therefore, varies from transaction to transaction. The various types of ancillary agreements typically fall within one of five categories:

1. Strategic agreements
2. Agreements related to the transition of responsibility to the vendor ("transition agreements")
3. Related service agreements
4. Agreements pursuant to which the vendor acquires additional resources or expertise necessary to provide the business process service ("vendor resource agreements")
5. Agreements related to the use or access of proprietary information, methodologies, or technology ("Access Agreements")

A list of the types of agreements that may fall within these five categories is set forth in Exhibit 10.3. A more detailed discussion of each of these types of agreements is provided in Exhibit 10.4. Exhibits 10.3 and 10.4 are not intended to identify every possible ancillary agreement that may be entered into in connection with a BPO transaction but rather are intended to be illustrative of the types of agreement that the customer and the vendor may need to consider when structuring the BPO relationship.

STRATEGIC AGREEMENTS

- Joint Venture Agreement
- Joint Marketing Agreement
- Gainsharing Agreement

TRANSITION AGREEMENTS

- Agreement for Temporary Provision of Staff
- Agreement with respect to Employee Transfers
- Asset Purchase Agreement
- Equipment Acquisition Agreement
- Equipment Lease Agreement
- Facility Purchase Agreement
- Facility Lease Agreement
- Assumption of Third-Party Contracts
- Amendment to Existing Third-Party Agreement (e.g., software licenses, equipment leases, facility leases, maintenance agreements)
- Transition Agreement

RELATED SERVICE AGREEMENTS

- Business Recovery Agreement
- Data Conversion Agreement
- Security Agreement
- Agreement for Training
- Consulting Services Agreement
- Business Reengineering Agreement
- Termination Services Agreement

VENDOR RESOURCE AGREEMENTS

- Teaming Agreement
- Subcontracting Agreement
- Maintenance Agreement

ACCESS AGREEMENTS

- Technology/Methodology License
- Agreement for Use of Developed Product by Third Party
- Confidentiality/Nondisclosure Agreement
- Technology Escrow Agreement

Exhibit 10.3   List of Ancillary Agreements

AGREEMENT TYPE	DESCRIPTION	
Joint Venture Agreement	Purpose	To document a business relationship pursuant to which a new entity is formed to provide services; customer and vendor typically each hold equity stake
	Parties	• Customer and vendor
		• In some instances may include customer/vendor affiliates or vendor's subcontractor
Joint Marketing Agreement	Purpose	If vendor will be developing new methodologies or technology, agreement pursuant to which parties agree to market and license such methodologies or technology to third parties
	Parties	• Customer and vendor
		• In some instances may include vendor's subcontractors or be directly between customer and vendor's subcontractor

(Continued)

Exhibit 10.4   Detailed Chart of Supplemental Agreements

AGREEMENT TYPE	DESCRIPTION	
Gainsharing Agreement	Purpose	To document business understanding pursuant to which customer or vendor receives incentives based on performance or cost savings (see Chapter 6)
	Parties	Customer and vendor
Agreement for Temporary Provision of Staff	Purpose	To provide fill-in or supplementary staff in the event that customer is operating at below critical staffing levels during negotiation period; used mostly if a large number of staff leaves prior to contract signing or if customer has imposed hiring freeze in light of the BPO contract
	Parties	Typically the preferred vendor will enter into an agreement to provide temporary staff; customer may also engage "body shops" or consulting agencies to provide the temporary staff
	Comment	• Provides means of increasing staffing levels to above critical levels on a temporary basis; alleviates some of the time pressure on signing the deal quickly due to staffing crises • If using vendor personnel, allows vendor access to customer's organization; customer may lose some negotiation leverage since once in the organization it is more difficult from an internal perspective to look to another vendor
Agreement with respect to Employee Transfers	Purpose	If the parties do not wish to include the provisions relevant to the transfer of employees in the BPO contract (typically done if the employee provisions are of a particular confidential nature)
	Parties	• Customer and vendor • In some instances may be between customer and vendor's subcontractor
	Comment	• May aid in maintaining confidentiality of human resource provisions • Since many of the human resources terms are closely linked to other terms of the BPO contract, it is often easier to include the human resources provisions in the main BPO contract
Asset Purchase Agreement	Purpose	If, as part of the outsourcing deal, the vendor will be purchasing some or all of the customer's existing assets, it is typical for the parties to enter into a side agreement relating to the transfer of the assets. This may be done for tax purposes, as well as to separate the legal terms specific to assets transfers not relevant to the rest of the outsourcing deal.
	Parties	• Customer and vendor • In some instances vendor's subcontractor may purchase some of the assets, in which case the parties may be the customer and the subcontractor with some type of guarantee of payment from the vendor
	Comment	May be beneficial to segregate the outsourcing transaction from the asset transfer for tax reasons; allows parties to separate asset transfer issues from service issues (many times different teams will negotiate the two agreements)
Equipment Acquisition Agreement	Purpose	To provide a standard form agreement pursuant to which the customer may acquire/purchase equipment from the vendor during the term of the BPO contract
	Parties	• Customer and vendor • In some instances may be between customer and a vendor's subcontractor
	Comment	• Advantageous for customer since parties agree to standard acquisition or purchase terms upfront at a time when customer has the most leverage (e.g., regarding risk of loss, shipping, insurance).

(Continued)

Exhibit 10.4   Detailed Chart of Supplemental Agreements *(Continued)*

AGREEMENT TYPE	DESCRIPTION	
		• However, the downside is that there may be instances where customer may wish to deviate from the standard terms and may be prevented from doing so due to standard form agreement.
Equipment Lease Agreement	Purpose	To provide a standard form lease pursuant to which the customer will lease equipment from the vendor during the term of the BPO contract (Note: The lease agreement should include termination, escalation, or assignment rights in the event of a termination of the outsourcing agreement.)
	Parties	• Customer and vendor
		• In some instances may be between customer and a vendor's subcontractor
	Comment	• Parties agree to lease terms upfront at a time when customer has the most leverage
		• However, the downside is that there may be instances where customer may wish to deviate from the standard terms and may be prevented from doing so due to standard form agreement.
Facility Purchase Agreement	Purpose	If, as part of the outsourcing deal, the vendor will be purchasing some or all of the customer's existing facilities, it is typical for the parties to enter into a side agreement relating to the transfer of the facilities. This may be done for tax purposes, as well as to separate the legal terms specific to facilities transfers not relevant to the rest of the outsourcing deal.
	Parties	• Customer and vendor
		• In some instances vendor's subcontractor may purchase some of the facilities, in which case the parties may be the customer and the subcontractor with some type of guarantee of payment from the vendor
Facility Lease Agreement	Purpose	Used when customer or vendor leases space in connection with the provision of services (e.g., if agreement states that customer must provide minimum space for vendor project staff and customer does not have necessary space; if vendor needs space in a location where it does not have offices; if vendor occupies—but does not purchase—an entire facility of customer)
	Parties	• Customer and vendor
		• Customer or vendor and a third party if customer or vendor does not have the necessary space
	Comment	May be beneficial to segregate the outsourcing transaction from the facility lease obligations for tax reasons; allows parties to separate facility issues from service issues (many times different teams will negotiate the two agreements)
Assumption of Third-Party Contracts	Purpose	To transfer all of the customer's rights and obligations under certain third party contracts to vendor
	Parties	• Customer and vendor
		• May be three way agreement between customer, vendor, and third party
	Comment	• Under the BPO contract, vendor may assume all responsibility for the third party contracts. Therefore, customer will have to negotiate new contracts if the BPO contract terminates or negotiate some type of assignment back to customer in the event of a termination.

(Continued)

Exhibit 10.4   Detailed Chart of Supplemental Agreements *(Continued)*

AGREEMENT TYPE	DESCRIPTION	
Amendment to Existing Third-Party Agreement		• Contracts will likely require third party vendor consent to assumption by vendor (third party vendor may refuse consent or demand a consent fee); if do not obtain consent, may be in violation of contracts
	Purpose	To modify terms of customer's existing agreement; may be necessary if customer would be in violation of third party agreement due to outsourcing transaction (e.g., software licenses prohibiting third-party operation of software, equipment leases prohibiting third-party operation of equipment)
	Parties	• Customer and third party • May be three way agreement between customer vendor and third party
	Comment	• Agreement of third party to allow vendor certain access/use rights • Third party may refuse consent or require consent fee (many customers attempt to amend their contracts through consent letters)
Transition Agreement	Purpose	To document responsibilities of customer and vendor in connection with the transfer of control from customer to vendor (e.g., testing, cutover, implementation)
	Parties	Customer and vendor
Teaming Agreement	Purpose	Used by vendor when using another party or parties to help prepare bid and, if accepted, to provide services under the BPO contract
	Parties	Vendor and third party
Subcontracting Agreement	Purpose	To provide additional staff or provide certain services under the BPO contract
	Parties	Vendor and third party
	Comment	In some instances, customers may not want certain services to be subcontracted (this should be negotiated into the BPO contract)
Maintenance Agreement	Purpose	To provide support services (scope may vary widely depending upon business deal)
	Parties	• Customer and vendor • Customer or vendor and a third party
Business Recovery Agreement	Purpose	To provide business continuation services
	Parties	• Customer and vendor • Customer or vendor and a third party
Data Conversion Agreement	Purpose	To convert data for use in one environment to another environment; typically used when customer is migrating to new systems/environment and existing data must be re-entered or converted for use on new systems/environment
	Parties	• Customer and vendor • Customer or vendor and a third party
	Comment	Allows customer to segregate data conversion from the base services and contract for services on an as-needed basis; allows customer to look to third parties for such services
Security Agreement	Purpose	To provide party with formal security interest in assets of the other party; may be used by a party if selling equipment to customer which is not paid in full upfront to secure rights in equipment until equipment is paid in full
	Parties	Customer and vendor
	Comment	• Evidences security interest in assets until assets are paid in full • Selling party may have a purchase mortgage security interest by operation of law

(Continued)

Exhibit 10.4   Detailed Chart of Supplemental Agreements *(Continued)*

AGREEMENT TYPE	DESCRIPTION	
Agreement for Training	Purpose	To outline specific training services to be provided to customer
	Parties	• Customer and vendor
		• Customer or vendor and a third party
Consulting Services Agreement	Purpose	To outline specific consulting services to be provided to customer
	Parties	• Customer and vendor
		• Customer or vendor and a third party
Business Reengineering Agreement	Purpose	To describe business re-engineering services to be provided to customer prior to or in connection with the BPO contract
	Parties	• Customer and vendor
		• Customer or vendor and a third party
Termination Services Agreement	Purpose	To document vendor's obligations with respect to the provision of services upon expiration or termination of the BPO contract
	Parties	Customer and vendor
Technology/Methodology License	Purpose	To license the right to use technology or methodology (scope of license may vary widely depending upon business deal—e.g., may be user, site, or enterprise license or may be object only or object and source code license)
	Parties	• Customer and vendor
		• Customer or vendor and a third party
	Comment	• Often used if customer or vendor is licensing third party technology or methodology as part of the provision of services
		• May be used as form license pursuant to which vendor will license certain technology or methodology to customer upon termination or expiration of the BPO contract
Agreement for Use of Developed Product by Third Party	Purpose	Used if, as part of the BPO contract, vendor will market or license developed product to its other customers or third parties and customer will receive portion of royalty (may be instances where both parties have the right to market/license product and royalties are due the non-licensing party)
	Parties	Customer or vendor and a third party
	Comment	• Specifies terms upon which third party may use product
		• Nonlicensing party may wish to retain approval rights or negotiate minimum, standard terms or nonlicensing party may lose control over licensing of developed product
Confidentiality/Non-Disclosure Agreement	Purpose	Typically used if third parties or auditors need access to certain confidential information of a party
	Parties	• Customer and vendor
		• Customer or vendor and a third party
	Comment	• Protects confidential information
		• If form of agreement not agreed to in advance, may allow party who is providing access to confidential information to impose onerous terms
Technology Escrow Agreement	Purpose	Used if certain technology will be placed in the custody of a third-party for release upon the occurrence of certain events (e.g., bankruptcy, failure to perform)
	Parties	Customer or vendor and a third party
	Comment	Typically used for software source code

Exhibit 10.4   Detailed Chart of Supplemental Agreements (*Continued*)

CHAPTER **11**

POSTNEGOTIATION ACTIVITIES

11.1 CONTRACT SIGNING

Having agreed on the terms and conditions on which the services will be provided, the parties are ready to move into contract execution mode. Typically, the parties have undergone tough, time-consuming negotiations—often away from home or off-site—and are eager to firm the deal up. There may be a few final due diligence and internal tasks to be completed in order to prepare for the signing. The following is a quick list to check off before moving onto contract signing.

- In accordance with policy, notify or obtain approvals from senior management and board of directors. (If board notification or approval is necessary, coordinate signing with board meeting.)
- Determine who will sign the BPO contract(s) for the customer and the vendor. Make sure the signing party is authorized to sign on behalf of the company.
- Identify date for signing and make sure all necessary parties are available. A number of considerations must be coordinated:
  - Determine whether any other internal events must be coordinated with signing (public offering, announcement of business reorganization).
  - Determine whether announcement will have an effect on stock prices and assess best time for announcement.
  - If signing requires all parties to be in one location, make sure that all necessary parties can be in that location. Confirm travel plans and itineraries.
  - Coordinate with internal, employee, and press communications.
- Identify location for signing. Confirm the signing particulars (lunch, number of people).
- Determine how many copies of the documentation will be signed and make sure that number is ready and available at signing.
- If the parties have a formal signing with all parties present, confirm who should be invited to signing and ensure invitations are made.
- Prepare, gain approval of and implement internal notification or announcement plan. This should include a general announcement, management announcements, and affected employee announcements. The affected employee announcements may be phased (general and individual) so ensure that timing is coordinated.
- Determine whether a press release will be issued. Prepare content and obtain approval. Determine when and how press release will be made. Determine whether press will be invited to signing.

- Determine how communications will be made to customer's third-party vendors affected by outsourcing transaction. Determine schedule for distributing consent letters to third parties from whom consent is necessary to allow outsourcing vendor access to third-party assets or manage third-party contracts (if applicable).

11.2 PRESS RELEASE

In many instances, particularly with respect to large outsourcing transactions, the parties agree to issue a press release outlining the major objectives and highlights of the transaction. In other transactions, the parties choose not to alert the press—typically with respect to smaller transactions or where the customer does not wish to draw attention to the transaction or is concerned that the outsourcing, coupled with other corporate events, will be viewed negatively by the press.

If the parties agree to issue a press release, one of the parties will need to take control of the drafting (bigger companies or organizations will turn the task over to their public relations departments). Both parties will need to review and approve the content and form of the release, as well as to whom the release will be issued and the mechanics of the release. An outline of a brief press release is provided in Exhibit 11.1.

In addition to issuing a press release, the parties will need to consider how inquiries *from* the press and outside parties will be handled. Typically, each party prepares procedures that should be followed by all employees and subcontractors receiving inquiries from the press. These procedures should be disseminated in an employee newsletter or bulletin so that employees and subcontractors are put on notice. In most cases, inquiries must be directed to a particular manager or to the public relations department who will then have (to the extent possible) prepared, preapproved responses to inquiries.

11.3 AUTOPSY

Depending on the availability of the outsourcing team, performing an "autopsy" of the RFP, proposal, and negotiation process can be a useful exercise to determine whether the team achieved its objectives and to identify the strengths and weaknesses of the team's positions and tactics. If the team elects to do an autopsy, it should prepare an outline of the objectives of the autopsy and what areas will be reviewed. (This process also allows the team to vent its

---

Contact:

FOR IMMEDIATE RELEASE

[CUSTOMER] CHOOSES [VENDOR] TO MANAGE
[BUSINESS PROCESS] OPERATIONS

[ADDRESS; DATE]—[Customer] chose [Vendor], a [***] company, to provide [***] services in a $_____outsourcing agreement. The outsourcing agreement will cover Customer's operations in [***].

[DESCRIBE CUSTOMER'S BUSINESS AND BUSINESS OBJECTIVES IN OUTSOURCING]

[QUOTE FROM CUSTOMER/VENDOR:] [NAME] of [Customer] [Vendor] who is [***] noted that [***].

The agreement covers [DESCRIBE HIGHLIGHTS OF DEAL].

Exhibit 11.1 Framework for Brief Press Release

frustrations and share its positive experiences—often a healthy idea for a bunch of people who have been working around the clock in a closed area for a number of months.)

The first step in performing the autopsy is to retrieve the initial objectives prepared by management and the outsourcing team. The team should review the objectives one by one and analyze whether each objective was achieved. For example, consider cost reduction— what are the overall projected savings? The analysis should take into account the customer's retained responsibilities (financial and administrative) as well as value-added services that the customer would not have been able to do with its own resources. Other areas that the team may wish to consider in the autopsy include:

- Dissect each part of the process—the RFP, the proposal, proposal evaluation, vendor selection, employee communications and negotiations. What were the high points? What was done well? What could have been done better? How?
- Look at the different components of the deal—the legal provisions, the description of services, projects, service levels, project management, staffing, pricing.
- Look at the organization of the outsourcing team. Was it the right group of people? Should other areas have been involved?
- Look at the performance of the different parts of the outsourcing team—management, team leaders, technical, financial, human resources, risk assessment, audit, public relations, consultants, legal.

11.4 RISK ANALYSIS

Another useful task (that can be done immediately before or after contract signing) is to analyze the potential risks of the transaction and how the contract handles such risks. Often the general counsel's office, senior management, or the board will ask for such an analysis (usually followed by a recommendation as to whether the benefits outweigh the risks). An example of a risk analysis is provided in Exhibit 11.2. The terms in the risk

---

**[BUSINESS PROCESS] SERVICES AGREEMENT
BETWEEN [CUSTOMER] AND [VENDOR]**

A. RISK ASSESSMENT

**1. RISK: SERVICE FAILURES.
CONTRACT PROVISIONS FOR REDUCING RISK:**

a. Service level requirements (with associated liquidated damages in the event of a failure to meet such service level requirements and the right to terminate if the liquidated damages exceed certain amounts)
b. Critical milestone requirements for migration/project implementations
c. Root cause analysis in the event of a failure to meet service levels

**2. RISK: LOSS OF CONTROL OVER OPERATIONS.
CONTRACT PROVISIONS FOR REDUCING RISK:**

a. Flexibility to use third-party package methodologies or technologies rather than newly developed methodologies/technologies
b. Approval rights over:
  - Any material changes to the services and the methodologies or technologies
  - New service locations
  - Project executive and certain key employees
c. Service levels
d. Benchmarking

(Continued)

Exhibit 11.2   Risk Assessment

    e. Customer satisfaction survey

    f. Audit rights of services and charges

3. RISK: ABILITY TO INSOURCE OR CONTRACT WITH A THIRD PARTY FOR SERVICES
CONTRACT PROVISIONS FOR REDUCING RISK:

    a. Right to contract with third parties

    b. Termination assistance

    c. Rights to use methodologies or technologies upon termination

4. RISK: CHANGES IN CUSTOMER BUSINESS/REGULATORY REQUIREMENTS
CONTRACT PROVISIONS FOR REDUCING RISK:

    a. Right to increase or decrease services

    b. Right to add or delete business units

    c. Renegotiation rights if change in usage is above or below certain percentages

    d. Parties' responsibilities for changes in laws/regulations

5. RISK: INFLEXIBLE PRICING
CONTRACT PROVISIONS FOR REDUCING RISK:

    a. Right to use discretionary resources for additional work or new projects

    b. Adjustments of baselines/fees to reflect increases or decreases in services

    c. Sharing in savings resulting from new methodologies or technologies

    d. Benchmarking

6. RISK: ABILITY TO TERMINATE CONTRACT
CONTRACT PROVISIONS FOR REDUCING RISK:

    a. Convenience in whole or in part

    b. Change in control

    c. Cause

    d. Failure to provide critical services

    e. Insolvency

7. RISK: POTENTIAL LIABILITY
CONTRACT PROVISIONS FOR REDUCING RISK:

    a. Indemnities

    b. Deferral rights or liquidated damages for failures to meet critical milestones or service levels

    c. Insurance

B. AREAS OF SIGNIFICANT EXPOSURE

1. CONDITIONS PRECEDENT OR CHANGES IN CIRCUMSTANCES

    a. Provision of the services

    b. Effect on roll-out of new methodologies or technologies

    c. Effect on human resources

    d. Additional costs

2. CUSTOMER READINESS FOR ROLL-OUT OF NEW METHODOLOGIES/
TECHNOLOGIES

3. VENDOR AS EXCLUSIVE PROVIDER OF SERVICES

4. CONSENTS

5. HUMAN RESOURCE ISSUES

    a. Transition

    b. Severance

    c. Litigation exposure

6. COST OF LIVING ADJUSTMENTS

7. TAXES

8. LIMITATION OF LIABILITY

Exhibit 11.2 **Risk Assessment** (*Continued*)

analysis are for illustrative purposes only and would need to be modified to reflect the particular transaction.

11.5 CONTRACT ADMINISTRATION

The contract is executed and the vendor is commencing work. Each party's most important task now (in addition to managing the impact of the change) is administering the contract. A great contract is of little help to either party if it is not followed effectively. Depending on the size and scope of the transaction, each party may want to appoint an individual or team responsible for contract administration, including following up on any to-be-determined items in the schedules to the contract, tracking customer and vendor tasks that are to be performed, tracking deliverables, managing customer use of vendor resources, and auditing invoices. The customer's contract administrator(s) may be part of the customer's team responsible for strategical decisions and issuing approvals or a separate administrative team. A thorough understanding of the contract is key to successful contract administration. If possible, the contract administrator(s) should be involved in contract negotiations.

As a starting point, each party may wish to prepare several documents for its internal purposes and use that have proven to be helpful in the understanding and management of the contract:

> *The executive summary.* A summary of the key contract provisions. This document can serve as a big picture checklist for the contract administrators and serve as a useful tool when briefing senior management on the terms of the contract as well as the status of key items.
> *Tracking the TBD list.* A list of items in the contract that at contract signing were not agreed upon due to insufficient information. Examples of such items include service levels for which there was no historical data, project definition, deliverables, and milestones for projects that were only in the conceptual stage as of contract signing. This list will need to be revised and updated on a regular basis.
> *Tracking the deliverables.* A list of items to be provided by the vendor during the term of the contract. Examples include project deliverables, new equipment (including pursuant to refreshes), inventory lists, and reports. This list will need to be revised and updated on a regular basis.

11.6 IMPLEMENTING THE TRANSITION PLAN

The first of the vendor's tasks will be to manage the transition of responsibility for the business process being outsourced from the customer to the vendor, as well as to manage the transfer of employees from the customer to the vendor (if applicable). In some instances, the transition plan will include the migration from a customer to vendor site. If the vendor will continue operations at a customer site for a period of time prior to migration to a vendor site, the migration plan may be provided in a separate document with separate completion dates.

11.7 NOTIFYING THIRD PARTIES

Often an action item that is part of the transition plan is the notification of third parties of the transaction. The third parties to be notified should have been identified during due diligence and contract negotiations. Relevant third parties may include:

> *Third-party vendors.* If the vendor requires access to assets licensed or leased from a third party or if certain contracts are being transferred to the vendor, are consent letters to the

relevant third-party vendors being sent out? If not, should certain vendors at a minimum be notified of the transaction (particularly those whose invoices will now be paid by the vendor)? Have any addresses for the purposes of invoicing, sending notices changed? Have contact names changed? Are any third-party vendors being terminated? Are any third-party vendors duties changing? If so, the parties should consider which vendors should be notified and how the notifications should be sent out. Examples of two types of consent letters (one where the vendor requires access to assets, the other where the contract for the assets being transferred to vendor) are provided in Appendices 11.1 and 11.2. The customer should note that the effect of the consent letters is questionable if the third-party vendor does not respond that it consents. It is not clear whether silent consent would be deemed effective. If consent is not obtained, the customer is at risk of violating the terms of the applicable licensing or service agreement.

Government or regulatory authorities. Are there any government, regulatory, or taxing authorities that should be notified or whose approval is necessary (typically as a condition precedent to the commencement of services)? For example, it is typical in an outsourcing transaction involving a financial institution that the financial institution notify (and possibly obtain the consent of) certain regulatory authorities. (The financial institution should assess the timing of this notice, which in some instances must be made prior to the vendor providing outsourcing services.)

Stockholders. The customer and the vendor should consider whether it needs to notify its stockholders of the transaction (or at least include it in securities reports). The customer and the vendor should also consider whether any special securities filings are necessary as a result of the transaction. This is particularly applicable to large transactions and transactions with large asset pieces.

Customer's clients. Does the customer have any obligation to notify or obtain the approval of any of its clients prior to or in conjunction with the outsourcing (e.g., is approval necessary to permit access to confidential information or data)?

CHAPTER 12

RENEGOTIATION AND TERMINATION

12.1 OVERVIEW

The contract is signed, operations are being or have been transferred to the outsourcing vendor, and, in many cases, employees have been transitioned and/or assets have been sold or disposed of—the customer essentially has handed over to the outsourcing vendor ownership of the infrastructure used to manage the business process on a day-to-day basis. Then something unanticipated happens. There is an organizational change or a real or perceived performance problem. The customer feels vulnerable and the vendor feels overburdened, causing both parties to become at least a little defensive. Although this is an unpleasant and dreaded scenario (and one that neither party wants to think about during the precontract courtship phase), it is a common one. A surprisingly high percentage of outsourcing contracts are renegotiated during the first few years of the term. Although fewer contracts are actually terminated (at least in their entirety), it is not unheard of for outsourcing contracts to be terminated for convenience or for breach.

While there are no prescribed reasons that drive a party's desire to renegotiate, we have attempted to highlight in Exhibit 12.1 some of the more common reasons for renegotiating the BPO arrangement from both the customer's *and* the vendor's perspective.

While termination is a more draconian consequence than renegotiation in the event of an organizational change or dissatisfaction with the BPO arrangement, many of the reasons underlying a party's desire to terminate the BPO contract are the same as the reasons for renegotiating highlighted in Exhibit 12.1. In fact, termination is often viewed as the next step if renegotiation is not a successful or viable option. A common, often effective strategy is for the customer or the vendor to head down the path to termination, when the party's real objective is to bring the other party to the table to renegotiate. (This strategy, however, is typically effective only if there are substantive reasons for termination.)

A number of the more common reasons that both the customer and the vendor seek to terminate the BPO contract are set forth in Exhibit 12.2.

12.2 THE RENEGOTIATION/TERMINATION PROCESS

Once a party has decided to consider renegotiating or terminating the outsourcing contract, the next step is to outline the renegotiation or termination process. As was the case when negotiating the contract that is now the subject of renegotiation or termination, the party's objectives underlying renegotiation or termination will in large part drive the

CUSTOMER REASONS FOR RENEGOTIATING

- Unrealized cost savings
- Unanticipated charges
- Excessive pricing (real or perceived)
- Change in management (with new management having different objectives)
- Unsatisfactory performance (real or perceived)
- Inadequate service levels
- Change in organizational structure
- Acquisition, merger, or divestiture
- Increased or reduced volumes
- New projects (not reflected in contract)
- Implementation of new environment (not reflected in contract)
- Delay or cancellation of roll-out of new environment
- Desire to bring certain services in-house
- Change in scope or project definition
- Change in strategic or infrastructure direction
- Desire to restructure relationship
- Contract expiration

VENDOR REASONS FOR RENEGOTIATING

- Unanticipated costs
- Unrealized profit
- Need for additional resources
- Unsatisfactory input from the customer
- Acquisition, merger or divestiture
- Increased or reduced volumes
- Desire to increase or decrease scope
- New projects (not reflected in contract)
- Implementation of new environment (not reflected in contract)
- Delay or cancellation of roll-out of new environment
- Change in scope or project definition
- Desire to restructure relationship
- Means to avoid termination
- Desire to increase length of term

Exhibit 12.1   Reasons for Renegotiating

CUSTOMER REASONS FOR SEEKING TERMINATION

- Excessive pricing (real or perceived)
- Unsatisfactory performance (real or perceived)
- Change in organization structure
- Acquisition, merger, or divestiture
- Implementation of new environment
- Failure to roll-out of new environment
- Poor customer or vendor relations
- Change in scope or project definition
- Change in strategic or infrastructure direction
- Means to initiate renegotiation

VENDOR REASONS FOR SEEKING TERMINATION

- Unanticipated costs
- Acquisition, merger, or divestiture
- Nonpayment by the customer

Exhibit 12.2   Reasons for Seeking Termination

process. For example, if a customer's primary objective in renegotiating is to obtain better pricing, the process will be different than if it is renegotiating to adjust the contract to reflect a change in scope. Some of the action items that each of the parties should consider as part of any renegotiation or termination are provided in Exhibit 12.3.

12.3 WHAT DOES THE CONTRACT SAY

When renegotiating or terminating a BPO contract, the precise language of the contract, which was once considered the dalliance of lawyers, is now extremely important. Seem-

- Define objectives
- Obtain management support
- Obtain support from business process department
- Obtain empowerment from management
- Identify point people for renegotiations or termination discussions
  - Management
  - Technical
  - Financial
- Involve legal counsel
- Involve human resources (if there are personnel issues)
- Review the contract (all provisions!) (see Section 12.3)
- Review all ancillary agreements with vendor
- Review the file
  - Correspondence
  - Memoranda
  - Amendments
  - Change orders
  - New service orders
  - Invoices
- Know the history of the deal
  - Original goals in outsourcing
  - The vendor's primary commitments
  - Concessions by the customer
  - Concessions by the vendor
  - Financial engineering
  - Customer promises or representations
  - Vendor promises or representations
- Document problems
  - Nonperformance
  - Failure to meet service levels
  - Failure to provide deliverables
  - Customer/vendor relations
  - Churning of employees
- Anticipate other party's objectives
- Develop strategy
  - Assess current and future business needs
  - Assess strength of any nonperformance or breach claims
  - Calculate any credits or fees owing for nonperformance or delayed performance
  - Identify and access alternatives
    - Insource
    - Resource
  - Determine the customer's willingness or ability to use a third party
  - Determine impact of termination on other business processes of the customer
  - Initiate contact or dialogue with the other party

Exhibit 12.3   Action Items

ingly innocuous provisions are being closely reviewed and dissected. Each party is looking for contractual support, however thin, to bolster its position. The document that was intended to forge the outsourcing relationship is now being used to dissolve or at least restructure it. The use of the contract to dissolve or restructure the outsourcing relationship is an important point to keep in mind during renegotiation or termination, as well as during the initial negotiation and structuring of the BPO contract.

The following list provides an overview of some of the key provisions typically included in the BPO contract that each of the parties should review when renegotiation or termination is being considered.

Term of Agreement

The parties should review the contract provision setting out the term of the contract. How long is the relationship supposed to go for under the terms of the contract? Is there an expiration date? Is there a pilot period with an early out right? What are the renewal options and have they been exercised? An additional issue to consider is how the length of the term came to be agreed upon. For example, did the parties agree to a shorter or longer term with the understanding that the customer would receive some financial relief in the early years or that the vendor would recoup upfront costs over the term of the contract? What other commitments were made as part of the negotiations around term? Were there any incentives to agreeing to a longer term?

Right to Renegotiate/Terminate

Renegotiation. Is there any contractual basis for requesting a renegotiation (e.g., a provision that calls for renegotiation if volumes exceed or go below a certain amount)? Has there been any event of termination (discussed next) that could be used as a lever to request renegotiation?

Termination. What events may trigger a termination right (e.g., convenience, change of control, regulatory event, breach)? Has any termination event occurred? If the basis for a termination for breach exists, what are the procedural requirements (e.g., has the cure period passed, has proper notice been given)?

Termination Fees

The BPO contract typically includes a specific termination fee or formula that is applicable upon termination for certain events (e.g., termination for convenience). What types of termination trigger the termination fee? The applicability of a termination fee may drive the strategy pursued by each of the parties. For example, if a termination fee applies for termination without cause and does not apply for termination for cause, the customer will likely argue that there has been a breach and the vendor will argue that the customer is terminating for convenience.

Data

The contractual provisions relating to ownership and return of data are very important when renegotiating or terminating an outsourcing contract. The customer may have a weakened negotiating position if it does not own its data (in any modified form) or does not have the right to obtain copies of its data on demand (whether at any time during the term or upon termination). It is undesirable, from the customer's perspective, to be in a position where it is threatening to go to another service provider when it does not have copies of its data necessary to maintain business operations. A related issue is the cost of recovering data (e.g., delivery charges, storage, media costs).

Intellectual Property

As part of renegotiation and termination discussions, both parties will want to review the intellectual property provisions in the BPO contract to determine their ownership and use rights of certain key intellectual property (e.g., software, methodologies, tools, documentation) upon termination. Some of the issues that should be considered include:

- Who owns new developments?
- Who owns modifications or enhancements to the customer's intellectual property (including methodologies, technology, and documentation)?
- Who owns modifications or enhancements to the vendor's intellectual property (including methodologies, technology, and documentation)?
- Does the customer have the right to use the vendor's proprietary intellectual property during the term? Upon termination?
- Does the customer's right to use the vendor's proprietary intellectual property include software object and source code (if applicable)? Does it include the right to maintain the software?
- What are the customer's rights to use intellectual property licensed by the vendor from a third party during the term? Upon termination? Is there any associated cost (e.g., transfer or consent fee)?
- What are the customer's rights to use tools used to provide the services? During the term? Upon termination?
- Who owns work product?
- What are the customer's rights to require the vendor to transfer knowledge (e.g., training, configuration designs) to the customer or its designee during the term? Upon termination?
- What are the customer's rights to request copies of all work product? To request an inventory?
- What are the vendor's rights to use residual knowledge?

Equipment/Facilities

Similar to intellectual property, each of the parties should review the provisions in the BPO contract to determine its rights with respect to key equipment and facilities. If the agreement were to terminate, what are the party's ongoing rights? A number of issues to consider are:

- Who owns equipment acquired in connection with the provision of the services?
- Who owns upgrades, enhancements, and add-ons to the customer's equipment or facilities?
- Who owns upgrades, enhancements, and add-ons to the vendor's equipment or facilities?
- Does the customer have the right to access or use vendor-owned equipment or facilities during the term? Does the customer have a purchase right upon expiration or termination? At what cost?
- What are the customer's rights to access/use equipment or facilities leased by the vendor from a third party during the term? Upon termination?
- Does the vendor occupy any customer space? Has the vendor leased any facilities in connection with the provision of services?

Third-Party Service Contracts

The parties will need to assess their respective rights under third party service contracts in the event of a termination of the BPO contract. For example, are there any limitations on the customer's rights to use the vendor's subcontractors upon the termination of the BPO contract? What are the customer's rights to assume the vendor's third-party service contracts upon termination? Are there any associated cost (e.g., transfer or consent fee)?

Service Levels

For a customer seeking to assert a claim that the vendor has failed to perform, key provisions to focus on are the provisions relating to service levels. What are the vendor's obligations with respect to service levels? Has the vendor met all of its service level obligations? Under what circumstances is the vendor excused from performance? Is the vendor obligated to perform a root cause analysis of the service failure upon the customer's request? Is there a termination right associated with the failure to meet service levels (in addition to the right to terminate for material breaches)? Does the customer have the right to request liquidated damages?

Customer Satisfaction

More and more BPO contracts include a provision regarding customer satisfaction. Both parties should review the BPO contract (and the exhibits) to determine if there are any obligations for the vendor to conduct a customer satisfaction survey. Has the vendor complied with these obligations? What do the results of the survey reveal? Is the vendor obligated to improve customer satisfaction? If so, have such improvements been achieved?

Deliverables or Milestones

Often at the center of renegotiation or termination discussions is a project that was not successfully implemented, not implemented on time, delayed, or cancelled. The parties will need to review the BPO contract to determine each party's obligations with respect to the project and the impact on the BPO contract if the project was not implemented as designed or on schedule or was delayed or cancelled. As is frequently the case with projects, the parties will find that a number of TBDs were never completed. Issues for the parties to consider include:

- Has the vendor provided all deliverables in a timely manner? Has the vendor met all required milestones?
- Is there a termination right associated with the failure to provide deliverables or meet milestones (in addition to the right to terminate for material breaches)?
- Does the customer have the right to request liquidated damages?
- Are there any third parties that did not perform that have impacted project implementation? If so, which party bore the risk of third-party nonperformance?
- If a party delayed or cancelled a project, how was the contract impacted? Is there an adjustment or renegotiation mechanism?
- Have the fees associated with the project been segregated or bundled into one base fee?

Fees

Many renegotiations or terminations are driven by a dispute over the fees. The customer may believe that it is being overcharged, the vendor may feel that it is not making the profits that it anticipated or either or both parties may think that the deal has changed so that the pricing structure in the contract is no longer appropriate. Issues to consider when reviewing the contract provisions relating to fees include:

- How is the customer charged?
- Are there fixed rates for additional or reduced resource usage?
- Can baselines be adjusted?
- Are there any minimum revenue commitments?
- Are there any cost of living adjustments?
- Who is responsible for what taxes?
- How is termination assistance charged?
- Does the customer have any right to offset, withhold, or escrow payments?
- What are the customer's rights to audit? Have such rights been exercised?

Benchmarking

In instances where the customer feels that it is being overcharged compared to other organizations receiving similar services, the parties will need to review the contract to determine whether there is a benchmarking provision. If so, has a benchmark been performed? Do the results reveal inconsistencies with industry standards? Do the benchmarking results allow either party to request a readjustment of pricing/services or implementation of new methodologies or technology?

Gainsharing

Were any gainsharing provisions negotiated as part of the business deal? For example:

- Does the contract contain any guaranteed savings?
- Are there any shared benefits or shared risks?
- Does the contract contain a profitability index?
- Are there any cross-marketing opportunities that have been exercised? That should have been exercised?

If there are gainsharing provisions, have they been implemented? Are they still appropriate in light of the overall business deal?

Damages

If a party is claiming that the other party has not performed as a basis for renegotiation or termination, each of the parties should assess its liability in the event of nonperformance. Accordingly, an in-depth review of the damages provisions in the contract should be reviewed. What is each party's liability for failure to perform? Are there any types of damages that *cannot* be recovered?

Confidential Information

Often during renegotiation and termination discussions, a number of outside parties will need access to confidential information. What does the contract say regarding disclosing information to consultants, lawyers, etc.? In addition, if there is a termination, the parties should determine their obligations regarding proprietary data and confidential information upon termination.

Dispute Resolution

Most renegotiations and terminations are preceded by a dispute that is not resolved and gets escalated. What are the dispute procedures in the contract? Must dispute claims be made in writing and referred to certain individuals? Is there an escalation track? Can action be taken without going to management committee/senior management? Has proper notice been given? Must disputes be arbitrated or litigated?

Continued Performance

The parties will need to review the BPO contract to assess each party's obligations to continue to perform. Does the vendor have any right to cease performance (e.g., nonpayment)? Are there any protections that would prohibit the vendor from ceasing to perform (particularly during a dispute)? Often, parties are excused from performance upon the occurrence of certain events beyond their control (e.g., *force majeure* events). What constitutes a *force majeure* event? Has one occurred? What constitutes a disaster? What are the parties' obligations upon the occurrence of a disaster? Has a disaster taken place?

Termination or Transition Assistance

Each of the parties should determine what, in the event renegotiation or termination discussions go sour, the vendor's obligations are to provide assistance to the customer in connection with the termination of the BPO arrangement and the transition back in-house or to another service provider. Issues to consider include:

- What in-scope services is the vendor obligated to perform?
- What out-of-scope services is the vendor obligated to perform?
- What is the extent of the vendor's assistance obligations? Does it include cooperation with third parties? Do third-party vendors need to sign a confidentiality agreement?
- What are the costs of termination or transition assistance?
- Can the customer hire the vendor personnel?

Rights to Resource/Insource

Does the customer have any contractual right to source services to a third party? Does the customer have any contractual right to bring any of the services back in-house? If so, the customer may be able to use these rights to prompt renegotiation or implement a partial termination.

Assignment

Renegotiation and termination are often driven by an organizational change (e.g., merger, acquisition). What are each of the party's rights to assign the agreement, in whole or in part, to a new entity or organization?

Employee Issues

As part of the BPO transaction, the customer's employees responsible for the day-to-day operations of the business process have been transferred to the vendor. The vendor in effect has employed most, if not all, of the persons with residual knowledge of the customer's operations and has trained its own employees in any new operational requirements.

The customer at best has retained some high-level understanding about how things are run. Issues to consider relating to employees and personnel include:

- What are the customer's rights to hire the vendor's employees?
  - Right to rehire employees transferred to the vendor by the customer
  - Right to hire the vendor's employees assigned to the customer's account (Is there a restriction on vendor employees primarily assigned to the customer's account? Determine time contribution of employees that the customer is interested in hiring.)
  - Right to hire other vendor employees
- Are there any exceptions from the restrictions on hiring for blind solicitations (e.g., through newspapers)?
- If there is a partial termination, customer should ascertain whether hiring restrictions or allowances only apply upon full termination.
- May third-party service providers assuming responsibility for part or all of the services hire any vendor employees previously assigned to the customer's account?
- Are there any restrictions on the use by the customer or its third-party service provider of the vendor's subcontractors?
- What are the vendor's rights to hire the customer's employees?
- Are there any noncompete provisions in the contract?

Stategic Alliance or Joint Venture

The parties will need to determine if a strategic alliance or joint venture has been formed and, if so, review any documents relating to the formation and operations of the strategic alliance or joint venture. What are the cross-negotiation or termination rights (if any)? Are there any other rights in the strategic alliance or joint venture documents that would impact/affect or have to be amended in connection with renegotiation or termination?

Ancillary Agreements

In addition to the BPO contract and any strategic alliance or joint venture documents discussed earlier, the parties should be sure to review other agreements entered into in conjunction with the transaction (e.g., reengineering, specific projects, consulting, training). Would any of these agreements be impacted by a renegotiation or termination? What are the termination rights in these agreements?

12.4 ADDITIONAL ISSUES TO CONSIDER

In addition to the issues raised in the BPO contract documents, there are other external factors that the parties should consider when considering renegotiation or termination. A number of these issues are summarized below. The applicability and importance of these issues will vary from deal to deal and depend largely on the type and scope of transaction at issue.

Internal Politics

Who or what is driving renegotiation or termination? Is this a senior management directive? Is there senior management support? Is there a general corporate reorganization taking place? What are the reasons underlying renegotiation or termination? Is there a corporate initiative to cut cost? The "who" and "what" driving renegotiation or termination will shape how discussions proceed and how serious each party addresses the other party's concerns. Another political issue to consider is the status of other relationships that the party has with the other party. For example, if this BPO contract is small compared to a larger, unrelated relationship between the two parties, the parties may be more cautious about how discussions proceed.

Publicity

What is the potential impact to the parties if news of renegotiation or termination leaks internally or to the press? How would negative publicity impact the customer's and the vendor's ability to do or obtain additional business? Would there be any impact on stock price?

Termination/Transition Costs

Implementing the termination of a BPO contract will undoubtedly cause each of the parties to incur additional costs. The questions then are:

- Does the additional cost outweigh the risk or cost of not terminating?
- How much are the costs and can they be mitigated?

Examples of such costs may include additional fees to the vendor for providing termination services, such as maintaining parallel environments and training of customer employees.

Transition Timeframe

In the event of a termination, both parties will need to consider the tasks necessary to complete transition back to the customer or to another service provider. How long will transition take? How will service levels be impacted? Will users be impacted? How much transition can the customer's organization absorb?

Assessing In-House Capabilities

As part of renegotiation, the customer should assess whether the in-house capabilities that it maintains are in fact sufficient to manage the BPO contract and whatever other business process functions that it retained. Too often the customer transfers all of its business process personnel to the vendor and does not maintain enough staff to effectively manage and administer the outsourcing contract. Renegotiation may give the customer an opportunity to assess whether additional resources are necessary. If the customer is terminating the BPO contract, the customer should assess whether it has the capabilities to bring the business process back in-house (which it typically does not) and, when transitioning to another vendor, what additional resources are necessary.

Other Service Providers

If the customer is considering terminating and does not wish to or does not have the capabilities to bring the business process back in-house, it will need to determine whether any other service providers can provide the services. In assessing the strengths and weaknesses of other service providers, the customer should investigate whether the service provider has successfully transitioned services from another service provider (as opposed to from a customer's in-house operations). For example, how would the service provider handle staffing issues?

12.5 TERMINATION PLAN

If the parties are moving toward termination, it is in both parties' interest to develop a termination plan (a plan outlining each party's rights and obligations upon termination, including the obligation to provide termination assistance, transition assistance, and ongoing services). Just as important as the content of such plans is how any services provided under them will be paid for.

The vendor is typically contractually obligated to provide reasonable assistance for a period of time after the termination date. Termination assistance services may include:

- Continued provision of certain services for a period of time
- Parallel environments
- Testing
- User acceptance
- Provision of back-up tapes
- Provision of operating documentation
- Freezing of all methodology or technology changes
- List of procedures to be followed during transition
- Review of all systems libraries
- Analysis of space required for databases and systems libraries
- Unloading of production and test databases
- Return of customer equipment
- Return of customer software or tools
- Return of customer data
- Copies of all methodologies or technology used to provide the services
- Generation of reports during transition
- Maintenance of service levels during transition

The BPO contract may also require the vendor to provide assistance to the customer and its third-party service provider in transitioning services to the third-party service provider. Transition assistance may be in addition to termination assistance. Examples of transition assistance services include:

- Making vendor employees available for consultation
- Making vendor subcontractors available for consultation
- Providing copies of all customer owned and licensed methodologies or technology (for software: object and source code)
- Providing access to vendor methodologies or technology and copies of all vendor methodologies or technology to be licensed to the customer or the customer's designee
- Providing access to vendor tools and copies of all vendor tools to be licensed to the customer or the customer's designee
- Providing documentation of customer configurations
- Providing manuals
- Providing procedures
- Providing passwords or security codes
- Providing access to vendor hardware
- Providing access to facilities
- Allowing third party service provider to hire vendor employees assigned to customer account

- Providing an inventory
  - Equipment
  - Methodologies
  - Software
  - Networks
  - Tools
  - Cabling or Lines
  - Documentation
  - Manuals
  - Configurations
  - Procedures
  - Work product
  - Third-party agreements (e.g., licenses, leases, service contracts, tariff agreements)
- Identifying which party owns which assets and how ownership was determined (i.e., under which contract provision)
- Identifying whether assets are used in dedicated/shared environment
- Identifying where assets are being used
- Identifying which customer entity the asset is being used for
- List of vendor employees or subcontractors used to provide services
- Identification of key personnel
- List of works in progress, including a status report and report as to the work necessary to complete the project
- List of any contract negotiations in progress, including status report and name and contact person for other negotiating parties
- List of all facilities
- List of all reports generated

LETTER AGREEMENT FOR DISCLOSURE OF INFORMATION IN CONNECTION WITH EVALUATION OF POSSIBLE BPO TRANSACTION (MUTUAL PROTECTION)

CONFIDENTIAL

[ADDRESSEE]
[ADDRESS]

Dear _____ :

In connection with the evaluation, discussion, and negotiation of a potential arrangement with Customer pursuant to which Vendor would provide Customer with certain **[SPECIFY BUSINESS PROCESS]** services (the "Transaction"), each of Customer and Vendor hereby agrees as follows:

1. To keep secret and confidential all information, specifications, know-how, trade secrets, materials, data and other communications, oral or written, ("*Confidential Information*") of the other Party and not reveal such Confidential Information to any person except such responsible employees of the Party as may be necessary for the purposes of evaluating, discussing and negotiating the Transaction.
2. To ensure that it treat the Confidential Information of the other Party in the same manner and with the same degree of care as it applies with respect to its own confidential information of a similar character.
3. Not to use the Confidential Information of the other Party in any way whatsoever anywhere in the world except for the purpose stated in paragraph 1 above.
4. To keep safe all documents and other tangible property comprised within the Confidential Information of the other Party and not to release them or it out of its possession.
5. To immediately notify the other Party upon learning of any unauthorized use or disclosure of any Confidential Information.
6. That Confidential Information being disclosed by the Parties pursuant to this Letter Agreement is with the express understanding that Parties shall not be obligated to enter into any further agreement. That should the Parties not enter into any agreement to return to the other Party all Confidential Information supplied by such Party on demand within 24 hours, and immediately cease all use whatsoever of the Confidential Information of the other Party.

7. Each Party agrees that the Confidential Information of the other Party and all copyright and other proprietary rights therein shall remain such Party's property at all times and that the receiving Party shall on demand return it to the disclosing Party within 24 hours of a written or oral demand.

8. The undertakings and agreements made by each of the Parties hereunder shall continue to be binding for a minimum period of **[SPECIFY TIME PERIOD]** whether or not the Confidential Information has been returned to the other Party until such time (if ever) as the Confidential Information falls into the public domain otherwise than as a result of or arising from any disclosure by the receiving Party.

9. Each of Customer and Vendor recognize that the disclosure of Confidential Information of the other party may give rise to irreparable injury and acknowledge that remedies other than injunctive relief may not be adequate. Accordingly, each of Customer and Vendor has the right to equitable and injunctive relief to prevent the unauthorized disclosure of its Confidential Information, as well as such damages or other relief as is occasioned by such unauthorized use or disclosure.

10. This Letter Agreement shall be governed by and construed in accordance with the laws of **[SPECIFY LAW]**.

11. Each of Customer and Vendor represents that it has the full authority and right to enter into this Letter Agreement and to disclose to the other party Confidential Information and that such disclosure will not violate the rights of any third party.

12. This Letter Agreement sets forth the entire agreement between Customer and Vendor as to the subject matter of this Letter Agreement. The terms of this Letter Agreement shall not be amended or modified except in writing signed by each of Customer and Vendor.

Please evidence your agreement with this Letter Agreement by executing in the space provided and returning to Vendor one of the two original copies of this Letter Agreement sent to you.

Sincerely yours,

[VENDOR]

By:_____
   Name:
   Title:

Date: _____

ACKNOWLEDGED AND AGREED:

[CUSTOMER]

By:_____
   Name:
   Title:

Date: _____

Appendix 2.2

QUESTIONNAIRE FOR ASSESSING LEGAL RESOURCES REQUIRED (CUSTOMER FORM)

CONFIDENTIAL
FOR INTERNAL [CUSTOMER] USE ONLY

[CUSTOMER]

QUESTIONNAIRE FOR ASSESSING NECESSARY
LEGAL RESOURCES TO BE ASSIGNED TO BPO TRANSACTION

The purpose of this questionnaire is to provide to the [CUSTOMER] Legal Department general background information regarding the proposed BPO transaction. The information gathered through this questionnaire is intended to assist the [CUSTOMER] Legal Department in assessing the types and amount of legal resources that should be assigned or made available to the particular transaction. Please take the time to review this questionnaire and provide as much information as possible, with the understanding that the transaction and the required legal resources may change over the course of the transaction.

  1. KEY OBJECTIVES: (List key objectives for outsourcing, e.g., cost savings, move to new environment)

  2. CONTRACT STRUCTURE: (Describe proposed contract structure, e.g., two-phase transaction, including business process reengineering and ongoing day-to-day operations and services; joint venture/strategic alliance)

  3. SCOPE OF SERVICES: (Describe scope of services to be outsourced)

4. GEOGRAPHIC SCOPE: (List all states/countries from which services will be provided, as well as all states/countries to which services will be provided)

5. AFFECTED SITES: (Name all [CUSTOMER] sites that will be outsourced)

6. TRANSFER OF EMPLOYEES: (If employees will be transferred to the vendor or a vendor subcontractor or affiliate, specify approximate number of employees to be transferred (by [CUSTOMER] location if possible) and describe any other personnel issues)

7. SALE/LEASE:

(A) ASSETS: (If any assets will be sold/leased to the vendor, specify types of assets and general terms of sale/lease if known)

(B) FACILITIES: (If any facilities will be sold/leased to the vendor, specify facilities and general terms of sale/lease if known)

8. VALUE OF TRANSACTION: (Specify proposed value of outsourcing contract)

9. DEGREE OF "CRITICALNESS": (Indicate the importance of the outsourcing arrangement to [CUSTOMER], e.g., contract value may be small but vendor non-performance would greatly damage [CUSTOMER])

10. PROPOSED TERM: (Specify proposed term of transaction)

11. RELEVANT ISSUES: (Specify any particular concerns in the following areas)

(A) REGULATORY COMPLIANCE

(B) PERMITS/LICENSES

(C) ENVIRONMENTAL

(D) AUDIT

(E) TAX

(F) DATA PRIVACY

(G) INSURANCE

(H) SPECIAL ISSUES

12. CORPORATE ACTIONS: (Specify any corporate actions that are required (if known), e.g., board approval)

13. COMMUNICATIONS/PR: (Specify any particular communications/public relation actions that have been or will be taken, e.g., employee communication plan, press release)

14. TRANSACTION STATUS: (Describe status of transaction, e.g., RFP prepared; RFP issued)

15. SELECTION OF VENDOR: (Indicate whether a vendor(s) has (have) been selected (at least preliminarily))

16. HISTORY WITH VENDOR: (Describe any existing or previous relationships between [CUSTOMER] and preferred vendor(s))

17. TIMELINE: (Describe the proposed schedule for the outsourcing process)

18. ROLE OF COUNSEL: (Describe desired role that counsel should take in transaction, e.g., review documents, negotiate)

19. DESIRED LEGAL RESOURCES/TIME COMMITMENT: (Indicate any specific legal resources desired at this time)

20. DRAFTING RESPONSIBILITY: (Indicate whether **[CUSTOMER]** or the vendor will have drafting responsibility for the contract (if known))

21. EXHIBIT REVIEW: (Describe the resources to be used to review the exhibits to the contract, e.g., technical experts, business team members; define the anticipated role legal will have in the exhibit review)

22. TEAM MEMBERS:

  (A) **[CUSTOMER]** TEAM (Specify all of the members of the **[CUSTOMER'S]** outsourcing team)

  (B) VENDOR TEAM (Specify all of the members of the vendor's outsourcing team)

23. LOCATION OF DUE DILIGENCE/NEGOTIATIONS: (Specify the location where due diligence and negotiations will take place)

24. OTHER CONCERNS/NOTES: (List any additional concerns or comments)

Appendix **2.3**

QUESTIONNAIRE FOR ASSESSING LEGAL RESOURCES REQUIRED (VENDOR FORM)

[VENDOR]

QUESTIONNAIRE FOR ASSESSING NECESSARY LEGAL RESOURCES TO BE ASSIGNED TO BPO TRANSACTION

The purpose of this questionnaire is to provide to the [VENDOR] Legal Department general background information regarding the proposed BPO transaction. The information gathered through this questionnaire is intended to assist the [VENDOR] Legal Department in assessing the types and amount of legal resources that should be assigned or made available to the particular transaction. Please take the time to review this questionnaire and provide as much information as possible, with the understanding that the transaction and the required legal resources may change over the course of the transaction.

1. **NAME OF CUSTOMER/TRANSACTION:** (Identify name of the customer (if possible) and provide a general description of transaction)

2. **CONTRACT STRUCTURE:** (Describe proposed contract structure, e.g., two-phase transaction, including business process reengineering and ongoing day-to-day operations and services; joint venture/strategic alliance)

3. **SCOPE OF SERVICES:** (Describe scope of services to be outsourced)

4. AFFECTED SITES: (Identify all customer sites that will be outsourced (by state/country))

5. GEOGRAPHIC SCOPE: (List all states/countries from which services will be provided, as well as all states/countries to which services will be provided)

6. TRANSFER OF EMPLOYEES: (If employees will be transferred to **[VENDOR]** or a **[VENDOR]** subcontractor or affiliate, specify approximate number of employees to be transferred (by location if possible) and describe any other personnel issues)

7. SALE/LEASE:

(A) ASSETS: **(**If any assets will be sold/leased to **[VENDOR],** specify types of assets and general terms of sale/lease if known)

(B) FACILITIES: (If any facilities will be sold/leased to the **[VENDOR],** specify facilities and general terms of sale/lease if known)

8. VALUE OF TRANSACTION: (Specify proposed value of outsourcing contract)

9. PROPOSED TERM: (Specify proposed term of transaction)

10. RELEVANT ISSUES: (Specify any particular concerns in the following areas)

(A) REGULATORY COMPLIANCE

(B) PERMITS/LICENSES

(C) ENVIRONMENTAL

(D) AUDIT

(E) TAX

(F) DATA PRIVACY

(G) INSURANCE

(H) SPECIAL ISSUES

11. CORPORATE ACTIONS: (Specify any corporate actions that are required (if known), e.g., board approval)

12. COMMUNICATIONS/PR: (Specify any particular communications/public relation actions that have been or will be taken, e.g., employee communication plan, press release)

13. TRANSACTION STATUS: (Describe status of transaction, e.g., RFP prepared; RFP issued)

14. HISTORY WITH VENDOR: (Describe any existing or previous relationships between **[VENDOR]** and the customer)

15. TIMELINE: (Describe the proposed schedule for the outsourcing process)

16. DESIRED LEGAL RESOURCES/TIME COMMITMENT: (Describe desired role that counsel should take in transaction, e.g., review documents; negotiate, indicate any specific legal resources desired at this time)

17. DRAFTING RESPONSIBILITY: (Indicate whether **[VENDOR]** or the customer will have drafting responsibility for the contract (if known))

18. EXHIBIT REVIEW: (Describe the resources to be used to review the exhibits to the contract, e.g., technical experts, business team members; define the anticipated role legal will have in the exhibit review)

19. TEAM MEMBERS:

(A) **[VENDOR]** TEAM (Specify all of the members of **[VENDOR'S]** outsourcing team)

(B) CUSTOMER TEAM (Specify all of the members of the customer's outsourcing team)

20. LOCATION OF DUE DILIGENCE/NEGOTIATIONS: (Specify the location where due diligence and negotiations will take place)

21. OTHER CONCERNS/NOTES: (List any additional concerns or comments)

Appendix **2.4**

REQUEST FOR INFORMATION

[NAME OF CUSTOMER OR, IF CUSTOMER WISHES TO RETAIN ANONYMITY, DESCRIBE TYPE OF COMPANY/ORGANIZATION, E.G., A MULTINATIONAL MANUFACTURING COMPANY] is considering outsourcing its [DESCRIBE FUNCTIONS] in [SPECIFY GEOGRAPHIC LOCATIONS]. [CUSTOMER OR A CONSULTANT ON CUSTOMER'S BEHALF] is issuing this request for information (this "RFI") to gain information regarding qualified outsourcing vendors.

All questions and comments relating to this RFI should be directed to [NAME OF CONTACT] at [CONTACT PHONE NUMBER/ADDRESS]. Responses are due by [TIME] on [DATE]. Responses should be sent to: [FILL IN CONTACT NAME AND ADDRESS]

Customer is interested in obtaining information about the vendor relating to the general categories identified below. More specific questions and requests for information are set forth in the pages that follow. Please format your response so that it corresponds to the numbers in this RFP. If there is additional information that you think would be helpful, please attach the information to your response as appendices.

1. *VENDOR HISTORY*	[OBJECTIVE: What is the vendor's history? How long has it been in business? What has its market share been during the period that it has been in business? Have there been any unusual peaks/valleys? Has the vendor been in any significant/relevant disputes/litigations?]
2. *FINANCIAL STANDING/ STABILITY*	[OBJECTIVE: Is the vendor financially secure? What is the vendor's market share? Has the vendor acquired/divested entities recently? Ask for a copy of the most recent financial statements, annual report. Are there any pending or threatened claims that could effect the vendor's financial standing.]
3. *ORGANIZATION*	[OBJECTIVE: How is the vendor organized? By Industry? By value of contract? Is there one international outsourcing entity or is there a network of local entities that work together?]

4. *EXPERIENCE—SERVICES*	[OBJECTIVE: Does the vendor have experience providing the types of services that the customer wishes to outsource? Ask for references by type of service, industry and transaction value.]
5. *EXPERIENCE— METHODOLOGIES/ TECHNOLOGY*	[OBJECTIVE: Does the vendor have experience with your current/future environment? Does the vendor have the capabilities to provide other services (e.g., reengineering)? Ask for examples and references.]
6. *EXPERIENCE—INDUSTRY*	[OBJECTIVE: Does the vendor have experience dealing with customers in your particular industry? Ask for examples and references.]
7. *RESOURCE DISTRIBUTION*	[OBJECTIVE: Where are the vendor's service centers? Where are the vendor's employees located? Does the vendor have resources in the locations that your organization requires them? What is the extent of these resources (e.g., does the vendor really have an office in Singapore?)?]
8. *EMPLOYEE TRANSITION* (if applicable)	[OBJECTIVE: What is the vendor's experience transitioning employees? How many transitions has the vendor done? In what states/countries? Has the vendor ever been sued in connection with a transition?]
9. *SUBCONTRACTORS*	[OBJECTIVE: Does the vendor typically partner with another entity to provide certain services? Who? What is the relationship with the partner?]
10. *CUSTOMER BASE/ REFERENCES*	[OBJECTIVE: Obtain references and contact names.]

1. *VENDOR HISTORY*

a. Please provide marketing and other information regarding the vendor's business.

b. Please describe the vendor's background, including how long it has been in business.

2. *FINANCIALS*

a. Please provide the **[SPECIFY YEAR]** annual report and (if available) the latest quarterly audited financial statements for your company.

b. If applicable, please provide the **[SPECIFY YEAR]** annual report and (if available) the latest quarterly financial statement for your parent.

c. Specify any recent acquisitions, divestitures, and downsizings.

d. Specify whether there are any pending or threatened claims that could affect the vendor's financial standing.

3. *ORGANIZATION*

    a. Please describe how the vendor is organized, e.g., by industry, by value of contract.

    b. Please identify the vendor's main offices and service locations.

    c. **[FOR INTERNATIONAL DEALS]** Please describe the vendor's global organization.

4. *EXPERIENCE—SERVICES*

    a. Please list those transactions where the vendor has provided **[DESCRIBE BUSINESS PROCESS SERVICES]**. Categorize industry and such transaction by customer name (if permissable), transaction value.

    b. Please describe the number and types of resources used to staff **[DESCRIBE BUSINESS PROCESS SERVICES]** transactions.

    c. If possible, describe in general terms how the vendor would structure a **[DESCRIBE BUSINESS PROCESS SERVICES]** transaction.

5. *EXPERIENCE—METHODOLOGIES/TECHNOLOGY*
[DESCRIBE CURRENT AND FUTURE METHODOLOGIES/TECHNOLOGY OF CUSTOMER]

    a. Please specify the number of vendor personnel trained to operate/use **[DESCRIBE METHODOLOGIES/TECHNOLOGY]**.

    b. Please specify the vendor's experience in implementing **[DESCRIBE FUTURE ENVIRONMENTS]**.

    c. Please specify the software and hardware tools and methodologies used by the vendor.

    d. **[CUSTOMER]** may decide to expand the scope of its outsourcing efforts, please describe other areas in which the vendor has particular expertise.

6. *EXPERIENCE—INDUSTRY*

    a. Please describe the vendor's experience dealing with customers in **[DESCRIBE INDUSTRY]** in **[LIST LOCATIONS]**.

b. Please provide **[SPECIFY NUMBER]** examples and contact names/numbers.

7. *RESOURCE DISTRIBUTION*

a. Customer has sites in the following locations: **[SPECIFY]**. Please indicate the locations where the vendor has service centers. Please indicate the locations where the vendor has employees located and the number of employees in each location.

b. Please indicate the annual revenue of the vendor allocable to each location listed pursuant to (a) above.

c. Provide a list of customers for whom the vendor provides services in **[LIST LOCATION]**.

8. *EMPLOYEE TRANSITION*

a. Please specify the types and numbers of employee transitioned that the vendor has managed.

b. Please identify the states and countries in which the vendor has managed employee transitions.

c. Please indicate any litigation/disputes arising in connection with a transition that the vendor has been involved in.

9. *SUBCONTRACTORS/PARTNERS*

a. Please indicate whether the vendor typically subcontracts or enters into a teaming arrangement to provide part of the services.

b. Specify the functional areas and locations for which the subcontractor/partner is typically responsible.

10. *CUSTOMER BASE/REFERENCES*

Appendix **2.5**

REQUEST FOR PROPOSAL[a]

[CUSTOMER]

[SPECIFY TYPE OF BUSINESS PROCESS]
SERVICES REQUEST FOR PROPOSAL

[DATE]

THIS DOCUMENT CONTAINS PROPRIETARY AND CONFIDENTIAL INFOR-
MATION OF CUSTOMER AND MAY NOT BE DUPLICATED, USED OR
DISCLOSED, IN WHOLE OR IN PART, WITHOUT THE WRITTEN PERMISSION
OF CUSTOMER.

\# ____ Submitted to _____

TABLE OF CONTENTS

---

[a] Note: The information provided in this document is illustrative only. It is intended to provide the customer with the general format of an RFP. It is not intended to address all of the issues that should be covered in an RFP for a particular business process. The specific content and scope of the RFP will vary from transaction to transaction and should be reviewed and edited by appropriate representatives of the customer (e.g., representatives from business, finance, audit, legal, human resources, environmental, and tax).

175

1. **INTRODUCTION AND VENDOR INSTRUCTIONS**
  1.1 Overview

    [CUSTOMER] has prepared this Request for Proposal (this "RFP") to provide an overview of Customer's current and proposed **[SPECIFY TYPE OF BUSINESS PROCESS]** environments that are to be addressed and supported in the vendor's Proposal.

    This RFP reflects Customer's current plan to outsource the following areas: **[LIST AREAS]**

  1.2 Objectives

    Customer's overall business objective is to **[DESCRIBE]**.

    Customer's primary objectives in entering into an outsourcing arrangement are to:

      [FOR ILLUSTRATIVE PURPOSES ONLY]

- Rapidly enhance its **[SPECIFY TYPE OF BUSINESS PROCESS]** infrastructure in order to improve overall business performance, flexibility and responsiveness
- Substantially reduce Customer's overall **[SPECIFY TYPE OF BUSINESS PROCESS]** costs and expenditures
- Continuously improve the levels of service provided to users without increasing **[SPECIFY TYPE OF BUSINESS PROCESS]** costs

  1.3 Evaluation Criteria

    The evaluation of the Proposals will involve both an objective and subjective process. Key evaluation criteria will include:

[FOR ILLUSTRATIVE PURPOSES ONLY]

- Resources and ability to support and manage Customer's current and long term **[SPECIFY TYPE OF BUSINESS PROCESS]** needs
- Improved management of resources
- Total cost advantage to Customer
- Ability to provide continuous, measurable and improving service
- Transition approach and plan
- Sensitive handling of employees
- Provision of cost-effective access to new methodologies/technology on an "as-needed" basis
- Vendor traits and characteristics

1.4 **DISCLAIMER**

THIS RFP AND THE DATA PROVIDED BY CUSTOMER IS BELIEVED BY CUSTOMER TO BE ACCURATE. EACH VENDOR IS RESPONSIBLE FOR MAKING ITS OWN EVALUATION OF ALL INFORMATION, CIRCUMSTANCES AND DATA IN PREPARING AND SUBMITTING RESPONSES TO THIS RFP. IF DURING THE COURSE OF ITS EVALUATION, A VENDOR BECOMES AWARE OF AN ERROR IN THIS RFP OR THE DATA PROVIDED BY CUSTOMER, THE VENDOR SHOULD NOTIFY CUSTOMER OF SUCH ERROR. NEITHER CUSTOMER NOR ANY OF ITS DIRECTORS, OFFICERS, EMPLOYEES OR AGENTS IS REPRESENTING THE ACCURACY OR COMPLETENESS OF THIS RFP OR THE DATA PROVIDED.

1.5 Confidentiality

The vendor should treat as confidential all information contained in this RFP and obtained in subsequent communications with Customer. In addition, the vendor should regard Customer's process of evaluating outsourcing opportunities as strictly confidential business information. None of the information described in this Section 1.5 may be duplicated, used or disclosed, in whole or in part, without the written permission of Customer.

[Prior to the receipt of this RFP, the vendor has entered into a Confidentiality Agreement with Customer. The information described in this Section 1.5 will be deemed confidential information for the purposes of such Confidentiality Agreement.]

The vendor may not make any public announcement or release any information regarding Customer's outsourcing process without Customer's written permission.

1.6 Proposal Due Date and Time Table

All Proposals must be received by **[TIME] [a.m.] [p.m.]** (**[SPECIFY TIME STANDARD]**) on **[DATE]**. Customer reserves the right to reject any proposal received after the due date (and time).

Other key dates include:

RFP Issued	**[DATE]**
Proposals Due	**[DATE]**
Proposal Presentations (if requested)	**[DATE]**
Due Diligence (data room)	**[DATE]**

1.7   Delivery of Proposals
In order to facilitate the preparation of your Proposal, a 3-1/2" diskette containing this RFP has been included. The text files on this diskette are in **[SPECIFY FORMAT]** format.

The vendor must submit **[NUMBER]** printed copies in loose-leaf binders and one electronic copy (on **[DESCRIBE FORMAT]**) of its Proposal to:
[SPECIFY CONTACT NAME AND ADDRESS]

1.8   Binding Offer
The vendor's Proposal will remain valid until **[TIME]** (**[SPECIFY TIME STANDARD]**) on **[DATE]**.

1.9   Vendor Costs and Selection
The vendor will assume all costs it incurred or incurs in providing responses to Customer's requests for proposals, in providing any additional information required by Customer to facilitate the evaluation process and in connection with performing due diligence. The issuance of this RFP does not obligate Customer to accept any of the resulting proposals. Customer makes no commitments, implied or otherwise, that this RFP process will result in a business transaction with one or more of the vendors.

1.10   Presentations
The vendor will, upon Customer's request, provide an oral presentation of the key elements of the vendor's response to this RFP. If requested to provide an oral presentation, Customer will make up to **[SPECIFY TIME]** hours available at Customer's **[SPECIFY LOCATION]** facility at an agreed upon date and time.

1.11   Amendments to this RFP
The vendor is advised that subsequent to issuance of this RFP, additional information may become available and provided to you. The vendor will be required to consider such information in their response, or if such information is provided by Customer after the Proposal Due Date, the vendor will amend its response as appropriate.

1.12   Communications/Clarifications
All aspects of the vendor's Proposal, and subsequent questions and responses, must be submitted in writing to be considered part of the final vendor Proposal.

THE INDIVIDUALS INCLUDED BELOW WILL BE INVOLVED IN THIS PROJECT IN DIFFERENT ROLES AND TO VARYING DEGREES. INFORMATION ABOUT THIS PROJECT SHOULD NOT BE DISCUSSED WITH ANY CUSTOMER'S PERSONNEL OR AGENTS OTHER THAN THOSE DESIGNATED BELOW AT THE CONTACT NUMBERS PROVIDED. ONLY **[SPECIFY NAME]** IS AUTHORIZED TO CONSIDER REQUESTS FOR DIRECT CONTACT WITH OTHER PERSONNEL OR AGENTS OF CUSTOMER.
[SPECIFY NAMES, ADDRESSES, AND TELEPHONE NUMBERS]

1.13   Due Diligence and Negotiations
As part of the vendor's initial due diligence, Customer intends to provide each of the vendors access to certain information and data, including third-party contracts, asset listings and financial information, relating to Cus-

tomer's **[SPECIFY TYPE OF BUSINESS PROCESS]** functions to be outsourced pursuant to this RFP. Such information and data will be made available in a data room at Customer's **[SPECIFY LOCATION]** facility at dates and times agreed upon by Customer and the vendor. Any information or data provided to vendor in connection with this due diligence shall be deemed Customer's confidential information and shall be treated as such in accordance with Section 1.5. The vendors may not duplicate any of the information or data provided in the data room. Upon Customer's request, the vendor will immediately destroy or cause to be destroyed all notes, memoranda, summaries, analyses, compilations, or other writings relating to this due diligence prepared by it or its agents. Such destruction shall be certified in writing by an authorized officer of the vendor supervising the destruction.

The vendor will notify Customer of any inaccurate or incomplete information revealed during due diligence.

The vendor must be prepared to enter into negotiations with Customer and take the appropriate action to conduct such negotiations within a reasonable time period at Customer's **[SPECIFY LOCATION]** facility. The vendor's response should also include a statement indicating the vendor's understanding of this requirement, as well as indicating the names and positions of persons granted authority to negotiate on behalf of and to contractually bind the vendor.

1.14   Guidelines
The vendor is advised that it should present its most favorable solutions, pricing, and terms and conditions it is prepared to offer.

With respect to those items that are statements specifying Customer's requirements (as opposed to requiring the vendor to respond to a particular request), please confirm the vendor's agreement to comply with such requirements. If the requirement is not accepted as stated, the vendor should propose specific alternative language that would be acceptable. Failure to provide a response to an item will be treated as the vendor's acceptance of the item.

Where the vendor is presented with a specific approach, the vendor must not only state its conformity, but also how it intends to conform. Where a statement of nonconformity is provided, the vendor must indicate its reasons for doing so, describe its proposed alternative and explain the benefit to Customer in its proposed approach. Failure to provide a response to an item will be treated as the vendor's acceptance of the item.

1.15   Proposal Format
So that Customer is able to fairly evaluate all proposals, we request a uniform proposal format. The proposal sections are listed below and, except for Sections 1, 2 and 13, correspond to the numbers in this RFP. Except with respect to Sections 1, 2 and 13 of the vendor's response, the requirements of which are described below, the sections of the Proposal should contain the vendor's response to all items listed in the corresponding section of this RFP. The vendor may provide additional information relevant to a section, not specifically requested in the section of this RFP, at the end of such section of the vendor's response.

Section 1. Cover Letter.   Submit a cover letter on your letterhead signed by an authorized representative of your organization, certifying the accuracy of all information in your proposal and acknowledging your agreement to be bound by and comply with the terms set forth in Section 1 of this RFP.

Section 2. Executive Summary.   Submit an executive summary of your proposal, covering the main features and benefits that distinguish it.

Section 3. Vendor-Specific Information.

Section 4. Services to Be Provided.

Section 5. Performance Specifications and Service Levels.

Section 6. Transition Plan.

Section 7. Business Recovery.

Section 8. Services to Be Provided by Customer.

Section 9. Project Staff and Management.

Section 10. Human Resources.

Section 11. Financial Information.

Section 12. Terms and Conditions.

Section 13. Appendices.   Appendices are optional. The vendor may wish to submit additional material that it believes will clarify or enhance its proposal.

2. CUSTOMER—BACKGROUND INFORMATION AND STRATEGY

2.1   Background Information

[STATISTICAL INFORMATION RE: CUSTOMER, E.G., TYPE OF BUSINESS, SIZE, LOCATION]

2.2   Customer's **[SPECIFY TYPE OF BUSINESS PROCESS]** Strategy
[FOR ILLUSTRATIVE PURPOSES ONLY]

Over the past several years, consolidation and standardization have been Customer's primary thrusts to support a business strategy of **[DESCRIBE].** Now the Customer businesses are seeking significant improvements in the **[SPECIFY TYPE OF BUSINESS PROCESS]** infrastructure to support their aggressive business plans.

To address these major business imperatives, Customer has developed the following principles:

[DESCRIBE STRATEGY]

3. VENDOR-SPECIFIC INFORMATION

3.1   Vendor Background

3.1.1   Provide an overview of your company, including the relationship of the vendor to the parent company (if applicable).

3.1.2   Provide specific details about your company's organization, including details of your corporate culture, current strategic plans, current major contracts (by industry sector), status of any current, recent, or relevant litigation and any other information that could support or impact Customer's selection of your company.

3.2   Vendor Organization

Provide detailed information regarding your organization, including an organizational chart of the vendor, a chart of specific organizations used to service the account and the resumes of key employees to be assigned to the Customer account. Similar information, including an organizational chart, should be provided for all other vendors and subcontractors used to provide the services.

3.3   Resources

3.3.1   Document your company's US **[and global]** presence and approach to management of Customer's **[worldwide]** contract.

3.3.2 Describe your experience with the methodologies, equipment and technology used by Customer.

3.4 Financial Performance

3.4.1 Attach financial statements for the last **[SPECIFY TIME PERIOD]** years. Certified financial statements of annual reports must be submitted for all identified vendors and subcontractors to be used by the vendor to provide services to Customer.

3.4.2 Provide detailed information on lines of business, revenues, profitability and any other measures that would provide Customer with a better sense of the vendor's performance in the outsourcing business and the financial resources that it has available.

3.5 Multi-Vendor Proposals

3.5.1 In the event the vendor anticipates using other vendors or subcontractors to provide **[SPECIFY TYPE OF BUSINESS PROCESS]** services to Customer, such other vendors and subcontractors must be clearly identified in the vendor's Proposal. In addition, the Proposal must clearly state the legal and operational relationship of such other vendors and subcontractors and the areas of work such other vendors and subcontractors will be responsible for under the direction of the vendor.

3.5.2 Specify the scope and duration of any third-party arrangements for the provision of services to Customer.

3.5.3 Specify the material conditions, restrictions and warranties which apply to any third-party arrangements for the provision of services to Customer.

3.5.4 The vendor will retain all responsibility for services provided to Customer by third parties.

3.6 Audit Reports

Attach recent third-party audit (control review) reports of those areas related to the in-scope services.

3.7 References

3.7.1 Provide at least five references from current clients who have similar or "nearest fit" arrangements in size, scope and geographical dispersement of services. The references should include:
- Name
- Profile of the BPO Arrangement
- Date Contracted
- Term of Contract
- Contact, Title, Address, and Telephone Number

3.7.2 Provide the above information for at least two BPO clients who have deconverted and are no longer using the vendor's services.

4. SERVICES TO BE PROVIDED

4.1 Operations and Management

4.1.1 Customer **[ENVIRONMENT/LOCATIONS]**

Customer's **[[SPECIFY TYPE OF BUSINESS PROCESS] [operations] [facilities]]** are located at **[SPECIFY LOCATION]**. The

[SPECIFY LOCATION] facility includes [DESCRIBE NUMBER OF USERS/FACILITY].
[DESCRIBE CUSTOMER'S ENVIRONMENT/LOCATIONS]

4.1.2 [Operations]
[DESCRIBE OPERATIONAL RESPONSIBILITIES]

4.1.3 [Production Control]
[DESCRIBE IF APPLICABLE]
[THE FOLLOWING ITEMS ARE FOR ILLUSTRATIVE PURPOSES ONLY:]

4.1.__ Inventory Management
This function includes the development and maintenance of a database that includes all Customer [SPECIFY TYPE OF BUSINESS PROCESS] assets. The inventory includes [FOR EXAMPLE: FURNITURE, EQUIPMENT, HARDWARE AND PC SOFTWARE.]

The inventory will be used to access information on an as-needed basis to verify billing reports and plan upgrades of assets and to maintain information on our infrastructure. We would expect this to be an on-line system that we would use in a read only manner with download capability.

We expect that you will develop and maintain an inventory of all Customer [SPECIFY TYPE OF BUSINESS PROCESS] assets and leases. This information is to be made available to Customer as described above.

4.1.__ Change Management
This process provides the method of controlling the introduction of change.

The nature of the Customer business requires service [SPECIFY TIME PERIOD] hours a day, [SPECIFY TIME PERIOD] days a week. It is important that change is introduced with as minimum impact as possible. It is expected that measures on change activities will be provided to verify the effectiveness and quality of the change process.

In view of the above definition and scope, please explain in detail the change management process you will include as part of the outsourcing agreement.

4.1.__ Problem Management
This process addresses the method used to manage the problem determination, escalation, and resolution activities. Included in this process are problem reporting, problem assignment, problem resolution, problem escalation, dispatching repair personnel, and other associated problem management activities. As part of the definitive agreement, we expect to have measurements of the effectiveness of the problem management process.

Explain the problem management methods you will include as part of the definitive agreement. Describe how your problem management repository will integrate with inventory, asset, and change management repositories.

4.1.__ Capacity Planning/Analysis
This function is responsible for determining future resource requirements.

4.1.__ Distribution Services

The functions associated with this activity include the distribution activities of all output media including hard copy, microfiche tapes and graphics, if required. Distribution services activities are conducted at Customer's **[SPECIFY LOCATION]** facility and at other locations serving other operating facilities. This function will be required at each location and will require multiple shifts.

Describe the vendor's plan for supporting Customer's distribution services requirements.

Describe the organization and operating characteristics of your distribution services facility(ies). Your description should address the following: Does the vendor support distribution packaging software products? Do they include online viewing capabilities? What products are supported?

Describe the hardware and network products used by the vendor to support remote high speed output services, including laser printing, microfiche and graphics products.

4.1.__ Software

Your bid must include the cost of all systems and applications software license and maintenance fees. Many of Customer's software licenses have been paid for the remainder of fiscal **[SPECIFY YEAR]**. Your bid should be reduced to reflect these payments. The vendor will have financial and administrative responsibility for all software licenses retained by Customer.

If conversion to alternate system software/application package software is required, the vendor will be financially responsible for the conversion and any associated training, installation and testing.

The vendor will consult with Customer prior to the introduction of any new software, which must be approved by Customer.

The vendor will assume financial responsibility for all contract termination and lease termination charges.

We require vendors to maintain software at existing or supported levels unless otherwise requested by Customer.

The vendor will be required to pay for all software upgrades.

The vendor will be financially responsible for any required data conversion.

[You have been provided with an inventory of systems software installed on the [SPECIFY] CPU.] Will you continue support for all of this software? Vendor will be responsible for paying the costs of obtaining any consents required in connection with such software.

4.1.__ Security

Data security is a function required to protect, restrict and assess risk associated with access to information.

Standard requirements include use of user IDs and passwords with various levels of data access authority and virus protection, appropriate levels of audit trails and reporting through backup facilities. **[The vendor will use the same data security product utilized by Customer which is [SPECIFY PRODUCT].**

Prior to migrating or relocating any Services to a shared environment, vendor will provide, for Customer's approval, a proposal for such migration or relocation, including benefits or risks to Customer during the term of the BPO agreement.

Vendor shall provide necessary security to prevent unauthorized access to any networks that process Customer information.

Vendor will implement arrangements, satisfactory to Customer, to ensure that competitors of Customer will not have access to Customer's information.

4.1.__ Migration/Consolidation

We expect the vendor to provide, as part of the base fee, all migration and consolidation activities.

Any of the following expenses incurred in connection with moves will be included in the base fee:

- Disconnection
- Packaging
- Transportation
- Insurance
- Installation
- Recertification
- Any deductible amount on the insurance, in case of a claim

You are expected to be responsible for planning and executing the migration and for this process to be completed within **[SPECIFY TIME PERIOD]** months of the effective date.

The vendor will be financially responsible for any other conversion or migration costs related to migration.

4.1.__ Hardware

The vendor will assume financial and management responsibility for all hardware maintenance.

The vendor will assume financial responsibility for all contract termination and lease termination charges.

Will Customer personnel be expected to support communications equipment in any way?

4.2 Help Desk

4.2.1 Customer Environment

The Client Support Center is located at **[SPECIFY LOCATION]** and is responsible for providing help desk support for **[DESCRIBE]**. This function must be staffed **[SPECIFY TIME PERIOD]** days a week, **[SPECIFY TIME PERIOD]** hours a day, with a single phone number for all users. As part of the definitive agreement, we would expect to have responsibility assumed for all **[SPECIFY TIER]** tier support as well as **[SPECIFY TIER]** tier support for all outsourced functions. These functions must be performed on a global basis and calls must be answered in the first **[SPECIFY NUMBER]** rings, in the language of the calling party (e.g., English, French, German, Spanish). The Help Desk must be transitioned to the successful vendor location within six months of the effective date.

4.2.2 Staffing

How long will Customer staff be retained by you to transition the Help Desk functions to your support staff?

4.2.3 Help Desk Location
Where will the Help Desk(s) be geographically located?

4.2.4 Support Services
The Help Desk must provide support for **[DESCRIBE]**.
How will priorities and severity levels be assigned?
Additional support services that must be addressed by the Help Desk include the following:
- Configuration assistance
- Moves, adds, and changes to the workstation
- User instructions and guidelines
- Management reports, trends, performance statistics
- Call follow-up
- Password resets

4.2.5 Monitoring/Quality Control
What measures will you use to determine the effectiveness of the Help Desk and the problem management process?

4.2.6 Automation Tools
What type of hardware/software automation tools are used in the Help Desk functions?

4.3 General Services

4.3.1 Long Range Information Technology Plan
The vendor will assist Customer in developing and maintaining a long range plan. The objectives of this plan are to:
- Develop an understanding and confirm the business requirements
- Identify new projects, accompanied by a high-level cost benefit analysis and a preliminary schedule
- Review and where appropriate update Customer hardware, software, and network architectures

4.3.2 Value-Added Services
Customer expects the vendor will bring added value to areas in addition to those identified in this RFP. The vendor should describe any unique capabilities it possesses for assisting Customer in achieving additional improvements and describe how it would make such capabilities available to Customer.

5. PERFORMANCE SPECIFICATIONS AND SERVICE LEVELS

5.1 Commitment and Approach
The vendor should describe its commitment and approach to each of the following:
- Initial service level commitments
- Commitment to improving service levels
- Approach to defining missing service levels
- Commitment to provide measurement tools
- Service level reporting

5.2 Specific Service Level Requirements
[DESCRIBE REQUIREMENTS]

5.3 Management and Adjustment
5.3.1 Describe the practices and procedures that the vendor will use to manage and monitor service levels.

5.3.2 All service levels must be reviewed quarterly and adjusted as required annually.

5.4 Performance Credits

The vendor is required to describe its approach to defining and calculating performance credits in the event of a failure to meet agreed-to service levels and other performance measurement standards. Include any contemplated formula for calculating performance credits and the approach by which these amounts will be paid or credited to Customer.

5.5 Root Cause Analysis

In the event the vendor fails to provide the services in accordance with the service levels, the vendor will, at no cost to Customer (1) perform root cause analysis to identify the cause of such failure, (2) correct such failure, (3) provide Customer with a report detailing the cause of, and procedure for correcting, such failure and (4) provide Customer with reasonable evidence that such failure will not recur.

5.6 Customer Satisfaction Survey

Describe the vendor's proposed approach for administering and evaluating customer satisfaction surveys, including how the survey results will be used by the vendor to improve performance.

5.7 Benchmarking

Customer expects the vendor to engage at vendor's cost an independent party agreed upon by Customer to conduct benchmarking of Customer pricing, methodologies/technology, and service levels. Describe the vendor's proposed use of benchmarking to measure Customer pricing, methodologies/technology, and service levels.

6. TRANSITION PLAN

Transition of workloads to the management of the vendor will be a critical element of the project plan. The Customer global user community demands a very low level of down time. We expect that the transition process you propose will take these requirements into consideration and provide for as seamless a transition as possible.

The vendor will perform all functions and services necessary to accomplish a smooth transition of the outsourcing of the identified services.

The vendor will perform the transition such that during the process of the transition, Customer will not experience any additional costs or expenses or any degradation in services or performance.

During and following the transition, the vendor will not change the way any services are performed or processes in a manner that materially and adversely impacts the way Customer conducts its business operations, including procedures for inputting data or formats of reports, without Customer's consent.

During the transition, the vendor will meet or exceed the service levels provided prior to the commencement of the transition.

Provide a detailed transition plan with key dates and responsibilities, including:
- Overall approach
- Major activities and schedules
- Specific staffing plan during transition
- Testing processes

7. BUSINESS RECOVERY
[DESCRIBE REQUIREMENTS]

8. SERVICES TO BE PROVIDED BY CUSTOMER

8.1 Overview

Customer will retain responsibility for the following areas:

[FOR ILLUSTRATIVE PURPOSES ONLY]

* Strategy and planning
* Business process design
* Application development
* Approval for changes

8.2 Facilities

Describe Customer's responsibilities with respect to facilities, office equipment, and computer equipment. The vendor's proposal should be as flexible as possible, with alternative approaches for Customer to consider. In any case, the vendor will be responsible for all equipment upgrades, replacements and additions in use by all vendor personnel, including the transitioned personnel.

8.3 Other Areas

Please detail any other areas that for which Customer will retain responsibility.

9. PROJECT STAFF AND MANAGEMENT

9.1 Structure

9.1.1 Please describe the vendor's proposed account management structure.

9.1.2 Please describe the vendor's proposed staffing plans.

9.2 Project Manager

The selected vendor will appoint a project executive to Customer's account. Customer must approve of such appointment. In addition, the vendor will not replace or reassign the project executive without Customer's consent.

9.3 Key Employees

Customer will designate certain members of the vendor's project staff as key employees. The vendor will not replace or reassign any of the key employees without Customer's consent.

9.4 Subcontractors

The selected vendor will not subcontract any of the services to be provided without Customer's consent. In addition, specify any proposed subcontractors and the services they will provide.

9.5 Procedures Manuals and Periodic Management Reports

Describe your approach to developing, providing and maintaining a procedures manual and periodic management reports.

10. HUMAN RESOURCES
[ADD LANGUAGE FROM APPENDIX 7.2]

11. FINANCIAL INFORMATION

11.1 General Guidelines

[FOR ILLUSTRATIVE PURPOSES ONLY:]

11.1.1 **[The vendor is required to develop and present an overall base charge, presented as fixed annual payments over the term.]**

11.1.2 At a minimum, the vendor's base charges should include services that Customer provides for itself through its own personnel as of the date of the BPO agreement, as such services may evolve during the term.

11.1.3 **[The base charges should include a compounded annual growth rate of [SPECIFY PERCENTAGE] percent.]**

11.1.4 **[The vendor must reconcile its final pricing structure to Customer's [SPECIFY YEAR] budget which is attached as Appendix ____.]**

11.1.5 Any areas of base responsibility or costs that are excluded from the vendor's proposal must be explicitly detailed, as to the nature, estimated cost, estimated period of operation, and the designated responsible party.

11.1.6 All cost areas including vendor responsible, pass-through, and Customer retained cost areas should be detailed by subarea over each of the years of the term.

11.1.7 In addition to the base cost proposal, the vendor is required to provide detailed information on the guidelines and methods for operational and structural changes that could impact pricing. These changes could include: periodic fluctuations in resource consumption, permanent changes in baseline consumption volumes, shifts in methodologies/technology, capital projects, and peripheral discretionary expenditures.

11.1.8 The vendor may expand this framework to supply additional information. It is Customer's goal to fully define the pricing structure, processes, and guidelines so that both Customer and the vendor may operate in a defined, predictable environment.

11.2 Base Charges

The vendor is required to provide a base charge, broken down into separate pricing for each of the following sub-areas for each of the years of the term:

[LIST]

11.3 Incremental Usage

Describe how increased/reduced usage will be handled. Provide units rates that will be charged for any additional resources used and that will be credited for any resources not used by Customer (including hourly, daily, weekly, monthly rates). Rates will be the same for increased and reduced usage.

11.4 Baseline Adjustments

Customer wishes to have the flexibility to adjust the resource baselines upon notice to the vendor, with an appropriate adjustment to the fees. Describe the mechanism pursuant to which baselines will be adjusted.

11.5 Inflation

[DESCRIBE INFLATIONARY ADJUSTMENTS, IF ANY]

11.6 New Services

11.6.1 Provide a detailed description of the approach, method and treatment of the new services. These descriptions should be illustrated with examples whenever possible.

11.6.2 Customer reserves the right to solicit, negotiate, and award those capital and discretionary projects and services, which are outside the scope of this RFP, to a third-party vendor at its sole discretion.

11.7   Continuous Cost Reduction
The vendor will continuously seek ways to reduce and minimize the total **[SPECIFY BUSINESS PROCESS]** expenses. Accordingly, the vendor will explore and identify opportunities to improve the services and reduce the costs of services being provided under the BPO agreement. The vendor will notify Customer of such opportunities and estimate the potential savings.

11.8   Gain Sharing
Customer is interested in achieving breakthrough improvements and savings. Identify how such improvements and savings will be achieved.

11.9   Guaranteed Price Reductions
Customer expects a **[SPECIFY PERCENTAGE]** percent or more reduction in total **[SPECIFY TYPE OF BUSINESS PROCESS]** expenses during the first year of the BPO agreement and **[SPECIFY PERCENTAGE]** percent or more during each subsequent year. Describe how the vendor will meet these requirements.

11.10 Taxes
[CUSTOMER] **[VENDOR]** will be responsible for all worldwide taxes (other than for taxes based on Customer's net income) levied on payments made by Customer to the vendor or services provided by the vendor.

11.11 Currency
All payments will be in currencies designated by Customer.

11.12 Invoice Requirements
11.12.1   All invoices must identify costs by the following categories, within a cost center/department and within a location. Customer has approximately **[SPECIFY]** cost center/departments and approximately **[SPECIFY]** locations.
Service cost categories:
[LIST]
Invoices will be directed to each location with a detailed summary copy to Customer. In addition, the vendor will provide an electronic file of the detailed summary information.
11.12.2   Customer will pay vendor fees within **[SPECIFY TIME PERIOD]** days of the end of the month following the month during which services were provided.
11.12.3   Vendor pricing methodology, cost elements and cost data will be provided to Customer in sufficient detail to permit reconciliation of actual costs to prices.

11.13 Chargeback Requirements
One of Customer's major objectives for outsourcing is to make users more accountable for their use of resources by implementing a chargeback system based on variable charges and easy to understand pricing. The vendor should

describe how its invoicing system will meet Customer's requirements and what type of chargeback capabilities will be provided as part of the base contract.

11.14 Most Favored Customer
The vendor will provide Customer with its most favored customer status and benefits to Customer.

11.15 Services for Newly Acquired Customer Enterprise or Additional Customer Work
Customer reserves the right to add or remove business units to or from the scope of the BPO agreement.

11.16 Treatment of Disputed Amounts
Describe the procedure used to settle disputed payments or credit amounts, including the period of time to settle disputes, the process of verifying these disputed items and the process of resolving disputes that cannot be resolved during the normal procedures specified above. The parties will be required to continue to perform under the BPO agreement in the event of a good faith dispute.

11.17 Expenses
All vendor expenses should be included in the base fee, including expenses for consummables such as printed forms, computer paper, tape and ribbons.

12. TERMS AND CONDITIONS
Key terms and conditions are set forth in the Term Sheet attached as Appendix ___. As part of your response, please indicate whether you accept the terms and conditions specified and, if not, indicate reasons for non-acceptance and alternative language. **[A SAMPLE TERM SHEET IS PROVIDED IN APPENDIX 4.2]**

13. APPENDICES
[FOR ILLUSTRATIVE PURPOSES ONLY:]
Asset/Inventory List
Project Staff
    Customer Organization Charts
Human Resources
    Personal Information
    Customer Benefits Materials
Miscellaneous
    Customer Annual Report

Appendix **3.1**

EVALUATION OF VENDOR PROPOSALS RELATING TO THE PROVISION OF BPO SERVICES

A. OVERVIEW OF VENDORS BEING CONSIDERED

Vendor	Vendor Representative	Address	Status

B. SCREENING CRITERIA [TO BE MODIFIED BY CUSTOMER PROJECT TEAM]

Criteria		Explanation

Examples of criteria:

1. **Vendor Resources** (Financial stability of Vendor; ability of Vendor to meet its commitments over the term of the contract)
2. **International Presence** (Experience and resources providing services outside of the United States and supporting users in other countries)
3. **Experience in Customer's Industry** (Specialized skills in Customer's industry to ensure quality)
4. **Previous Experience with Customer** (Past experience Customer has with Vendor that may impact selection)
5. **Financial Considerations** (Anticipated savings, improved cash flow, increased revenues)
6. **Services to Be Provided** (Experience, resources and ability of Vendor to provide in-scope services)
7. **Human Resources** (Transition of Customer employees to Vendor; terms of offers)
8. **Terms and Conditions** (Responses to Customer's terms and conditions)

C. *OVERALL WEIGHTED RANKING* **[TO BE MODIFIED BY CUSTOMER PROJECT TEAM]**

Criteria	Weight	Justification
1. Vendor Resources		
2. International Presence		
3. Experience in Customer's Industry		
4. Previous Experience with Customer		
5. Financial Considerations		
6. Services to Be Provided		
7. Human Resources		
8. Terms & Conditions		
Total	100%	

D. VENDOR RESOURCES

Vendor	Annual Revenue	Parent Company Revenue	Overall Rank

Key:

10	=	Superior
8	=	Very Good
6	=	Good
4	=	Adequate
2	=	Fair
0	=	Poor

E. INTERNATIONAL PRESENCE

Vendor	[AREA]	[AREA]	Europe	Asia	Overall Rank

194

F. EXPERIENCE IN CUSTOMER'S INDUSTRY

Vendor	Related Experience— United States	Related Experience— International	Overall Rank

G. PREVIOUS EXPERIENCE WITH CUSTOMER[a]

Vendor	Description of Work	Fees	Comments	Overall Rank

[a] This shall be a brief description of any services provided by the relevant Vendor to Customer prior to the date of the RFP and any services currently being provided by Vendor to Customer.

H. FINANCIAL CONSIDERATIONS

Vendor	Cost Structure	Cash Flow	Increased Revenue	Comments	Overall Ranking

I. SERVICES TO BE PROVIDED

	[FUNCTION]		[FUNCTION]		[FUNCTION]		[FUNCTION]		[FUNCTION]		Overall Ranking
Weight	%		%		%		%		%		100%
	Raw Score	Weighted Score	Raw Score	Weighted Score	Raw Score	Weighted Score	Raw Score	Weighted Score	Raw Score	Weighted Score	Total of Weighted Scores

1. *Weighting for "Services to Be Provided" Category* **[TO BE MODIFIED BY CUSTOMER PROJECT TEAM]**

Criteria	Weight	Justification
1. [FUNCTION]		
2. [FUNCTION]		
3. [FUNCTION]		
4. [FUNCTION]		
5. [FUNCTION]		
Total	100%	

1. **[FUNCTION 1]**

Vendor	Experience	Resources	Ability	Overall Rank

2. [FUNCTION 2]

Vendor	Experience	Resources	Ability	Overall Rank

3. [FUNCTION 3]

Vendor	Experience	Resources	Ability	Overall Rank

4. [FUNCTION 4]

Vendor	Experience	Resources	Ability	Overall Rank

5. [FUNCTION 5]

Vendor	Experience	Resources	Ability	Overall Rank

J. HUMAN RESOURCES

Vendor	Transition	Terms of Offer	Overall Rank

K. TERMS AND CONDITIONS

Vendor	Compliance with RFP Requirements	Overall Rank

L. OVERALL RANKING OF VENDOR

Weight	Vendor Resources		International Presence		Experience in Customer Industry		Previous Experience with Customer		Financial Considerations		Services to Be Provided		Human Resources		Terms and Conditions		Overall Ranking
		%		%		%		%		%		%		%		%	100%
	Raw Score	Weighted Score	Raw Score	Weighted Score	Raw Score	Weighted Score	Raw Score	Weighted Score	Raw Score	Weighted Score	Raw Score	Weighted Score	Raw Score	Weighted Score	Raw Score	Weighted Score	Total of Weighted Scores[a]

[a] Represents final score for each vendor for this ballot. To tally scores of all of the ballots, add final scores together. For example,

	Vendor #1	Vendor #2
Ballot #1		
Ballot #2		
Ballot #3		
Ballot #4		
Ballot #5		
Total Score:	_____	_____

201

Appendix 3.2

LETTER OF INTENT (CUSTOMER FORM)

[DATE]

CONFIDENTIAL

[NAME]
[TITLE]
[ADDRESS]

Dear _____:

1. This letter is addressed to **[VENDOR]** ("Vendor") to confirm the interest of Vendor and **[CUSTOMER]** ("Customer") in entering into a **[SPECIFY TYPE OF BUSINESS PROCESS]** services agreement (the "Services Agreement") for Vendor's provision of certain **[SPECIFY TYPE OF BUSINESS PROCESS]** and related services to Customer.

2. Formalization of our relationship is subject to appropriate corporate approvals by Customer **[and its parent]** and final preparation and execution of the Services Agreement. If the Services Agreement has not been executed or has not received the appropriate corporate approvals of Customer **[and its parent]** on or before **[DATE]**, this letter shall be of no further force and effect, except as provided herein with respect to the terms of paragraphs 3, 5 and 6.

3. During the pendency of formal corporate approvals from Customer **[and its parent]** and final preparation and execution of the Services Agreement, it is expected the parties will exchange confidential information. The parties agree to treat such confidential information in accordance with the confidentiality provisions attached as *Attachment 1*. Substantially similar provisions will be included in the Services Agreement. In addition, the parties agree that negotiations which are intended to result in a definitive agreement are taking place between Customer and Vendor and the terms, conditions or other facts with respect to such possible agreement, including the status thereof, shall be treated as "Confidential Information" in accordance with the same confidentiality provisions.

4. [In connection with the proposed transaction between Customer and Vendor, Customer intends to transition certain of its employees to Vendor (the "Transitioned Employees"). In the event Customer and Vendor execute the Services Agreement, Customer and Vendor wish to complete the transition of the Transitioned Employees to Vendor on [DATE]. In order to complete such a transition, it will be necessary for Vendor to commence pre-employment screenings and similar employee-related tasks prior to the date of the Services Agreement between Customer and Vendor. In this regard, Customer and Vendor have agreed to certain terms and conditions relating to the transition of the Transitioned Employees, attached as *Attachment 2*. Substantially similar terms and conditions will be included in the Services Agreement between Customer and Vendor in the event the Services Agreement is executed. The agreement of Customer and Vendor on such terms and conditions does not in any way obligate Customer and Vendor to enter into the Services Agreement.]

5. Each party shall indemnify the other party against and hold the other party harmless from any claims by the Transitioned Employees arising out of such party's conduct or representations during the period through **[DATE]**.

6. In the event Customer and Vendor do not execute the Services Agreement, each of the parties will bear its own costs and expenses incurred in negotiating the Services Agreement, including any costs and expenses relating to the preliminary work performed by Vendor in connection with the proposed transition of the Transitioned Employees.

7. It is understood that while this letter constitutes a statement of mutual intentions of Customer and Vendor with respect to the proposed provision of certain **[SPECIFY TYPE OF BUSINESS PROCESS]** and related services by Vendor to Customer, it does not constitute an obligation binding on either side, nor does it contain all matters upon which agreement must be reached and, except with respect to paragraphs 3, 5, and 6, this letter shall create no rights in favor of either party. A binding commitment with respect to the proposed project will result only from the execution of the Services Agreement.

Very truly yours,

[CUSTOMER]

By:_____
[NAME]
[TITLE]

AGREED TO AND ACCEPTED THIS
___ DAY OF _____, _____

[VENDOR]

By:_____
[NAME]
[TITLE]

Appendix **3.3**

LETTER OF INTENT (VENDOR FORM)

[VENDOR LETTERHEAD]

[DATE]

CONFIDENTIAL

[NAME]
[TITLE]
[ADDRESS]

Dear _____:

   This letter (this "*Letter Agreement*") is addressed to **[CUSTOMER]** ("*Customer*") to confirm the interest of Customer in entering into a services agreement with **[VENDOR]** ("*Vendor*") (the "*Services Agreement*") for Vendor's provision of **[DESCRIBE SERVICES]** (the "*Services*") to Customer.

   [IF EXCLUSIVE NEGOTIATIONS: In consideration of the time and efforts of each of the parties in negotiating the Services Agreement, Customer agrees and acknowledges that it will negotiate exclusively with Vendor for the provision of the Services, and will not contact, respond to proposals from, or negotiate with any other vendor or third party for or in connection with the provision of the Services, as of the date of this Letter Agreement and continuing up to and including **[SPECIFY DATE]** (the "*Exclusivity Period*"). **[IF CERTAIN RATES/TERMS ARE FIRM DURING EXCLUSIVITY PERIOD:** The rates set forth in **[SPECIFY DOCUMENT]** are only applicable during the Exclusivity Period only, unless otherwise agreed upon by the parties.] If the Services Agreement has not been executed before the expiration of the Exclusivity Period, the parties shall agree to either: (a) agree upon an extension to the Exclusivity Period, (b) continue to negotiate the Services Agreement in accordance with the terms of this Letter Agreement on a non-exclusive basis or (c) cease negotiations and terminate this Letter Agreement, subject to the terms of this Letter Agreement.]

   [IF SERVICES WILL BE COMMENCED PRIOR TO EXECUTION OF SERVICES AGREEMENT: Customer desires Vendor to commence the provision of **[OPTION 1:** those Services described in **[SPECIFY DOCUMENT]** (the "*Interim Services*")] **[OPTION**

204

2: the resources described in **[SPECIFY DOCUMENT]** (the *"Interim Resources"*)] as of **[SPECIFY DATE]** until the earlier of the execution of the Services Agreement and the termination of this Letter Agreement (the *"Interim Service Period"*). Customer agrees and acknowledges that time is critical and that Vendor agrees to provide the **[OPTION 1:** Interim Services] **[OPTION 2:** Interim Resources] to Customer solely as a convenience to Customer. Vendor shall therefore not be liable for any damages incurred in connection with the provision of the **[OPTION 1:** Interim Services] **[OPTION 2:** Interim Resources] and Customer agrees to indemnify Vendor in connection with any claims relating to the provision of the Services pursuant to paragraph ___ below. Customer shall pay the fees for the **[OPTION 1:** Interim Services] **[OPTION 2:** Interim Resources] during the Interim Service Period **[OPTIONS FOR PRICING: [OPT A:** set forth in **[SPECIFY DOCUMENT]** on the terms and according to the time frames set forth in **[SPECIFY DOCUMENT]] [OPT B:** as agreed upon by the parties or where not so agreed in advance fair and reasonable renumeration when directed to do so by Vendor] **[OPT C:** on a time and materials basis] **[OPT D:** at Vendor's then-current commercial rates]. **[Vendor may change the fees upon ___ days' notice to Customer.]]**

During the negotiation of the Services Agreement, it is expected the parties will exchange confidential information. The parties agree to treat such confidential information in accordance with the confidentiality provisions set forth in **[SPECIFY DOCUMENT]**. Substantially similar provisions will be included in the Services Agreement. In addition, the parties agree that negotiations which are intended to result in a definitive agreement are taking place between Customer and Vendor and the terms, conditions, or other facts with respect to such possible agreement, including the status thereof, shall be treated as "Confidential Information" in accordance with the same confidentiality provisions.

[IF EMPLOYEE TRANSFERS WILL COMMENCE PRIOR TO EXECUTION OF SERVICES AGREEMENT: In connection with the proposed transaction between Customer and Vendor, Customer intends to transition certain of its employees to Vendor (the *"Transitioned Employees"*). In the event Customer and Vendor execute the Services Agreement, Customer and Vendor wish to complete the transition of the Transitioned Employees to Vendor on **[SPECIFY DATE]**. In order to complete such a transition, it will be necessary for Vendor to commence pre-employment screenings and similar employee-related tasks prior to the date of the Services Agreement between Customer and Vendor. In this regard, Customer and Vendor have agreed to certain terms and conditions relating to the transition of the Transitioned Employees, set forth in **[SPECIFY DOCUMENT]**. Substantially similar terms and conditions will be included in the Services Agreement between Customer and Vendor in the event the Services Agreement is executed. The agreement of Customer and Vendor on such terms and conditions does not in any way obligate Customer and Vendor to enter into the Services Agreement.]

[IF INTERM SERVICES OR EMPLOYEE TRANSFER PARAGRAPHS INCLUDED: Customer shall indemnify Vendor against and hold Vendor harmless from any claims (a) relating to the provision of services described in paragraph ___ above and (b) by or relating to the Transitioned Employees.]

Upon the termination of this Letter Agreement, **[OPTION 1:** each of the parties will bear its own costs and expenses incurred in negotiating the Services Agreement.] **[OPTION 2:** Customer shall (a) reimburse Vendor for any costs and expenses relating to **[the negotiation and due diligence performed in connection with the Services Agreement [up to [SPECIFY DOLLAR AMOUNT] and] [IF EMPLOYEE TRANSFER PARAGRAPH APPLIES:** the preliminary work performed by Vendor in connection with the proposed transition of the Transitioned Employees] **[IF INTERIM SERVICES PARAGRAPH APPLIES:** and (b) pay to Vendor any amounts incurred in connection with the provision of the services described in paragraph ___].] This paragraph and paragraphs **[LIST CON-FIDENTIALITY AND INDEMNITY]** shall survive the termination of this Letter Agreement.

[When the Services Agreement is executed, the terms and conditions of the Services Agreement shall apply retroactively to any work performed under this Letter Agreement.] This Letter Agreement shall be governed by, and construed in accordance with, the laws of **[SPECIFY LAW].**

Upon your understanding of and agreement to the foregoing, please sign the two original copies of this Letter Agreement provided to you and return one fully executed original to me.

Very truly yours,

[CUSTOMER]

By:_____
[NAME]
[TITLE]

AGREED TO AND ACCEPTED THIS
___ DAY OF _____, _____

[VENDOR]

By:_____
[NAME]
[TITLE]

DUE DILIGENCE AGREEMENT[a]

[NAME]
[TITLE]
[ADDRESS]

Dear _____ :

I am writing to confirm that **[Customer]** ("Customer") and **[Vendor]** ("Vendor") have agreed to proceed with negotiations for the provision by Vendor of certain **[SPECIFY TYPE OF BUSINESS PROCESS]** services to Customer. In connection with such negotiations and prior to the execution of a definitive agreement (the "Definitive Agreement"), Vendor will perform due diligence, as described in more detail in the due diligence plan prepared by Vendor set forth in *Appendix 1*, ("Due Diligence") to (a) verify the data and information provided by Customer in its Request for Proposal, dated **[DATE]**, as amended by **[SPECIFY NAME AND DATE OF AMENDMENTS]**, (collectively, the "RFP"), (b) verify certain assumptions made by Vendor in its Proposal, dated **[DATE]**, as amended by **[SPECIFY NAME AND DATE OF AMENDMENTS]**, (collectively, the "Proposal") and (c) enable Vendor to offer services, pricing and baselines that reflect Customer's existing and future **[SPECIFY TYPE OF BUSINESS PROCESS]** environments.

This letter agreement (this "Letter Agreement") shall set forth the terms and conditions governing Due Diligence. In this regard:

1. *Due Diligence Representative.* Vendor shall appoint an individual who shall (a) be in charge of performing Due Diligence, (b) serve as the primary contact for Customer in dealing with Vendor with respect to Due Diligence and (c) be empowered to act and make decisions on behalf of Vendor in connection with Due Diligence.

---

[a] Note: The provisions in this due diligence agreement are for illustrative purposes only. The specific content and scope of a due diligence agreement will vary from transaction to transaction. In addition, the terms of the due diligence agreement may need to be modified to comply with the requirements of the local jurisdiction. Legal counsel should be consulted prior to entering into any due diligence agreement.

2. *Due Diligence Objectives.* Due Diligence shall be performed in respect of the following Customer locations: **[SPECIFY LOCATIONS]**. Due Diligence shall involve the evaluation of the following functions: **[SPECIFY FUNCTIONS]**. Due Diligence shall include an evaluation of the following areas: (a) Customer's budget items, (b) operating expenses, (c) inventories of associated assets including **[DESCRIBE ASSETS]**, (d) third party leases, licenses, maintenance and services agreements, (e) Customer's existing and proposed future environments, (f) chargeback procedures, (g) **[ADD ADDITIONAL ITEMS]**. A more detailed description of the activities to be performed during due diligence is set forth in *Appendix 1*.

3. *Scheduling.* Customer and Vendor shall agree upon the times during which and locations where Due Diligence shall take place. Vendor shall not contact any Customer employee or agent or attempt access to any Customer data, information, or facilities without Customer's consent. Customer reserves the right, in its sole discretion, to deny access to any facility or data and withhold consent to any due diligence activity. Customer shall cooperate with Vendor to identify other means for achieving the objectives of such activity.

4. *Completion.* Vendor shall complete all Due Diligence by **[DATE]**.

5. *Documentation.* By **[DATE]**, Vendor shall submit to Customer a detailed report summarizing the due diligence performed and documenting the findings and results of such due diligence.

6. *Discrepancies/Additional Information.* Vendor shall be responsible for informing Customer of any discrepancies, inaccuracies, errors or omissions learned or disclosed during Due Diligence. Customer shall not be responsible for any discrepancies, inaccuracies, errors, or omissions that it is not informed of prior to the execution of the Definitive Agreement.

7. **[OPTIONAL: In connection with the proposed transaction between Customer and Vendor, Customer intends to transition certain of its employees to Vendor (the "Transitioned Employees"). In the event Customer and Vendor execute the Definitive Agreement, Customer and Vendor wish to complete the transition of the Transitioned Employees to Vendor on [DATE]. In order to complete such a transition, it will be necessary for Vendor to commence pre-employment screenings and similar employee-related tasks prior to the date of the Definitive Agreement between Customer and Vendor. In this regard, Customer and Vendor have agreed to certain terms and conditions relating to the transition of the Transitioned Employees, attached as *Appendix 2*. Substantially similar terms and conditions will be included in the Definitive Agreement between Customer and Vendor in the event the Definitive Agreement is executed. The agreement of Customer and Vendor on such terms and conditions does not in any way obligate Customer and Vendor to enter into the Definitive Agreement. Each party shall indemnify the other party against and hold the other party harmless from any claims by the Transitioned Employees arising out of such party's conduct or representations during the period through [DATE].]**

8. *Customer's Responsibilities.* Customer shall cooperate with Vendor as may be necessary to enable Vendor to perform Due Diligence. Vendor acknowledges and agrees that completion of Due Diligence is **[primarily]** the responsibility of Vendor and **[that Customer shall not be required to expend any significant level of effort or resources toward Due Diligence] [that Customer shall be responsible for providing the following resources: [IDENTIFY]]**.

9. *Binding Nature.* It is understood that while this letter constitutes a statement of mutual intentions of Customer and Vendor with respect to the proposed provision of certain **[SPECIFY TYPE OF BUSINESS PROCESS]** and related services by Vendor to Customer, it does not constitute an obligation binding on either side, nor

does it contain all matters upon which agreement must be reached and, except with respect to Paragraphs 7, 10, and 11, this Letter Agreement shall create no rights in favor of either party. A binding commitment with respect to the proposed project will result only from the execution of the Definitive Agreement.

10. *Expenses.* In the event Customer and Vendor do not execute the Definitive Agreement, each of the parties will bear its own costs and expenses incurred in negotiating the Definitive Agreement, including any costs and expenses relating to the preliminary work performed by Vendor in connection with the proposed transition of the Transitioned Employees.

11. *Confidentiality.* During the pendency of formal corporate approvals from Customer **[and its parent]** and final preparation and execution of the Definitive Agreement, it is expected the parties will exchange confidential information, including business data, budgets, inventories, strategies, customer information ("Confidential Information"). In addition, the parties agree that negotiations which are intended to result in the Definitive Agreement and the terms, conditions or other facts with respect to such possible agreement, including the status thereof, shall be treated as Confidential Information **[and covered under the Confidentiality Agreement entered into between the parties on [DATE]]. [Each of the parties undertakes and agrees to (a) keep secret and confidential all Confidential Information and not reveal such Confidential Information to any person except such responsible employees as may be necessary for the purposes of performing Due Diligence, (b) ensure that it treats the Confidential Information in the same manner and with the same degree of care as it applies with respect to its own confidential information of a similar character, (c) to keep safe all documents and other tangible property comprised within the Confidential Information and not to release them or it out of its possession, (d) immediately notify the other party upon learning of any unauthorized use or disclosure of such party's Confidential Information and (e) return all Confidential Information on demand within 24 hours and immediately cease all use whatsoever of the Confidential Information.]**

12. *Term of Agreement.* Formalization of this relationship is subject to appropriate corporate approvals by Customer **[and its parent]** and final preparation and execution of the Definitive Agreement. If the Definitive Agreement has not been executed or has not received the appropriate corporate approvals of Customer **[and its parent]** on or before **[DATE]**, this letter shall be of no further force and effect, except as provided herein with respect to the terms of Paragraphs 7, 10, and 11.

13. *Miscellaneous.*

(a) *Publicity.* Each party shall not publish or use any advertising, written sales promotion, press releases, or other publicity matters relating to this Letter Agreement in which the other party's name or mark is mentioned or language from which the connection of said name or mark may be inferred or implied without the other party's consent.

(b) *Entire Agreement.* This Letter Agreement represents the entire agreement between the parties with respect to its subject matter, and there are no other representations, understandings or agreements between the parties relative to such subject matter. No amendment to, or change, waiver, or discharge of, any provision of this Letter Agreement shall be valid unless in writing and signed by an authorized representative of the party against which such amendment, change, waiver or discharge is sought to be enforced.

(c) *Counterparts.* This Letter Agreement may be executed in any number of counterparts, all of which taken together shall constitute one single agreement between the parties.

(d) *Exclusivity*. Neither this Letter Agreement nor any other arrangement between the parties grants Vendor any exclusive right to negotiate with Customer.

(e) *Assignment/Subcontracting*. Neither party may assign or subcontract its rights or obligations under this Letter Agreement in whole or in part without the consent of the other party. Any purported assignment in contravention of this Paragraph shall be null and void.

(f) *Governing Law*. **THIS LETTER AGREEMENT AND THE RIGHTS AND OBLIGATIONS OF THE PARTIES HEREUNDER SHALL BE CONSTRUED IN ACCORDANCE WITH AND BE GOVERNED BY THE LAWS OF THE STATE OF [SPECIFY LAW].**

Please evidence your agreement and acceptance of the terms and conditions of this Letter Agreement by signing both of the two copies enclosed and returning one of the original, fully executed copies to me.

Sincerely yours,

[CUSTOMER]

By:_____
[NAME]
[TITLE]

AGREED TO AND ACCEPTED THIS
___ DAY OF _____, _____

[VENDOR]

By:_____
[NAME]
[TITLE]

Appendix **4.2**

MODEL TERM SHEET[a]

SUMMARY OF KEY TERMS AND CONDITIONS

Agreement Structure

The parties will enter into a [services agreement] [master services agreement "MSA"] that will set out the [*if a MSA*: general] terms and condition applicable to Vendor's provision of services to Customer.

[*If a MSA*: Vendor and Customer will enter into specific service agreements [for each Customer site] [describing the responsibilities and obligations specific to the applicable services].]

The parties will simultaneously enter into [DESCRIBE ANY OTHER AGREEMENTS THAT WILL BE ENTERED INTO AS PART OF THE TRANSACTION, E.G., LEASES, PURCHASE AND SALE, CONSULTING SERVICES]

[*If the parties will be forming a joint venture or strategic alliance*: The parties will enter into an agreement to form [DESCRIBE JV/STRATEGIC ALLIANCE].]

Term

The term of the [services agreement] [MSA] will commence on [SPECIFY DATE] and continue until [SPECIFY DATE].

[*If a MSA*: The term of [IDENTIFY SPECIFIC SERVICE AGREEMENTS] will commence on [SPECIFY DATE] and continue until [SPECIFY DATE].]

Scope of Services

Vendor [will provide] [will be the exclusive provider of] the following services to Customer (the "Services"): [PROVIDE GENERAL DESCRIPTION OF SERVICES]

Vendor will have responsibility for: [DESCRIBE ANY KEY RESPONSIBILITIES THAT WILL IMPACT PRICE,

---

[a] Note: These sample terms and conditions are intended to illustrate the types of legal issues that customers and vendors typically wish to address in connection with BPO transactions. The provisions included in these sample terms and conditions, while comprehensive, may not cover all of the issues relevant to a particular transaction. Legal issues will vary depending on the type of business process being outsourced and the scope of the outsourcing transaction. These sample terms and conditions, or any part thereof, should only be used after consultation with your legal counsel. You should consult legal counsel prior to entering into or negotiating any outsourcing transaction.

E.G., UPGRADES, REFRESHES, NEW/ADDITIONAL EQUIPMENT, BUSINESS RECOVERY]

The following services are expressly excluded from scope: [LIST EXCLUDED SERVICES]

Customer Sites/Entities Receiving Services

Vendor will provide the Services to the following Customer sites: [LIST SITES]

The Customer entities receiving the Services under the [services agreement] [MSA] will be: [LIST ENTITIES]

Permits/Licenses/ Consents

[Customer] [Vendor] will be responsible for obtaining at its cost all governmental and third party operating, discharge, release and other permits, licenses and consents required [or desirable] in connection with the provision and receipt of the Services.

[ADD LANGUAGE RE: LIENS IF APPLICABLE]

Projects

Vendor will have the following project responsibilities: [DESCRIBE PROJECTS IF APPLICABLE]

The fees for the projects are [included] [not included] in the [base fees].

Contract Administration

Vendor will have [administrative] [financial] responsibility for the third party contracts specified in Exhibit __.

Transition of Employees

[DETERMINE WHETHER CUSTOMER EMPLOYEES WILL BE TRANSFERRED TO VENDOR OR VENDOR SUBCONTRACTOR; IF SO, DETERMINE TERMS OF HIRING BY VENDOR; ALLOCATE SEVERANCE/REDUNDANCY RESPONSIBILITIES]

Staffing

[SPECIFY ANY SPECIAL STAFFING REQUIREMENTS; ANY RESTRICTIONS ON SUBCONTRACTING]

Purchase of Assets/ Facility(ies)

Vendor will purchase from Customer the following [assets] [facility(ies)] : [LIST ASSETS/FACILITY(IES)]

Vendor will pay to Customer the following amounts in consideration of such purchase on [SPECIFY DATE]: [SPECIFY PURCHASE PRICE]

Service Levels

Vendor will perform the Services in accordance with [SPECIFY SERVICE LEVELS]

If Vendor fails to meet the service levels specified above, [DESCRIBE CONSEQUENCES FOR PERFORMANCE FAILURE]

Customer Responsibilities

Customer will retain the following responsibilities: [DESCRIBE RETAINED RESPONSIBILITIES OF CUSTOMER, E.G., PROVISION OF SPACE, OFFICE EQUIPMENT, SUPPLIES].

Pricing

In consideration for providing the Services, Customer will pay to Vendor the following amounts: [DESCRIBE PRICING STRUCTURE]

Payment Terms

Vendor will deliver an invoice on or about the [first] day of each month for the Services [to be performed during such month] [performed during the preceding month] and each such invoice will be due within [FILL IN NUMBER OF DAYS] of receipt by Customer.]

Taxes

Except for Vendor's obligation to pay employee related taxes and taxes owed by Vendor measured by the net income of Vendor, all payments of compensation made by Customer hereunder will [be exclusive of] [include] any withholdings and of any federal, state or local sales or use tax, or any other tax or similar charge based upon or measured by Vendor's gross receipts. [DISCUSS STATE LAW CONCERNS]

Benchmarking

[DESCRIBE ANY BENCHMARKING OR CUSTOMER SATISFACTION PROVISIONS]

Proprietary Rights

Customer Intellectual Property: Customer will grant to Vendor a nonexclusive right to use any intellectual property owned or licensed by Customer and used in connection with the provision of the Services.

Vendor Intellectual Property: Vendor will grant to Customer a nonexclusive right to use any intellectual property owned or licensed by Vendor and used in connection with the provision of the Services. [DETERMINE RIGHTS DURING TERM AND AFTER EXPIRATION/TERMINATION]

Developments: All intellectual property developed by Vendor as part of the Services will become the property of [Customer] [Vendor].

[*Tools*: Vendor will retain all right, title and interest in and to any and all ideas, concepts, know-how, development tools, methodologies, processes, procedures, technologies or algorithms ("Tools") which are based upon trade secrets or proprietary information of Vendor.]

Audits

Verification of Fees: Upon reasonable notice from Customer, Vendor will provide Customer access to all relevant documentation and facilities for the purpose of confirming that fees billed are in accordance with the terms of the [services agreement] [MSA].

Access: Upon reasonable notice from Customer, Vendor will provide Customer access to all relevant facilities and equipment for the purpose of auditing the services and service levels.

Termination

By Vendor: Vendor will have the right to terminate the [services agreement] [MSA] if: (1) Customer fails to pay any amounts due or (2) Customer enters into bankruptcy.

By Customer: Customer will have the right to terminate the [services agreement] [MSA] if: (1) Vendor fails to perform any of its material obligations and does not cure such default within [SPECIFY NUMBER OF DAYS] or (2) Vendor enters into bankruptcy

[SPECIFY ANY OTHER TERMINATION RIGHTS, E.G., TERMINATION FOR CONVENIENCE]

Rights upon Termination

Vendor will provide transition services to be agreed to Vendor for up to [SPECIFY NUMBER OF DAYS] [before] [after] the effective date of termination of the Service Agreement.

[SPECIFY ANY RIGHTS/OBLIGATIONS WITH RESPECT TO THE TRANSFER OF ASSETS OR AGREEMENTS AND THE RIGHT TO USE INTELLECTUAL PROPERTY]

[SPECIFY ANY RESTRICTIONS ON THE SOLICITATION OF EMPLOYEES]

Indemnification

The [services agreement] [MSA] will provide appropriate indemnification provisions for items such as intellectual property infringement, tangible and personal property damage, [environmental compliance] and other items to be agreed.

Dispute Resolution [SPECIFY DISPUTE ESCALATION PROCEDURES]

Force Majeure [ADD APPLICABLE *FORCE MAJEURE* PROVISION]

Insurance [SPECIFY INSURANCE REQUIREMENTS]

Standard The [services agreement] [MSA] will include standard provisions regarding, e.g., confidentiality, notice, assignment, governing law, compliance with laws.

   Miscellaneous

   Provisions

Appendix 5.1

CHECKLIST: KEY ISSUES IN BPO AGREEMENTS (GENERAL)[a]

KEY ISSUES IN
BUSINESS PROCESS OUTSOURCING AGREEMENTS
(GENERAL)

1. Structure of the BPO Agreement
    * How will the BPO agreement be structured?
        * A single services agreement
        * A master agreement with site-specific, country specific or entity-specific service agreements
        * Separate agreements for business process reengineering, development, and ongoing business process management
        * Separate agreements documenting the terms applicable to a joint venture/ strategic alliance relationship and the terms applicable to ongoing services
    * What is the inter-relationship between these agreements if separate, e.g., cross-termination, payment?
    * Factors that may affect the agreement structure include:
        * Scope of services: will Vendor be providing any business process reengineering or development services?
        * Geographic scope: single country vs. international agreement
        * Scope of services at specific sites: will all Customer sites receive the same services or will each Customer site receive different services?
        * Types of entities receiving/delivering the services: is the contracting entity for each of the parties able to bind the entities that will receive/deliver the services or must each of the recipient/delivering entities agree to be bound by the master agreement?

---

[a] Note: This checklist is intended to illustrate the types of legal issues that may arise in connection with business process outsourcing transactions. The issues identified in this checklist, while comprehensive, may not cover all of the issues relevant to a particular transaction. Legal issues will vary depending on the type of business process being outsourced and the scope of the outsourcing transaction. This checklist or any part thereof should only be used after consultation with your legal counsel. You should consult legal counsel prior to entering into or negotiating any outsourcing transaction.

- Cost allocation: are there any cost allocation requirements internal to customer that would drive separate site/entity agreements?
- Taxes: are there any tax requirements that would drive separate service agreements?

2. Contracting Party
   - Who will sign the agreement on behalf of Customer? On behalf of Vendor?
   - If there is a master agreement with separate service agreements, will the same party that signs the master agreement sign the service agreements?

3. Entities Receiving Services from Vendor
   - Determine who will receive services from Vendor
   - Entities may include:
     - Customer affiliates
     - Joint ventures/alliances
     - Contractors
     - Suppliers
     - Clients of Customer

   - Will Customer have the option of adding/deleting entities over the term?
   - How will mergers/acquisitions/divestitures be handled? What will Customer's and Vendor's ongoing obligations be?
   - Which entity(ies) will have payment obligations? Are recipients of services third party beneficiaries?

4. Entities Providing Services to Customer
   - Determine which entity (or entities) will provide the services to Customer.
   - Will there be any subcontracting/teaming relationships?
   - For international deals, how will Vendor provide resources/services in each country? Will Vendor use affiliated entities or subcontractors?
   - What are Customer's rights to approve/remove subcontractors?
   - Which entity(ies) will have performance/indemnification obligations?

5. Term
   - What is the commencement date of services? Will there be one commencement date for all sites? Will there be one commencement date for all services (e.g., business process reengineering, development and ongoing business process management)?
   - How long is the term of the agreement? If the transaction includes multiple agreements, are all of the agreements co-terminus? If there is a master agreement with separate site/service agreements, are all of the agreements co-terminus?
   - Will there be a pilot period?
   - What are each party's renewal rights? What type of notice is required for renewal?

6. Scope of Services
   - Determine the general scope of services to be provided by Vendor.
   - Determine those services which will be provided in-house by Customer or to Customer by a third party.
   - Describe in detail the services (typically by service category) to be provided by Vendor.

- Define Customer's responsibilities with respect to the services to be provided by Vendor (i.e., definition of requirements, strategic direction, approvals).
- Define existing and future requirements (e.g., capacity requirements, volume changes, business changes). Allocate managerial and financial responsibility.

7. Transition Plan
   - How will the transition of services to Vendor be handled?
   - Will there be any redundant/parallel environments?
   - Determine the performance standards during transition.
   - How long will the transition period be?

8. Methodologies
   - Assess methodologies to be used by Vendor. Are the methodologies proprietary to Vendor or licensed from a third party? If licensed from a third party, are there any use restrictions? What are Customer's rights to use during the term and after expiration/termination?
   - Will any of Customer's methodologies continue to be used during the term of the transaction? What are Vendor's use rights (e.g., use in connection with services to Customer only; use in connection with other customers)?
   - How will Vendor transition Customer to Vendor's methodologies (if applicable)?
   - How will the methodologies introduced by Vendor be integrated with Customer's existing and future methodologies (with respect to the applicable business function as well as other business areas, e.g., information systems)?
   - Will Vendor be developing/providing any new methodologies? If so, how will ownership/use rights be allocated? How will new methodologies be rolled out (e.g., define time period, consequences for failure to meet deadlines, each party's responsibilities)?

9. Technology
   - Assess technology to be used by Vendor. Is the technology proprietary to Vendor or licensed from a third party? If licensed from a third party, are there any use restrictions? What are Customer's rights to use during the term and after expiration/termination?
   - Will any of Customer's technology continue to be used during the term of the transaction? What are Vendor's use rights (e.g., use in connection with services to Customer only; use in connection with other customers)?
   - Will the environment be dedicated/shared?
   - How will Vendor transition Customer to Vendor's technology (if applicable)?
   - How will the technology introduced by Vendor be integrated with Customer's existing or future technology, e.g., is Vendor technology compatible with technology used by Customer's information system group?
   - Will Vendor be developing/providing any new technology? If so, how will ownership/use rights be allocated? How will new technology be rolled out (e.g., define time period, consequences for failure to meet deadlines, each party's responsibilities)?

10. Assets
    - Will Vendor be purchasing any of Customer's assets (e.g., equipment, real estate)? If so, when will purchase be made (e.g., on date of signing)?
    - How will assets be valued (e.g., book value, fair market value)?
    - Is the transfer of assets necessary in conjunction with the transfer of employees in order to constitute an "automatic transfer" under the particular country's employment/redundancy laws?

11. Projects
    * Identify any projects that Vendor will be responsible for implementing/managing as part of the transaction.
    * Will Vendor be responsible for any business process reengineering in connection with its provision of business process services? If so, what are each party's responsibilities? What are the consequences if the reengineering is not successful or performed by deadlines specified?
    * What is the inter-relationship of Vendor's business process reengineering responsibilities and Vendor's business process service responsibilities (e.g., are they cross-terminable)?
    * Will Vendor be responsible for any new implementations? If so, what are each party's responsibilities? What are the consequences if the reengineering is not successful or performed by deadlines specified?
    * Which party will be responsible for purchase/license of third-party methodologies/technologies (if applicable)?

12. Integration
    * How will the methodologies/technologies introduced by Vendor be integrated with other methodologies/technologies used by Customer?
    * Have other Customer business areas been contacted for input (e.g., information systems, human resources)?

13. Transfer of Employees
    * Determine whether any or all Customer employees will be offered employment by, or transitioned to, Vendor or a Vendor subcontractor.
    * Identify group of retained employees.
    * Review Customer's severance/redundancy policy, if any, to determine whether a transition to Vendor may invoke severance obligations. (If so, factor into Customer's cost analysis.)
    * Are there any claims with respect to any of the transitioned employees?
    * Compare Customer and Vendor benefits. Are any adjustments necessary?
    * Does Vendor require any special screening of employees (e.g., drug testing)?
    * Will Vendor require transitioned employees to sign an employment agreement?
    * Develop an employee communication plan.
    * Determine whether any stay bonuses/incentives are necessary.

14. Project Staff
    * Identify management structure of Vendor as well as Customer in connection with the provision/receipt of services.
    * Are there any limitations/restrictions with respect to reassignment/replacement of key Vendor personnel?
    * Are there any limitations/restrictions with respect to "churning" of employees?
    * How will Customer complaints regarding Vendor personnel be handled?
    * Are there any special clearances of Vendor personnel necessary?
    * Are there any limitations/restrictions with respect to subcontractors?

15. Retained Assets
    * Identify which assets Vendor will manage and, of those assets, which assets Vendor will have financial responsibility for.
    * Identify which assets Customer will continue to manage and, of those assets, whether Vendor will have any financial responsibility.

- How will the parties act in the event it is not clear where a problem originates from (e.g., root cause analysis)?

16. Agreements to be Reviewed
    - Identify any third-party agreements/relationships that may be impacted by the outsourcing, including:
      - Maintenance agreements
      - Subcontracting relationships
      - Other service agreements
      - Methodology/technology licenses
      - Equipment/asset leases
      - Real estate leases/subleases
    - Are there any restrictions with respect to third-party management/access or assignment to a third party?
    - What are the terms relating to termination/renewal?
    - What are the pricing terms and will they be impacted by the transaction?
    - Develop a strategy for notifying third parties, if applicable.

17. Third Party Consents
    - Are any third-party consents necessary in connection with the commencement of the transaction? If so, which party is responsible for obtaining such consents and how will financial responsibility be allocated?
    - How will third-party consents be obtained upon the expiration/termination of the transaction (in order to transition agreements/assets back to Customer or Customer's designee)? How will financial responsibility be allocated?

18. Performance Standards
    - Identify those services which will have performance standards.
    - How will Vendor's performance be measured? Will existing performance standards be used or will performance standards be established on a going forward basis?
    - Identify any permitted downtime and testing.
    - How will failures to meet performance standards be handled (e.g., liquidated damages or termination)?
    - Will there be any procedures for assessing/determining causes of failures to meet performance standards (e.g., root cause analysis)?
    - What performance standards will apply during transition/implementation?

19. Customer Satisfaction
    - Will Vendor be responsible for any type of customer satisfaction reporting?
    - Determine pool of employees surveyed (e.g., management, end-users).
    - How will the results of such surveys be used (e.g., as basis for performance standard)?

20. Benchmarking
    - Determine whether the agreement will include any benchmarking procedures (e.g., benchmarking of services or prices).
    - Develop benchmarking procedures (e.g., scope of benchmark, group against which services/prices will be benchmarked).
    - Identify benchmarker (e.g., third party, Vendor group).
    - How will benchmarking results be reviewed and how will changes, if applicable, be implemented?

21. Gainsharing
    - Determine whether any gainsharing provisions will be included in the agreement (e.g., bonuses tied to stock price).
    - Develop procedures for implementing gainsharing agreement.
    - How will disputes be handled?

22. Compliance Issues
    - Identify any regulatory/governmental requirements (e.g., timing, notice, consent). (Note: These requirements are typically driven by the type of transaction, e.g., rules governing accounting services, and the type of organization receiving services, e.g., rules governing financial institutions. In addition, compliance issues may vary from country to country or if the transaction involves more than one country.)
    - Are there any year 2000 issues? Will Vendor have any year 2000 remediation responsibilities?
    - Are there any Euro compliance issues?
    - Determine which party is responsible for ensuring compliance. Allocate costs of compliance due to changes in laws, rules or regulations after commencement.
    - Identify any license/permits required to be obtained by Customer and/or Vendor.
    - Consult with legal, regulatory, tax, and audit departments.

23. Transaction-Specific Issues
    - Identify any business-process specific requirements (e.g., for warehouse distribution transactions, provisions regarding liens; for real estate management transactions, insurance and environmental obligations; for accounting services transactions, provisions regarding accounting standards and filing deadlines).
    - Consult with legal, regulatory, tax, and audit departments.

24. Customer Responsibilities
    - Identify Customer's responsibilities (e.g., provision of supplies, computers, parking).
    - Will Customer be providing any space/facilities to house Vendor's employees? What are the terms of Vendor's use (e.g., sublease)?
    - Is Customer retaining staff necessary to perform the retained responsibilities (e.g., management, definition of requirements, approvals)?

25. Service Locations
    - Where will Vendor be providing the services from? If such locations are not Customer locations, are there any restrictions on where Vendor may provide services from?
    - Will the service locations be dedicated to Customer or shared facilities?
    - Describe physical security requirements. Are uniforms or other identification required? Does Customer or Vendor have specific codes of conduct?
    - How will breaches of security be handled?
    - Are there any environmental concerns?

26. Management Procedures
    - Will the parties develop management procedures to be used in connection with the provision of the services?
    - How will change control be handled?

27. Reports
    - Identify the performance and other reports that Customer currently generates or receives with respect to the services being outsourced.

- Identify those reports that Customer wishes to receive from Vendor.
- Establish deadlines for each report.
- Will Customer be required to review the reports within a specific time period?
- How will errors in reports be handled?

28. Data
    - Discuss procedures for handling Customer data. What are Vendor's use rights?
    - How will errors in Customer data be handled?
    - Describe data security requirements at service locations. Are passwords required?
    - How will breaches of security be handled?

29. Proprietary Rights
    - Establish Vendor's right to use Customer proprietary methodologies and technology during the term and after expiration/termination of the agreement.
    - Establish Vendor's right to use during the term and after expiration/termination of the agreement methodologies and technology licensed by Customer from third parties and used in connection with the provision of the services.
    - Establish Customer's right to use Vendor's proprietary methodologies and technology during the term and after expiration/termination of the agreement.
    - Establish Customer's right to use during the term and after expiration/termination of the agreement methodologies and technology licensed by Vendor from third parties and used in connection with the provision of the services.
    - Establish each party's ownership/use rights with respect to methodologies and technology developed or acquired as part of or in connection with the provision of the services.
    - Establish any restrictions governing the use of confidential information.
    - Establish any restrictions governing the use of mentally retained information.
    - Discuss whether noncompetition provisions are appropriate.

30. Audit
    - What are Customer's rights to audit the services and the service locations? How often may Customer exercise any such audit rights?
    - How will the results of any such audit be dealt with?
    - What are Customer's rights to audit the fees?
    - How will overpayments/underpayments be handled?
    - Will interest be charged?

31. Fees
    - Determine the applicable fee structure.
    - Customer should assess actual cost savings, if any. Such analysis should include any new taxes, employee transfer costs, and other expenses resulting from the outsourcing.
    - Vendor should assess actual profit margin.
    - Other Fee Provisions:
        - If a base fee structure is used, determine structure for increasing and decreasing fees/resources.
        - Determine the rights of the parties to set off monies owed.
        - To what extent, if any, will Customer be responsible for Vendor expenses, e.g., travel? Will Vendor use Customer or Vendor expense guidelines?
        - Will there be any cost of living adjustments?
        - For international deals, is there any currency risk?
        - Consider a most favored customer provision.

- How will fees be paid, e.g., in what currency, in what manner and according to what schedule?
- How, when and to what Customer entity(ies) will invoices be issued? Determine the degree of detail to be included on invoices.
- How will disputed fees/credits be handled, e.g., escrow? What are the parties' obligations to perform in the event of a dispute?
- How will changes in business volumes be handled?

32. Taxes
    - Determine liability for sales, use, and other taxes.
    - Determine liability for additional taxes resulting from Vendor's relocation of service locations or rerouting of services.

33. Additional Services
    - How will the provision of additional services be handled? Will Vendor be required to submit a bid? Will there be any rights of first refusal granted to Vendor?
    - What type of detail must be included in a Vendor proposal?
    - To what extent does Customer wish to reserve the right to contract with third parties?

34. Insurance
    - Specify Vendor's insurance requirements, e.g.:
      - Errors and omissions
      - Liability
      - Workers' compensation
      - Automobile
      - Environmental
    - Specify any specific bonding requirements.
    - Determine whether any parental or other type of guarantee is appropriate.

35. Termination
    - Consider early termination rights, e.g.:
      - Termination for convenience in whole
      - Partial termination for convenience
      - Termination upon change of control of Vendor
      - Termination upon change of control of Customer
      - Termination for breach
      - Termination for nonpayment
      - Termination for failure to provide critical services
      - Termination for failure to meet the performance standards
      - Termination for substantial changes in business
      - Termination upon the occurrence of a regulatory event
      - Cross-termination with other agreements
    - Determine whether and in what instances termination fees are applicable. If so, establish formula for determining applicable termination fees.

36. Exit Rights

    - Determine each party's ongoing rights after expiration/termination with respect to proprietary and third-party methodologies, technology, equipment, facilities, subcontracting arrangements, and third-party service agreements.

- Determine which party will be responsible for transfer/assignment fees imposed by third parties.
- If Customer has right to purchase certain Vendor assets used to provide the services, how will the purchase price be determined?

37. Termination Assistance
    - Determine the types of assistance Vendor and/or its subcontractors will provide Customer upon expiration/termination.
    - Determine duration of Vendor's termination assistance obligations.
    - How will termination assistance be paid for (e.g., fee schedule, time schedule for payment)?

38. Liability Provisions
    - Assess liability exposure.
    - Determine any liquidated damages to be imposed upon Vendor (e.g., for failure to meet performance standards, for failure to meet implementation schedules).
    - What are each party's indemnification obligations (e.g., for claims of infringement, employee claims).
    - Determine the representations and warranties to be made by each party.

39. Dispute Resolution
    - How will disputes be handled? Will the agreement include an escalation procedure?
    - Will unresolved disputes be handled through arbitration or litigation?

40. Business Recovery
    - Will Vendor have any business recovery responsibilities?
    - What are Customer's existing business recovery plan? Will Customer's plans be terminated?
    - Specify response times for delivery of business recovery services. Describe escalation procedures.

41. Assignment
    - Specify each party's right to assign its rights/obligations under the agreement in whole or in part.
    - Will there be any special assignment rights in the event of a merger/acquisition/divestiture?
    - May either party assign to an affiliate/related entity?

42. Solicitation of Employees
    - Will there be any limitations/restrictions on Customer's or Vendor's right to solicit and/or hire the other party's employees?
    - When will such limitations/restrictions apply (e.g., during the term, after expiration/termination)?
    - Will there be any exceptions for blind solicitations (e.g., newspaper advertisements)?

43. Miscellaneous Provisions
    - *Notices*: How will notices be given (e.g., by hand, by facsimile)? To whom (e.g., to business manager and/or counsel)?
    - *Publicity*: Limitations/restrictions on each party's ability to make public statements regarding the other party and/or the transaction.

- *Governing Law*: Determine which state/country law will govern the transaction (or if international transaction with multiple documents, determine which law will govern each part of the transaction).
- *Venue*: Will there be a requirement that any action be brought in a particular venue?
- *Import/Export*: Provide any limitations/restrictions on the export/import of data and/or technology.
- *Interpretation of Documents*: How will the transaction documents be interpreted in the event of a dispute (e.g., the main agreement will take precedence over the exhibits/schedules, change orders will take precedence over earlier dated documents)?
- *Counterparts*: Specify whether the various transaction documents may be executed in counterparts.
- *Relationship of the Parties*: Specify that Vendor is an independent contractor to Customer and that the provision of services does not constitute any type of partnership or joint venture (unless that is expressly the intent).
- *Severability*: Specify that if any provision is held to be invalid that the remaining provisions shall remain in full force and effect.
- *Waivers*: Specify that any delay or omission does not constitute a waiver of rights and that any waiver should not be construed to be a waiver of a subsequent breach/covenant.
- *Entire Agreement*: Specify that the transaction documents constitute the entire agreement between the parties.
- *Amendments*: Specify how the transaction documents may be amended (e.g., by writing signed by both parties).
- *Survival*: Specify which provisions of the agreement will survive termination and/or expiration of the agreement.
- *Third-Party Beneficiaries*: Expressly state that there will not be any third-party beneficiaries under the transaction documents or, if there will be third-party beneficiaries, identify such beneficiaries.
- *Covenant of Further Assurances*: Expressly state that each party will execute any documents or perform any actions necessary to effectuate the purposes of the agreement.

CHECKLIST: KEY ISSUES IN BPO AGREEMENTS (ACCOUNTING SERVICES)[a]

KEY ISSUES IN
BUSINESS PROCESS OUTSOURCING AGREEMENTS
(ACCOUNTING SERVICES)

1. Structure of the Accounting Services Agreement
   * How will the agreement be structured?
     * A single services agreement
     * A master agreement with site-specific, country specific or entity-specific service agreements
     * Separate agreements for reengineering, development, and ongoing accounting services
     * Separate agreements documenting the terms applicable to a joint venture/ strategic alliance relationship and the terms and applicable to ongoing accounting services
   * What is the inter-relationship between these agreements if separate, e.g., cross-termination, payment?
   * Factors that may affect the agreement structure include:
     * Scope of services: will Vendor be providing any business process reengineering or development services?
     * Geographic scope: single country vs. international agreement
     * Scope of services at specific sites: will all Customer sites receive the same accounting services or will each Customer site receive different services?
     * Types of entities receiving/delivering the services: is the contracting entity for each of the parties able to bind the entities that will receive/deliver the services or must each of the recipient/delivering entities agree to be bound by the master agreement?

---

[a] Note: This checklist is intended to illustrate the types of legal issues that may arise in connection with accounting services outsourcing transactions. The issues identified in this checklist, while comprehensive, may not cover all of the issues relevant to a particular transaction. Legal issues will vary depending on the type of business process being outsourced and the scope of the outsourcing transaction. This checklist or any part thereof should only be used after consultation with your legal counsel. You should consult legal counsel prior to entering into or negotiating any outsourcing transaction.

- Cost allocation: are there any cost allocation requirements internal to customer that would drive separate site/entity agreements?
- Taxes: are there any tax requirements that would drive separate service agreements?
- SEC requirements: are there any SEC or other regulations that would drive separate service agreements?

2. Contracting Party
   - Who will sign the agreement on behalf of Customer? On behalf of Vendor?
   - If there is a master agreement with separate service agreements, will the same party that signs the master agreement, sign the service agreements?

3. Entities Receiving Services from Vendor
   - Determine who will receive services from Vendor
   - Entities may include:
     - Customer affiliates
     - Joint ventures/alliances
     - Contractors
     - Suppliers
     - Clients of Customer
   - Will Customer have the option of adding/deleting entities over the term?
   - How will mergers/acquisitions/divestitures be handled? What will Customer's and Vendor's ongoing obligations be?
   - Which entity(ies) will have payment obligations? Are recipients of services third-party beneficiaries?

4. Entities Providing Services to Customer
   - Determine which entity (or entities) will provide the services to Customer.
   - Will there be any subcontracting/teaming relationships?
   - For international deals, how will Vendor provide resources/services in each country? Will Vendor use affiliated entities or subcontractors?
   - What are Customer's rights to approve/remove subcontractors?
   - Which entity(ies) will have performance/indemnification obligations?

5. Term
   - What is the commencement date of services? Will there be one commencement date for all sites? Will there be one commencement date for all services (e.g., business process reengineering, development and ongoing accounting services)?
   - How long is the term of the agreement? If the transaction includes multiple agreements, are all of the agreements co-terminus? If there is a master agreement with separate site/service agreements, are all of the agreements co-terminus?
   - Will there be a pilot period?
   - What are each party's renewal rights? What type of notice is required for renewal?

6. Scope of Services
   - Determine the general scope of services to be provided by Vendor. For example:
     - General Accounting
     - Payroll
     - Treasury/Cash Management
     - Accounts Payable
     - Accounts Receivable

- Credit
- Fixed Assets
- Contract Maintenance
- Collections
- Financial Systems
- Tax Compliance
- Budgeting
- SEC Reporting
- Determine those services which will be provided in-house by Customer or to Customer by a third party.
- Describe in detail the services (typically by service category) to be provided by Vendor. For example:
  - Managerial activities
    — monthly/quarterly closing
    — routine management/reporting
    — internal audit
    — outside travel services
    — budget
    — forecasting
    — corporate initiatives
    — functional support
  - General accounting
    — general ledger maintenance
    — expense accounting
    — cash accounting/reconciliation
    — fixed asset accounting
    — company accounting
    — intercompany accounting
    — earned by unbilled accounting
  - Treasury
    — beginning cash position
    — expected cash position
    — end cash position forecast
    — forecasting
    — variance analysis
    — third-party excess funds
    — forgery
  - Cash management
    — beginning cash position
    — expected cash position
    — end cash position forecast
    — forecasting
    — variance analysis
    — third-party excess funds
    — forgery
    — outgoing wires
    — paid without invoices
    — stop pay
    — receipt processing
    — manual check preparation and mailing
    — documentation requests

      — journal edits
      — check issuance files
      — banking structure/relationships
      — cash policies
      — credit management
      — facilities and real estate
      — risk management

- Accounts Payable
  - invoice payment requests
  - approved invoice entry
  - travel and expense reports
  - manual journal entries
  - manual payroll checks
  - automated check generation and distribution
- Define Customer's responsibilities with respect to the services to be provided by Vendor (i.e., definition of requirements, strategic direction, approvals).
- Define existing and future requirements (e.g., capacity requirements, volume changes, business changes). Allocate managerial and financial responsibility.

7. Transition Plan
   - How will the transition of services to Vendor be handled?
   - Will there be any redundant/parallel environments?
   - Determine the performance standards during transition.
   - How long will the transition period be?

8. Methodologies
   - Assess methodologies to be used by Vendor. Are the methodologies proprietary to Vendor or licensed from a third party? If licensed from a third party, are there any use restrictions? What are Customer's rights to use during the term and after expiration/termination?
   - Will any of Customer's methodologies continue to be used during the term of the transaction? What are Vendor's use rights (e.g., use in connection with services to Customer only; use in connection with other customers)?
   - How will Vendor transition Customer to Vendor's methodologies (if applicable)?
   - How will the methodologies introduced by Vendor be integrated with Customer's existing and future methodologies (with respect to the applicable business function as well as other business areas, e.g., information systems)?
   - Will Vendor be developing/providing any new methodologies? If so, how will ownership/use rights be allocated? How will new methodologies be rolled out (e.g., define time period, consequences for failure to meet deadlines, each party's responsibilities)?

9. Technology
   - Assess technology to be used by Vendor. Is the technology proprietary to Vendor or licensed from a third party? If licensed from a third party, are there any use restrictions? What are Customer's rights to use during the term and after expiration/termination?
   - Will any of Customer's technology continue to be used during the term of the transaction? What are Vendor's use rights (e.g., use in connection with services to Customer only; use in connection with other customers)?
   - Will the environment be dedicated/shared?
   - How will Vendor transition Customer to Vendor's technology (if applicable)?

- How will the technology introduced by Vendor be integrated with Customer's existing or future technology, e.g., is Vendor technology compatible with technology used by Customer's information system group?
- Will Vendor be developing/providing any new technology? If so, how will ownership/use rights be allocated? How will new technology be rolled out (e.g., define time period, consequences for failure to meet deadlines, each party's responsibilities)?

10. Assets
- Will Vendor be purchasing any of Customer's assets (e.g., equipment, real estate)? If so, when will purchase be made (e.g., on date of signing)?
- How will assets be valued (e.g., book value, fair market value)?
- Is the transfer of assets necessary in conjunction with the transfer of employees in order to constitute an "automatic transfer" under the particular country's employment/redundancy laws?

11. Projects
- Identify any projects that Vendor will be responsible for implementing/managing as part of the transaction.
- Will Vendor be responsible for any business process reengineering in connection with its provision of accounting services? If so, what are each party's responsibilities? What are the consequences if the reengineering is not successful or performed by deadlines specified?
- What is the inter-relationship of Vendor's business process reengineering responsibilities and Vendor's accounting service responsibilities (e.g., are they cross-terminable)?
- Will Vendor be responsible for any new implementations? If so, what are each party's responsibilities? What are the consequences if the reengineering is not successful or performed by deadlines specified?
- Which party will be responsible for purchase/license of third-party methodologies/technologies (if applicable)?

12. Integration
- How will the methodologies/technologies introduced by Vendor be integrated with other methodologies/technologies used by Customer?
- Have other Customer business areas been contacted for input (e.g., information systems, human resources)?
- How will Vendor work with Customer's third-party vendor's?

13. Transfer of Employees
- Determine whether any or all Customer employees will be offered employment by, or transitioned to, Vendor or a Vendor subcontractor.
- Identify group of retained employees.
- Review Customer's severance/redundancy policy, if any, to determine whether a transition to Vendor may invoke severance obligations. (If so, factor into Customer's cost analysis.)
- Are there any claims with respect to any of the transitioned employees?
- Compare Customer and Vendor benefits. Are any adjustments necessary?
- Does Vendor require any special screening of employees (e.g., drug testing)?
- Will Vendor require transitioned employees to sign an employment agreement?

* Develop an employee communication plan.
* Determine whether any stay bonuses/incentives are necessary.

14. Project Staff
    * Identify management structure of Vendor as well as Customer in connection with the provision/receipt of services.
    * Are there any limitations/restrictions with respect to reassignment/replacement of key Vendor personnel?
    * Are there any limitations/restrictions with respect to "churning" of employees?
    * How will Customer complaints regarding Vendor personnel be handled?
    * Are there any special clearances of Vendor personnel necessary?
    * Are there any limitations/restrictions with respect to subcontractors?

15. Retained Assets
    * Identify which assets Vendor will manage and, of those assets, which assets Vendor will have financial responsibility for.
    * Identify which assets Customer will continue to manage and, of those assets, whether Vendor will have any financial responsibility.
    * How will the parties act in the event it is not clear where a problem originates from (e.g., root cause analysis)?

16. Agreements to be Reviewed
    * Identify any third-party agreements/relationships that may be impacted by the outsourcing, including:
        * Maintenance agreements
        * Subcontracting relationships
        * Other service agreements
        * Methodology/technology licenses
        * Equipment/asset leases
        * Real estate leases/subleases
    * Are there any restrictions with respect to third-party management/access or assignment to a third party?
    * What are the terms relating to termination/renewal?
    * What are the pricing terms and will they be impacted by the transaction?
    * Develop a strategy for notifying third parties, if applicable.

17. Third-Party Consents
    * Are any third-party consents necessary in connection with the commencement of the transaction? If so, which party is responsible for obtaining such consents and how will financial responsibility be allocated?
    * How will third-party consents be obtained upon the expiration/termination of the transaction (in order to transition agreements/assets back to Customer or Customer's designee)? How will financial responsibility be allocated?

18. Performance Standards
    * Identify those services which will have performance standards (e.g., general ledger maintenance—time to initiate account changes, journal entries, table maintenance).
    * How will Vendor's performance be measured? Will existing performance standards be used or will performance standards be established on a going forward basis?
    * Identify any permitted downtime and testing.

- How will failures to meet performance standards be handled (e.g., liquidated damages or termination)?
- Will there be any procedures for assessing/determining causes of failures to meet performance standards (e.g., root cause analysis)?
- What performance standards will apply during transition/implementation?

19. Customer Satisfaction
    - Will Vendor be responsible for any type of customer satisfaction reporting?
    - Determine pool of employees surveyed (e.g., management, end-users).
    - How will the results of such surveys be used (e.g., as basis for performance standard)?

20. Benchmarking
    - Determine whether the agreement will include any benchmarking procedures (e.g., benchmarking of services or prices).
    - Develop benchmarking procedures (e.g., scope of benchmark, group against which services/prices will be benchmarked).
    - Identify benchmarker (e.g., third party, Vendor group).
    - How will benchmarking results be reviewed and how will changes, if applicable, be implemented?

21. Gainsharing
    - Determine whether any gainsharing provisions will be included in the agreement (e.g., bonuses tied to stock price).
    - Develop procedures for implementing gainsharing agreement.
    - How will disputes be handled?

22. Accounting Principles
    - What are Vendor's responsibilities with respect to defining, identifying and following accounting principles and practices applicable to corporate and statutory reporting requirements of Customer?
    - Will Vendor have any responsibilities with respect to maintaining internal account controls.

23. Compliance Issues
    - Identify any regulatory requirements.
    - Are there any year 2000 issues? Will Vendor have any year 2000 remediation responsibilities?
    - Are there any Euro compliance issues?
    - Determine which party is responsible for ensuring compliance. Allocate costs of compliance due to changes in laws, rules, or regulations after commencement.
    - Identify any license/permits required to be obtained by Customer and/or Vendor.
    - Consult with legal, regulatory, tax, and audit departments.

24. Customer Responsibilities
    - Identify Customer's responsibilities (e.g., provision of information, supplies, computers, parking).
    - Will Customer be providing any space/facilities to house Vendor's employees? What are the terms of Vendor's use (e.g., sublease)?
    - Is Customer retaining staff necessary to perform the retained responsibilities (e.g., management, definition of requirements, approvals)?

25. Service Locations
    - Where will Vendor be providing the services from? If such locations are not Customer locations, are there any restrictions on where Vendor may provide services from?
    - Will the service locations be dedicated to Customer or shared facilities?
    - Describe physical security requirements. Are uniforms or other identification required? Does Customer or Vendor have specific codes of conduct?
    - How will breaches of security be handled?
    - Are there any environmental issues?

26. Management Procedures
    - Will the parties develop management procedures to be used in connection with the provision of the services?
    - How will change control be handled?

27. Reports/Records
    - Identify any reporting requirements (e.g., SEC filings, tax filings).
    - Identify performance reports that Customer currently generates or receives with respect to the services being outsourced.
    - Establish deadlines for each report.
    - Will Customer be required to review the reports within a specific time period?
    - How will errors in reports be handled?
    - What are Customer's record retention requirements?

28. Data
    - Discuss procedures for handling Customer data. What are Vendor's use rights?
    - How will errors in Customer data be handled?
    - Describe data security requirements at service locations. Are passwords required?
    - How will breaches of security be handled?

29. Proprietary Rights
    - Establish Vendor's right to use Customer proprietary methodologies and technology during the term and after expiration/termination of the agreement.
    - Establish Vendor's right to use during the term and after expiration/termination of the agreement methodologies and technology licensed by Customer from third parties and used in connection with the provision of the services.
    - Establish Customer's right to use Vendor's proprietary methodologies and technology during the term and after expiration/termination of the agreement.
    - Establish Customer's right to use during the term and after expiration/termination of the agreement methodologies and technology licensed by Vendor from third parties and used in connection with the provision of the services.
    - Establish each party's ownership/use rights with respect to methodologies and technology developed or acquired as part of or in connection with the provision of the services.
    - Establish any restrictions governing the use of confidential information.
    - Establish any restrictions governing the use of mentally retained information.
    - Discuss whether noncompetition provisions are appropriate.

30. Audit
    - What are Customer's rights to audit the services and the service locations? How often may Customer exercise any such audit rights?

- How will the results of any such audit be dealt with?
- What are Customer's rights to audit the fees?
- How will overpayments/underpayments be handled?
- Will interest be charged?

31. Fees
    - Determine the applicable fee structure.
    - Customer should assess actual cost savings, if any. Such analysis should include any new taxes, employee transfer costs, and other expenses resulting from the outsourcing.
    - Vendor should assess actual profit margin.
    - Other Fee Provisions:
        - If a base fee structure is used, determine structure for increasing and decreasing fees/resources.
        - Determine the rights of the parties to set off monies owed.
        - To what extent, if any, will Customer be responsible for Vendor expenses, e.g., travel? Will Vendor use Customer or Vendor expense guidelines?
        - Will there be any cost of living adjustments?
        - For international deals, is there any currency risk?
        - Consider a most favored customer provision.
        - How will fees be paid, e.g., in what currency, in what manner and according to what schedule?
        - How, when and to what Customer entity(ies) will invoices be issued? Determine the degree of detail to be included on invoices.
        - How will disputed fees/credits be handled, e.g., escrow? What are the parties' obligations to perform in the event of a dispute?
        - How will changes in business volumes be handled?

32. Taxes
    - Determine liability for sales, use, and other taxes.
    - Determine liability for additional taxes resulting from Vendor's relocation of service locations or rerouting of services.

33. Additional Services
    - How will the provision of additional services be handled? Will Vendor be required to submit a bid? Will there be any rights of first refusal granted to Vendor?
    - Examples of additional services include:
        - Actuarial services
        - Investment accounting
        - Data warehousing
        - Data center services
    - What type of detail must be included in a Vendor proposal?
    - To what extent does Customer wish to reserve the right to contract with third parties?

34. Insurance
    - Specify Vendor's insurance requirements, e.g.:
        - Errors and omissions
        - Liability
        - Worker's compensation
        - Automobile

- Specify any specific bonding requirements.
- Determine whether any parental or other type of guarantee is appropriate.

35. Termination
    - Consider early termination rights, e.g.:
      - Termination for convenience in whole
      - Partial termination for convenience
      - Termination upon change of control of Vendor
      - Termination upon change of control of Customer
      - Termination for breach
      - Termination for nonpayment
      - Termination for failure to provide critical services
      - Termination for failure to meet the performance standards
      - Termination for substantial changes in business
      - Termination upon the occurrence of a regulatory event
      - Cross-termination with other agreements
    - Determine whether and in what instances termination fees are applicable. If so, establish formula for determining applicable termination fees.

36. Exit Rights
    - Determine each party's ongoing rights after expiration/termination with respect to proprietary and third-party methodologies, technology, equipment, facilities, subcontracting arrangements, and third-party service agreements.
    - Determine which party will be responsible for transfer/assignment fees imposed by third parties.
    - If Customer has right to purchase certain Vendor assets used to provide the services, how will the purchase price be determined?

37. Termination Assistance
    - Determine the types of assistance Vendor and/or its subcontractors will provide Customer upon expiration/termination.
    - Determine duration of Vendor's termination assistance obligations.
    - How will termination assistance be paid for (e.g., fee schedule, time schedule for payment)?

38. Liability Provisions
    - Assess liability exposure.
    - Determine any liquidated damages to be imposed upon Vendor (e.g., for failure to meet performance standards, for failure to meet implementation schedules).
    - What are each party's indemnification obligations (e.g., for claims of infringement, employee claims).
    - Determine the representations and warranties to be made by each party.

39. Dispute Resolution
    - How will disputes be handled? Will the agreement include an escalation procedure?
    - Will unresolved disputes be handled through arbitration or litigation?

40. Business Recovery
    - Will Vendor have any business recovery responsibilities?
    - What are Customer's existing business recovery plan? Will Customer's plans be terminated?

- Specify response times for delivery of business recovery services. Describe escalation procedures.

41. Assignment
    - Specify each party's right to assign its rights/obligations under the agreement in whole or in part.
    - Will there be any special assignment rights in the event of a merger/acquisition/divestiture?
    - May either party assign to an affiliate/related entity?

42. Solicitation of Employees
    - Will there be any limitations/restrictions on Customer's or Vendor's right to solicit and/or hire the other party's employees?
    - When will such limitations/restrictions apply (e.g., during the term, after expiration/termination)?
    - Will there be any exceptions for blind solicitations (e.g., newspaper advertisements)?

43. Miscellaneous Provisions
    - *Notices*: How will notices be given (e.g., by hand, by facsimile)? To whom (e.g., to business manager and/or counsel)?
    - *Publicity*: Limitations/restrictions on each party's ability to make public statements regarding the other party and/or the transaction.
    - *Governing Law*: Determine which state/country law will govern the transaction (or if international transaction with multiple documents, determine which law will govern each part of the transaction).
    - *Venue*: Will there be a requirement that any action be brought in a particular venue?
    - *Import/Export*: Provide any limitations/restrictions on the export/import of data and/or technology.
    - *Interpretation of Documents*: How will the transaction documents be interpreted in the event of a dispute (e.g., the main agreement will take precedence over the exhibits/schedules, change orders will take precedence over earlier dated documents)?
    - *Counterparts*: Specify whether the various transaction documents may be executed in counterparts.
    - *Relationship of the Parties*: Specify that Vendor is an independent contractor to Customer and that the provision of services does not constitute any type of partnership or joint venture (unless that is expressly the intent)
    - *Severability*: Specify that if any provision is held to be invalid that the remaining provisions shall remain in full force and effect.
    - *Waivers*: Specify that any delay or omission does not constitute a waiver of rights and that any waiver should not be construed to be a waiver of a subsequent breach/covenant.
    - *Entire Agreement*: Specify that the transaction documents constitute the entire agreement between the parties.
    - *Amendments*: Specify how the transaction documents may be amended (e.g., by writing signed by both parties).
    - *Survival*: Specify which provisions of the agreement will survive termination and/or expiration of the agreement.

- *Third Party Beneficiaries*: Expressly state that there will not be any third-party beneficiaries under the transaction documents or, if there will be third-party beneficiaries, identify such beneficiaries.
- *Covenant of Further Assurances*: Expressly state that each party will execute any documents or perform any actions necessary to effectuate the purposes of the agreement.

CHECKLIST: KEY ISSUES IN BPO AGREEMENTS (HUMAN RESOURCE SERVICES)[a]

KEY ISSUES IN
BUSINESS PROCESS OUTSOURCING AGREEMENTS
(HUMAN RESOURCE SERVICES)

1. Structure of the Human Resource Services Agreement
   - How will the agreement be structured?
     - A single services agreement
     - A master agreement with site-specific, country-specific, or entity-specific service agreements
     - Separate agreements for business process reengineering, development and ongoing human resources services
     - Separate agreements documenting the terms applicable to a joint venture/ strategic alliance and the terms applicable to ongoing human resource services
   - What is the inter-relationship between these agreements if separate, e.g., cross-termination, payment?
   - Factors that may affect the agreement structure include:
     - Scope of services: will Vendor be providing any business process reengineering or development services?
     - Geographic scope: single country vs. international agreement
     - Scope of services at specific sites: will all Customer sites receive the same services or will each Customer site receive different services?
     - Types of entities receiving/delivering the services: is the contracting entity for each of the parties able to bind the entities that will receive/deliver the services or must each of the recipient/delivering entities agree to be bound by the master agreement?
     - Cost allocation: are there any cost allocation requirements internal to customer that would drive separate site/entity agreements?

---

[a] Note: This checklist is intended to illustrate the types of legal issues that may arise in connection with human resource outsourcing transactions. The issues identified in this checklist, while comprehensive, may not cover all of the issues relevant to a particular transaction. Legal issues will vary depending on the type of business process being outsourced and the scope of the outsourcing transaction. This checklist or any part thereof should only be used after consultation with your legal counsel. You should consult legal counsel prior to entering into or negotiating any outsourcing transaction.

- Taxes: are there any tax requirements that would drive separate service agreements?

2. Contracting Party
   - Who will sign the agreement on behalf of Customer? On behalf of Vendor?
   - If there is a master agreement with separate service agreements, will the same party that signs the master agreement, sign the service agreements?

3. Entities Receiving Services from Vendor
   - Determine who will receive services from Vendor
   - Entities may include:
     - Customer affiliates
     - Joint ventures/alliances
     - Contractors
     - Suppliers
     - Clients of Customer
   - Will Customer have the option of adding/deleting entities over the term?
   - How will mergers/acquisitions/divestitures be handled? What will Customer's and Vendor's ongoing obligations be?
   - Which entity(ies) will have payment obligations? Are recipients of services third-party beneficiaries?

4. Entities Providing Services to Customer
   - Determine which entity (or entities) will provide the services to Customer.
   - Will there be any subcontracting/teaming relationships?
   - For international deals, how will Vendor provide resources/services in each country? Will Vendor use affiliated entities or subcontractors?
   - What are Customer's rights to approve/remove subcontractors?
   - Which entity(ies) will have performance/indemnification obligations?

5. Term
   - What is the commencement date of services? Will there be one commencement date for all sites? Will there be one commencement date for all services (e.g., business process reengineering, development and ongoing human resource services)?
   - How long is the term of the agreement? If the transaction includes multiple agreements, are all of the agreements co-terminus? If there is a master agreement with separate site/service agreements, are all of the agreements co-terminus?
   - Will there be a pilot period?
   - What are each party's renewal rights? What type of notice is required for renewal?

6. Scope of Services
   - Determine the general scope of services to be provided by Vendor. For example:
     - Payroll process
     - Payroll financial services
     - Governmental reporting
     - Timekeeping solutions
     - Customer service
     - Benefits management
     - HR systems development
     - Training
     - Job posting and placement

- Out placement
- Employee relations
- Employee absence management
- Resource planning
- Strategic HR planning
- Employee data management
- Expatriate administration

- Determine those human resource services which will be provided in-house by Customer or to Customer by a third party.
- Describe in detail the human resource services (typically by service category) to be provided by Vendor. For example:
  - Payroll process
    — Pay calculation
    — Checking printing and distribution
    — Direct deposit
    — Third-party remittances
    — Savings bonds
    — Variable pay
    — W-2s
  - Payroll Financial Services
    — Tax payments and reports
    — Payroll general ledger account analysis
    — Bank reconciliations
    — Labor expense allocations
  - Benefits Management
    — Monitoring of services provided by external providers
    — Payments to external providers
    — Short-term disability
    — Pensionable wage calculation and verification
- Define Customer's responsibilities with respect to the services to be provided by Vendor (i.e., definition of requirements, strategic direction, approvals).
- Define existing and future requirements (e.g., capacity requirements, number of employees, business changes). Allocate managerial and financial responsibility.

7. Transition Plan
   - How will the transition of services to Vendor be handled?
   - Will there be any redundant/parallel environments?
   - Determine the performance standards during transition.
   - How long will the transition period be?

8. Methodologies
   - Assess methodologies to be used by Vendor. Are the methodologies proprietary to Vendor or licensed from a third party? If licensed from a third party, are there any use restrictions? What are Customer's rights to use during the term and after expiration/termination?
   - Will any of Customer's methodologies continue to be used during the term of the transaction? What are Vendor's use rights (e.g., use in connection with services to Customer only; use in connection with other customers)?
   - How will Vendor transition Customer to Vendor's methodologies (if applicable)?

- How will the methodologies introduced by Vendor be integrated with Customer's existing and future methodologies (with respect to the applicable business function as well as other business areas, e.g., information systems)?
- Will Vendor be developing/providing any new methodologies? If so, how will ownership/use rights be allocated? How will new methodologies be rolled out (e.g., define time period, consequences for failure to meet deadlines, each party's responsibilities)?

9. Technology
   - Assess technology to be used by Vendor. Is the technology proprietary to Vendor or licensed from a third party? If licensed from a third party, are there any use restrictions? What are Customer's rights to use during the term and after expiration/termination?
   - Will any of Customer's technology continue to be used during the term of the transaction? What are Vendor's use rights (e.g., use in connection with services to Customer only; use in connection with other customers)?
   - Will the environment be dedicated/shared?
   - How will Vendor transition Customer to Vendor's technology (if applicable)?
   - How will the technology introduced by Vendor be integrated with Customer's existing or future technology, e.g., is Vendor technology compatible with technology used by Customer's information system group?
   - Will Vendor be developing/providing any new technology? If so, how will ownership/use rights be allocated? How will new technology be rolled out (e.g., define time period, consequences for failure to meet deadlines, each party's responsibilities)?

10. Assets
    - Will Vendor be purchasing any of Customer's assets (e.g., equipment, real estate)? If so, when will purchase be made (e.g., on date of signing)?
    - How will assets be valued (e.g., book value, fair market value)?
    - Is the transfer of assets necessary in conjunction with the transfer of employees in order to constitute an "automatic transfer" under the particular country's employment/redundancy laws?

11. Projects
    - Identify any projects that Vendor will be responsible for implementing/managing as part of the transaction.
    - Will Vendor be responsible for any business process reengineering in connection with its provision of human resource services? If so, what are each party's responsibilities? What are the consequences if the reengineering is not successful or performed by deadlines specified?
    - What is the inter-relationship of Vendor's business process reengineering responsibilities and Vendor's human resource service responsibilities (e.g., are they cross-terminable)?
    - Will Vendor be responsible for any new implementations? If so, what are each party's responsibilities? What are the consequences if the reengineering is not successful or performed by deadlines specified?
    - Which party will be responsible for purchase/license of third-party methodologies/technologies (if applicable)?

12. Integration
    - How will the methodologies/technologies introduced by Vendor be integrated with other methodologies/technologies used by Customer?

- Have other Customer business areas been contacted for input (e.g., information systems, human resources)?

13. Transfer of Employees
    - Determine whether any or all Customer employees will be offered employment by, or transitioned to, Vendor or a Vendor subcontractor.
    - Identify group of retained employees.
    - Review Customer's severance/redundancy policy, if any, to determine whether a transition to Vendor may invoke severance obligations. (If so, factor into Customer's cost analysis.)
    - Are there any claims with respect to any of the transitioned employees?
    - Compare Customer and Vendor benefits. Are any adjustments necessary?
    - Does Vendor require any special screening of employees (e.g., drug testing)?
    - Will Vendor require transitioned employees to sign an employment agreement?
    - Develop an employee communication plan.
    - Determine whether any stay bonuses/incentives are necessary.

14. Project Staff
    - Identify management structure of Vendor as well as Customer in connection with the provision/receipt of services.
    - Are there any limitations/restrictions with respect to reassignment/replacement of key Vendor personnel?
    - Are there any limitations/restrictions with respect to "churning" of employees?
    - How will Customer complaints regarding Vendor personnel be handled?
    - Are there any special clearances of Vendor personnel necessary?
    - Are there any limitations/restrictions with respect to subcontractors?

15. Retained Assets
    - Identify which assets Vendor will manage and, of those assets, which assets Vendor will have financial responsibility for.
    - Identify which assets Customer will continue to manage and, of those assets, whether Vendor will have any financial responsibility.
    - How will the parties act in the event it is not clear where a problem originates from (e.g., root cause analysis)?

16. Agreements to be Reviewed
    - Identify any third-party agreements/relationships that may be impacted by the outsourcing, including:
        - Employment agreements
        - Consulting agreements
        - Maintenance agreements
        - Subcontracting relationships
        - Other service agreements
        - Methodology/technology licenses
        - Equipment/asset leases
        - Real estate leases/subleases
    - Are there any restrictions with respect to third-party management/access or assignment to a third party?
    - What are the terms relating to termination/renewal?
    - What are the pricing terms and will they be impacted by the transaction?
    - Develop a strategy for notifying third parties, if applicable.

17. Third-Party Consents
    * Are any third-party consents necessary in connection with the commencement of the transaction? If so, which party is responsible for obtaining such consents and how will financial responsibility be allocated?
    * How will third-party consents be obtained upon the expiration/termination of the transaction (in order to transition agreements/assets back to Customer or Customer's designee)? How will financial responsibility be allocated?

18. Performance Standards
    * Identify those services which will have performance standards (e.g., paycheck delivery, customer service).
    * How will Vendor's performance be measured? Will existing performance standards be used or will performance standards be established on a going forward basis?
    * Identify any permitted downtime and testing.
    * How will failures to meet performance standards be handled (e.g., liquidated damages or termination)?
    * Will there be any procedures for assessing/determining causes of failures to meet performance standards (e.g., root cause analysis)?
    * What performance standards will apply during transition/implementation?

19. Customer Satisfaction
    * Will Vendor be responsible for any type of customer satisfaction reporting?
    * Determine pool of employees surveyed (e.g., management, end-users).
    * How will the results of such surveys be used (e.g., as basis for performance standard)?

20. Benchmarking
    * Determine whether the agreement will include any benchmarking procedures (e.g., benchmarking of services or prices).
    * Develop benchmarking procedures (e.g., scope of benchmark, group against which services/prices will be benchmarked).
    * Identify benchmarker (e.g., third party, Vendor group).
    * How will benchmarking results be reviewed and how will changes, if applicable, be implemented?

21. Gainsharing
    * Determine whether any gainsharing provisions will be included in the agreement (e.g., bonuses tied to stock price).
    * Develop procedures for implementing gainsharing agreement.
    * How will disputes be handled?

22. Compliance Issues
    * Identify any compliance issues arising from law, rule or regulation, including ERISA issues.
    * Are there any year 2000 issues? Will Vendor have any year 2000 remediation responsibilities?
    * Are there any Euro compliance issues?
    * Determine which party is responsible for ensuring compliance. Allocate costs of compliance due to changes in laws, rules or regulations after commencement.
    * Identify any license/permits required to be obtained by Customer and/or Vendor.
    * Consult with legal, regulatory, tax and audit departments.

23. Customer Responsibilities
    - Identify Customer's responsibilities (e.g., provision of supplies, computers, parking).
    - Will Customer be providing any space/facilities to house Vendor's employees? What are the terms of Vendor's use (e.g., sublease)?
    - Is Customer retaining staff necessary to perform the retained responsibilities (e.g., management, definition of requirements, approvals)?

24. Service Locations
    - Where will Vendor be providing the services from? If such locations are not Customer locations, are there any restrictions on where Vendor may provide services from?
    - Will the service locations be dedicated to Customer or shared facilities?
    - Describe physical security requirements. Are uniforms or other identification required? Does Customer or Vendor have specific codes of conduct?
    - How will breaches of security be handled?
    - Are there any environmental issues?

25. Management Procedures
    - Will the parties develop management procedures to be used in connection with the provision of the services?
    - How will change control be handled?

26. Reports
    - Identify the performance and other reports that Customer currently generates or receives with respect to the services being outsourced.
    - Identify those reports that Customer wishes to receive from Vendor.
    - Establish deadlines for each report.
    - Will Customer be required to review the reports within a specific time period?
    - How will errors in reports be handled?
    - Identify record retention requirements.

27. Data
    - Discuss procedures for handling Customer data. Identify any laws/regulations pertaining to data privacy. What are Vendor's access rights? Is employee consent/notice required?
    - How will errors in Customer data be handled?
    - Describe data security requirements at service locations. Are passwords required?
    - How will breaches of security be handled?

28. Proprietary Rights
    - Establish Vendor's right to use Customer proprietary methodologies and technology during the term and after expiration/termination of the agreement.
    - Establish Vendor's right to use during the term and after expiration/termination of the agreement methodologies and technology licensed by Customer from third parties and used in connection with the provision of the services.
    - Establish Customer's right to use Vendor's proprietary methodologies and technology during the term and after expiration/termination of the agreement.
    - Establish Customer's right to use during the term and after expiration/termination of the agreement methodologies and technology licensed by Vendor from third parties and used in connection with the provision of the services.

- Establish each party's ownership/use rights with respect to methodologies and technology developed or acquired as part of or in connection with the provision of the services.
- Establish any restrictions governing the use of confidential information.
- Establish any restrictions governing the use of mentally retained information.
- Discuss whether noncompetition provisions are appropriate.

29. Audit
    - What are Customer's rights to audit the services and the service locations? How often may Customer exercise any such audit rights?
    - How will the results of any such audit be dealt with?
    - What are Customer's rights to audit the fees?
    - How will overpayments/underpayments be handled?
    - Will interest be charged?

30. Fees
    - Determine the applicable fee structure.
    - Customer should assess actual cost savings, if any. Such analysis should include any new taxes, employee transfer costs and other expenses resulting from the outsourcing.
    - Vendor should assess actual profit margin.
    - Other Fee Provisions:
      - If a base fee structure is used, determine structure for increasing and decreasing fees/resources.
      - Determine the rights of the parties to set off monies owed.
      - To what extent, if any, will Customer be responsible for Vendor expenses, e.g., travel? Will Vendor use Customer or Vendor expense guidelines?
      - Will there be any cost of living adjustments?
      - For international deals, is there any currency risk?
      - Consider a most favored customer provision.
      - How will fees be paid, e.g., in what currency, in what manner and according to what schedule?
      - How, when and to what Customer entity(ies) will invoices be issued? Determine the degree of detail to be included on invoices.
      - How will disputed fees/credits be handled, e.g., escrow? What are the parties' obligations to perform in the event of a dispute?
      - How will changes in business volumes be handled?

31. Taxes
    - Determine liability for sales, use, and other taxes.
    - Determine liability for additional taxes resulting from Vendor's relocation of service locations or rerouting of services.

32. Additional Services
    - How will the provision of additional services be handled? Will Vendor be required to submit a bid? Will there be any rights of first refusal granted to Vendor?
    - What type of detail must be included in a Vendor proposal?
    - To what extent does Customer wish to reserve the right to contract with third parties?

33. Insurance
    - Specify Vendor's insurance requirements, e.g.:

- Errors and omissions
- Liability
- Worker's compensation
- Automobile
- Specify any specific bonding requirements.
- Determine whether any parental or other type of guarantee is appropriate.

34. Termination
   - Consider early termination rights, e.g.:
     - Termination for convenience in whole
     - Partial termination for convenience
     - Termination upon change of control of Vendor
     - Termination upon change of control of Customer
     - Termination for breach
     - Termination for nonpayment
     - Termination for failure to provide critical services
     - Termination for failure to meet the performance standards
     - Termination for substantial changes in business
     - Termination upon the occurrence of a regulatory event
     - Cross-termination with other agreements
   - Determine whether and in what instances termination fees are applicable. If so, establish formula for determining applicable termination fees.

35. Exit Rights
   - Determine each party's ongoing rights after expiration/termination with respect to proprietary and third-party methodologies, technology, equipment, facilities, subcontracting arrangements, and third-party service agreements.
   - Determine which party will be responsible for transfer/assignment fees imposed by third parties.
   - If Customer has right to purchase certain Vendor assets used to provide the services, how will the purchase price be determined?

36. Termination Assistance
   - Determine the types of assistance Vendor and/or its subcontractors will provide Customer upon expiration/termination.
   - Determine duration of Vendor's termination assistance obligations.
   - How will termination assistance be paid for (e.g., fee schedule, time schedule for payment)?

37. Liability Provisions
   - Assess liability exposure.
   - Determine any liquidated damages to be imposed upon Vendor (e.g., for failure to meet performance standards, for failure to meet implementation schedules).
   - What are each party's indemnification obligations (e.g., for claims of infringement, employee claims).
   - Determine the representations and warranties to be made by each party.

38. Dispute Resolution
   - How will disputes be handled? Will the agreement include an escalation procedure?
   - Will unresolved disputes be handled through arbitration or litigation?

39. Business Recovery
    * Will Vendor have any business recovery responsibilities?
    * What are Customer's existing business recovery plan? Will Customer's plans be terminated?
    * Specify response times for delivery of business recovery services. Describe escalation procedures.

40. Assignment
    * Specify each party's right to assign its rights/obligations under the agreement in whole or in part.
    * Will there be any special assignment rights in the event of a merger/acquisition/divestiture?
    * May either party assign to an affiliate/related entity?

41. Solicitation of Employees
    * Will there be any limitations/restrictions on Customer's or Vendor's right to solicit and/or hire the other party's employees?
    * When will such limitations/restrictions apply (e.g., during the term, after expiration/termination)?
    * Will there be any exceptions for blind solicitations (e.g., newspaper advertisements)?

42. Miscellaneous Provisions
    * *Notices*: How will notices be given (e.g., by hand, by facsimile)? To whom (e.g., to business manager and/or counsel)?
    * *Publicity*: Limitations/restrictions on each party's ability to make public statements regarding the other party and/or the transaction.
    * *Governing Law*: Determine which state/country law will govern the transaction (or if international transaction with multiple documents, determine which law will govern each part of the transaction).
    * *Venue*: Will there be a requirement that any action be brought in a particular venue?
    * *Import/Export*: Provide any limitations/restrictions on the export/import of data and/or technology.
    * *Interpretation of Documents*: How will the transaction documents be interpreted in the event of a dispute (e.g., the main agreement will take precedence over the exhibits/schedules, change orders will take precedence over earlier dated documents)?
    * *Counterparts*: Specify whether the various transaction documents may be executed in counterparts.
    * *Relationship of the Parties*: Specify that Vendor is an independent contractor to Customer and that the provision of services does not constitute any type of partnership or joint venture (unless that is expressly the intent).
    * *Severability*: Specify that if any provision is held to be invalid that the remaining provisions shall remain in full force and effect.
    * *Waivers*: Specify that any delay or omission does not constitute a waiver of rights and that any waiver should not be construed to be a waiver of a subsequent breach/covenant.
    * *Entire Agreement*: Specify that the transaction documents constitute the entire agreement between the parties.

- *Amendments*: Specify how the transaction documents may be amended (e.g., by writing signed by both parties).
- *Survival*: Specify which provisions of the agreement will survive termination and/or expiration of the agreement.
- *Third Party Beneficiaries*: Expressly state that there will not be any third-party beneficiaries under the transaction documents or, if there will be third-party beneficiaries, identify such beneficiaries.
- *Covenant of Further Assurances*: Expressly state that each party will execute any documents or perform any actions necessary to effectuate the purposes of the agreement.

CHECKLIST: KEY ISSUES IN THE BPO AGREEMENTS (WAREHOUSE MANAGEMENT SERVICES)[a]

KEY ISSUES IN
BUSINESS PROCESS OUTSOURCING AGREEMENTS
(WAREHOUSE MANAGEMENT SERVICES)

1. Structure of the Warehouse Management Agreement
   * How will the agreement be structured?
     * A single services agreement
     * A single services agreement for multiple facilities
     * A master agreement with facility-specific, country-specific, or entity-specific service agreements
     * Separate agreements for business process reengineering, development and ongoing warehouse management
     * Separate agreements documenting the terms applicable to a joint venture/ strategic alliance relationship and the terms of ongoing warehouse management services
   * What is the interrelationship between these agreements if separate, e.g., cross-termination, payment?
   * Factors that may affect the agreement structure include:
     * Scope of services: will Vendor be providing any business process re-engineering or development services?
     * Geographic scope: single country vs. international agreement
     * The number of facilities: will agreement cover one or multiple facilities?
     * Scope of services at specific facilities: will all Customer facilities receive the same services or will each Customer facility receive different services?
     * Types of entities receiving/delivering the services: is the contracting entity for each of the parties able to bind the entities that will receive/deliver the services or must each of the recipient/delivering entities agree to be bound by the master agreement?

---

[a] Note: This checklist is intended to illustrate the types of legal issues that may arise in connection with warehouse management outsourcing transactions. The issues identified in this checklist, while comprehensive, may not cover all of the issues relevant to a particular transaction. Legal issues will vary depending on the type of business process being outsourced and the scope of the outsourcing transaction. This checklist or any part thereof should only be used after consultation with your legal counsel. You should consult legal counsel prior to entering into or negotiating any outsourcing transaction.

- Cost allocation: are there any cost allocation requirements internal to customer that would drive separate facility/entity agreements?
- Taxes: are there any tax requirements that would drive separate service agreements?

2. Contracting Party
   - Who will sign the agreement on behalf of Customer? On behalf of Vendor?
   - If there is a master agreement with separate service agreements, will the same party that signs the master agreement, sign the service agreements?

3. Entities Receiving Services from Vendor
   - Determine who will receive services from Vendor
   - Entities may include:
     - Customer affiliates
     - Joint ventures/alliances
     - Contractors
     - Suppliers
     - Clients of Customer
   - Will Customer have the option of adding/deleting entities/facilities over the term?
   - How will mergers/acquisitions/divestitures be handled? What will Customer's and Vendor's ongoing obligations be?
   - Which entity(ies) will have payment obligations? Are recipients of services third-party beneficiaries?

4. Entities Providing Services to Customer
   - Determine which entity (or entities) will provide the services to Customer.
   - Will there be any subcontracting/teaming relationships?
   - For international deals, how will Vendor provide resources/services in each country? Will Vendor use affiliated entities or subcontractors?
   - What are Customer's rights to approve/remove subcontractors?
   - Which entity(ies) will have performance/indemnification obligations?

5. Term
   - What is the commencement date of services? Will there be one commencement date for all facilities? Will there be one commencement date for all services (e.g., business process reengineering, development and ongoing warehouse management services)?
   - How long is the term of the agreement? If the transaction includes multiple agreements, are all of the agreements co-terminus? If there is a master agreement with separate facility/service agreements, are all of the agreements co-terminus?
   - Will there be a pilot period?
   - What are each party's renewal rights? What type of notice is required for renewal?

6. Scope of Services
   - Determine the general scope of services to be provided by Vendor. For example:
     - General Warehouse Services
     - Transportation Management (inbound)
     - Receiving of Inbound Products
     - Storage
     - Order-pricing
     - Shipment of Orders
     - Inventory Management

- Packaging
- Product disposal
- Procurement of materials
- Handling equipment/supplies
- Determine those services which will be provided in-house by Customer or to Customer by a third party.
- Describe in detail the services (typically by service category) to be provided by Vendor. For example:
  - General Warehouse Services
    — Schedule orders
    — Pick and pack product
    — Schedule inbound deliveries (e.g., monitoring inbound notifications, scheduling deliveries, planning and managing trailer yard and delivery door activities, maintaining yard and carrier delivery data)
    — Unload and locate finished product from inbound trailers/containers
    — Consolidate and store products
    — Provide supply chain reporting
  - Transportation Management (inbound)
    — Monitor arrival and accuracy of import and shipment documentation (bill of landing, invoice, c/o, and packing list)
    — Contact carrier/forwarder and schedule delivery
    — Monitor and document carrier/forwarder performance and compliance
    — Participate in carrier/forwarder review
    — Provide Customer with shipping reports and information
    — Insurance and claim management
  - Receiving of inbound products
    — Customer will ship products to itself in care of Vendor
    — Check for over, short and damaged items
    — Accept/reject items
    — Issue claims
    — Add to inventory
  - Shipment of Orders
    — Receive order
    — Check inventory
    — Adjust inventory
    — Check and comply with insurance and delivery requirements
    — Ship product
    — Receive returns
  - Inventory Management
    — Provide audit trail of inventory adjustments
    — Create inventory swap shots for inventory reconciliation
    — Perform cycle counts
- Define Customer's responsibilities with respect to the services to be provided by Vendor (i.e., definition of requirements, strategic direction, approvals).
- Define existing and future requirements (e.g., capacity requirements, volume changes, business changes). Allocate managerial and financial responsibility.

7. Service Locations
   - Where will Vendor be providing the services from? If such locations are not Customer locations, are there any restrictions on where Vendor may provide services from?

- Will the service locations be dedicated to Customer or shared facilities?
- Describe physical security requirements. Are uniforms or other identification required? Does Customer or Vendor have specific codes of conduct?
- How will breaches of security be handled?

8. Assets/Facilities
   - Will Vendor be purchasing/leasing any of Customer's assets (e.g., equipment, real estate)? If so, when will purchase be made (e.g., on date of signing)?
   - For asset purchase transactions, how will assets be valued (e.g., book value, fair market value)?
   - Is the transfer of assets necessary in conjunction with the transfer of employees in order to constitute an "automatic transfer" under the particular country's employment/redundancy laws?
   - Will Customer or Vendor have any construction obligations, e.g.:
     - Site preparation
     - Building construction
     - Fixture installation
     - Electrical work
   - Are there any environmental issues? (*see* #24 below)

9. Transition Plan
   - How will the transition of services to Vendor be handled?
   - Will there be any redundant/parallel environments?
   - Determine the performance standards during transition.
   - How long will the transition period be?

10. Methodologies
    - Assess methodologies to be used by Vendor. Are the methodologies proprietary to Vendor or licensed from a third party? If licensed from a third party, are there any use restrictions? What are Customer's rights to use during the term and after expiration/termination?
    - Will any of Customer's methodologies continue to be used during the term of the transaction? What are Vendor's use rights (e.g., use in connection with services to Customer only; use in connection with other customers)?
    - How will Vendor transition Customer to Vendor's methodologies (if applicable)?
    - How will the methodologies introduced by Vendor be integrated with Customer's existing and future methodologies (with respect to the applicable business function as well as other business areas, e.g., information systems)?
    - Will Vendor be developing/providing any new methodologies? If so, how will ownership/use rights be allocated? How will new methodologies be rolled out (e.g., define time period, consequences for failure to meet deadlines, each party's responsibilities)?

11. Technology
    - Assess technology to be used by Vendor (e.g., outline inventory system). Is the technology proprietary to Vendor or licensed from a third party? If licensed from a third party, are there any use restrictions? What are Customer's rights to use during the term and after expiration/termination?
    - Will any of Customer's technology continue to be used during the term of the transaction? What are Vendor's use rights (e.g., use in connection with services to Customer only; use in connection with other customers)?

- Will the environment be dedicated/shared?
- How will Vendor transition Customer to Vendor's technology (if applicable)?
- How will the technology introduced by Vendor be integrated with Customer's existing or future technology, e.g., is Vendor technology compatible with technology used by Customer's information system group?
- Will Vendor be developing/providing any new technology? If so, how will ownership/use rights be allocated? How will new technology be rolled out (e.g., define time period, consequences for failure to meet deadlines, each party's responsibilities)?

12. Projects
    - Identify any projects that Vendor will be responsible for implementing/managing as part of the transaction.
    - Will Vendor be responsible for any business process reengineering in connection with its provision of warehouse management services? If so, what are each party's responsibilities? What are the consequences if the re-engineering is not successful or performed by deadlines specified?
    - What is the inter-relationship of Vendor's business process reengineering responsibilities and Vendor's warehouse management service responsibilities (e.g., are they cross-terminable)?
    - Will Vendor be responsible for any new implementations? If so, what are each party's responsibilities? What are the consequences if the reengineering is not successful or performed by deadlines specified?
    - Which party will be responsible for purchase/license of third-party methodologies/technologies (if applicable)?

13. Integration
    - How will the methodologies/technologies introduced by Vendor be integrated with other methodologies/technologies used by Customer?
    - Have other Customer business areas been contacted for input (e.g., information systems, human resources)?

14. Transfer of Employees
    - Determine whether any or all Customer employees will be offered employment by, or transitioned to, Vendor or a Vendor subcontractor.
    - Identify group of retained employees.
    - Review Customer's severance/redundancy policy, if any, to determine whether a transition to Vendor may invoke severance obligations. (If so, factor into Customer's cost analysis.)
    - Are there any claims with respect to any of the transitioned employees?
    - Compare Customer and Vendor benefits. Are any adjustments necessary?
    - Does Vendor require any special screening of employees (e.g., drug testing)?
    - Will Vendor require transitioned employees to sign an employment agreement?
    - Develop an employee communication plan.
    - Determine whether any stay bonuses/incentives are necessary.

15. Project Staff
    - Identify management structure of Vendor as well as Customer in connection with the provision/receipt of services.
    - Are there any limitations/restrictions with respect to reassignment/replacement of key Vendor personnel?
    - Are there any limitations/restrictions with respect to "churning" of employees?

- How will Customer complaints regarding Vendor personnel be handled?
- Are there any special clearances of Vendor personnel necessary?
- Are there any limitations/restrictions with respect to subcontractors?

16. Retained Assets
    - Identify which assets Vendor will manage and, of those assets, which assets Vendor will have financial responsibility for.
    - Identify which assets Customer will continue to manage and, of those assets, whether Vendor will have any financial responsibility.
    - How will the parties act in the event it is not clear where a problem originates from (e.g., root cause analysis)?

17. Agreements to be Reviewed
    - Identify any third-party agreements/relationships that may be impacted by the outsourcing, including:
      - Maintenance agreements
      - Subcontracting relationships
      - Other service agreements
      - Methodology/technology licenses
      - Equipment/asset leases
      - Real estate leases/subleases
    - Are there any restrictions with respect to third-party management/access or assignment to a third party?
    - What are the terms relating to termination/renewal?
    - What are the pricing terms and will they be impacted by the transaction?
    - Develop a strategy for notifying third parties, if applicable.

18. Third-Party Consents
    - Are any third-party consents necessary in connection with the commencement of the transaction? If so, which party is responsible for obtaining such consents and how will financial responsibility be allocated?
    - How will third-party consents be obtained upon the expiration/termination of the transaction (in order to transition agreements/assets back to Customer or Customer's designee)? How will financial responsibility be allocated?

19. Performance Standards
    - Identify those services which will have performance standards (e.g., inventory accuracy, inventory damage, order picking, delivery).
    - How will Vendor's performance be measured? Will existing performance standards be used or will performance standards be established on a going forward basis?
    - Identify any permitted downtime and testing.
    - How will failures to meet performance standards be handled (e.g., liquidated damages or termination)?
    - Will there be any procedures for assessing/determining causes of failures to meet performance standards (e.g., root cause analysis)?
    - What performance standards will apply during transition/implementation?

20. Customer Satisfaction
    - Will Vendor be responsible for any type of customer satisfaction reporting?
    - Determine pool of employees surveyed (e.g., management, end-users).
    - How will the results of such surveys be used (e.g., as basis for performance standard)?

21. Benchmarking
    * Determine whether the agreement will include any benchmarking procedures (e.g., benchmarking of services or prices).
    * Develop benchmarking procedures (e.g., scope of benchmark, group against which services/prices will be benchmarked).
    * Identify benchmarker (e.g., third party, Vendor group).
    * How will benchmarking results be reviewed and how will changes, if applicable, be implemented?

22. Gainsharing
    * Determine whether any gainsharing provisions will be included in the agreement (e.g., bonuses tied to stock price).
    * Develop procedures for implementing gainsharing agreement.
    * How will disputes be handled?

23. Compliance Issues
    * Identify any regulatory requirements.
    * Is Vendor considered a "freight forwarder" as defined under the U.S. Code? If so what is impact of Code on parties rights and liabilities?
    * Identify any regulatory/governmental requirements (e.g., OSHA requirements).
    * Are there any year 2000 issues? Will Vendor have any year 2000 remediation responsibilities?
    * Are there any Euro compliance issues?
    * Determine which party is responsible for ensuring compliance. Allocate costs of compliance due to changes in laws, rules, or regulations after commencement.
    * Identify any license/permits required to be obtained by Customer and/or Vendor.
    * Consult with legal, regulatory, tax, and audit departments.

24. Environmental
    * Are there any environmental compliance issues (e.g., with respect to product destruction or disposal)?
    * Will Vendor be handling any hazardous materials?

25. Liens
    * What liens will attach to facilities or products by law (e.g., warehouseman lien)? Can any of these liens be waived?
    * What is risk of Vendor's subcontractors/creditors placing a lien on Customer's products?

26. Customer Responsibilities
    * Identify Customer's responsibilities (e.g., provision of supplies, computers, parking).
    * Will Customer be providing any space/facilities to house Vendor's employees? What are the terms of Vendor's use (e.g., sublease)?
    * Is Customer retaining staff necessary to perform the retained responsibilities (e.g., management, definition of requirements, approvals)?

27. Management Procedures
    * Will the parties develop management procedures to be used in connection with the provision of the services?
    * How will change control be handled?

28. Reports
    - Identify the performance and other reports that Customer currently generates or receives with respect to the services being outsourced.
    - Identify those reports that Customer wishes to receive from Vendor.
    - Establish deadlines for each report.
    - Will Customer be required to review the reports within a specific time period?
    - How will errors in reports be handled?

29. Data
    - Discuss procedures for handling Customer data. What are Vendor's use rights?
    - How will errors in Customer data be handled?
    - Describe data security requirements at service locations. Are passwords required?
    - How will breaches of security be handled?

30. Proprietary Rights
    - Determine ownership of any improvements made to warehouse facilities.
    - Establish each party's right to use proprietary and third-party methodologies and technology during the term and after expiration/termination of the agreement.
    - Establish each party's ownership/use rights with respect to methodologies and technology developed or acquired as part of or in connection with the provision of the services.
    - Determine ownership of work product (e.g., models, illustrations, documents, analyses, drawings, and specifications).
    - Establish any restrictions governing the use of confidential information.
    - Establish any restrictions governing the use of mentally retained information.
    - Discuss whether noncompetition provisions are appropriate.

31. Audit
    - What are Customer's rights to audit the services and the service locations? How often may Customer exercise any such audit rights?
    - How will the results of any such audit be dealt with?
    - What are Customer's rights to audit the fees?
    - How will overpayments/underpayments be handled?
    - Will interest be charged?

32. Fees
    - Determine the applicable fee structure (e.g., fee based on number of items stripped and/or cost per unit).
    - Customer should assess actual cost savings, if any. Such analysis should include any new taxes, employee transfer costs, and other expenses resulting from the outsourcing.
    - Vendor should assess actual profit margin.
    - Other Fee Provisions:
        - If a base fee structure is used, determine structure for increasing and decreasing fees/resources.
        - Determine the rights of the parties to set off monies owed.
        - To what extent, if any, will Customer be responsible for Vendor expenses, e.g., travel? Will Vendor use Customer or Vendor expense guidelines?
        - Will there be any cost-of-living adjustments?
        - For international deals, is there any currency risk?
        - Consider a most favored customer provision.

- How will fees be paid, e.g., in what currency, in what manner and according to what schedule?
- How, when and to what Customer entity(ies) will invoices be issued? Determine the degree of detail to be included on invoices.
- How will disputed fees/credits be handled (e.g., escrow)? What are the parties' obligations to perform in the event of a dispute?
- How will changes in business volumes be handled?

33. Taxes
    - Determine liability for sales, use and other taxes.
    - Determine liability for additional taxes resulting from Vendor's relocation of service locations or rerouting of services.

34. Additional Services
    - How will the provision of additional services be handled? Will Vendor be required to submit a bid? Will there be any rights of first refusal granted to Vendor?
    - What type of detail must be included in a Vendor proposal?
    - To what extent does Customer wish to reserve the right to contract with third parties?

35. Risk of Loss
    - When will Vendor assume responsibility to loss of/damage to products received by Vendor? For example:
      - Upon acceptance from shipper/carrier at the warehouse distribution facilities
      - Damage/loss due to poor facilities management, improper storage or handling
      - Damage/loss due to employee theft or fraud
    - When will Customer be responsible for loss of/damage to products? For example:
      - Improper packaging
      - Breakage
      - Crating
      - Wear and tear
      - Leakage
      - Force majeure event (i.e., acts of God, fire, flood, moths, vermin)

36. Insurance
    - Specify each party's insurance requirements, e.g.:
      - Errors and omissions
      - Commercial general liability
      - Worker's compensation
      - Automobile
      - "All risks" property
      - Warehouse legal liability
      - Theft
      - Casualty
    - Specify any specific bonding requirements.
    - Determine whether any parental or other type of guarantee is appropriate.

37. Termination
    - Consider early termination rights, e.g.:
      - Termination for convenience in whole
      - Partial termination for convenience

- Termination upon change of control of Vendor
- Termination upon change of control of Customer
- Termination for breach
- Termination for non-payment
- Termination of lease
- Termination for failure to provide critical services
- Termination for failure to meet the performance standards
- Termination for substantial changes in business
- Cross-termination with other agreements
- Determine whether and in what instances termination fees are applicable. If so, establish formula for determining applicable termination fees.

38. Termination Obligations/Rights
    - Determine each party's ongoing rights after expiration/termination with respect to:
      - Proprietary and third-party methodologies
      - Proprietary and third-party technology
      - Equipment
      - Facilities
      - Subcontracting arrangements
      - Third-party service agreements
    - Determine which party will be responsible for transfer/assignment fees imposed by third parties.
    - If Customer has right to purchase certain Vendor assets used to provide the services, how will the purchase price be determined?

39. Termination Assistance
    - Determine the types of assistance Vendor and/or its subcontractors will provide Customer upon expiration/termination.
    - Determine duration of Vendor's termination assistance obligations.
    - How will termination assistance be paid for (e.g., fee schedule, time schedule for payment)?

40. Liability Provisions
    - Assess liability exposure.
    - Determine any liquidated damages to be imposed upon Vendor (e.g., for failure to meet performance standards, for failure to meet implementation schedules).
    - What are each party's indemnification obligations (e.g., for claims of infringement, employee claims).
    - Determine the representations and warranties to be made by each party.

41. Dispute Resolution
    - How will disputes be handled? Will the agreement include an escalation procedure?
    - Will unresolved disputes be handled through arbitration or litigation?

42. Business Recovery
    - Will Vendor have any business recovery responsibilities?
    - What are Customer's existing business recovery plan? Will Customer's plans be terminated?

* Specify response times for delivery of business recovery services. Describe escalation procedures.

43. Assignment
    * Specify each party's right to assign its rights/obligations under the agreement in whole or in part.
    * Will there be any special assignment rights in the event of a merger/acquisition/divestiture?
    * May either party assign to an affiliate/related entity?

44. Solicitation of Employees
    * Will there be any limitations/restrictions on Customer's or Vendor's right to solicit and/or hire the other party's employees?
    * When will such limitations/restrictions apply (e.g., during the term, after expiration/termination)?
    * Will there be any exceptions for blind solicitations (e.g., newspaper advertisements)?

45. Miscellaneous Provisions
    * *Notices*: How will notices be given (e.g., by hand, by facsimile)? To whom (e.g., to business manager and/or counsel)?
    * *Publicity*: Limitations/restrictions on each party's ability to make public statements regarding the other party and/or the transaction.
    * *Governing Law*: Determine which state/country law will govern the transaction (or if international transaction with multiple documents, determine which law will govern each part of the transaction).
    * *Venue*: Will there be a requirement that any action be brought in a particular venue?
    * *Import/Export*: Provide any limitations/restrictions on the export/import of data and/or technology.
    * *Interpretation of Documents*: How will the transaction documents be interpreted in the event of a dispute (e.g., the main agreement will take precedence over the exhibits/schedules, change orders will take precedence over earlier dated documents)?
    * *Counterparts*: Specify whether the various transaction documents may be executed in counterparts.
    * *Relationship of the Parties*: Specify that Vendor is an independent contractor to Customer and that the provision of services does not constitute any type of partnership or joint venture (unless that is expressly the intent)
    * *Severability*: Specify that if any provision is held to be invalid that the remaining provisions shall remain in full force and effect.
    * *Waivers*: Specify that any delay or omission does not constitute a waiver of rights and that any waiver should not be construed to be a waiver of a subsequent breach/covenant.
    * *Entire Agreement*: Specify that the transaction documents constitute the entire agreement between the parties.
    * *Amendments*: Specify how the transaction documents may be amended (e.g., by writing signed by both parties).
    * *Survival*: Specify which provisions of the agreement will survive termination and/or expiration of the agreement.

- *Third-Party Beneficiaries*: Expressly state that there will not be any third-party beneficiaries under the transaction documents or, if there will be third-party beneficiaries, identify such beneficiaries.
- *Covenant of Further Assurances*: Expressly state that each party will execute any documents or perform any actions necessary to effect the purposes of the agreement.

Appendix 5.5

CHECKLIST: KEY ISSUES IN BPO AGREEMENTS (PROPERTY MANAGEMENT SERVICES)[a]

KEY ISSUES IN
BUSINESS PROCESS OUTSOURCING AGREEMENTS
(PROPERTY MANAGEMENT SERVICES)

1. Structure of the Property Management Agreement
   - How will the agreement be structured?
     - A single services agreement for a single property
     - A singe services agreement for multiple properties
     - A master agreement with property-specific, country-specific, or entity-specific service agreements
     - Separate agreements for different services (e.g., cafeteria, security, parking)
     - Separate agreements documenting the terms applicable to a joint venture/ strategic alliance relationship and the terms applicable to ongoing property management services
   - What is the inter-relationship between these agreements if separate, e.g., cross-termination, payment?
   - Factors that may affect the agreement structure include:
     - Scope of services: will one manager be providing full service outsourcing services or will there be multiple managers?
     - Number of properties: will there be more than one property being outsourced?
     - Scope of services at specific properties: will all Owner properties receive the same services or will each Owner property receive different services?
     - Geographic scope: single country vs. international agreement
     - Types of entities receiving/delivering the services: is the contracting entity for each of the parties able to bind the entities that will receive/deliver the services or must each of the recipient/delivering entities agree to be bound by the master agreement?

---

[a] Note: This checklist is intended to illustrate the types of legal issues that may arise in connection with property management outsourcing transactions. The issues identified in this checklist, while comprehensive, may not cover all of the issues relevant to a particular transaction. Legal issues will vary depending on the type of business process being outsourced and the scope of the outsourcing transaction. This checklist or any part thereof should only be used after consultation with your legal counsel. You should consult legal counsel prior to entering into or negotiating any outsourcing transaction.

- Cost allocation: are there any cost allocation requirements internal to customer that would drive separate property/entity agreements?
- Taxes: are there any tax requirements that would drive separate service agreements?

2. Contracting Party
   - Who will sign the agreement on behalf of Owner? On behalf of Manager?
   - If there is a master agreement with separate service agreements, will the same party that signs the master agreement, sign the service agreements?

3. Entities Providing Services to Owner
   - Determine which entity (or entities) will provide the services to Owner.
   - Will there be any subcontracting/teaming relationships?
   - For international deals, how will Manager provide resources/services in each country? Will Manager use affiliated entities or subcontractors?
   - What are Owner's rights to approve/remove subcontractors?
   - Which entity(ies) will have performance/indemnification obligations?

4. Term
   - What is the commencement date of services (e.g., the date on which the owner acquires fee title to the property)? Will there be one commencement date for all services? If there are multiple properties, will there be one commencement date for all properties?
   - How long is the term of the agreement? If the transaction includes multiple agreements, are all of the agreements co-terminus? If there is a master agreement with separate site/service agreements, are all of the agreements co-terminus?
   - Will there be a pilot period?
   - What are each party's renewal rights? What type of notice is required for renewal?

5. Scope of Services
   - Determine the general scope of services to be provided by Manager (e.g., operation, maintenance and repair of the property).
   - What are Manager's obligations with respect to:
     - Tenants, Licensees, Concessionaires and Other Occupants, and Users of the Property
     - Collection of Rents and Charges (including office rental, retail rental, storage space rental, escalation rentals, utility charges, vending machines, pay telephones, parking charges, merchant association dues, common area maintenance charges)
     - Compliance with Leases
     - Compliance with Insurance Requirements
     - Leasing of Space (including design and production of advertising and leasing materials, placement of advertising)
   - Determine those services which will be provided in-house by Owner or to Owner by a third party.
   - Describe in detail the services (typically by service category) to be provided by Manager. For example, maintenance and repair may include:
     - Interior and Exterior Cleaning
     - Painting and Decorating
     - Plumbing
     - Carpentry

- Define Owner's responsibilities with respect to the services to be provided by Manager (i.e., definition of requirements, strategic direction, approvals).
- Define existing and future requirements (e.g., capacity requirements, volume changes, business changes). Allocate managerial and financial responsibility.

6. Procurement
   - What are Vendor's procurement responsibilities?
   - Are there restrictions on the third-party vendors that Manager procures services or goods from (e.g., affiliates or agents)?
   - Are there any competitive bidding requirements?

7. Third Party Contracts
   - Identify any third-party agreements/relationships that may be impacted by the outsourcing, including:
     - Utility agreements (e.g., water, electricity, gas, telephone, extermination, trash removal, heating, ventilating, and or conditioning maintenance and security)
     - Maintenance agreements
     - Subcontracting relationships
     - Other service agreements
     - Methodology/technology licenses
     - Equipment/asset leases
     - Real estate leases/subleases
   - Will Customer retain any approval rights over the third-party contracts that Manager enters into on Owner's behalf (contracts over a certain amount)?
   - Are there any restrictions with respect to third-party management/access or assignment to a third party?
   - What are the terms relating to termination/renewal?
   - What are the pricing terms and will they be impacted by the transaction?
   - Develop a strategy for notifying third parties, if applicable.

8. Security
   - Describe physical security requirements. Are uniforms or other identification required? Does Owner or Manager have specific codes of conduct?
   - How will breaches of security be handled?

9. Transition Plan
   - How will the transition of services to Manager be handled?
   - Will there be any redundant/parallel environments?
   - Determine the performance standards during transition.
   - How long will the transition period be?

10. Techniques/Methodologies
    - Assess practices/techniques/methodologies to be used by Manager. Are the practices/techniques/methodologies proprietary to Manager or licensed from a third party? If licensed from a third party, are there any use restrictions? What are Owner's rights to use during the term and after expiration/termination?
    - Will any of Owner's practices/techniques/methodologies continue to be used during the term of the transaction? What are Manager's use rights (e.g., use in connection with services to Owner only; use in connection with other customers)?

- How will Manager transition Owner to Manager's practices/techniques/methodologies (if applicable)?
- Will Manager be developing/providing any new practices/techniques/methodologies? If so, how will ownership/use rights be allocated? How will new practices/techniques/methodologies be rolled out (e.g., define time period, consequences for failure to meet deadlines, each party's responsibilities)?

11. Technology
    - Assess technology to be used by Manager. Is the technology proprietary to Manager or licensed from a third party? If licensed from a third party, are there any use restrictions? What are Owner's rights to use during the term and after expiration/termination?
    - Will any of Owner's technology continue to be used during the term of the transaction? What are Manager's use rights (e.g., use in connection with services to Owner only; use in connection with other customers)?
    - Will the environment be dedicated/shared?
    - How will Manager transition Owner to Manager's technology (if applicable)?
    - How will the technology introduced by Manager be integrated with Owner's existing or future technology, e.g., is Manager technology compatible with technology used by Owner's information system group?
    - Will Manager be developing/providing any new technology? If so, how will ownership/use rights be allocated? How will new technology be rolled out (e.g., define time period, consequences for failure to meet deadlines, each party's responsibilities)?

12. Assets/Properties
    - Will Manager be purchasing any of Owner's assets (e.g., equipment, real estate)? If so, when will purchase be made (e.g., on date of signing)?
    - How will assets be valued (e.g., book value, fair market value)?
    - Is the transfer of assets necessary in conjunction with the transfer of employees in order to constitute an "automatic transfer" under the particular country's employment/redundancy laws?
    - What are Manager's construction obligations, e.g.:
      - Building installation
      - Fixture installation
      - Electrical work

13. Projects
    - Identify any projects that Manager will be responsible for implementing/managing as part of the transaction.
    - What is the inter-relationship of Manager's project responsibilities and Manager's service responsibilities (e.g., are they cross-terminable)?

14. Integration
    - How will the methodologies/technologies introduced by Manager be integrated with other methodologies/technologies used by Owner?
    - Have other Owner business areas been contacted for input (e.g., information systems, human resources)?

15. Transfer of Employees
    - Determine whether any or all Owner employees will be offered employment by or transitioned to Manager or a Manager subcontractor.

- Identify group of retained employees.
- Review Owner's severance/redundancy policy, if any, to determine whether a transition to Manager may invoke severance obligations. (If so, factor into Owner's cost analysis.)
- Are there any claims with respect to any of the transitioned employees?
- Compare Owner and Manager benefits. Are any adjustments necessary?
- Does Manager require any special screening of employees (e.g., drug testing)?
- Will Manager require transitioned employees to sign an employment agreement?
- Develop an employee communication plan.
- Determine whether any stay bonuses/incentives are necessary.

16. Project Staff
    - Identify management structure of Manager as well as Owner in connection with the provision/receipt of services.
    - Identify organizational structure of Manager (e.g., number/types of personnel).
    - Identify any union issues. Which party will be responsible for negotiating with applicable unions?
    - Are there any limitations/restrictions with respect to reassignment/replacement of key Manager personnel?
    - Are there any limitations/restrictions with respect to "churning" of employees?
    - How will Owner complaints regarding Manager personnel be handled?
    - Are there any special clearances of Manager personnel necessary?
    - Are there any limitations/restrictions with respect to subcontractors?

17. Retained Assets
    - Identify which assets Manager will manage and, of those assets, which assets Manager will have financial responsibility for.
    - Identify which assets Owner will continue to manage and, of those assets, whether Manager will have any financial responsibility.
    - How will the parties act in the event it is not clear where a problem originates from (e.g., root cause analysis)?

18. Third-Party Consents
    - Are any third-party consents necessary in connection with the commencement of the transaction? If so, which party is responsible for obtaining such consents and how will financial responsibility be allocated?
    - How will third-party consents be obtained upon the expiration/termination of the transaction (in order to transition agreements/assets back to Owner or Owner's designee)? How will financial responsibility be allocated?

19. Performance Standards
    - Identify those services which will have performance standards.
    - How will Manager's performance be measured? Will existing performance standards be used or will performance standards be established on a going-forward basis?
    - Identify any permitted downtime and testing.
    - How will failures to meet performance standards be handled (e.g., liquidated damages or termination)?
    - Will there be any procedures for assessing/determining causes of failures to meet performance standards (e.g., root cause analysis)?
    - What performance standards will apply during transition/implementation?

20. Customer Satisfaction
    - Will Manager be responsible for any type of customer satisfaction reporting?
    - Determine pool of employees surveyed (e.g., management, end-users).
    - How will the results of such surveys be used (e.g., as basis for performance standard)?

21. Benchmarking
    - Determine whether the agreement will include any benchmarking procedures (e.g., benchmarking of services or prices).
    - Develop benchmarking procedures (e.g., scope of benchmark, group against which services/prices will be benchmarked).
    - Identify benchmarker (e.g., third party, Manager group).
    - How will benchmarking results be reviewed and how will changes, if applicable, be implemented?

22. Gainsharing
    - Determine whether any gainsharing provisions will be included in the agreement (e.g., bonuses tied to stock price).
    - Develop procedures for implementing gainsharing agreement.
    - How will disputes be handled?

23. Compliance Issues
    - Identify any regulatory requirements.
    - Identify any federal, state, and municipal requirements relating to the leasing, use, operation repair, and maintenance of the property. Are there any special bodies whose rules/regulations govern the services to be provided, e.g., local Board of Five Underwriters, State Fire Marshal.
    - Are there any year 2000 issues? Will Vendor have any year 2000 remediation responsibilities?
    - Are there any Euro compliance issues?
    - Identify any mortgage compliance issues.
    - Determine which party is responsible for ensuring compliance. Allocate costs of compliance due to changes in laws, rules, or regulations after commencement.
    - Identify any license/permits required to be obtained by Owner and/or Manager.
    - Consult with legal, regulatory, tax, and audit departments.

24. Environmental
    - Are there any environmental compliance issues?
    - Will Manager be handling or be exposed to any hazardous materials?

25. Owner Responsibilities
    - Identify Owner's responsibilities, e.g., provision of:
      - Office space
      - Supplies
      - Computers
      - Parking
    - Will Owner be providing any space/facilities to house Manager's employees? What are the terms of Manager's use (e.g., sublease)?
    - Is Owner retaining staff necessary to perform the retained responsibilities (e.g., management, definition of requirements, approvals)?

26. Management and Control
    - Will each party identify an individual to be the "Contract Manager"? Who will be the primary contact person?
    - Will Customer wish to retain the right to appoint an individual or organization to serve as its "manager" of the property management services agreement?
    - Will the parties develop management procedures to be used in connection with the provision of the services?
    - How will change control be handled?

27. Records/Reports
    - Specify Manager's recording requirements.
    - Which documents will Manager be required to maintain in connection with the operation and management of the property, e.g.:
        - Statements
        - Receipts
        - Invoices
        - Checks
        - Leases
        - Contracts
        - Worksheets
        - Financial statements
        - Books and records
    - Specify Manager's reporting requirements, e.g., preparation of monthly, quarterly and annual operation reports. Items that may be included in such reports may include:
        - Key operational and financial matters (including financial and physical condition of the property)
        - Balance sheet
        - Statement of income and expense
        - Cash flow statement
        - Budget vs. Actual variance report
        - Bank statements and reconciliations
        - Accounts receivable listing
        - Status report on capital improvements, tenant improvements, and leasing commissions
        - Accounts payable listing
        - Annual review and analysis of all recovery income accruals
        - Fees payable to manager
        - Rent roll
        - Lease expiration report
        - Space availability report
        - Site plans with tenant information
        - Property maintenance report
        - Cash receipts and disbursements journals
        - Monthly general ledgers
        - Invoices for capital expenditures and unrecurring items
        - Paid bills
        - Trial balance
        - Record of all security deposits
        - Theft, error or intentional misconduct (e.g., Theft of assets; penalties, interest and loss due to late payment; overpayments; unauthorized use of facilities)

- Will Owner be required to review the reports within a specific time period?
- How will errors in reports be handled?

28. Data
    - Discuss procedures for handling Owner and tenant data. What are Manager's use rights?
    - How will errors in Owner and tenant data be handled?
    - Describe data security requirements at service locations. Are passwords required?
    - How will breaches of security be handled?

29. Proprietary Rights
    - Determine which party will own books, records, computer disks, invoices, and other documents prepared or acquired in connection with the property management services agreement.
    - Establish Manager's right to use proprietary and third-party methodologies and technology during the term and after expiration/termination of the agreement.
    - Establish each party's ownership/use rights with respect to methodologies and technology developed or acquired as part of or in connection with the provision of the services.
    - Establish any restrictions governing the use of confidential information.
    - Establish any restrictions governing the use of mentally retained information.
    - Discuss whether noncompetition provisions are appropriate.

30. Audit
    - What are Owner's rights to audit the services and the service locations? How often may Owner exercise any such audit rights?
    - How will the results of any such audit be dealt with?
    - What are Owner's rights to audit the fees?
    - How will overpayments/underpayments be handled?
    - Will interest be charged?

31. Fees
    - Determine the applicable fee structure (e.g., management fee, reimbursement of personnel expenses and other costs).
      Examples of reimbursable expenses:
        - Salary and wages, payroll taxes, insurance, worker's compensation, and other benefits
        - Printed forms and supplies used at the property
        - Real estate and personal property taxes and improvement assessments
        - Correction of any violation of federal, state, and municipal laws/regulations
        - Repairs, decorations and alterations
        - Capital expenditures
        - Leasing commissions payable to third parties
        - Utilities
        - Service and related contracts
        - Rent collection
        - Insurance premiums
        - Consultants
      Examples of non-reimbursable expenses:
        - General accounting and reporting services

- Printed forms and supplies not used at the property
- Computers
- Travel
- Equipment used by Manager to perform duties
- Will there be an "approved budget"?
- Owner should assess actual cost savings, if any. Such analysis should include any new taxes, employee transfer costs, and other expenses resulting from the outsourcing.
- Manager should assess actual profit margin.
- What types of accounts will Owner be required to set-up and maintain, e.g.:
  - Deposit account
  - Operating account
- Other Fee Provisions:
  - Determine the rights of the parties to set off monies owed.
  - Will there be any cost of living adjustments?
  - For international deals, is there any currency risk?
  - Consider a most favored customer provision.
  - How will fees be paid, e.g., in what currency, in what manner and according to what schedule?
  - How, when and to what Owner entity(ies) will invoices be issued? Determine the degree of detail to be included on invoices.
  - How will disputed fees/credits be handled (e.g., escrow)? What are the parties' obligations to perform in the event of a dispute?
  - How will changes in the number of tenants/sites be handled?

32. Taxes
    - Determine liability for sales, use, and other taxes.
    - Determine liability for additional taxes resulting from Manager's relocation of service locations or rerouting of services.

33. Additional Services
    - How will the provision of additional services be handled? Will Manager be required to submit a bid? Will there be any rights of first refusal granted to Manager?
    - What type of detail must be included in a Manager proposal?
    - To what extent does Owner wish to reserve the right to contract with third parties?

34. Insurance
    - Specify Manager's insurance requirements, e.g.:
      - All insurance required by law
      - Liability
      - Commercial (or comprehensive) general liability
      - Worker's compensation
      - Automobile
      - Employee fidelity insurance
      - Crime
    - Specify Owner's insurance requirements.
    - Specify minimum amounts of insurance required.
    - Determine whether any subcontractors should be required to obtain special insurance in addition to or in lieu of the types of insurance required to be obtained by Manager, e.g.:

- Medical expenses
- Excess liability coverage
- Transit coverage
- Completed operations coverage
- Specify any specific bonding requirements.
- Determine whether any parental or other type of guarantee is appropriate.

35. Termination
    - Consider early termination rights, e.g.:
        - Termination for convenience in whole
        - Partial termination for convenience
        - Termination upon change of control of Manager
        - Termination upon change of control of Owner
        - Termination for breach
        - Termination for nonpayment
        - Termination for conviction of a crime and other acts
        - Termination for theft by Manager employee
        - Termination for re-possession by lender
        - Termination for failure to provide critical services
        - Termination for failure to meet the performance standards
        - Termination for substantial changes in business
        - Termination upon the occurrence of a regulatory event
        - Cross-termination with other agreements
    - Determine whether and in what instances termination fees are applicable. If so, establish formula for determining applicable termination fees.

36. Rights/Obligations upon Termination
    - Determine each party's payment obligations upon expiration/termination particularly with respect to third-party contracts.
    - Determine each party's ongoing rights after expiration/termination with respect to proprietary and third-party methodologies, technology, equipment, facilities, subcontracting arrangements, and third-party service agreements.
    - Determine which party will be responsible for transfer/assignment fees imposed by third parties.
    - If Owner has right to purchase certain Manager assets used to provide the services, how will the purchase price be determined?

37. Termination Assistance
    - Determine the types of assistance Manager and/or its subcontractors will provide Owner upon expiration/termination.
    - Determine duration of Manager's termination assistance obligations.
    - How will termination assistance be paid for (e.g., fee schedule, time schedule for payment)?

38. Liability Provisions
    - Assess liability exposure.
    - Determine any liquidated damages to be imposed upon Manager (e.g., for failure to meet performance standards, for failure to meet implementation schedules).
    - What are each party's indemnification obligations (e.g., for claims of infringement, employee claims).
    - Determine the representations and warranties to be made by each party.

39. Dispute Resolution
    - How will disputes be handled? Will the agreement include an escalation procedure?
    - Will unresolved disputes be handled through arbitration or litigation?

40. Business Recovery
    - Will Manager have any business recovery responsibilities?
    - What are Owner's existing business recovery plan? Will Owner's plans be terminated?
    - Specify response times for delivery of business recovery services. Describe escalation procedures.

41. Assignment
    - Specify each party's right to assign its rights/obligations under the agreement in whole or in part.
    - Will there be any special assignment rights in the event of a merger/acquisition/divestiture?
    - May either party assign to an affiliate/related entity?

42. Solicitation of Employees
    - Will there be any limitations/restrictions on Owner's or Manager's right to solicit and/or hire the other party's employees?
    - When will such limitations/restrictions apply (e.g., during the term, after expiration/termination)?
    - Will there be any exceptions for blind solicitations (e.g., newspaper advertisements)?

43. Miscellaneous Provisions
    - *Notices*: How will notices be given (e.g., by hand, by facsimile)? To whom (e.g., to business manager and/or counsel)?
    - *Publicity*: Limitations/restrictions on each party's ability to make public statements regarding the other party and/or the transaction.
    - *Governing Law*: Determine which state/country law will govern the transaction (or if international transaction with multiple documents, determine which law will govern each part of the transaction).
    - *Venue*: Will there be a requirement that any action be brought in a particular venue?
    - *Import/Export*: Provide any limitations/restrictions on the export/import of data and/or technology.
    - *Interpretation of Documents*: How will the transaction documents be interpreted in the event of a dispute (e.g., the main agreement will take precedence over the exhibits/schedules, change orders will take precedence over earlier dated documents)?
    - *Counterparts*: Specify whether the various transaction documents may be executed in counterparts.
    - *Relationship of the Parties*: Specify that Manager is an independent contractor to Owner and that the provision of services does not constitute any type of partnership or joint venture (unless that is expressly the intent)
    - *Severability*: Specify that if any provision is held to be invalid that the remaining provisions shall remain in full force and effect.
    - *Waivers*: Specify that any delay or omission does not constitute a waiver of rights and that any waiver should not be construed to be a waiver of a subsequent breach/covenant.

- *Entire Agreement*: Specify that the transaction documents constitute the entire agreement between the parties.
- *Amendments*: Specify how the transaction documents may be amended (e.g., by writing signed by both parties).
- *Survival*: Specify which provisions of the agreement will survive termination and/or expiration of the agreement.
- *Third-Party Beneficiaries*: Expressly state that there will not be any third-party beneficiaries under the transaction documents or, if there will be third-party beneficiaries, identify such beneficiaries.
- *Covenant of Further Assurances*: Expressly state that each party will execute any documents or perform any actions necessary to effectuate the purposes of the agreement.

Appendix 5.6

BUSINESS PROCESS OUTSOURCING AGREEMENT (CUSTOMER FORM)ᵃ

[SPECIFY TYPE OF BUSINESS PROCESS SERVICES TO BE OUTSOURCED]
AGREEMENT

by and between

[CUSTOMER]

and

[VENDOR]

Dated as of **[SPECIFY DATE]**

TABLE OF CONTENTS

ᵃ Note: This sample agreement is intended to illustrate the types of legal issues that customers typically wish to address in connection with business process outsourcing transactions. The provisions included in this sample agreement, while comprehensive, may not cover all of the issues that may arise in a particular transaction. Legal issues will likely vary depending on the type of business process being outsourced and the scope of the outsourcing transaction. This sample agreement or any part thereof should only be used after consultation with your legal counsel. You should consult legal counsel prior to entering into or negotiating any outsourcing transaction.

TABLE OF EXHIBITS

This **[SPECIFY TYPE OF BUSINESS PROCESS SERVICES TO BE OUTSOURCED] AGREEMENT,** dated as of **[SPECIFY DATE],** is by and between **CUSTOMER** and **VENDOR.**

WITNESSETH:

WHEREAS, in response to the RFP, Vendor submitted the Proposal;

WHEREAS, based on the Proposal, Customer and Vendor have engaged in extensive negotiations and discussions that have culminated in the formation of the relationship described in this Agreement; and

WHEREAS, Vendor desires to provide to Customer, and Customer desires to obtain from Vendor, the **[SPECIFY TYPE OF BUSINESS PROCESS SERVICES TO BE OUTSOURCED]** and related services described in this Agreement on the terms and conditions set forth in this Agreement.

NOW, THEREFORE, for and in consideration of the agreements set forth below, Customer and Vendor agree as follows:

ARTICLE 1   DEFINITIONS AND CONSTRUCTION.

1.01   *Definitions.* The following defined terms used in this Agreement shall have the meanings specified below:

"*Additional Resource Charges*" shall mean the resource charges specified in *Exhibit 11* for the use of Services above the resource baselines set forth in *Exhibit 11*.

"*Affected Employees*" shall mean those Customer Employees set forth in *Exhibit 7*.

[**"*Affected Project Staff Member*"** shall have the meaning set forth in *Section 28.03.*]

[*"Affected Resources"* shall have the meaning set forth in *Section 28.04.*]

"Affiliate" shall mean, as to any entity, any other entity that, directly or indirectly, Controls, is Controlled by, or is under common Control with such entity.

"Agreement" shall mean this **[SPECIFY TYPE OF BUSINESS PROCESS SERVICES TO BE OUTSOURCED]** by and between Customer and Vendor.

[*"Assets"* **shall mean the [facilities] equipment, technology and related assets set forth in *Exhibit 2*.]**

"Assigned Agreements" shall mean the third-party agreements that are assigned, in whole or in part, to Vendor and that are set forth in *Exhibit 3*.

"Benchmarker" shall mean the third party designated by Customer from time to time **[upon [SPECIFY TIME PERIOD] days' notice to Vendor]** to conduct the Benchmarking Process.

"Benchmarking Process" shall mean the objective measurement and comparison process (utilizing baselines and industry standards agreed upon by Customer and Vendor) established by Customer and Vendor.

"Benchmark Results" shall mean the final results of the Benchmarking Process delivered by the Benchmarker in a written report to each of Customer and Vendor, including any supporting documentation requested by Customer or Vendor to analyze the results of the Benchmarking Process.

"Benchmark Review Period" shall mean the **[SPECIFY TIME PERIOD]** period following receipt by Customer and Vendor of the Benchmark Results.

[*"Century Compliant"* **shall mean, with respect to Software, Tools and Machines, that such Software, Tools and Machines shall be capable of accounting for all calculations using a century and date sensitive algorithm for the year 2000 and the fact that the year 2000 is a leap year.]**

"Change(s)" shall mean any change to the Services **[or the Systems]** that would materially alter the functionality, performance standards **[or technical environment of the Systems,]** the manner in which the Services are provided, the composition of the Services or the cost to Customer of the Services.

"Change Control Procedures" shall mean the written description of the change control procedures applicable to any Changes under this Agreement.

"Change in Control" shall mean the (1) consolidation or merger of a Party with or into any entity (other than the consolidation or merger of a Party with an Affiliate of such Party in which such Party is the surviving entity); (2) sale, transfer or other disposition of all or substantially all of the assets of a Party; or (3) acquisition by any entity, or group of entities acting in concert, of beneficial ownership of **[SPECIFY PERCENT]** or more (or such lesser percentage that constitutes Control) of the outstanding voting securities or other ownership interests of a Party.

"Confidential Information" of Customer or Vendor shall mean all information and documentation of Customer and Vendor, respectively, whether disclosed to or accessed by Customer or Vendor in connection with this Agreement, including (1) with respect to Customer, all Customer Data and all information of Customer or its customers, suppliers, contractors and other third parties doing business with Customer, (2) with respect to Customer and Vendor, the terms of this Agreement and (3) any information developed by reference to or use of Customer's or Vendor's information, provided, however, that except to the extent otherwise provided by Law, the term "Confidential Information" shall not include information that (a) is independently developed by the recipient, as demonstrated by the recipient's written records, without violating the disclosing Party's proprietary rights, (b) is or becomes publicly known (other than through unauthorized disclosure), (c) is disclosed by the owner of such information to a third party free of any obligation of confidentiality, (d) is already known by the recipient at the time of disclosure, as demonstrated by the recipient's written records, and the recipient has no obligation of confidentiality other than pursuant to this Agreement or

any confidentiality agreements between Customer and Vendor entered into before the Effective Date or (e) is rightfully received by a Party free of any obligation of confidentiality, provided that (i) such recipient has no knowledge that such information is subject to a confidentiality agreement and (ii) such information is not of a type or character that a reasonable person would have regarded it as confidential.

"*Consents*" shall mean all licenses, consents, authorizations and approvals that are necessary to allow (1) Vendor and Vendor Agents to use (a) Customer's owned and leased assets, (b) the services provided for the benefit of Customer under Customer's third-party services contracts, (c) the Customer IP, (d) the Vendor IP and (e) any assets owned or leased by Vendor, (2) Customer to assign the Assigned Agreements to Vendor pursuant to *Section 7.03* and Vendor to manage and administer the Customer Third-Party Contracts pursuant to *Article 7*, (3) Vendor and Vendor Agents to (a) use any third-party services retained by Vendor to provide the Services during the Term and the Termination Assistance Period and (b) assign to Customer the New IP **[and (4) after the expiration, termination or partial termination of this Agreement or the insourcing or resourcing of any portion of the Services, (i) Customer and its designee(s) to use the Vendor IP or, with respect to any Vendor IP that Vendor has licensed, leased or otherwise obtained from third parties pursuant to *Section 28.02(c)*, Vendor to transfer, assign or sublicense such Vendor IP, (ii) Vendor and Vendor Agents assign the agreements and Vendor Machines to Customer and its designee(s) pursuant to *Section 28.02(e)* and *Section 28.02(f)*]**.

"*Contract Year*" shall mean each 12-month period commencing, in the case of the first Contract Year, on the Effective Date and thereafter upon the completion of the immediately preceding Contract Year.

"*Control*" shall mean, with respect to any entity, the possession, directly or indirectly, of the power to direct or cause the direction of the management and policies of such entity, whether through the ownership of voting securities (or other ownership interest), by contract or otherwise.

"*Critical Services*" shall mean those services described as Critical Services in *Exhibit 4*.

"*Customer*" shall mean **[CUSTOMER NAME]**, a **[SPECIFY TYPE, E.G., DELAWARE] [corporation] [partnership] [other]**.

"*Customer Agents*" shall mean the agents, subcontractors and representatives of Customer, other than Vendor and Vendor Agents.

["*Customer Budget*" shall mean the [SPECIFY YEAR] budget for [SPECIFY TYPE OF BUSINESS PROCESS] services set forth in *Exhibit 8*.]

"*Customer Contract Manager*" shall have the meaning set forth in *Section 6.01*.

"*Customer Data*" shall mean all data and information (1) submitted to Vendor or Vendor Agents by or on behalf of Customer, (2) obtained, developed or produced by Vendor or Vendor Agents in connection with this Agreement or (3) to which Vendor or Vendor Agents have access in connection with the provision of the Services.

"*Customer IP*" shall mean the IP **[including the IP set forth in *Exhibit 5*]** used in connection with the provision of the Services that is (1) owned, acquired, or developed by Customer or (2) licensed or leased by Customer from a third party.

"*Customer's Regulatory Requirements*" shall mean the Laws to which Customer is required to submit or voluntarily submits from time to time.

"*Customer Service Location(s)*" shall mean any Customer service location set forth in *Exhibit 6* and any other service location owned or leased by Customer for which Vendor has received Customer's approval in accordance with *Section 10.01(3)*.

"*Customer Third Party Contracts*" shall mean the Managed Agreements and the Assigned Agreements, collectively.

"*Data Safeguards*" shall have the meaning set forth in *Section 10.03*.

"Default Cure Period" shall have the meaning set forth in *Section 26.04(1)*.

"Default Notice" shall have the meaning set forth in *Section 26.04(1)*.

"Designated Fees" shall mean the fees for the Designated Services set forth in *Exhibit 9*.

"Designated Service Levels" shall mean the service levels and standards for the performance of the Designated Services as described in *Exhibit 10*.

"Designated Services" shall have the meaning set forth in *Section 3.01*.

[**"*Developed Software*" shall mean any Software, modifications or enhancements to Software and Related Documentation developed pursuant to this Agreement by or on behalf of (1) Vendor, (2) Vendor Agents, (3) Vendor and Customer or Customer Agents jointly, (4) Vendor Agents and Customer or Customer Agents jointly or (5) Vendor, Vendor Agents, Customer and Customer Agents jointly.**]

"DRP" shall mean the disaster recovery plan.

"Effective Date" shall mean **[SPECIFY DATE]**.

[**"*EMU Compliant*" shall mean, with respect to Software, Tools and Machines, that such Software, Tools and Machines shall be capable of processing calculations relating to conversions of any currency to a European Monetary Unit.**]

"End Date" shall have the meaning set forth in *Section 28.02*.

"End-Users" shall mean users of the Services, as specified by Customer.

"Extension Period" shall have the meaning set forth in *Section 2.02*.

"Fees" shall mean the Designated Fees, the Additional Resource Charges and any other amounts payable by Customer to Vendor pursuant to this Agreement.

[**"*Force Majeure Event*" shall have the meaning set forth in *Section 17.02*.**]

"Governmental Approval" shall mean any license, consent, permit, approval, or authorization of any person or entity, or any notice to any person or entity, the granting of which is required by Law, including Customer's Regulatory Requirements, for the consummation of the transactions contemplated by this Agreement.

"Governmental Authority" shall mean any federal, state, municipal, local, territorial, or other governmental department, regulatory authority, judicial or administrative body, domestic, international, or foreign.

"Improvements" shall mean any developments, including new developments in IP and Machines, that could reasonably be expected to have an impact on Customer's business, to the extent known and made available within or by Vendor.

"Indemnified Party" shall have the meaning set forth in *Section 29.03*.

"Indemnifying Party" shall have the meaning set forth in *Section 29.03*.

"Initial Agreement Expiration Date" shall mean **[SPECIFY DATE]**.

"Initial Customer Satisfaction Survey" shall have the meaning set forth in *Section 9.01*.

"Initial Term" shall have the meaning set forth in *Section 2.01*.

"Interest" shall mean interest at a rate of **[SPECIFY PERCENT]** per annum more than the prime rate established by Customer, but in no event to exceed the highest lawful rate of interest.

"IP" shall mean any (1) processes, methodologies, procedures, and trade secrets, (2) Software, Tools and machine-readable texts and files and (3) literary work or other work of authorship, including documentation, reports, drawings, charts, graphics and other written documentation.

"Key Personnel" shall mean the Vendor Contract Manager and such other individuals specified in *Exhibit 13*, collectively.

"Law" shall mean any declaration, decree, directive, legislative enactment, order, ordinance, regulation, rule or other binding restriction of or by any Governmental Authority.

"Losses" shall mean any and all damages, fines, penalties, deficiencies, losses, liabilities (including settlements and judgments) and expenses (including interest, court costs, rea-

sonable fees and expenses of attorneys, accountants and other experts or other reasonable fees and expenses of litigation or other proceedings or of any claim, default, or assessment).

"*Machines*" shall mean equipment used to provide the Services, including **[computers and related equipment, such as central processing units and other processors, controllers, modems, communications and telecommunications equipment (voice, data and video), cables, storage devices, printers, terminals, other peripherals and input and output devices, and other tangible mechanical and electronic equipment intended for the processing, input, output, storage, manipulation, communication, transmission and retrieval of information and data.]**

[BROADEN DEFINITION FOR PROPERTY MANAGEMENT TRANSACTIONS TO INCLUDE OTHER EQUIPMENT USED TO PROVIDE SERVICES]

"*Managed Agreement Invoice(s)*" shall mean any invoice submitted by third parties in connection with the Managed Agreements.

"*Managed Agreements*" shall mean the third-party agreements for which Customer retains financial responsibility and that are set forth in *Exhibit 3*.

"*Management Committee*" shall have the meaning set forth in *Section 13.01*.

"*New IP*" shall mean the IP developed or acquired by Vendor or Vendor Agents under this Agreement or in connection with the provision or delivery of the Services.

"*New Service(s)*" shall mean any service that is outside the scope of the Designated Services.

"*New Service Level(s)*" shall mean any service level established by Vendor and Customer in connection with a New Service.

"*Parties*" shall mean Customer and Vendor, collectively.

"*Party*" shall mean either Customer or Vendor, as the case may be.

"*Performance Credits*" shall mean the performance credits set forth in *Exhibit 10*.

"*Privileged Work Product*" shall have the meaning set forth in *Section 22.02*.

"*Procedures Manual*" shall have the meaning set forth in *Section 13.02*.

"*Project Staff*" shall mean the personnel of Vendor and Vendor Agents who provide the Services.

["*Proposal*" shall mean the Proposal, dated [SPECIFY DATE] and set forth in *Exhibit 12*, submitted by Vendor in response to the RFP.]

"*Reduced Resource Credits*" shall mean the credits in the amounts equal to the Additional Resource Charges specified in *Exhibit 11* for the use of Services below the resource baselines set forth in *Exhibit 11*.

"*Related Documentation*" shall mean, with respect to Software and Tools, all materials, documentation, specifications, technical manuals, user manuals, flow diagrams, file descriptions, and other written information that describes the function and use of such Software or Tools, as applicable.

["*RFP*" shall mean the Request for Proposal distributed by Customer that is set forth in *Exhibit 12*.]

"*Service Levels*" shall mean the Designated Service Levels and the New Service Levels, collectively.

"*Service Location(s)*" shall mean any Customer Service Location or Vendor Service Location, as applicable.

"*Services*" shall mean, collectively, the Designated Services, the New Services being provided by Vendor pursuant to this Agreement, and, during the Termination Assistance Period, the Termination Assistance Services.

["*Software*" shall mean the source code and object code versions of any applications programs, operating system software, computer software languages, utilities, other computer programs and Related Documentation, in whatever form or media, including the tangible media upon which such applications programs, operating system software, computer software languages, utilities, other computer programs and Related Documentation are

recorded or printed, together with all corrections, improvements, updates and releases thereof.]

["*Systems*" shall mean the IP and the Machines, collectively, used to provide the Services.]

"*Term*" shall mean the Initial Term and any renewal or extension of the Initial Term pursuant to *Section 2.02*.

"*Termination Assistance Period*" shall mean a reasonable period of time designated by Customer during which Vendor shall provide the Termination Assistance Services in accordance with *Article 28*.

"*Termination Assistance Services*" shall mean (1) the terminated, insourced or resourced Services (and any replacements thereof or substitutions therefore), to the extent Customer requests such Services during the Termination Assistance Period, (2) Vendor's cooperation with Customer or another service provider designated by Customer in the transfer of the terminated, insourced or resourced Services to Customer or such other service provider in order to facilitate the transfer of the terminated, insourced or resourced Services to Customer or such other service provider and (3) any New Services requested by Customer in order to facilitate the transfer of the terminated, insourced or resourced Services to Customer or another service provider designated by Customer.

["*Tools*" shall mean any Software development and performance testing tools, know-how, methodologies, processes, technologies, or algorithms and Related Documentation used by Vendor in providing the Services and based upon trade secrets or proprietary information of Vendor or otherwise owned or licensed by Vendor.]

"*Transition Plan*" shall mean the high-level transition plan set forth in *Exhibit 14*.

"*Transition Schedule*" shall mean the schedule for the transition of services and functions to Vendor from Customer, as set forth in the Transition Plan.

"*Transition Services*" shall have the meaning set forth in *Section 4.01*.

"*Use*" shall mean the right to load, execute, store, transmit, display, copy, maintain, modify, enhance, create derivative works, make, and have made.

"*Variable Fee Report*" shall mean the detailed invoice provided to Customer by Vendor on a monthly basis describing the Variable incurred by Customer and Vendor during the preceding month.

"*Variable Fees*" shall mean the Additional Resource Charges and the Reduced Resource Credits, collectively.

"*Vendor*" shall mean [VENDOR NAME], a [SPECIFY TYPE] [corporation] [partnership] [other].

"*Vendor Agents*" shall mean the agents, subcontractors and representatives of Vendor.

"*Vendor Contract Manager*" shall have the meaning set forth in *Section 12.01*.

"*Vendor IP*" shall mean the IP used in connection with the Services or with Customer IP which is (1) owned, acquired or developed by or on behalf of Vendor or (2) licensed, leased or otherwise obtained by Vendor from a third party, excluding in each case Customer IP and New IP.

"*Vendor Machines*" shall mean those Machines leased or owned by Vendor and Vendor Agents that are used by Vendor and Vendor Agents to provide the Services.

"*Vendor Service Location(s)*" shall mean any Vendor service location set forth in *Exhibit 6* and any other service location approved by Customer pursuant to *Section 10.01(3)*.

1.02   *References.* In this Agreement and the Exhibits to this Agreement:

(1)   the Exhibits to this Agreement shall be incorporated into and deemed part of this Agreement and all references to this Agreement shall include the Exhibits to this Agreement;

(2)   references to an Exhibit, Section, or Article shall be to such Exhibit to, Section, or Article of this Agreement, unless otherwise provided;

(3) references to any Law shall mean references to such Law in changed or supplemented form or to a newly adopted Law replacing a previous Law; and

(4) references to and mentions of the word "including" or the phrase "e.g." shall mean "including, without limitation."

1.03   *Headings.* The Article and Section headings, Table of Contents and Table of Exhibits are for reference and convenience only and shall not be considered in the interpretation of this Agreement.

1.04   *Interpretation of Documents.* Except as otherwise expressly set forth in the body of this Agreement or in any of the Exhibits, in the event of a conflict between the provisions in the body of the this Agreement and the Exhibits, the provisions in the body of this Agreement shall prevail.

ARTICLE 2   TERM.

2.01   *Initial Term.* The initial term of this Agreement shall commence on the Effective Date and continue until 23:59 (**[SPECIFY TIME STANDARD]**) on the Initial Agreement Expiration Date, or such earlier date upon which this Agreement may be terminated pursuant to *Article 26* (the "*Initial Term*").

2.02   *Renewal and Extension.* Unless this Agreement is terminated earlier pursuant to *Article 26*, Customer shall notify Vendor at least **[SPECIFY TIME PERIOD]** prior to the Initial Agreement Expiration Date as to whether Customer desires to renew this Agreement. If Customer provides Vendor with notice that it does not desire to renew this Agreement, this Agreement shall expire on the Initial Agreement Expiration Date. If Customer provides Vendor with notice that it desires to renew this Agreement and the Parties have not agreed on the terms and conditions applicable to the renewal of this Agreement **[SPECIFY TIME PERIOD]** prior to the Initial Agreement Expiration Date, then the term of this Agreement shall extend for a period as determined by Customer (the "*Extension Period*") of up to **[SPECIFY TIME PERIOD]** from the Initial Agreement Expiration Date, at the charges, terms and conditions in effect as of the Initial Agreement Expiration Date. If during the Extension Period the Parties are unable to reach agreement on the terms and conditions applicable to the renewal of this Agreement, this Agreement shall expire at the end of the Extension Period.

ARTICLE 3   DESIGNATED SERVICES.

3.01   *Generally.* Commencing on the Effective Date and continuing throughout the Term, Vendor shall be responsible for providing to Customer:

(1) the services described in this Agreement (including the services, functions, responsibilities and projects described in the Statement of Work set forth as *Exhibit 1*);

(2) the services, functions and responsibilities being performed prior to the Effective Date by the Affected Employees or such other Customer employees whose services, functions or responsibilities were eliminated as a result of this Agreement, even if the service, function or responsibility is not specifically described in this Agreement; **[NOTE: MAY NEED TO ADDRESS CONTRACTORS]**

(3) **[the business process services, functions and responsibilities reflected in and contemplated by the Customer Budget;]**and

(4) any services, functions or responsibilities not specifically described in this Agreement, but which are required for the proper performance and delivery of the Services (clauses (1) through (4) of this Section, collectively, the "*Designated Services*").

Subject to *Section 18.02*, Vendor shall increase or decrease the amount of the Services according to Customer's request for the Services.

3.02   *Provision of Methodologies/Technology.* In providing methodologies, technology and the Services to Customer, Vendor shall (1) jointly with Customer, identify the least cost/highest benefit methods to implement proven methodologies and technology changes and, upon Customer's approval, implement proven methodologies and technology changes, (2) maintain a level of methodologies and technology that allows Customer to take advantage of advances in order to remain competitive in the markets which Customer serves, (3) provide to Customer the Improvements for Customer's evaluation in connection with the Services and (4) meet with Customer at least once during every **[SPECIFY TIME PERIOD]** during the Term in accordance with the procedures agreed upon by the Customer Contract Manager and the Vendor Contract Manager to inform Customer of any new methodologies and technology Vendor is developing or trends and directions of which Vendor is otherwise aware that could reasonably be expected to have an impact on Customer's business.

3.03   *Vendor Licenses and Permits.* Vendor shall obtain and maintain all Governmental Approvals. Upon Vendor's request, Customer shall cooperate with and assist Vendor in obtaining any such Governmental Approvals, to the extent reasonably possible.
[ADD LANGUAGE RE: LIENS IF APPLICABLE]

3.04   *Changes in Law and Regulations.*
(1)   Vendor shall promptly identify and notify Customer of any changes in Law, including Customer's Regulatory Requirements, that may relate to Customer's use of the Services or Vendor's delivery of the Services. Vendor and Customer shall work together to identify the impact of such changes on how Customer uses, and Vendor delivers, the Services. Vendor shall be responsible for any fines and penalties arising from any noncompliance with any Law relating to the delivery or use of the Services, except as set forth in the following sentence. Customer shall be responsible for any fines and penalties arising from any noncompliance by Customer with any Law relating to Customer's use of the Services, to the extent (a) Vendor notifies Customer in a timely manner of changes in such Law in accordance with this subsection and (b) such noncompliance was not caused by Vendor.
(2)   Vendor shall perform the Services regardless of changes in Law, including Customer's Regulatory Requirements. If such changes prevent Vendor from performing its obligations under this Agreement, Vendor shall develop and, upon Customer's approval, implement a suitable workaround until such time as Vendor can perform its obligations under this Agreement without such workaround; provided, however, that if such workaround results in an increase in the charges to Customer under this Agreement, then Customer shall have the right to terminate the affected portion of Customer's obligations without regard to *Section 26.04(1)* **[and *Section 26.05*]**. Upon the implementation of such workaround, the Parties shall negotiate and implement an equitable adjustment to the applicable Fees.

3.05   **[*Technical Architecture and Product Standards.* Vendor shall comply with Customer's information management technical architecture and product standards set forth in *Exhibit 15*, as the same may be modified by Customer from time to time during the Term and the Termination Assistance Period.]**

3.06   *Knowledge Sharing.* At least once every Contract Year, or on request after at least **[SPECIFY TIME PERIOD]** notice from Customer, Vendor shall meet with representatives of Customer in order to **[(1) explain how the Systems work and should be operated,]** (2) explain how the Services are provided and (3) provide such training and documentation as Customer may require for Customer to **[understand and operate the Systems and]** understand and provide the Services after the expiration or termination of this Agreement.

3.07   *Insourcing.* Upon at least **[SPECIFY TIME PERIOD]** notice to Vendor, Customer may insource or obtain from a third party all, or any portion, of the Services.

3.08   **[*Asset Transfer.* On the Effective Date, Vendor shall purchase the Assets for the purchase price specified in *Exhibit 16.* Vendor shall be responsible for and shall pay all sales, use and other similar taxes arising out of or in connection with the transfer of the Assets by Customer to Vendor on the Effective Date. On the Effective Date, Customer shall assign and transfer to Vendor good and valid title in and to the Assets free and clear of all liens, except permitted liens, by delivery of one or more general assignments and bills of sale in the form of *Exhibit 16,* duly executed by Customer and Vendor.]**

3.09   *Reports.* Vendor shall provide to Customer, in a form acceptable to Customer, the **[on-line]** reports set forth in *Exhibit 17,* and such other reports as Customer may request from time to time.

ARTICLE 4   TRANSITION.
4.01   *Transition Services.* Vendor shall perform all functions and services necessary to accomplish the transition of Customer's business process operations and capabilities to Vendor on or before **[SPECIFY DATE]** (the *"Transition Services"*). The Transition Services shall be performed in accordance with the Transition Plan and without causing a material disruption to Customer's business. Vendor shall designate an individual for each of Customer's facilities and functions being transitioned in accordance with this Agreement who shall be responsible for managing and implementing the Transition Services with respect to such functions or services. Until the completion of the applicable Transition Services, each individual shall review with the Customer Contract Manager the status of the Transition Services for which that individual is responsible as often as may be reasonably requested by the Customer Contract Manager.

4.02   *Extensions to the Transition Schedule.* Upon notice from Customer that Customer desires Vendor to extend the Transition Schedule by more than **[SPECIFY TIME PERIOD]** days, or if the Transition Schedule is extended for more than **[SPECIFY TIME PERIOD]** days as a result of delays caused by Customer or Customer Agents or as a result of Customer's Regulatory Requirements, (1) Vendor shall extend the Transition Schedule for the applicable period of time and (2) Customer shall pay to Vendor an amount equal to Vendor's direct and actual costs associated with extending the Transition Schedule pursuant to this subsection, including any of Vendor's direct and actual costs that would otherwise have been reduced or eliminated if the transition had occurred as scheduled.

(a)   In the event the Transition Schedule is extended for more than **[SPECIFY TIME PERIOD]** as a result of delays caused by Vendor or Vendor Agents, (i) Customer shall continue to pay the Designated Fees, subject to Customer's deferral rights in accordance with *Section 18.06,* and (ii) Vendor shall pay to Customer an amount equal to Customer's direct and actual costs associated with extending the Transition Schedule in accordance with this subsection, including payment of occupancy expenses at the applicable Customer facilities and such other direct and actual costs retained by Customer that would have otherwise been reduced or eliminated if the transition had occurred as scheduled.

(b)   In the event Customer and Vendor agree to extend the Transition Schedule, Customer, and Vendor shall negotiate an appropriate adjustment to the Fees.

(c) In the event Customer or Vendor incurs costs in connection with the extension of the Transition Schedule for which the other Party will be responsible pursuant to this Section, the Party incurring the costs shall be obligated to use all commercially reasonable efforts to minimize such costs.

ARTICLE 5 NEW SERVICES.

5.01 *New Services.* Customer may from time to time during the Term request that Vendor perform a New Service. Upon receipt of such a request from Customer, Vendor shall provide Customer with a written proposal for such New Service which shall include:

(1) a description of the services, function, and responsibilities Vendor anticipates performing in connection with such New Service;

(2) a schedule for commencing and completing such New Service;

(3) Vendor's prospective charges for such New Service, including a detailed breakdown of such charges;

(4) when appropriate, a description of any new IP or Machines to be provided by Vendor in connection with such New Service;

(5) a description of the human resources necessary to provide the New Service;

(6) when appropriate, a list of any existing IP or Machines included in or to be used in connection with such New Service;

(7) when appropriate, acceptance test criteria and procedures for **[any new Software]** or any products, packages or services; and

(8) such other information requested by Customer.

Vendor shall not begin performing any New Service until Customer has provided Vendor with authorization to perform the New Service from the Customer Contract Manager.

[CONSIDER WHETHER THERE ARE CERTAIN SERVICES THAT VENDOR SHOULD BE OBLIGATED TO PROVIDE IF REQUESTED BY CUSTOMER]

5.02 *Third Party Services.* Notwithstanding any request made to Vendor by Customer pursuant to *Section 5.01* or any other provision in this Agreement, Customer shall have the right to contract with a third party to perform any New Service, including services to augment or supplement the Services. Upon Customer's request, Vendor shall assist Customer in identifying qualified third-party suppliers to provide New Services. In the event Customer contracts with a third party to perform any New Service, Vendor shall cooperate in good faith with Customer and any such third party, to the extent reasonably required by Customer, including by providing:

(1) in writing, applicable requirements, standards and policies for the Services, to the extent available;

(2) assistance and support services to such third party; and

(3) **[access to the Systems, to the extent that such access is required for the New Service and does not materially and adversely affect Vendor's ability to perform its obligations pursuant to this Agreement.]**

5.03 *Additional Business Units.* Customer reserves the right to add business units to this Agreement. Customer shall share such information with Vendor as may be necessary for Vendor to determine which resources will be required to meet Customer's needs. Customer shall not be obligated to obtain the Services from Vendor with respect to any additional entity or business unit or pursuant to an acquisition.

ARTICLE 6 CUSTOMER RESPONSIBILITIES.

6.01 *Customer Contract Manager.* Customer shall appoint an individual (the "*Customer Contract Manager*") who from the date of this Agreement shall serve as the primary Customer representative under this Agreement. The Customer Contract Manager shall (1) have overall responsibility for managing and coordinating the performance of Customer's obligations under this Agreement and (2) be authorized to act for and on behalf of Customer with respect to all matters relating to this Agreement. Notwithstanding the foregoing, the Customer Contract Manager may, upon notice to Vendor, delegate such of his or her responsibilities to other Customer employees, as the Customer Contract Manager deems appropriate.

6.02   [*Customer Resources.* **Commencing on the Effective Date and continuing for so long as Vendor requires the same for the performance of the Services, Customer shall provide to Vendor, at no charge to Vendor and subject to *Section 6.03*, the following:**
(1)   **the use of the space in Customer's premises that was utilized by the Affected Employees as of the Effective Date and any additional space in Customer's premises that Vendor may from time to time reasonably require in connection with the performance of the Services (in accordance with Customer's corporate policy), together with office furnishings, telephone equipment and services, janitorial services, utilities and office-related equipment, supplies and duplicating services reasonably required in connection with the performance of the Services;**
(2)   **for use by personnel employed or managed by Vendor on Customer's premises, those personal computers, workstations, terminals, printers and other equipment utilized by the Affected Employees as of the Effective Date, other than the Assets. Vendor shall maintain and replace such equipment, at its own expense, as may be necessary to perform the Services in accordance with the Service Levels. All equipment provided by Customer shall remain the property of Customer or its lessor; provided, however, that, to the extent that Vendor upgrades such equipment or replaces parts included in such equipment, Customer shall own the upgrades and replacement parts and Vendor shall own the replaced or removed equipment.]**

6.03   [*Use of Customer Facilities.* **Except as expressly provided in this Agreement, Vendor shall use the Customer Service Locations for the sole and exclusive purpose of providing the Services. Use of such facilities by Vendor does not constitute a leasehold interest in favor of Vendor or any of Vendor's customers.**
(1)   **Vendor shall use the Customer Service Locations in a reasonably efficient manner. To the extent that Vendor operates the space in a manner that unnecessarily increases facility costs incurred by Customer, Customer reserves the right to set-off the excess utility costs of such practices.**
(2)   **Vendor and Vendor Agents shall keep the Customer Service Locations in good order, not commit or permit waste or damage to such facilities, not use such facilities for any unlawful purpose or act and comply with all of Customer's standard policies and procedures as in effect from time to time, including procedures for the physical security of the Customer Service Locations.**
(3)   **Vendor shall permit Customer and Customer Agents to enter into those portions of the Customer Service Locations occupied by Vendor's staff at any time to perform facilities-related services.**
(4)   **Vendor shall not make any improvements or changes involving structural, mechanical or electrical alterations to the Customer Service Locations without Customer's approval. [OWNERSHIP OF IMPROVEMENTS/CHANGES TO FACILITIES]**
(5)   **When the Customer Service Locations are no longer required for performance of the Services, Vendor shall return such locations to Customer in substantially the same condition as when Vendor began using such locations.]**
[ADD OBLIGATIONS RE: HAZARDOUS MATERIALS/ENVIRONMENTAL COMPLIANCE]

ARTICLE 7   CONTRACT ADMINISTRATION. **[IF APPLICABLE]**

7.01   *Managed Agreements.* Vendor shall manage, administer and maintain the Managed Agreements. Vendor shall provide Customer with reasonable notice of any renewal, termination or cancellation dates and fees with respect to the Managed Agreements. Vendor shall not renew, modify, terminate or cancel, or request or grant any consents or waivers under, any Managed Agreements without the consent of the appropriate entity or unit of Customer. Any fees or charges or other liability or obligation imposed upon Customer in connection with any such renewal, modification, termination or cancellation of, or consent or waiver under, the Managed Agreements, obtained or given without Customer's consent, shall be paid or discharged, as applicable, by Vendor.

7.02   *Managed Agreement Invoices.* Vendor shall (1) receive all Managed Agreement Invoices, (2) review and correct any errors in any such Managed Agreement Invoices in a timely manner and (3) submit such Managed Agreement Invoices to Customer within a reasonable period of time prior to the due date or, if a discount for payment is offered, the date on which Customer may pay such Managed Agreement Invoice with a discount. Customer shall pay the Managed Agreement Invoices received and approved by Vendor. Customer shall only be responsible for payment of the Managed Agreement Invoices and shall not be responsible to Vendor for any management, administration or maintenance fees of Vendor in connection with the Managed Agreement Invoices. Customer shall be responsible for any late fees in respect of the Managed Agreement Invoices, provided that Vendor submitted the applicable Managed Agreement Invoices to Customer for payment within a reasonable period of time prior to the date any such Managed Agreement Invoice is due, but in no event later than **[SPECIFY TIME PERIOD]** prior to the due date of such Managed Agreement Invoice. If Vendor fails to submit a Managed Agreement Invoice to Customer for payment in accordance with the preceding sentence, Vendor shall be responsible for any discount not received or any late fees in respect of such Managed Agreement Invoice.

7.03   *Assigned Agreements.* As of the Effective Date, Vendor shall assume all responsibility for the Assigned Agreements. Vendor may, to the extent permitted by the Assigned Agreements, renew, modify, terminate or cancel, or request or grant any consents or waivers under, any such Assigned Agreements. Any modification, termination, or cancellation fees or charges imposed upon Customer in connection with any modification, termination or cancellation of, or consent or waiver under, the Assigned Agreements shall be paid by Vendor.

7.04   *Assigned Agreement Invoices.* Vendor shall pay the invoices submitted by third parties in connection with the Assigned Agreements and shall be responsible for any late fees in respect of such third-party invoices.

7.05   *Performance Under Agreements.* Vendor shall promptly notify Customer of any breach of, or misuse or fraud in connection with, any Managed Agreements of which Vendor becomes aware and shall cooperate with Customer to prevent or stay any such breach, misuse, or fraud. Vendor shall pay all amounts due for any penalties or charges (including amounts due to a third party as a result of Vendor's failure to promptly notify Customer pursuant to the preceding sentence), associated taxes, legal expenses, and other incidental expenses incurred by Customer as a result of Vendor's nonperformance of its obligations under this Agreement with respect to the Customer Third-Party Contracts.

ARTICLE 8   SERVICE LEVELS.

8.01   *Designated Service Levels.* Vendor shall perform the Designated Services in accordance with the Designated Service Levels and in accordance with *Exhibit 10.*

8.02   *New Service Levels.* Vendor shall provide the New Services in accordance with the New Service Levels applicable to such New Services.

8.03   *Adjustment of Service Levels.* The Management Committee (1) shall review the Service Levels for the preceding 12 months during the last calendar quarter of every Contract Year, (2) with respect to any Service Levels that require periodic adjustment pursuant to this Agreement or are no longer appropriate because of an increase, decrease or change to the Services, shall adjust the Service Levels for the subsequent Contract Year and (3) with respect to all other Service Levels, may adjust the Service Levels for the subsequent Contract Year. In addition, either Party may, at any time upon notice to the other Party, initiate negotiations to review and, upon agreement by the Management Committee, adjust any Service Level which such Party in good faith believes is inappropriate at the time.

8.04   *Root-Cause Analysis.* Upon receipt of a notice from Customer with respect to Vendor's failure to provide the Services in accordance with the applicable Service Levels, Vendor shall, as soon as reasonably practicable, (1) perform a root-cause analysis to identify the cause of such failure, (2) provide Customer with a report detailing the cause of, and procedure for correcting, such failure, (3) implement such procedure and (4) provide Customer with assurance satisfactory to Customer that such failure will not recur following the completion of the implementation of the procedure.

8.05   *Measurement and Monitoring Tools.* As of the Effective Date, Vendor shall implement the measurement and monitoring Tools and procedures required to measure and report Vendor's performance of the Services against the applicable Service Levels. Such measurement and monitoring and procedures shall (1) permit reporting at a level of detail sufficient to verify compliance with the Service Levels and (2) be subject to audit by Customer or its designee. Vendor shall provide Customer and its designees with information concerning access to such measurement and monitoring Tools and procedures upon request, for inspection and verification purposes.

8.06   *Continuous Improvement and Best Practices.* Vendor shall, on a continuous basis (1) as part of its total quality management process, identify ways to improve the Service Levels and (2) identify and apply proven techniques and Tools from other installations within its operations that would benefit Customer either operationally or financially. Vendor shall, from time to time, include updates with respect to such improvements, techniques and Tools in the reports provided to Customer pursuant to *Section 3.09.*

8.07   *Performance Credits.* In the event of a failure to provide the Services in accordance with the applicable Service Levels, Vendor shall incur the Performance Credits identified in and according to the schedule set forth in *Exhibit 10.* The Performance Credits shall not limit Customer's right to recover, in accordance with this Agreement, other damages incurred by Customer as a result of such failure. If the Performance Credits incurred exceed $**[SPECIFY DOLLAR AMOUNT]** in any **[SPECIFY TIME PERIOD]** period during the Term, Customer may, upon notice to Vendor, terminate this Agreement, in whole or in part, without regard to *Section 26.04(1).* Nothing in this Section shall be deemed to limit or obviate Customer's right to terminate this Agreement pursuant to *Section 26.04(1).*

ARTICLE 9   CUSTOMER SATISFACTION AND BENCHMARKING.
9.01   *Initial Customer Satisfaction Survey.* During the **[SPECIFY TIME PERIOD]** period after the Effective Date, Vendor shall submit to Customer, for Customer's approval, the identity of the unaffiliated third party that shall conduct a initial customer satisfaction sur-

vey. Upon Customer's approval of such third party, Vendor shall engage such third party to conduct a initial customer satisfaction survey as approved by Customer for affected End-Users approved by Customer (the "*Initial Customer Satisfaction Survey*"). The Initial Customer Satisfaction Survey shall be (1) of the content and scope set forth in *Exhibit 18*, (2) administered in accordance with the procedures set forth in *Exhibit 18* and (3) subject to Customer's approval. The results of the Initial Customer Satisfaction Survey shall be the baseline for measurement of the performance improvements described in *Section 9.02*.

9.02   *Customer Satisfaction Survey.*

(1)   At least once every Contract Year during the Term, Vendor shall, upon Customer's request, engage an unaffiliated third party approved by Customer to conduct a customer satisfaction survey in respect of those aspects of the Services designated by Customer. The survey shall, at a minimum, cover a representative sampling of End-Users and senior management of Customer, in each case as specified by Customer. The timing, content, scope, and method of the survey shall be consistent with the Initial Customer Satisfaction Survey and subject to Customer's approval. Vendor agrees that **[(a)]** increased measured customer satisfaction shall be a key performance incentive for the compensation of the Key Personnel **[and (b) customer satisfaction shall be measured as a service level pursuant to *Section 8.01*]**.

(2)   **[In the event that Customer disputes the results of the customer satisfaction survey, Customer may engage a third party, reasonably acceptable to Vendor, to conduct the customer satisfaction survey pursuant to this Section. The results of such survey shall be binding on the Parties.]**

9.03   *Benchmarking Overview.* The Benchmarking Process shall be conducted by the Benchmarker. In the event (1) a Benchmarker is no longer providing the services required to conduct the Benchmarking Process, (2) Customer and Vendor agree that the Benchmarker should be replaced or (3) Customer and Vendor determine that another Benchmarker would be needed to take advantage of another system or methodology utilized by such Benchmarker to conduct the Benchmarking Process, Customer shall promptly designate a replacement Benchmarker. The fees and expenses charged by the Benchmarker shall be paid by Vendor.

9.04   *Benchmarking Process.* The Benchmarker shall conduct the Benchmarking Process annually in respect of each Contract Year. Within **[SPECIFY TIME PERIOD]** after the beginning of each Contract Year, or such later date agreed upon by the Parties, Customer and Vendor shall (1) agree upon the period during which the Benchmarking Process shall be conducted in such Contract Year and (2) review the Benchmarking Process used during the preceding Contract Year and adjust the Benchmarking Process as may be agreed upon by the Parties for the current Contract Year.

9.05   *Benchmark Results Review Period and Adjustments.* Customer and Vendor shall review the Benchmark Results during the Benchmark Review Period. In the event the Management Committee agrees with the Benchmark Results, the terms (e.g., the Fees or the Service Levels) of this Agreement shall be adjusted accordingly.

ARTICLE 10   SERVICE LOCATIONS.

10.01   *Service Locations.* The Services shall be provided **[(1) to the Customer Service Locations,]** (2) from the Vendor Service Locations and (3) from any other location for which Vendor has received Customer's approval. Any incremental expenses incurred by Customer as a result of a relocation to, or use of, any location other than the locations set forth on *Exhibit 6* shall, at Customer's sole discretion, be paid by Vendor or reimbursed to

Customer by Vendor. **[Except with respect to a Customer Service Location that Vendor is (a) the sole lessee of or (b) a sub-lessee and has management control of,]** Vendor and Vendor Agents may not provide or market services to a third-party from a Customer Service Location without Customer's consent.

10.02 *Safety and Security Procedures.* Vendor shall maintain and enforce at the Service Locations safety and security procedures that are at least equal to the most stringent of the following: (1) industry standards for locations similar to the Vendor Service Locations; (2) the procedures in effect at locations of other Vendor customers; (3) those procedures applicable to the Customer Service Locations as may be reasonably amended by Customer from time to time during the Term; and (4) any higher standard otherwise agreed upon by the Parties. Vendor shall comply with the safety and security procedures that are applicable to the Customer Service Locations, including the safety and security procedures set forth in *Exhibit 19.*

10.03 *Data Security.* Vendor shall establish and maintain safeguards against the destruction, loss or alteration of the Customer Data in the possession of Vendor (the "*Data Safeguards*") that shall be no less rigorous than those data security policies in effect as of the Effective Date at each applicable Customer Service Location in respect of such Customer Service Location and Vendor Service Location. Vendor shall revise and maintain the Data Safeguards at Customer's request. In the event Vendor intends to implement a change to the Data Safeguards (including pursuant to Customer's request), Vendor shall notify Customer and, upon Customer's approval, implement such change. In the event Vendor or Vendor Agents discovers or is notified of a breach or potential breach of security relating to the Customer Data, Vendor shall immediately (1) notify the Customer Contract Manager of such breach or potential breach and (2) if the applicable Customer Data was in the possession of Vendor or Vendor Agents at the time of such breach or potential breach, Vendor shall (a) investigate and remediate the effects of the breach or potential breach and (b) provide Customer with assurance satisfactory to Customer that such breach or potential breach will not recur.

10.04 *Security Relating to Competitors.* If (1) Vendor provides the Services to Customer from a Service Location that is shared with a third party or third parties or (2) any part of the business of Vendor or any such third party is now or is in the future competitive with Customer's business, then Vendor shall develop a process, subject to Customer's approval, to restrict access in any such shared environment to Customer's Confidential Information so that Vendor's employees or Vendor Agents providing services to such competitive business do not have access to Customer's Confidential Information.

ARTICLE 11   HUMAN RESOURCES.
Transitioning of employees of Customer to Vendor shall be effected in accordance with the terms and conditions set forth in *Exhibit 20.*

ARTICLE 12   VENDOR STAFF.
12.01 *Vendor Contract Manager.* Vendor shall appoint an individual (the "*Vendor Contract Manager*") who from the date of this Agreement shall serve, on a full-time basis, as the primary Vendor representative under this Agreement. Vendor's appointment of any Vendor Contract Manager shall be subject to Customer's prior approval. The Vendor Contract Manager shall (1) have overall responsibility for managing and coordinating the performance of Vendor's obligations under this Agreement and (2) be authorized to act for and on behalf of Vendor with respect to all matters relating to this Agreement.

12.02 *Key Personnel.* With respect to the Key Personnel set forth in *Exhibit 13*, the Parties agree as follows:

(1) Each Key Personnel shall be dedicated to the Customer account on a full-time basis.

(2) Before assigning an individual to a Key Personnel position, whether as an initial assignment or as a replacement, Vendor shall (a) notify Customer of the proposed assignment, (b) introduce the individual to appropriate representatives of Customer, (c) provide Customer with a résumé and any other information regarding the individual that may be reasonably requested by Customer and (d) obtain Customer's approval for such assignment. Vendor shall only assign an individual to a Key Personnel position who is approved by Customer.

(3) Vendor shall not replace or reassign (a) the Vendor Contract Manager for [SPECIFY TIME PERIOD] from the Effective Date or (b) the other Key Personnel for [SPECIFY TIME PERIOD] from the Effective Date, unless Customer consents to such reassignment or replacement or such Key Personnel (i) voluntarily resigns from Vendor, (ii) is dismissed by Vendor for misconduct (e.g., fraud, drug abuse, theft), (iii) fails to perform his or her duties and responsibilities pursuant to this Agreement, or (iv) dies or is unable to work due to his or her disability.

(4) If Customer decides that any Key Personnel should not continue in that position, then Customer may in its sole discretion and upon notice to Vendor require removal of such Key Personnel. Vendor shall, as soon as reasonably practicable, replace such Key Personnel.

(5) Vendor shall maintain backup procedures and conduct the replacement procedures for the Key Personnel in such a manner so as to assure an orderly succession for any Key Personnel who is replaced. Upon request, after a determination that a Key Personnel will be replaced, Vendor shall make such procedures available to Customer.

12.03 *Project Staff.* Vendor shall appoint individuals with suitable training and skills to perform the Services to the Project Staff. Vendor shall provide Customer with a list of all Vendor personnel dedicated full-time to the Project Staff at the end of every [SPECIFY TIME PERIOD] period after the Effective Date. Except as otherwise approved by Customer (in its sole discretion), those Vendor personnel located on Customer's premises may only provide services on such premises which support Customer's operations. Vendor shall notify Customer as soon as possible after dismissing or reassigning any member of the Project Staff whose normal work location is at a Customer Service Location.

12.04 *Subcontractors.*

(1) Prior to subcontracting any of the Services, Vendor shall notify Customer of the proposed subcontract and shall obtain Customer's approval of such subcontract. Prior to amending, modifying or otherwise supplementing any subcontract relating to the Services, Vendor shall notify Customer of the proposed amendment, modification or supplement and shall obtain Customer's approval thereof.

(2) No subcontracting shall release Vendor from its responsibility for its obligations under this Agreement. Vendor shall be responsible for the work and activities of each of the Vendor Agents, including compliance with the terms of this Agreement. Vendor shall be responsible for all payments to its subcontractors.

(3) Vendor shall promptly pay for all services, materials, equipment and labor used by Vendor in providing the Services and Vendor shall keep Customer's premises free of all liens.

12.05 *Conduct of Vendor Personnel.* While at the Customer Service Locations, Vendor and Vendor Agents shall (1) comply with the requests, standard rules and regulations of Customer regarding safety and health, personal and professional conduct (including the wearing of a particular uniform, identification badge or personal protective equipment and adhering to plant regulations and general safety practices or procedures) generally applicable to such Customer Service Locations and (2) otherwise conduct themselves in a businesslike manner. Vendor shall cause the Project Staff to maintain and enforce the confidentiality provisions of this Agreement. In the event that Customer determines that a particular member of the Project Staff is not conducting himself or herself in accordance with this Section, Customer may notify Vendor of such conduct. Upon receipt of such notice, Vendor shall promptly (a) investigate the matter and take appropriate action which may include (i) removing the applicable person from the Project Staff and providing Customer with prompt notice of such removal and (ii) replacing the applicable person with a similarly qualified individual or (b) take other appropriate disciplinary action to prevent a recurrence. In the event there are repeat violations of this Section by a particular member of the Project Staff, Vendor shall promptly remove the individual from the Project Staff as set forth above.

12.06 *Non-Competition.* Vendor shall not assign a Key Personnel or member of the Project Staff to the account of any competitor of Customer without Customer's prior consent (1) while such Key Personnel or member of the Project Staff, as the case may be, is assigned to the Customer account and (2) for a period of **[SPECIFY TIME PERIOD]** years following the date that such Key Personnel or member of the Project Staff, as the case may be, is removed from, or ceases to provide services in connection with, the Customer account.

ARTICLE 13   MANAGEMENT AND CONTROL.
13.01 *Management Committee.* Within **[SPECIFY TIME PERIOD]** of the Effective Date, the Customer Contract Manager and the Vendor Contract Manager shall appoint **[an equal number of]** representatives to serve on a management committee (the "*Management Committee*"). Customer shall designate one of its representatives on the Management Committee to act as the chairperson of the Management Committee. The Management Committee shall be authorized and responsible for (1) advising with respect to Customer's strategic and tactical decisions regarding the establishment, budgeting and implementation of Customer's priorities and plans for the Services and (2) monitoring and resolving disagreements regarding the provision of the Services and the Service Levels. A Party may change any of its representatives on the Management Committee upon notice to the other Party.

13.02 *Procedures Manual.* Within **[SPECIFY TIME PERIOD]** after the Effective Date, Vendor shall deliver to Customer **[for Customer's approval]**, in the form and scope agreed upon by Customer and Vendor, a management procedures manual (the "*Procedures Manual*"). Vendor shall periodically prepare and provide to Customer updates to such Procedures Manual to reflect any changes in the procedures described therein within a reasonable time after such changes are made.

13.03 *Change Control Procedures.* Prior to the Effective Date, Vendor shall deliver to Customer, for its review and approval, the Change Control Procedures. The Change Control Procedures shall provide, at a minimum, that:
(1)   No Change shall be implemented without Customer's approval, except as may be necessary on a temporary basis to maintain the continuity of the Services.
(2)   With respect to all Changes, Vendor shall (a) other than those Changes made on a temporary basis to maintain the continuity of the Services, schedule Changes so as not to unreasonably interrupt Customer's business operations, (b) prepare and deliver to Customer each month a rolling schedule for ongoing and planned Changes for the

next **[SPECIFY TIME PERIOD]** period and (c) monitor the status of Changes against the applicable schedule.

(3)   With respect to any Change made on a temporary basis to maintain the continuity of the Services, Vendor shall document and provide to Customer notification (which may be given orally provided that any oral notice must be confirmed in writing to Customer within five business days) of the Change no later than the next business day after the Change is made.

Vendor shall update the Change Control Procedures as necessary and shall provide such updated Change Control Procedures to Customer for its approval.

ARTICLE 14   PROPRIETARY RIGHTS.

14.01   *Customer IP.* Customer hereby grants to Vendor solely to provide the Services a nonexclusive, nontransferable, limited right to have access to and Use, to the extent permissible under the applicable third-party agreements, the Customer IP. Vendor may sublicense, to the extent permissible under the applicable third-party agreements, to Vendor Agents the right to have access to and Use the Customer IP solely to provide those Services that such Vendor Agents are responsible for providing and as may otherwise be agreed to by the Parties.

14.02   *Vendor IP.* Vendor shall provide Customer with access to the Vendor IP during the Term and during the Termination Assistance Period in accordance with *Article 28.* Customer shall have the right to approve any Vendor IP prior to Vendor's use of such Vendor IP to provide the Services. Vendor hereby grants to Customer a global, perpetual, irrevocable, fully paid-up, nonexclusive license to Use and sublicense, and to permit a third party to Use, solely in connection with providing goods or services to or purchasing goods or services from Customer, the Vendor IP being used to provide the Services as of the date of expiration or termination of this Agreement. Upon Customer's request, Vendor shall provide Customer with a list of all Vendor IP being used to provide the Services as of the date of such request.

14.03   *New IP.* New IP shall be owned by Customer. Customer shall have all right, title and interest, including worldwide ownership of copyright and patent, in and to the New IP and all copies made from it. Vendor hereby irrevocably assigns, transfers and conveys, and shall cause Vendor Agents to assign, transfer and convey, to Customer without further consideration all of its and their right, title and interest in and to such New IP, including all rights of patent, copyright, trade secret or other proprietary rights in such materials. Vendor acknowledges, and shall cause Vendor Agents to acknowledge, that Customer and the successors and permitted assigns of Customer shall have the right to obtain and hold in their own name any intellectual property rights in and to such New IP. Vendor agrees to execute, and shall cause Vendor Agents to execute, any documents or take any other actions as may reasonably be necessary, or as Customer may reasonably request, to perfect Customer's ownership of any such New IP.

ARTICLE 15   DATA.

15.01   *Ownership of Customer Data.* All Customer Data is, or will be, and shall remain the property of Customer and shall be deemed Confidential Information of Customer. Without Customer's approval (in its sole discretion), the Customer Data shall not be, (1) used by Vendor or Vendor Agents other than in connection with providing the Services, (2) disclosed, sold, assigned, leased or otherwise provided to third parties by Vendor or Vendor Agents or (3) commercially exploited by or on behalf of Vendor or Vendor Agents. Vendor hereby irrevocably assigns, transfers and conveys, and shall cause Vendor Agents to assign, transfer and convey, to Customer without further consideration all of its and their right, title and interest in and to the Customer Data. Upon request by Customer, Vendor shall execute and deliver, and shall cause Vendor Agents to execute and deliver, any financing statements or other documents that may be necessary or desirable under any Law to preserve, or enable Customer to enforce, its rights hereunder with respect to the Customer Data.

15.02 *Correction of Errors.* Vendor shall promptly correct any errors or inaccuracies in the Customer Data and the reports delivered to Customer under this Agreement, to the extent caused by Vendor or Vendor Agents. At Customer's request and expense, Vendor shall promptly correct any other errors or inaccuracies in the Customer Data or such reports.

15.03 *Return of Data.* Upon request by Customer at any time during the Term and upon expiration or termination of this Agreement, Vendor shall (1) promptly return to Customer, in the format and on the media requested by Customer, all or any part of the Customer Data and (2) erase or destroy all or any part of the Customer Data in Vendor's possession, in each case to the extent so requested by Customer. Any archival tapes containing Customer Data shall be used by Vendor and Vendor Agents solely for back-up purposes.

ARTICLE 16   CONSENTS.
Vendor, at its own cost, shall obtain, maintain, and comply with all of the Consents.

ARTICLE 17   CONTINUED PROVISION OF SERVICES.
17.01 *Disaster Recovery Plan.* Vendor shall (1) develop, submit to Customer for Customer's review, and implement a DRP acceptable to Customer within **[SPECIFY TIME PERIOD]** of the Effective Date, (2) periodically update and test the operability of the DRP during every **[SPECIFY TIME PERIOD]** period that the DRP is fully operational, (3) certify to Customer at least **[SPECIFY TIME PERIOD]** during every **[SPECIFY TIME PERIOD]** period that the DRP is fully operational and (4) implement the DRP upon the occurrence of a disaster (as such term is defined in the DRP). Vendor shall reinstate the Critical Services within **[SPECIFY TIME PERIOD]** of the occurrence of a disaster. In the event the Critical Services are not reinstated within **[SPECIFY TIME PERIOD]**, Customer may terminate this Agreement, in whole or in part, without regard to *Section 26.04(1)*. In the event of a disaster, Vendor shall not increase its charges under this Agreement or charge Customer usage fees in addition to the Designated Fees or the Variable Fees.

17.02 *Force Majeure.* **[ADD APPLICABLE FORCE MAJEURE PROVISION]**

ARTICLE 18   PAYMENTS TO VENDOR.
18.01 *Designated Fees.* In consideration of Vendor providing the Designated Services, Customer shall pay to Vendor the Designated Fees. Except as expressly set forth in this Agreement, there shall be no charge or fees payable by Customer in respect of Vendor's performance of its obligations pursuant to this Agreement.

18.02 *Variable Fees and Adjustment of Baselines.* At the end of every month, Vendor shall review the amount of the Designated Services used by Customer during the preceding month. In the event Customer's use of such services (1) increases above the resource baselines set forth in *Exhibit 11*, Customer shall pay to Vendor, in addition to the Designated Fees, an amount equal to the Additional Resource Charges in connection with the services set forth in *Exhibit 11* or (2) decreases below the resource baselines set forth in *Exhibit 11*, Vendor shall credit Customer an amount equal to Reduced Resource Credits in connection with the services set forth in *Exhibit 11*. Upon notice to Vendor, and no more than once each Contract Year, Customer may adjust the resource baselines set forth in *Exhibit 11* and Customer and Vendor shall implement an appropriate adjustment to the Fees to reflect the adjustment of the resource baselines.

18.03   *Substantial Change in Baselines.* In the event that Customer's use of the Designated Services decreases or increases more than **[SPECIFY PERCENT]** in the aggregate from the baselines set forth in *Exhibit 11* for any consecutive **[SPECIFY TIME PERIOD]** period during the Term, Customer, and Vendor shall negotiate and implement an appropriate reduction or increase to the Designated Fees. Customer shall not be obligated to obtain the Services from Vendor with respect to any newly acquired or formed entity or business unit.

18.04   **[*Adjustments to Fees.* There shall be no periodic adjustments to the Fees.]**

18.05   *Expenses.* Except as expressly set forth in this Agreement, all costs and expenses relating to the Services (including all costs and expenses related to the acquisition, maintenance and enhancement of the IP and Machines) are included in the Fees and shall not be charged to or reimbursed by Customer.

18.06   *Critical Milestones.* In connection with the development of the Transition Plan, Customer and Vendor shall develop a list of milestones relating to Vendor's obligations pursuant to *Article 4* which are critical to Customer, and, for each milestone, (1) a description of the applicable triggering event from which achievement of that milestone shall be measured, (2) the duration of time from the triggering event for the completion of that milestone and (3) an amount of the Designated Fees that Customer may defer with respect to that milestone in accordance with this Section. *Exhibit 21* contains lists of events and related information that Customer and Vendor agree shall be included in the final list. After development of the final list, Customer may defer, upon Customer's election, the specified amount of the Designated Fees if, as a result of Vendor's failure to perform its obligations pursuant to this Agreement, Vendor fails by more than **[SPECIFY TIME PERIOD]** days to achieve any specified milestone by the specified completion date. If and when Vendor achieves the specified milestone, all deferred fees shall be promptly paid to Vendor. Customer's deferral rights described in this Section shall not limit Customer's right to recover other damages incurred by Customer as a result of such failure or to terminate this Agreement pursuant to *Section 26.04(1)*.

18.07   *Rights of Set-Off.* With respect to any amount that (1) should be reimbursed to Customer or (2) is otherwise payable to Customer pursuant to this Agreement, Customer may upon notice to Vendor deduct the entire amount owed to Customer against the charges otherwise payable or expenses owed to Vendor under this Agreement.

18.08   *Proration.* All periodic Fees or charges under this Agreement are to be computed on a calendar month basis and shall be prorated on a per diem basis for any partial month.

18.09   *Refundable Items; Prepaid Expenses.* In the event Vendor receives any refund, credit or other rebate (including deposits) in connection with a Customer Third Party Contract or the Assets that is attributable to periods prior to the Effective Date or for which Customer retained financial responsibility after the Effective Date, then Vendor shall promptly (1) notify Customer of such refund, credit or rebate and (2) pay to Customer the full amount of such refund, credit or rebate. Vendor shall reimburse Customer for all prepaid amounts related to the Services.

18.10 *Unused Credits.* Any unused credits against future payments owed to either Party by the other pursuant to this Agreement shall be paid to the applicable Party within 30 days of the earlier of the expiration or termination of this Agreement.

18.11 *Most Favored Customer.* Vendor's charges to Customer for the Services shall be at least as low as Vendor's lowest charges for similar services to Vendor's best customer. Upon Customer's request, Vendor shall notify Customer that this Section has not been contradicted by any transaction entered into by Vendor since the later of (1) the Effective Date or (2) the date of the most recent notice provided by Vendor pursuant to this Section. If Vendor is unable to provide such notice because of a transaction entered into by Vendor contradicting this Section, Vendor shall offer to Customer an adjustment to the terms of this Agreement, including, if appropriate, the lowest charges included in any such transaction.

ARTICLE 19 PAYMENT SCHEDULE AND INVOICES.

19.01 *Designated Fees.* Within **[SPECIFY TIME PERIOD]** of the last day of each month of the Term, Vendor shall invoice Customer for the Designated Services performed in accordance with this Agreement during that month. **[Vendor shall invoice the Designated Fees in the currency specified by Customer.]** The Designated Fees for the first month of the Term shall be due and payable to Vendor within **[SPECIFY TIME PERIOD]** after the Effective Date. The Designated Fees for each subsequent month during the Term shall be due and payable to Vendor within **[SPECIFY TIME PERIOD]** of the later of (1) the end of the month in which Vendor provided the Services and (2) the date that Customer receives Vendor's invoice.

19.02 *Variable Fees.* During the first week of each calendar month of the Term after the first such month, Vendor shall provide Customer with the Variable Fee Report and an invoice for payment of the Additional Resource Charges. Customer shall pay such invoice within **[SPECIFY TIME PERIOD]** of Customer's receipt of such invoice or, in the event the Reduced Resource Credits are in excess of the Additional Resource Charges, Vendor shall provide Customer with a credit as set forth in the invoice for the Designated Fees for the following month. In the event Customer disapproves of any of the Variable Fees set forth in the Variable Fee Report, Customer shall provide Vendor with a list of any Variable Fees of which Customer disapproves and Vendor shall adjust the Variable Fee Report to reflect the changes indicated by Customer and agreed to by Vendor.

19.03 *Time of Payment.* Any sum due Vendor pursuant to this Agreement for which payment is not otherwise specified shall be due and payable **[SPECIFY TIME PERIOD]** after receipt by Customer of an invoice from Vendor.

19.04 *Detailed Invoices.* Vendor shall provide invoices with varying degrees of detail (e.g., per end-user, department, project, site), as requested by Customer.

19.05 *Fee Dispute.* In the event of a dispute, Customer shall pay any undisputed amounts to Vendor and Vendor shall continue to perform its obligations under this Agreement.

ARTICLE 20 TAXES.

(1) The Fees paid to Vendor are inclusive of any applicable sales, use, gross receipts, excise, value-added, withholding, personal property or other taxes attributable to periods on or after the Effective Date based upon or measured by Vendor's cost in

acquiring or providing equipment, materials, supplies or services furnished or used by Vendor in performing or furnishing the Services, including all personal property and sales or use taxes, if any, due on the Vendor Machines. In the event that a sales, use, excise, gross receipts, or services tax is assessed on the provision of the Services by Vendor to Customer or on Vendor's charges to Customer under this Agreement, however levied or assessed, Vendor shall bear and be responsible for and pay the amount of any such tax. To the extent that any sales, use, gross receipts, excise, value-added, or services tax is required by Law to be separately identified in Vendor's billings to Customer, Vendor shall separately identify the tax and assume any and all responsibility for non-compliance, including tax, interest, and penalty assessments.

(2)   Any taxes assessed, as determined by Customer, including a gross-up thereon, on the provision of the Services for a particular site resulting from Vendor's relocating or rerouting the delivery of Services for Vendor's convenience to, from or through a location other than the Service Location used to provide the Services as of the Effective Date shall be paid by Customer and Customer shall receive a credit with respect to the Fees invoiced under this Agreement equal to such payments made pursuant to this subsection.

(3)   Customer and Vendor shall each bear sole responsibility for all taxes, assessments, and other real property–related levies on its owned or leased real property.

(4)   Customer and Vendor shall cooperate to segregate the Fees into the following separate payment streams: (a) those for taxable Services; (b) those for nontaxable Services; (c) those for which a sales, use or other similar tax has already been paid; and (d) those for which Vendor functions merely as a paying agent for Customer in receiving goods, supplies or services (including leasing and licensing arrangements) that otherwise are nontaxable or have previously been subject to tax. In addition, each of Customer and Vendor shall reasonably cooperate with the other to more accurately determine a Party's tax liability and to minimize such liability, to the extent legally permissible. Each of Customer and Vendor shall provide and make available to the other any resale certificates, information regarding out-of-state sales or use of equipment, materials or services, and any other exemption certificates or information requested by a Party.

ARTICLE 21   AUDITS.

21.01   *Services.* Upon notice from Customer, Vendor, and Vendor Agents shall provide Customer, Customer Agents, and any of Customer's regulators with access to and any assistance (including reports) that they may require with respect to the Service Locations and the Systems for the purpose of performing audits or inspections of the Services and the business of Customer relating to the Services. If any audit by an auditor designated by Customer, a Customer Agent or a regulatory authority results in Vendor being notified that Vendor or Vendor Agents are not in compliance with any Law or audit requirement, Vendor shall, and shall cause Vendor Agents to, promptly take actions to comply with such audit. Vendor shall bear the expense of any such response that is (1) required by a Law or audit requirement relating to Vendor's business or (2) necessary due to Vendor's noncompliance with any Law or audit requirement imposed on Vendor. To the extent the expense is not payable by Vendor pursuant to the preceding sentence, Customer shall bear the expense of any such compliance that is (a) required by any Law or audit requirement relating to Customer's business or (b) necessary due to Customer's noncompliance with any Law or audit requirement imposed on Customer.

21.02   *Fees.*

(1)   Upon notice from Customer, Vendor shall provide Customer and Customer Agents with access to such financial records and supporting documentation as may be

requested by Customer and Customer and Customer Agents may audit the Fees charged to Customer to determine if such Fees are accurate and in accordance with this Agreement (including *Section 18.11*).

(2) If, as a result of such audit, Customer determines that Vendor has overcharged Customer, Customer shall notify Vendor of the amount of such overcharge and Vendor shall promptly pay to Customer the amount of the overcharge, plus Interest calculated from the date of receipt by Vendor of the overcharged amount until the date of payment to Customer.

(3) In addition to Customer's rights set forth in *Section 21.02(2)*, in the event any such audit reveals an overcharge to Customer of five percent or more of a particular fee category, Vendor shall, at Customer's option, issue to Customer a credit against the Designated Fees or reimburse Customer for the cost of such audit.

21.03   *Record Retention.* Vendor shall retain records and supporting documentation sufficient to document the Services and the Fees paid or payable by Customer under this Agreement in accordance with Customer's then-current record retention procedures, as in effect from time to time.

21.04   *Facilities.* Vendor shall provide to Customer[,]Customer Agents **[and Customer's regulators]**, on Vendor's premises (or, if the audit is being performed of a Vendor Agent, the Vendor Agent's premises if necessary), space, office furnishings (including lockable cabinets), telephone and facsimile services, utilities, and office-related equipment and duplicating services as Customer or such Customer Agents may reasonably require to perform the audits described in this Article.

ARTICLE 22   CONFIDENTIALITY.

22.01   *General Obligations.* All Confidential Information relating to or obtained from Customer or Vendor shall be held in confidence by the recipient to the same extent and in at least the same manner as the recipient protects its own confidential information. Neither Customer nor Vendor shall disclose, publish, release, transfer, or otherwise make available Confidential Information of, or obtained from, the other in any form to, or for the use or benefit of, any person or entity without the disclosing Party's consent. Each of Customer and Vendor shall, however, be permitted to disclose relevant aspects of the other's Confidential Information to its officers, directors, agents, professional advisors, contractors (including the Benchmarker), subcontractors and employees and to the officers, directors, agents, professional advisors, contractors, subcontractors and employees of its affiliates, to the extent that such disclosure is not restricted under this Agreement, any Assigned Agreements, any Managed Agreements, any Consents or any Governmental Approvals and only to the extent that such disclosure is reasonably necessary for the performance of its duties and obligations, or exercise of its rights, under this Agreement; provided, however, that the recipient shall take all reasonable measures to ensure that Confidential Information of the disclosing Party is not disclosed or duplicated in contravention of the provisions of this Agreement by such officers, directors, agents, professional advisors, contractors, subcontractors and employees. The obligations in this Section shall not restrict any disclosure pursuant to any Law (provided that the recipient shall give prompt notice to the disclosing Party of such order).

22.02   *Attorney–Client Privilege.* Vendor recognizes that it may obtain access to client documents, data and databases created by and for Customer and associated communications related thereto (collectively, "*Privileged Work Product*") which are confidential attorney work product or subject to the attorney–client privilege. Vendor shall not intentionally reveal Privileged Work Product to third parties and Vendor shall institute adequate safeguards to prevent the unintentional disclosure of Privileged Work Product to third parties. The only Project Staff who may have access to Privileged Work Product shall be those for whom such access is necessary for the purpose of providing services to Customer as provided in this Agreement. All Project Staff who will need access to Privileged Work Product shall first sign and deliver to Customer a confidentiality agreement satisfactory to Customer. Vendor recognizes that Privileged Work Product has been prepared in anticipation of litigation and that Vendor is performing the Services in respect of Privileged Work Product as an agent of Customer, and that all matter related thereto is protected from disclosure by Rule 26 of the United States Federal Rules of Civil Procedure (or any similar Law in other local jurisdictions). Should Vendor ever be notified of any judicial or other proceeding seeking to obtain access to Privileged Work Product, Vendor shall (1) immediately notify Customer and (2) take such reasonable actions as may be specified by Customer to resist providing such access. Customer shall have the right and duty to represent Vendor in such resistance or to select and compensate counsel to so represent Vendor or to reimburse Vendor for reasonable attorneys' fees and expenses incurred in resisting such access.

22.03 *Unauthorized Acts.* Without limiting either Party's rights in respect of a breach of this Article, each Party shall:
(1) promptly notify the other Party of any unauthorized possession, use or knowledge, or attempt thereof, of the other Party's Confidential Information by any person or entity that may become known to such Party;
(2) promptly furnish to the other Party full details of the unauthorized possession, use or knowledge, or attempt thereof, and assist the other Party in investigating or preventing the recurrence of any unauthorized possession, use or knowledge, or attempt thereof, of Confidential Information;
(3) cooperate with the other Party in any litigation and investigation against third parties deemed necessary by the other Party to protect its proprietary rights; and
(4) promptly use its best efforts to prevent a recurrence of any such unauthorized possession, use or knowledge, or attempt thereof, of Confidential Information.
Each Party shall bear the cost it incurs as a result of compliance with this Section.

ARTICLE 23 REPRESENTATIONS AND WARRANTIES.
23.01 *By Customer.* Customer represents and warrants that:
(1) Customer is a **[corporation duly incorporated] [partnership duly organized,] [other,]** validly existing and in good standing under the Laws of **[SPECIFY LAWS]**;
(2) Customer has all requisite **[corporate] [partnership] [other]** power and authority to execute, deliver and perform its obligations under this Agreement;
(3) the execution, delivery, and performance of this Agreement by Customer (a) has been duly authorized by Customer and (b) will not conflict with, result in a breach of or constitute a default under any other agreement to which Customer is a party or by which Customer is bound;
(4) Customer is duly licensed, authorized, or qualified to do business and is in good standing in every jurisdiction in which a license, authorization, or qualification is required for the ownership or leasing of its assets or the transaction of business of the character transacted by it, except where the failure to be so licensed, authorized, or qualified would not have a material adverse effect on Customer's ability to fulfill its obligations under this Agreement;
(5) Customer is in compliance with all Laws applicable to Customer and has obtained all applicable permits and licenses required of Customer in connection with its obligations under this Agreement;
(6) Customer has not disclosed any Confidential Information of Vendor**[; and**

(7)   the Customer IP set forth in *Exhibit 5* does not infringe upon the proprietary rights of any third party].

[ADD ENVIRONMENTAL COMPLIANCE REP IF APPLICABLE]
[ADD ERISA COMPLIANCE REP IF APPLICABLE]

23.02   *By Vendor.* Vendor represents and warrants that:

(1)   Vendor is a **[corporation duly incorporated,]** **[partnership duly organized,]** **[other,]** validly existing and in good standing under the Laws of **[SPECIFY LAWS]**;

(2)   Vendor has all requisite **[corporate][partnership][other]** power and authority to execute, deliver, and perform its obligations under this Agreement;

(3)   the execution, delivery, and performance of this Agreement by Vendor (a) has been duly authorized by Vendor and (b) will not conflict with, result in a breach of or constitute a default under any other agreement to which Vendor is a party or by which Vendor is bound;

(4)   Vendor is duly licensed, authorized, or qualified to do business and is in good standing in every jurisdiction in which a license, authorization, or qualification is required for the ownership or leasing of its assets or the transaction of business of the character transacted by it, except where the failure to be so licensed, authorized, or qualified would not have a material adverse effect on Vendor's ability to fulfill its obligations under this Agreement;

(5)   Vendor is in compliance with all Laws applicable to Vendor and has obtained all applicable permits and licenses required of Vendor in connection with its obligations under this Agreement;

(6)   Vendor has not disclosed any Confidential Information of Customer;

(7)   there is no outstanding litigation, arbitrated matter or other dispute to which Vendor is a party which, if decided unfavorably to Vendor, would reasonably be expected to have a material adverse effect on Customer's or Vendor's ability to fulfill its respective obligations under this Agreement; and

(8)   the Vendor IP does not infringe upon the proprietary rights of any third party.

23.03   ***DISCLAIMER.* EXCEPT AS SPECIFIED IN *SECTION 23.01* AND *SECTION 23.02*, NEITHER CUSTOMER NOR VENDOR MAKES ANY OTHER WARRANTIES WITH RESPECT TO THE SERVICES OR THE SYSTEMS AND EACH EXPLICITLY DISCLAIMS ALL OTHER WARRANTIES, EXPRESS OR IMPLIED, INCLUDING THE IMPLIED WARRANTIES OF MERCHANTABILITY AND FITNESS FOR A SPECIFIC PURPOSE.**

ARTICLE 24   ADDITIONAL COVENANTS.

24.01   *By Customer.* Customer covenants and agrees with Vendor that during the Term and the Termination Assistance Period:

(1)   Customer shall comply with all Laws applicable to Customer and, except as otherwise provided in this Agreement, shall obtain all applicable permits and licenses required of Customer in connection with its obligations under this Agreement**[; and**

(2)   **the Customer IP set forth in *Exhibit 5* shall not infringe upon the proprietary rights of any third party (except as may have been caused by a modification by Vendor or Vendor Agents)].**

24.02   *By Vendor.* Vendor covenants and agrees with Customer that during the Term and the Termination Assistance Period:

(1)   Vendor shall comply with all Laws applicable to Vendor and shall obtain all applicable permits and licenses required of Vendor in connection with its obligations under this Agreement;

(2)   none of the Services, the New IP, the Vendor IP, the Vendor Machines, any enhancements or modifications to the Customer IP performed by Vendor or Vendor Agents

or any other resources or items provided to Customer by Vendor or Vendor Agents shall infringe upon the proprietary rights of any third party (except as may have been caused by a modification by Customer or Customer Agents).

(3) **[Vendor shall ensure that no viruses or similar items are coded or introduced into the Systems. Vendor agrees that, in the event a virus or similar item is found to have been introduced into the Systems, Vendor shall assist Customer in reducing the effects of the virus or similar item and, if the virus or similar item causes a loss of operational efficiency or loss of data, to assist Customer to the same extent to mitigate and restore such losses;]**

(4) **[without the consent of Customer, Vendor shall not insert into the Software used to provide the Services any code that would have the effect of disabling or otherwise shutting down all or any portion of the Services. Vendor further represents and warrants that, with respect to any disabling code that may be part of the Software used to provide the Services, Vendor shall not invoke such disabling code at any time, including upon expiration or termination of this Agreement, without Customer's consent;]**

(5) **[the Systems shall be Century Compliant on or before [SPECIFY DATE]. Vendor agrees that Customer may request test scripts from Vendor to validate that the Systems are century compliant and determine the latest future date such Systems are able to process;]** and

(6) **[If a European Monetary Unit is required under any Law, or is permitted under any Law and any country adopts such European Monetary Unit, then (a) to the extent required to provide the Services, the Systems shall be EMU Compliant and (b) upon Customer's request Vendor shall provide Customer with test scripts to validate that such Systems are EMU Compliant.]**

[ADD ENVIRONMENTAL COMPLIANCE COVENANT IF APPLICABLE]
[ADD ERISA COMPLIANCE COVENANT IF APPLICABLE]

ARTICLE 25   DISPUTE RESOLUTION.

25.01   *Contract Managers.* Any dispute arising under this Agreement shall be considered in person or by telephone by the Customer Contract Manager and the Vendor Contract Manager within **[SPECIFY TIME PERIOD]** of receipt of a notice from either Party specifying the nature of the dispute; provided, however, that a dispute relating to *Section 15.03* or *Article 22* shall not be subject to this Section. Unless the Customer Contract Manager and the Vendor Contract Manager otherwise agree in writing, either Party may pursue its rights and remedies under this Agreement after the occurrence of such meeting or telephone conversation.

25.02   *Continuity of Services.* Vendor acknowledges that the timely and complete performance of its obligations pursuant to this Agreement is critical to the business and operations of Customer. Accordingly, in the event of a dispute between Customer and Vendor, Vendor shall continue to so perform its obligations under this Agreement in good faith during the resolution of such dispute unless and until this Agreement is terminated in accordance with the provisions hereof.

25.03   *Expedited Dispute Resolution.* Notwithstanding anything to the contrary contained in this Agreement, in the event of a dispute relating to or arising out of a Default Notice, the dispute resolution process described in this Article must be commenced and completed within the applicable Default Cure Period.

ARTICLE 26   TERMINATION.

26.01   *Termination for Convenience.* Customer may terminate this Agreement, in whole or in part, for convenience effective as of any time after the Effective Date by giving Vendor notice of the termination at least **[SPECIFY TIME PERIOD]** prior to the termination date specified in the notice.

26.02 *Termination for Change in Control of Customer.* In the event of a Change in Control of Customer, Customer may terminate this Agreement by giving Vendor notice of the termination at least **[SPECIFY TIME PERIOD]** prior to the termination date specified in the notice.

26.03 *Termination for Change in Control of Vendor.* In the event of a Change in Control of Vendor, Customer may terminate this Agreement by giving Vendor notice of the termination at least **[SPECIFY TIME PERIOD]** prior to the termination date specified in the notice.

26.04 *Termination for Cause.*

(1) If Vendor defaults in the performance of any of its material obligations (or repeatedly defaults in the performance of any of its other obligations) under this Agreement (except as provided in *Section 26.05*), and does not cure such default within 30 days of receipt (the "*Default Cure Period*") of a notice of default (the "*Default Notice*"), then Customer may, by giving notice to Vendor, terminate this Agreement as of the termination date specified in the notice.

(2) If Customer fails to make undisputed payments due to Vendor under this Agreement and does not cure such default within 30 days of receipt of a Notice of Default from Vendor, then Vendor may, by giving notice to Customer, terminate this Agreement as of the Termination Date specified in the notice.

26.05 *Termination for Failure to Provide Critical Services.* If Vendor fails to provide (1) any Critical Service and does not, within **[SPECIFY TIME PERIOD]** after receipt of a notice from Customer with respect to such failure, cure such failure or, if such failure cannot be cured within **[SPECIFY TIME PERIOD]**, provide Customer with a workaround that allows Customer to receive such Critical Service or (2) any Critical Service more than **[SPECIFY TIME PERIOD]** times in any consecutive **[SPECIFY TIME PERIOD]** period during the Term, then Customer may, upon notice to Vendor, terminate this Agreement, in whole or in part, as of the termination date specified in the notice.
[ADD ADDITIONAL TERMINATION RIGHTS IF APPLICABLE]

26.06 *Other Terminations.* In addition to the provisions of this Article, this Agreement may be terminated as provided in *Section 3.04(2)*, *Section 8.07,* and *Section 17.01*.

ARTICLE 27 [TERMINATION FEES.]
27.01 *[Calculation of Termination Fees.]* **[Set forth in *Exhibit 22* are the only termination fees that would be payable to Vendor if this Agreement is terminated pursuant to *Section 26.01*, effective as of the end of any month during the remaining Contract Years during the Term. Any termination fees payable in accordance with this Article shall be due and payable on the End Date.]**

27.02 *[Fee Adjustment upon Partial Termination.]* **[If Customer terminates a portion of the Services pursuant to *Section 26.01* or any other provision of this Agreement, then the Designated Fees shall be adjusted in accordance with *Exhibit 22*.]**

27.03 *[Termination Fees.]* **[Except as otherwise specifically set forth in this Article, no termination fee shall be payable by Customer in connection with the termination of this Agreement.]**

ARTICLE 28 TERMINATION ASSISTANCE.

28.01 *Termination Assistance Services.* Vendor shall, upon Customer's request during the Termination Assistance Period, provide the Termination Assistance Services at Vendor's rates then in effect for such services immediately prior to the expiration, termination or partial termination of this Agreement, or the insourcing or resourcing of a portion of the Services, except to the extent that resources included in the Designated Fees being paid by Customer to Vendor after such expiration, termination, partial termination, insourcing, or resourcing can be used to provide the Termination Assistance Services. The quality and level of performance during the Termination Assistance Period shall not be degraded. After the expiration of the Termination Assistance Period, Vendor shall (1) answer questions from Customer regarding the terminated, insourced or resourced Services on an "as needed" basis at Vendor's then standard billing rates and (2) deliver to Customer any remaining Customer-owned reports and documentation relating to the terminated, insourced or resourced Services still in Vendor's possession.

28.02 *Exit Rights.* Upon the later of (1) the expiration, termination or partial termination of this Agreement or the insourcing or resourcing of a portion of the Services, and (2) the last day of the Termination Assistance Period (the "*End Date*"):

(a) The rights granted to Vendor and Vendor Agents in *Section 14.01* shall immediately terminate and Vendor shall, and shall cause Vendor Agents to, (i) deliver to Customer, at no cost to Customer, a current copy of the Customer IP in the form in use as of the End Date and (ii) destroy or erase all other copies of the Customer IP in Vendor's or Vendor Agents' possession. Vendor shall, upon Customer's request, certify to Customer that all such copies have been destroyed or erased.

(b) Vendor shall deliver to Customer a copy of the Vendor IP in the form in use as of the End Date, and Customer shall have the rights described in *Section 14.02.*

(c) Upon Customer's request, with respect to any Vendor IP that Vendor has licensed, leased or otherwise obtained from third parties, and is using to provide the Services as of the End Date, Vendor shall transfer, assign or sublicense such Vendor IP to Customer and its designee(s) at no additional cost.

(d) Vendor shall (i) deliver to Customer a copy of all of the New IP, in the form in use as of the End Date and (ii) destroy or erase all other copies of the New IP in Vendor's possession.

(e) Upon Customer's request, with respect to (i) any agreements for maintenance, disaster recovery services or other third-party services, and any Vendor Machines not owned by the Vendor, being used by Vendor or Vendor Agents to provide the Services as of the End Date and (ii) the Assigned Agreements (not otherwise covered in *Section 28.02(e)(i)*), Vendor shall, and shall cause Vendor Agents to, transfer or assign such agreements and Vendor Machines to Customer and its designee(s), on terms and conditions acceptable to all applicable parties.

(f) Upon Customer's request, Vendor shall sell to Customer or its designee(s) (i) the Vendor Machines being used by Vendor or Vendor Agents to perform the Services as of the End Date and (ii) any assets transferred by Customer to Vendor or Vendor Agents (not otherwise covered in *Section 28.02(f)(i)*), free and clear of all liens, security interests, or other encumbrances at the lesser of the fair market value, as shall be determined by an agreed-upon appraisal, and the book value.

28.03 *[Hiring of Project Staff.* **Upon the occurrence of the delivery to Vendor by Customer of a notice of intent to (1) terminate this Agreement, or (b) insource or resource a portion of the Services pursuant to *Section 3.07*, with respect to each then-current member of the Project Staff performing the portion of the Services that are being terminated, in-**

sourced or resourced (each an *"Affected Project Staff Member"*), **Vendor shall (a) not terminate, reassign or otherwise remove from the Project Staff any Affected Project Staff Member and (b) to the extent not prohibited by applicable laws or governmental rules or regulations, (i) provide Customer with the name of each Affected Project Staff Member's position and a description of job responsibilities, in accordance with Vendor's standard employment policies, (ii) provide Customer and its designees full access to such Affected Project Staff Members and (iii) allow Customer and its designees to meet with, solicit and hire such Affected Project Staff Members. Vendor shall waive any restrictions that may prevent Affected Project Staff Members from being hired by Customer or its designees pursuant to this Section.]**

28.04 *[Termination Assistance on Partial Termination.* **Where there is a partial termination of this Agreement, or an insourcing or resourcing of a portion of the Services pursuant to *Section 3.07*, then *Section 28.02* and *Section 28.03* shall apply only in relation to those resources and other items referred to in *Section 28.02* (the *"Affected Resources"*), and those Affected Project Staff Members, which are associated with the Services to be terminated, insourced, or resourced. As soon as practicable after Customer exercises its rights to partially terminate this Agreement, or insource or resource any Services, Vendor shall notify Customer if any such Affected Resources, or any such Affected Project Staff Members, are necessary for the provision of the remaining Services and cannot be duplicated; whereupon Customer and Vendor will agree on, and failing agreement within a reasonable time Customer will specify, an appropriate allocation of such Affected Resources and Affected Project Staff Members.]**

ARTICLE 29   INDEMNITIES.

29.01 *Indemnity by Customer.* Customer shall indemnify Vendor from, and defend and hold Vendor harmless from and against, any Losses suffered, incurred or sustained by Vendor or to which Vendor becomes subject, resulting from, arising out of or relating to any claim:

(1) **[That the Customer IP infringes upon the proprietary or other rights of any third party (except as may have been caused by a modification by Vendor or Vendor Agents).]**

(2) Relating to any duties or obligations of Customer or Customer Agents with respect to a third party.

(3) Relating to the inaccuracy, untruthfulness, or breach of any representation or warranty made by Customer under this Agreement.

(4) Relating to (a) a violation of Law for the protection of persons or members of a protected class or category of persons by Customer or Customer Agents, including unlawful discrimination, (b) work-related injury, except as may be covered by Customer's workers' compensation plan, or death caused by Customer or Customer Agents, (c) accrued employee benefits not expressly assumed by Vendor, (d) any representations, oral or written, made by Customer or Customer Agents to the Affected Employees and (e) any other aspect of the Affected Employees' employment relationship with Customer or termination of such employment relationship with Customer (including claims for breach of an express or implied contract of employment).

(5) Relating to any amounts, including taxes, interest and penalties, assessed against Vendor which are the obligation of Customer pursuant to *Article 20*.

(6) Relating to personal injury (including death) or property loss or damage resulting from Customer's or Customer Agents' acts or omissions.

(7) Relating to a breach of any of the covenants in *Section 24.01*.

[ADD ENVIRONMENTAL INDEMNITY IF APPLICABLE]

Customer shall indemnify Vendor from any costs and expenses incurred in connection with the enforcement of this Section.

29.02 *Indemnity by Vendor.* Vendor shall indemnify Customer from, and defend and hold Customer harmless from and against, any Losses suffered, incurred or sustained by Customer or to which Customer becomes subject, resulting from, arising out of or relating to any claim:

(1) That the Services, the New IP, the Vendor IP, the Vendor Machines, any enhancements or modifications to the Customer IP performed by Vendor or Vendor Agents or any other resources or items provided to Customer by Vendor or Vendor Agents infringe upon the proprietary or other rights of any third party (except as may have been caused by a modification by Customer or Customer Agents).

(2) Relating to any duties or obligations of Vendor or Vendor Agents in respect of a third party or any subcontractor of Vendor.

(3) By a third party arising from services **[or systems]** provided by Vendor or Vendor Agents from a Service Location.

(4) Relating to the inaccuracy, untruthfulness, or breach of any representation or warranty made by Vendor under this Agreement.

(5) Relating to Vendor's failure to obtain, maintain or comply with the Consents and Governmental Approvals.

(6) Relating to (a) a violation of Law for the protection of persons or members of a protected class or category of persons by Vendor or Vendor Agents, including unlawful discrimination, (b) work-related injury, except as may be covered by Vendor's workers' compensation plan, or death caused by Vendor or Vendor Agents, (c) accrued employee benefits not expressly retained by Customer, (d) any representations, oral or written, made by Vendor or Vendor Agents to Customer's employees, including the Affected Employees and (e) any other aspect of the Affected Employees' employment relationship with Vendor or the termination of the employment relationship with Vendor (including claims for breach of an express or implied contract of employment).

(7) Relating to inadequacies in the facilities and the physical and data security controls at (a) the Customer Service Locations, to the extent the same (i) are controlled or provided by Vendor or Vendor Agents after the Effective Date and (ii) relate to Vendor's or Vendor Agents' provision of the Services and (b) the Vendor Service Locations.

(8) Relating to any amounts, including taxes, interest and penalties, assessed against Customer that are the obligation of Vendor pursuant to *Article 20.*

(9) Relating to personal injury (including death) or property loss or damage resulting from Vendor's or Vendor Agents' acts or omissions.

(10) Relating to a breach of *Section 15.01* or *Section 15.03.*

(11) Relating to a breach of any of the covenants in *Section 24.02.*

[ADD ENVIRONMENTAL INDEMNITY IF APPLICABLE]

Vendor shall indemnify Customer from any costs and expenses incurred in connection with the enforcement of this Section.

29.03 *Indemnification Procedures.* If any third-party claim is commenced against a Party entitled to indemnification under *Section 29.01* or *Section 29.02* (the "*Indemnified Party*"), notice thereof shall be given to the Party that is obligated to provide indemnification (the "*Indemnifying Party*") as promptly as practicable. If, after such notice, the Indemnifying Party shall acknowledge that this Agreement applies with respect to such claim, then the Indemnifying Party shall be entitled, if it so elects, in a notice promptly delivered to the Indemnified Party, but in no event less than 10 days prior to the date on which a response to such claim is due, to immediately take control of the defense and investigation of such claim and to employ and engage attorneys reasonably acceptable to the Indemnified Party to handle and defend the same, at the Indemnifying Party's sole cost and expense. The Indemnified Party shall cooperate, at the cost of the Indemnifying Party, in all reasonable respects with the Indemnifying Party and its attorneys in the investigation, trial and defense of such claim and any appeal arising therefrom; provided, however, that the Indemnified Party may, at its own cost and expense, participate, through its attorneys or otherwise, in such investigation, trial, and defense of such claim and any appeal arising therefrom. No settlement of a claim that involves a remedy other than the payment of money by the Indemnifying Party shall be entered into without the consent of the Indemnified Party. After notice by the Indemnifying Party to the Indemnified Party of its election to assume full control of the defense of any such claim, the Indemnifying Party shall not be liable to the Indemnified Party for any legal expenses incurred thereafter by such Indemnified Party in connection with the defense of that claim. If the Indemnifying Party does not assume full control over the defense of a claim subject to such defense as provided in this Section, the Indemnifying Party may participate in such defense, at its sole cost and expense, and the Indemnified Party shall have the right to defend the claim in such manner as it may deem appropriate, at the cost and expense of the Indemnifying Party.

ARTICLE 30 INSURANCE.

30.01 *Insurance.* During the Term **[and the Termination Assistance Period]**, Vendor shall obtain and maintain at its own expense, and require Vendor Agents to obtain and maintain at their own expense or Vendor's expense, insurance of the type and in the amounts set forth below:

(1) statutory workers' compensation in accordance with all Federal, state, and local requirements;

(2) employer's liability insurance in an amount not less than $**[SPECIFY DOLLAR AMOUNT]** per occurrence, covering bodily injury by accident or disease, including death;

(3) commercial general liability (including contractual liability insurance) in an amount not less than $**[SPECIFY DOLLAR AMOUNT]**; and

(4) comprehensive automobile liability covering all vehicles that Vendor owns, hires or leases in an amount not less than $**[SPECIFY DOLLAR AMOUNT]** (combined single limit for bodily injury and property damage).

[ADD ADDITIONAL INSURANCE COVERAGE IF APPLICABLE]

30.02 *Insurance Documentation.* To the extent third-party insurance is obtained or maintained pursuant to *Section 30.01*, Vendor shall, upon Customer's request, furnish to Customer certificates of insurance or other appropriate documentation (including evidence of renewal of insurance) evidencing all coverages referenced in *Section 30.01* and, if and to the extent applicable, naming Customer as an additional insured. Such certificates or other documentation shall include a provision whereby 30 days' notice must be received by Customer prior to coverage cancellation or material alteration of the coverage by either Vendor or Vendor Agents or the applicable insurer. Such cancellation or material alteration shall not relieve Vendor of its continuing obligation to maintain insurance coverage in accordance with this Article.

30.03 *Risk of Loss.* Vendor is responsible for the risk of loss of, or damage to, any property of Customer at a Vendor Service Location, unless such loss or damage was caused by the acts or omissions of Customer or a Customer Agent. Customer is responsible for the risk of loss of, or damage to, any property of Vendor at a Customer Service Location, unless such loss or damage was caused by the acts or omissions of Vendor or a Vendor Agent.

ARTICLE 31 MISCELLANEOUS PROVISIONS.

31.01 *Assignment.*

(1) Neither Party shall, without the consent of the other Party, assign this Agreement or any amounts payable pursuant to this Agreement, except that Customer may assign this Agreement to an Affiliate or another entity or business unit of Customer or pur-

suant to a reorganization or Change in Control of Customer without such consent. Upon Customer's assignment of this Agreement to an Affiliate or another Customer entity or business unit or pursuant to a reorganization or Change in Control of Customer, Customer shall be released from any obligation or liability under this Agreement. The consent of a Party to any assignment of this Agreement shall not constitute such Party's consent to further assignment. This Agreement shall be binding on the Parties and their respective successors and permitted assigns. Any assignment in contravention of this subsection shall be void.

(2) **[In the event that Customer divests an entity or business unit of Customer, Vendor shall, for a period of up to two years from the effective date of such divestiture, at Customer's request, continue to provide the Services to such divested Customer entity or business unit at the Fees then in effect.]**

31.02 *Notices.* Except as otherwise specified in this Agreement, all notices, requests, consents, approvals, agreements, authorizations, acknowledgements, waivers and other communications required or permitted under this Agreement shall be in writing and shall be deemed given when sent by telecopy to the telecopy number specified below or delivered by hand to the address specified below. A copy of any such notice shall also be sent by express air mail on the date such notice is transmitted by telecopy to the address specified below:

In the case of Customer:
[ADDRESS]
Attention:
Telecopy No.:
In the case of Vendor:
[ADDRESS]
Attention:
Telecopy No.:

Either Party may change its address or telecopy number for notification purposes by giving the other Party **[SPECIFY TIME PERIOD]** notice of the new address or telecopy number and the date upon which it will become effective.

31.03 *Counterparts.* This Agreement may be executed in any number of counterparts, each of which will be deemed an original, but all of which taken together shall constitute one single agreement between the Parties.

31.04 *Relationship.* The Parties intend to create an independent contractor relationship and nothing contained in this Agreement shall be construed to make either Customer or Vendor partners, joint venturers, principals, agents (except as expressly set forth in *Article 7*) or employees of the other. No officer, director, employee, agent, affiliate, or contractor retained by Vendor to perform work on Customer's behalf under this Agreement shall be deemed to be an employee, agent or contractor of Customer. Neither Party shall have any right, power or authority, express or implied, to bind the other.

31.05 *Consents, Approvals, and Requests.* Except as specifically set forth in this Agreement, all consents and approvals to be given by either Party under this Agreement shall not be unreasonably withheld or delayed and each Party shall make only reasonable requests under this Agreement.

31.06 *Severability.* If any provision of this Agreement is held by a court of competent jurisdiction to be contrary to Law, then the remaining provisions of this Agreement, if capable of substantial performance, shall remain in full force and effect.

31.07 *Waivers.* No delay or omission by either Party to exercise any right or power it has under this Agreement shall impair or be construed as a waiver of such right or power. A waiver by any Party of any breach or covenant shall not be construed to be a waiver of any succeeding breach or any other covenant. All waivers must be signed by the Party waiving its rights.

31.08 *Remedies Cumulative.* No right or remedy herein conferred upon or reserved to either Party is intended to be exclusive of any other right or remedy, and each and every right and remedy shall be cumulative and in addition to any other right or remedy under this Agreement, or under applicable law, whether now or hereafter existing.

31.09 *Entire Agreement.* This Agreement and the Exhibits to this Agreement represent the entire agreement between the Parties with respect to its subject matter, and there are no other representations, understandings, or agreements between the Parties relative to such subject matter.

31.10 *Amendments.* No amendment to, or change, waiver or discharge of, any provision of this Agreement shall be valid unless in writing and signed by an authorized representative of each of the Parties.

31.11 *Survival.* The terms of **[TO BE FILLED IN]** shall survive the expiration or termination of this Agreement.

31.12 *Third-Party Beneficiaries.* Each Party intends that this Agreement shall not benefit, or create any right or cause of action in or on behalf of, any person or entity other than the Parties.

31.13 *Governing Law.* **[Except as required by Law in any jurisdiction outside of the United States,]** this Agreement and the rights and obligations of the Parties under this Agreement shall be governed by and construed in accordance with the Laws of the State of **[SPECIFY].**

31.14 *Sole and Exclusive Venue.* Each Party irrevocably agrees that any legal action, suit or proceeding brought by it in any way arising out of this Agreement must be brought solely and exclusively in **[the United States District Court for the [SPECIFY] District of [SPECIFY] or in the state courts of the State of [SPECIFY]]** and irrevocably accepts and submits to the sole and exclusive jurisdiction of each of the aforesaid courts in personam, generally and unconditionally with respect to any action, suit or proceeding brought by it or against it by the other Party; provided, however, that this Section shall not prevent a Party against whom any legal action, suit or proceeding is brought by the other Party in the state courts of the State of **[SPECIFY]** from seeking to remove such legal action, suit or proceeding, pursuant to applicable Federal Law, to the district court of the United States for the district and division embracing the place where the action is pending in the state courts of the State of **[SPECIFY]**, and in the event an action is so removed each Party irrevocably accepts and submits to the jurisdiction of the aforesaid district court. Each Party hereto further irrevocably consents to the service of process from any of the aforesaid courts by mailing copies thereof by registered or certified mail, postage prepaid, to such Party at its address designated pursuant to this Agreement, with such service of process to become effective 30 days after such mailing.

31.15 *Covenant of Further Assurances.* Customer and Vendor covenant and agree that, subsequent to the execution and delivery of this Agreement and, without any additional consideration, each of Customer and Vendor shall execute and deliver any further legal instruments and perform any acts that are or may become necessary to effectuate the purposes of this Agreement.

31.16 *Negotiated Terms.* The Parties agree that the terms and conditions of this Agreement are the result of negotiations between the Parties and that this Agreement shall not be construed in favor of or against any Party by reason of the extent to which any Party or its professional advisors participated in the preparation of this Agreement.

31.17 *Export.* Customer and Vendor shall not knowingly export or re-export any personal computer system, part, technical data or subelements under this Agreement, directly or indirectly, to any destinations prohibited by the United States Government. The term "technical data" in this context, means such data as is defined as technical data by applicable United States export regulations.

31.18 *Nonsolicitation.* Except as contemplated by *Article 11*, during the Term, Vendor shall not hire any individual while that individual is an employee of Customer.

31.19 *Conflict of Interest.* Vendor shall not pay any salaries, commissions, fees, or make any payments or rebates to any employee of Customer, or to any designee of such employee, or favor any employee of Customer, or any designee of such employee, with gifts or entertainment of significant cost or value or with services or goods sold at less than full market value. Vendor agrees that its obligation to Customer under this Section shall also be binding upon Vendor Agents. Vendor further agrees to insert the provisions of this Section in each contract with a Vendor Agent.

31.20 *Publicity.* **[Each Party shall (1) submit to the other all advertising, written sales promotions, press releases and other publicity matters relating to this Agreement in which the other Party's name or mark is mentioned or which contains language from which the connection of said name or mark may be inferred or implied and (2) not publish or use such advertising, sales promotions, press releases, or publicity matters without the other Party's consent.]**

* * * *

IN WITNESS WHEREOF, each of Customer and Vendor has caused this Agreement to be signed and delivered by its duly authorized representative.

[CUSTOMER]

By: _____
Name:
Title:

[VENDOR]

By: _____
Name:
Title:

Appendix 5.7

BUSINESS PROCESS OUTSOURCING AGREEMENT (VENDOR FORM)[a]

[SPECIFY TYPE OF BUSINESS PROCESS SERVICES TO BE OUTSOURCED]
AGREEMENT

by and between

[VENDOR]
and
[CUSTOMER]

Dated as of **[FILL IN DATE]**

TABLE OF CONTENTS

---

[a] Note: This sample agreement is intended to illustrate the types of legal issues that vendors typically wish to address in connection with business process outsourcing transactions. The provisions included in this sample agreement, while comprehensive, may not cover all of the issues that may arise in a particular transaction. Legal issues will likely vary depending on the type of business process being outsourced and the scope of the outsourcing transaction. This sample agreement or any part thereof should only be used after consultation with your legal counsel. Legal counsel should be consulted prior to entering into or negotiating any outsourcing transaction.

TABLE OF EXHIBITS

[Exhibit 10   Transferred Assets and Forms of General Assignment and Bill of Sale]
[Exhibit 11   Human Resources Provisions]
[Exhibit 12   Termination Assistance Services]

This **[SPECIFY TYPE OF BUSINESS PROCESS SERVICES TO BE OUT-SOURCED] AGREEMENT**, dated as of **[FILL IN DATE]**, is by and between **Vendor** and **Customer**.

NOW, THEREFORE, for and in consideration of the agreements set forth below, Vendor and Customer hereby agree as follows:

ARTICLE 1   DEFINITIONS AND CONSTRUCTION.

1.01   *Definitions.* The defined terms used in this Agreement shall have the meanings specified in *Exhibit 1*.

1.02   *Interpretation.*

(1)   In this Agreement and the Exhibits to this Agreement, the Exhibits to this Agreement shall be incorporated into and deemed part of this Agreement and all references to this Agreement shall include the Exhibits to this Agreement.

(2)   The Article and Section headings, Table of Contents and Table of Exhibits are for reference and convenience only and shall not be considered in the interpretation of this Agreement.

(3)   In the event of a conflict between the terms of this Agreement and the terms of any of the Exhibits, the terms of **[this Agreement] [the Exhibits]** shall prevail.

ARTICLE 2   TERM.

The initial term of this Agreement shall commence on the Effective Date and continue until 23:59 (**[SPECIFY TIME STANDARD]** Time) on **[SPECIFY DATE]**, or such earlier date upon which this Agreement may be terminated pursuant to *Article 17* (the "*Initial Term*"). Upon expiration of the Initial Term, the term of this Agreement shall automatically extend for successive one-year periods (each, a "*Renewal Term*") unless this Agreement is terminated earlier pursuant to *Article 17* or either Party gives the other Party notice at least 12 months prior to the expiration of the Initial Term or the applicable Renewal Term, as the case may be, that it does not desire to extend the term of this Agreement (the Initial Term and the Renewal Term collectively, the "*Term*").

ARTICLE 3   SERVICES.

3.01   *Generally.* **[IF REQUIREMENTS CONTRACT: During the Term, Vendor shall be the exclusive provider of, and Customer shall purchase from Vendor, all of Customer's requirements for the services described in *Exhibit 2* (the "*Services*"), all upon and subject to the terms and conditions set forth in this Agreement.] [FOR CONTRACTS THAT ARE NOT REQUIREMENTS-BASED: During the Term, Vendor shall provide to Customer, and Customer shall purchase from Vendor, the services described in *Exhibit 2* (the "*Services*").]**

3.02   *Service Locations.*

(1)   Vendor shall provide the Services to the Customer Service Locations.

(2)   Each Party, while on the other Party's premises, shall comply with the reasonable requests, standard rules and regulations of such Party regarding safety and health and personal and professional conduct generally applicable to such premises.

3.03   *Vendor Management.* During the Term, Vendor shall maintain an individual (the "*Vendor Account Manager*") who shall serve as the primary Vendor representative under this Agreement. The Vendor Account Manager shall (a) have overall responsibility for managing and coordinating the performance of Vendor's obligations under this Agreement and (b) be authorized to act for and on behalf of Vendor with respect to all matters relating to this Agreement.

3.04   *[Market Awareness.* **Vendor shall periodically meet with Customer in accordance with the procedures agreed upon by the Parties to inform Customer of any new developments or trends of which Vendor becomes aware that could reasonably be expected to have an impact on Customer's business. The acquisition and implementation of any such new assets, methodologies or technology by Vendor at Customer's request shall be an Out-of-Scope Service.]**

3.05   *[Asset Transfer.* **On [the Effective Date], Vendor shall purchase from Customer, the Transferred Assets for the purchase price set forth in *Exhibit 10*. [Customer] [Vendor] shall be responsible for and shall pay all sales, use and other similar taxes arising out of or in connection with the transfer of the Transferred Assets by Customer to Vendor on [the Effective Date]. On [the Effective Date], Customer shall assign, transfer and convey to Vendor good and valid title in and to the Transferred Assets free and clear of all liens by delivery of one of more general assignments and bills of sale in the form set forth in *Exhibit 10*, duly executed by Vendor and Customer.]**

ARTICLE 4   CONTRACT ADMINISTRATION.
4.01   *Third-Party Contracts.* Subject to Customer's obtaining and maintaining the Consents, Vendor shall have financial and administrative responsibility during the Term for the Third-Party Contracts. Vendor shall be responsible for the performance of all obligations of Customer under the Third-Party Contracts, including payment of all related expenses attributable to periods on or after the Effective Date, to the extent that such obligations were disclosed to Vendor on or before the Effective Date through receipt by Vendor of a copy of the relevant documents, including the applicable Third-Party Contracts. Customer represents and warrants that all obligations with respect to the Third-Party Contracts accruing prior to or attributable to periods prior to the Effective Date have been satisfied. Customer shall, upon Vendor's request from time to time, terminate any Third-Party Contracts and Vendor shall reimburse Customer for any termination charges arising out of any such terminations.

4.02   *Customer Obligations.* Commencing as of the earlier of the date this Agreement is executed by the Parties and the Effective Date, Customer shall not enter into any new or amend any existing agreements or arrangements, written or oral, affecting or impacting the Third-Party Contracts **[or the Transferred Assets],** without Vendor's consent.

ARTICLE 5   SERVICE LEVELS.
5.01   *Service Levels.* **[OPTION 1: Within [SPECIFY TIME PERIOD] days after the Effective Date, the Parties shall agree to the (1) service levels that Vendor shall meet in the performance of the Services in the categories set forth in *Exhibit 6* (the "*Service Levels*") and (2) time period during which the Service Levels shall be measured.] [OPTION 2: Vendor shall perform the Services in accordance with the service levels set forth in *Exhibit 6* (the "*Service Levels*").]**

5.02   *Reporting.* Vendor shall provide to Customer performance reports according to a schedule and in the format agreed upon by the Parties.

5.03   *Remedies.* **[OPTION 1: BE SILENT] [OPTION 2: Customer agrees that the remedies available to it in the event of a failure of Vendor to provide the Services in accordance with the Service Levels should be addressed to correcting problems that resulted in such** failure, rather than to penalizing Vendor. In recognition of this, (1) failures not of a general and consistent nature to meet a Service Level shall not be deemed a material breach by Vendor and (2) Customer's sole and exclusive remedies for such failure shall be as set forth in this Section and *Exhibit 6*. If Vendor fails to meet a Service Level for any Service, then Vendor shall (a) complete performance of the Service as near as reasonably possible to the applicable Service Level and (b) use commercially reasonable efforts to remedy the problem that caused it to fail to meet such Service Level.] [OPTION 3: In the event Vendor fails to provide the Services in accordance with the Service Levels, Vendor shall incur the performance credits identified in and according to the schedule set forth in *Exhibit 6*. Customer agrees that (1) Vendor shall not be obligated to issue a Performance Credit to Customer if the failure to meet the Service Level was not caused by Vendor or Vendor Agents, (2) any Performance Credit due to Customer shall be applied against amounts otherwise payable to Vendor by Customer pursuant to this Agreement within [90] days after the end of the applicable Contract Year, (3) the Performance Credits shall be Customer's sole and exclusive remedy for Vendor's failure to meet such Service Level and (4) such failure to meet such Service Level shall not be grounds for termination of this Agreement pursuant to *Section 17.02*.]

ARTICLE 6   CHANGES IN THE SERVICES.

(1)   Vendor reserves the right in its discretion to designate and make changes to the Services and the Service Levels (each, a "*Change*"); provided, however, that any such Change shall not have a material adverse impact on the Service Levels or cause a material increase to the Fees.

(2)   [OPTION 1: Subject to subsection (3) below, in the event Vendor intends to make a Change that would have a material adverse impact on the Service Levels or cause a material increase to the Fees, Vendor shall (a) notify Customer of the Change and its impact on the Service Levels and the Fees and, (b) if Customer requests within 15 days of receipt of such notice, discuss means to reduce any negative impact and implement such means as are practical and reasonable.]

   [OPTION 2: Except as set forth in subsection (1) above, in the event a Party wishes to make a Change, such Party shall submit a written proposal to the other Party describing such desired Change. The other Party shall reject or accept the proposal in writing within a reasonable period of time, but in no event more than 30 days after receipt of the proposal. In the event the proposal is rejected, the writing shall include the reason for the rejection. In the event the proposal is accepted, the Parties shall determine the additions or modifications to be made to this Agreement (including the Fees). Any such addition or modification shall be set forth in a written Change Order signed by the Parties. Neither Party shall be obligated to accept a proposal submitted by the other Party pursuant to this subsection. Vendor shall have no obligation to provide any service or otherwise act pursuant to any proposal submitted by Customer pursuant to this subsection, except to the extent such proposal is set forth in an executed Change Order.]

(3)   Customer shall promptly identify and notify Vendor of any changes in Law, including Customer's regulatory requirements, that may relate to Customer's use of the Services. The Parties shall work together to identify the impact of such changes on how Customer uses, and Vendor delivers, the Services. Customer shall be responsible for any fines and penalties arising from any noncompliance by Customer with any Law relating to Customer's use of the Services. Subject to the following sentence, if a change in Law prevents or delays Vendor from performing its obligations under this Agreement, the Parties shall develop and implement a suitable workaround until such time as Vendor can perform its obligations under this Agreement without such workaround. If a change in Law, including the development or implementation of a workaround, results in Vendor's use of additional resources or an increase in Vendor's

costs of providing the Services, Customer shall **[OPTION 1: pay for such additional resources and increased costs at rates agreed upon by the Parties][OPTION 2: reimburse Vendor for such additional resources and increased costs].**

ARTICLE 7   THIRD PARTY SERVICES.

7.01   *Vendor Opportunity.* **[OPTION 1: Vendor shall have the right to match the material terms of any third-party offer received by Customer with respect to any Out-of-Scope Service. If Vendor offers to provide such Out-of-Scope Service to Customer upon substantially similar terms as those set forth in such third-party offer, Vendor shall provide to Customer, and Customer shall purchase from Vendor, pursuant to a Change Order or separate agreement, as the case may be, such Out-of-Scope Services upon terms set forth in such Change Order or separate agreement, including Vendor's charges for such Out-of-Scope Service.] [OPTION 2: With respect to any Out-of-Scope Service, Customer shall (1) notify Vendor at or about the same time that it notifies other vendors that it is considering acquiring an Out-of-Scope Service and provide Vendor with the same information that it provides such other vendors and (2) allow Vendor the opportunity to compete with such other vendors for the provision of such Out-of-Scope Service. If Vendor is selected by Customer to provide such Out-of-Scope Service, Vendor and Customer shall negotiate a Change Order or separate agreement, as the case may be, including Vendor's charges for such Out-of-Scope Service.]**

7.02   *Cooperation with Third-Party Service Providers.* Upon Customer's request and reasonable notice, Vendor shall, as an Out-of-Scope Service, cooperate with third-party service providers of Customer; provided, however, that (1) such cooperation does not impact the Services or Vendor's ability to meet the Service Levels and (2) Vendor shall not be required to disclose any of Vendor's Confidential Information to such third-party service provider.

ARTICLE 8   HUMAN RESOURCES.

[The transition of employees of Customer to Vendor [or Vendor Agents] shall be effected in accordance with the terms and conditions set forth in *Exhibit 11*.]

ARTICLE 9   CUSTOMER RESPONSIBILITIES.

9.01   *Customer Project Manager.* During the Term, Customer shall maintain a senior executive of Customer (the "*Customer Project Manager*") who shall serve as the primary Customer representative under this Agreement. The Customer Project Manager shall (1) have overall responsibility for managing and coordinating the performance of Customer's obligations under this Agreement and (2) be authorized to act for and on behalf of Customer with respect to all matters relating to this Agreement.

9.02   *Customer Responsibilities.* During the Term and in connection with Vendor's performance of the Services under this Agreement, Customer shall, at its expense: (1) be responsible for the obligations and responsibilities set forth in *Exhibit 7*; (2) upon Vendor's request, make available to Vendor personnel familiar with Customer's business requirements; (3) provide to Vendor complete and accurate information regarding Customer's business requirements in respect of any work to be performed by Vendor under this Agreement; (4) respond within the time period specified in this Agreement (or if no time period is specified within three business days) to all deliverables presented to Customer by Vendor for Customer's approval, which approval shall not be unreasonably withheld (if Customer fails to respond within such three-day or other specified period, Customer shall be deemed to have accepted such deliverable); (5) cooperate with Vendor; (6) promptly notify Vendor of any (a) third-party claims that may have an impact on this Agreement and (b) invalid or nonexistent licenses or leases; and (7) perform all other obligations of Customer described in this Agreement.

9.03   *Customer Resources.* Commencing on the Effective Date and continuing for so long as Vendor requires the same for the performance of the Services, Customer shall provide to Vendor, at no charge to Vendor:

(1)   the use of the space in Customer's premises that Vendor may from time to time require in connection with the performance of the Services, together with office furnishings, telephone equipment and services, janitorial services, utilities and office-related equipment, supplies and duplicating services reasonably required in connection with the performance of the Services;

(2)   full access to, and use of, the Customer Assets; and

(3)   the resources set forth in *Exhibit 7*.

9.04   *Consents.* All Consents shall be obtained and maintained by Customer with Vendor's cooperation. Customer shall pay any costs of obtaining and maintaining the Consents.

9.05   *Use of Services.* Customer may not remarket or sell all or any portion of the Services provided under this Agreement, or make all or any portion of the Services available to any party other than Customer, without Vendor's consent.

ARTICLE 10   PROPRIETARY RIGHTS.

10.01   *[Customer Intellectual Property.* **Customer hereby grants to Vendor at no cost to Vendor a nonexclusive right to access and Use in connection with the provision of the Services (1) the Customer Proprietary Intellectual Property and (2) the Customer Third-Party Intellectual Property. Upon the later of the expiration of this Agreement or termination of this Agreement and the end of the Termination Assistance Period, the rights granted to Vendor in this Section shall immediately revert to Customer and Vendor shall, at Customer's cost and expense, deliver to Customer a current copy of all the Customer Intellectual Property (including any related source code in Vendor's possession) in the form in use as of such date. Customer shall pay all costs and expenses with respect to the Customer Intellectual Property, including the costs associated with maintenance, license payments, insurance, taxes and the Consents. [While Vendor shall manage the operation of the Customer Intellectual Property as described in *Exhibit 2*, Customer is responsible for maintaining, upgrading, and replacing the Customer Intellectual Property as necessary for Vendor to provide the Services. In the event that Customer does not comply with such obligations, Vendor shall be excused from its obligation to perform the Services, including Vendor's obligation to meet the Services Levels, to the extent that its inability to meet such obligation is caused by Customer's failure to comply with its obligations under this Section.]**

10.02   *Vendor Intellectual Property.* All Vendor Intellectual Property shall be and shall remain the exclusive property of Vendor or its licensor and Customer shall have no rights or interests in the Vendor Intellectual Property except as described in *Section 17.04*. Customer hereby irrevocably assigns to Vendor any and all rights or interests in the Vendor Intellectual Property. **[OPTION: Upon expiration or termination of this Agreement, if Customer has fully complied with all of its obligations and is not in default under this Agreement, Vendor hereby grants to Customer, to the extent possible and without additional cost to Vendor, a nonexclusive, nontransferable license to Use "as-is" the then-current, in-use versions of the Vendor Proprietary Intellectual Property set forth in Exhibit ___, in accordance with *Section 10*. Vendor makes no representations or warranties with respect to the Vendor Proprietary Intellectual Property.] [LIMIT RIGHT TO MODIFY/ENHANCE?]**

10.03   *Developments.* **[SEE OPTIONS IN APPENDIX 57A, "PROPRIETARY RIGHTS RIDER"]**

10.04   *Tools.* [**Notwithstanding anything contrary in this Agreement, Vendor shall retain all right, title and interest in and to any and all ideas, concepts, know-how, development tools, methodologies, processes, procedures, technologies or algorithms ("*Tools*") which are based upon trade secrets or proprietary information of Vendor. Nothing contained in this Agreement shall restrict Vendor from the use of any Tools which Vendor develops for Customer or has access to under this Agreement.**]

ARTICLE 11   PAYMENTS TO VENDOR.

11.01   *Fees.* In consideration of Vendor providing the Services, Customer shall pay to Vendor the Fees, as may be adjusted from time to time pursuant to this Agreement.

11.02   *Cost of Living Adjustment.* Customer shall pay a cost of living adjustment in accordance with *Exhibit 3*, beginning in the January following the Effective Date.

11.03   *Time of Payment.* Vendor shall deliver an invoice on or about the **[first]** day of each month for the Services to be performed during such month and each such invoice shall be due within **[SPECIFY TIME PERIOD]** days of receipt by Customer. Any sum due Vendor pursuant to this Agreement for which a time of payment is not otherwise specified shall be due and payable **[SPECIFY TIME PERIOD]** days after receipt by Customer of an invoice from Vendor. Any amounts not paid by Customer to Vendor when due shall bear interest **[at a rate of [SPECIFY PERCENTAGE] percent per year (or, if lesser, the maximum rate permissible by applicable law),] [at the Default Rate,]** measured from the date such amount was due until the date such amount is paid by Customer to Vendor. Without prejudice to any other rights it has under this Agreement, Vendor shall have the right to suspend the provision of the Services to Customer if Customer is more than **[SPECIFY TIME PERIOD]** days late in paying an invoice.

11.04   *Disputed Amounts.* If Customer, in good faith, disputes any invoice charges regarding the Services, it may withhold from its payment of the relevant invoice any such disputed amounts (except for applicable taxes), up to a maximum of the lesser of the amount for the Services to which the dispute relates and **[SPECIFY PERCENTAGE]** percent of the average monthly Fees for the previous 12 months. Customer shall pay to Vendor withheld amounts, plus interest **[at a rate of [SPECIFY PERCENTAGE] percent per year (or, if lesser, the maximum rate permissible by applicable law),] [at the Default Rate,]** measured from the date such amount was due until the date such amount is paid by Customer to Vendor, in accordance with the resolution of the dispute. Notwithstanding any dispute and in accordance with this Section, Customer shall remit to Vendor the invoiced amount, less the disputed amount, in accordance with this Section and *Section 11.03*.

11.05   *Permits and Approvals.* Customer shall be responsible for and carry the risk of obtaining all consents, permissions, approvals and assurances of whatever nature which may be needed to make payments as required under this Agreement.

11.06   *Expenses.* Unless otherwise agreed, Customer shall reimburse Vendor for all travel expenses, living, hotel and transportation allowances and other normally reimbursable expenses and allowances for any member of the Project Staff travelling in connection with the Services, all as reasonably incurred and in accordance with Vendor's generally applicable personnel practices and procedures.

11.07   *Proration.* All periodic charges under this Agreement are to be computed on a calendar month basis and shall be prorated on a per diem basis for any partial month.

11.08   Verification of Information. **[OPTION 1: The obligations of the Parties and the charges set forth in this Agreement are based upon information furnished by Customer to Vendor, but such information has not been independently verified by Vendor. Customer believes that such information is accurate and complete. However, if Vendor determines during the first Contract Year that any such information should prove to be inaccurate or incomplete in any adverse material respect, Vendor and Customer shall negotiate appropriate adjustments to the provisions of this Agreement, including the Fees.]**

[OPTION 2: The Services, Fees, and Service Levels are based on circumstances, estimates, metrics, principles, financial data, standards and general information disclosed by Customer or used by Vendor (collectively, "*Assumptions*"). Customer shall be responsible for the accuracy of any representation it made as part of the due diligence and negotiation process and on which the Assumptions are based. In the event of any material deviation from the Assumptions, Vendor and Customer shall negotiate to define and agree upon adjustments that shall be consistent with the intent of each of Vendor and Customer. Any such adjustments shall be set forth in a Change Order.]

11.09   *Taxes.* The Fees paid to Vendor are exclusive of any applicable sales, use, gross receipts, excise, value-added, withholding, personal property, or other taxes attributable to periods on or after the Effective Date. In the event that a sales, use, excise, gross receipts, or services tax is assessed on the provision of the Services by Vendor to Customer or on Vendor's charges to Customer under this Agreement, however levied or assessed, Customer shall bear and be responsible for and pay the amount of any such tax, or, if applicable, reimburse Vendor for the amount of any such tax.

11.10   *Extraordinary Changes in Workload.* If, during the Term, Customer experiences significant changes in the scope or nature of its business which have or are reasonably expected to have the effect of causing a sustained substantial decrease of **[SPECIFY PERCENTAGE]** percent or more in the amount of resources Vendor uses in performing the Services, provided such decreases are not due to Customer resuming the provision of such Services by itself or Customer transferring the provision of such Services to another vendor, Customer shall notify Vendor of any event or events which Customer believes may result in such sustained decrease and Vendor shall identify, in a plan that shall be submitted to Customer for review and acceptance, any changes that can be made to accommodate the extraordinary decrease of resource requirements in a cost-effective manner, without disruption to Customer's ongoing operations. Upon Customer's acceptance of Vendor's plan, Vendor shall make any applicable adjustments to the Fees to reflect the foregoing and distribute an amended *Exhibit 3* to Customer.

ARTICLE 12   AUDIT.

12.01   *Verification of Fees.* Upon 30 days' notice from Customer and not more than once during each Contract Year, Vendor shall furnish to Customer a certificate by Vendor's external auditors verifying the Fees. The cost of the verification shall be paid by Customer**[; provided however, that if an overcharge over [SPECIFY AMOUNT] is disclosed, Vendor shall reimburse such costs to Customer]**. Such certificate shall be conclusive. Any requests for verification of the Fees shall be made no later than **[SPECIFY TIME PERIOD]** years from the end of the Contract Year in which the Fees were incurred.

12.02   *Audit Expenses.* If Vendor is required to provide services or incur costs, other than of a routine nature, in connection with any audit pursuant to this Article, then Customer shall **[pay for such resources and costs at rates agreed upon by the Parties] [reimburse Vendor for such resources and costs]**.

ARTICLE 13 DATA AND REPORTS.

13.01 *Provision of Data.* Customer shall supply to Vendor, in connection with the Services, required data in the form and on such time schedules as may be agreed upon by Vendor and Customer ("*Customer Data*") in order to permit Vendor to perform the Services in accordance with the terms of this Agreement, including the Service Levels. All Customer Data is, or shall be, and shall remain the property of Customer.

13.02 *Inspection of Reports.* Customer shall use reasonable efforts to inspect and review reports and provide Vendor with notice of any errors or inaccuracies (1) in daily or weekly reports, within **[SPECIFY TIME PERIOD]** business days of receipt of such reports, and (2) in monthly or other reports, within **[SPECIFY TIME PERIOD]** business days of receipt of such reports. Vendor shall provide Customer with such documentation and information as may be requested by Customer in order to verify the accuracy of the reports. If Customer fails to reject any such report within the applicable period, Customer shall be deemed to have accepted such report.

13.03 *Correction of Errors.* Upon notice from Customer and at Customer's expense, Vendor shall promptly correct any errors or inaccuracies in Customer Data and reports prepared by Vendor as part of the Services, to the extent not caused by Vendor or Vendor Agents.

13.04 *Data Protection.* **[In the event the Services require the access to or use of personal data, each Party shall be responsible for taking all necessary steps required by applicable Law to ensure the protection of the privacy of such personal data to be accessed or used. In the event that applicable Law requires registration with a Governmental Authority, the Parties shall determine which Party shall register, or cause such registration, with such Governmental Authority.]**

ARTICLE 14 CONFIDENTIALITY AND SECURITY.

14.01 *General Obligations.*

(1) All Confidential Information relating to or obtained from Customer or Vendor shall be held in confidence by the recipient to the same extent and in at least the same manner as the recipient protects its own confidential or proprietary information.

(2) Neither Customer nor Vendor shall disclose, publish, release, transfer, or otherwise make available Confidential Information of, or obtained from, the other in any form to, or for the use or benefit of, any person or entity without the disclosing Party's consent. Each of Customer and Vendor shall, however, be permitted to disclose relevant aspects of the other's Confidential Information to its officers, directors, employees and Agents, to the extent that such disclosure is not restricted under this Agreement or any governmental approvals and only to the extent that such disclosure is reasonably necessary for the performance of its duties and obligations under this Agreement; provided, however, that the recipient shall be responsible or ensuring that such officers, directors, employees, and Agents abide by the provisions of this Agreement.

14.02 *Exclusions.* The obligations in *Section 14.01* shall not restrict any disclosure pursuant to any applicable Law or by order of any court or Governmental Authority (provided that the recipient shall give prompt notice to the disclosing Party of such order) and, except to the extent that local Law provides otherwise, shall not apply with respect to information that (1) is independently developed by the recipient without violating the disclosing Party's proprietary rights as shown by the recipient's written records, (2) is or becomes publicly known (other than through unauthorized disclosure), (3) is disclosed by the owner of such information to a third party free of any obligation of confidentiality, (4) is already known by the recipient at the time of disclosure, as shown by the recipient's written records, and the recipient has no obligation of confidentiality other than pursuant to this Agreement or any confidentiality agreements entered into before the Effective Date between Customer and Vendor or (5) is rightfully received by a Party free of any obligation of confidentiality.

14.03 *Unauthorized Acts.* Without limiting either Party's rights in respect of a breach of this Article, each Party shall:

(1) promptly notify the other Party of any unauthorized possession, use or knowledge, or attempt thereof, of the other Party's Confidential Information by any person or entity that may become known to such Party, including any incidents involving a breach of security, and any incidents that might indicate or lead to a threat to, or weakness in, security and any attempt to make unauthorized use of the Services or the Customer Data;

(2) promptly furnish to the other Party full details of the unauthorized possession, use or knowledge, or attempt thereof, and assist the other Party in investigating or preventing the recurrence of any unauthorized possession, use or knowledge, or attempt thereof, of Confidential Information;

(3) cooperate with the other Party in any litigation and investigation against third parties deemed necessary by the other Party to protect its proprietary rights; and

(4) promptly use its best efforts to prevent a recurrence of any such unauthorized possession, use or knowledge, or attempt thereof, of Confidential Information.

Each Party shall bear the cost it incurs as a result of compliance with this Section.

14.04 *Injunctive Relief.* Each Party recognizes that its disclosure of Confidential Information of the other Party may give rise to irreparable injury to such Party and acknowledges that remedies other than injunctive relief may not be adequate. Accordingly, each Party has the right to equitable and injunctive relief to prevent the unauthorized possession, use, disclosure or knowledge of any Confidential Information, as well as to such damages or other relief as is occasioned by such unauthorized possession, use, disclosure, or knowledge.

14.05 *Publicity.* **[OPTION 1: Neither Party shall use the other Party's name or refer to it directly or indirectly, without such Party's consent, which consent shall not be unreasonably withheld, in any media release, public announcement or public disclosure, except for promotional or marketing materials, customer lists or business presentations.][OPTION 2: BE SILENT]**

ARTICLE 15 REPRESENTATIONS AND ADDITIONAL COVENANTS.

15.01 *By Customer.* Customer represents and warrants that:

(1) it is either the owner of the Customer Data, each Transferred Asset, each Customer Asset and the Customer Intellectual Property or is authorized by its owner to include it under this Agreement; and

(2) it is authorized to permit Vendor access to and use of the Customer Service Locations used in connection with performing the Services, and Vendor is performing the Services for Customer at the Customer Service Locations at Customer's request.

   [ADD ENVIRONMENTAL AND ERISA COMPLIANCE REPS IF APPLICABLE]

15.02 *Mutual.* Each Party hereby represents and warrants that:

(1) it has all requisite corporate power and authority to enter into this Agreement and to carry out the transactions contemplated hereby;

(2)   the execution, delivery and performance of this Agreement and the consummation of the transactions contemplated hereby have been duly authorized by all requisite corporate action on the part of such Party;

(3)   this Agreement has been duly executed and delivered by such Party and (assuming the due authorization, execution and delivery hereof by the other Party) is a valid and binding obligation of such Party, enforceable against it in accordance with its terms; and

(4)   its entry into this Agreement does not violate or constitute a breach of any of its contractual obligations with third parties.

15.03   *Regulations.*

(1)   **[OPTION 1: Each Party shall obtain all necessary regulatory approvals applicable to its business, obtain any necessary permits, and comply with any regulatory requirements, in each case, applicable to the performance, or receipt, of the Services.]**

[OPTION 2: Customer shall obtain and furnish to Vendor any approvals, consents, licenses and permits required or recommended by any Law or Governmental Authority in connection with (a) the execution of this Agreement and (b) the performance and receipt of the Services.]

(2)   Each Party covenants and agrees that it shall comply with all applicable Laws applicable to such Party. **[ADD ACCOUNTING PRINCIPLES AND SEC REPORTING REQUIREMENTS IF APPLICABLE]**

15.04   *DISCLAIMERS.*

(1)   **[Vendor does not warrant the accuracy of any advice, report, data or other product delivered to Customer that is produced with or from Customer Data, Customer Assets or Intellectual Property provided by Customer. Such products are delivered "AS IS", and Vendor shall not be liable for any inaccuracy thereof.]**

(2)   **EXCEPT AS EXPRESSLY SET FORTH IN *SECTION 15.02*, VENDOR DOES NOT MAKE ANY OTHER WARRANTIES OR REPRESENTATIONS AND EXPRESSLY DISCLAIMS ALL OTHER REPRESENTATIONS AND WARRANTIES, EXPRESS OR IMPLIED, INCLUDING ANY IMPLIED WARRANTIES OF MERCHANTABILITY AND FITNESS FOR A SPECIFIC PURPOSE. VENDOR DOES NOT WARRANT THAT THE SERVICES SHALL MEET CUSTOMER'S REQUIREMENTS, THAT THE PERFORMANCE OF THE SERVICES SHALL BE UNINTERRUPTED OR ERROR-FREE, THAT ALL ERRORS IN THE SERVICES SHALL BE CORRECTED [OR THAT THE CUSTOMER ASSETS, CUSTOMER INTELLECTUAL PROPERTY, VENDOR INTELLECTUAL PROPERTY, DEVELOPMENTS OR SERVICES ARE OR SHALL BE YEAR 2000 READY OR COMPLIANT].**

ARTICLE 16   DISPUTE RESOLUTION.

16.01   *Customer Project Manager and Vendor Account Manager.* Any dispute arising under this Agreement shall be considered in person or by telephone by the Customer Project Manager and the Vendor Account Manager within **[seven]** business days of receipt of a notice from either Party specifying the nature of the dispute; provided, however, that a dispute relating to *Article 14* shall not be subject to this Section. **[Unless the Customer Project Manager and the Vendor Account Manager otherwise agree, either Party may pursue its rights and remedies under *Section 16.02* after the occurrence of such meeting or telephone conversation.]**

16.02   **[Resolution Procedures. ADD MEDIATION/ARBITRATION PROCEDURES IF APPLICABLE]**

ARTICLE 17 TERMINATION.

17.01 *By Vendor.* Vendor shall have the right to terminate this Agreement if: (1) Customer fails to pay any amounts payable under this Agreement when due, (2) Customer fails to perform any of its material non-monetary obligations under this Agreement, and does not cure such default within **[SPECIFY TIME PERIOD]** of receipt of notice of default from Vendor or (3) Customer becomes or is declared insolvent or bankrupt, is the subject of any proceedings relating to its liquidation, insolvency or for the appointment of a receiver or similar officer for it, makes an assignment for the benefit of all or substantially all of its creditors or enters into an agreement for the composition, extension or readjustment of all or substantially all of its obligations.

17.02 *By Customer.* If Vendor materially fails to perform any of its material obligations under this Agreement, Customer may give Vendor notice of such failure. Vendor shall within **[SPECIFY TIME PERIOD]** days of receipt of such notice remedy the failure specified therein. In the event Vendor fails to remedy the failure within such **[SPECIFY TIME PERIOD]** period, Customer may give a termination notice to Vendor and may terminate this Agreement under which the breach occurred; provided, however, that the time to cure a breach shall be extended if Vendor has promptly commenced to cure the breach and continues to use reasonable efforts to cure such breach.

17.03 *Termination Assistance.* Except in the event this Agreement is terminated by Vendor pursuant to *Section 17.01,* upon the expiration or termination of this Agreement, if (1) all payments due to Vendor under this Agreement have been paid and (2) Customer has requested termination assistance at least **[SPECIFY TIME PERIOD]** prior to the expiration of this Agreement or upon notice of termination of this Agreement, Vendor shall **[OPTION 1: (a) cooperate with Customer in effecting the orderly transfer of the Services to a third party or the resumption of the Services by Customer upon Customer 's request and (b) continue to perform such portion of the Services requested by Customer ((a) and (b) collectively, the "*Termination Assistance Services*").][OPTION 2: provide the services described in *Exhibit 12* (the "*Termination Assistance Services*").]** Except in the event this Agreement is terminated by Vendor pursuant to *Section 17.01*, Vendor shall provide the Termination Assistance Services for up to **[SPECIFY TIME PERIOD]** to the expiration of this Agreement or up to 90 days after the effective date of the termination of this Agreement by Customer (the "*Termination Assistance Period*"). To the extent such Termination Assistance Services cause Vendor to use resources beyond those otherwise then being provided by Vendor as part of the Services or incur additional costs, such Termination Assistance Services shall constitute and be performed as Out-of-Scope Services.

17.04 *Exit Rights.* Upon the expiration or termination of this Agreement (except in the event this Agreement is terminated by Vendor pursuant to *Section 17.01*):

(1) Vendor shall provide the Termination Assistance Services in accordance with *Section 17.03*;

(2) Customer shall allow Vendor to use, at no charge, those Customer facilities, Customer Assets and Customer Intellectual Property being used to perform the Termination Assistance Services for as long as Vendor is providing the Termination Assistance Services to enable Vendor to effect an orderly transition of Vendor's resources;

(3) each Party shall have the rights specified in *Article 10* to be applicable upon expiration or termination of this Agreement in respect of Intellectual Property;

(4) **[upon Customer's request, with respect to generally commercially available Vendor Third-Party Intellectual Property, which Vendor has licensed and is dedicated full-time to providing the Services as of the date of the expiration or termination of this Agreement, Vendor shall transfer, assign or sublicense such Vendor Third-Party Intellectual**

Property to Customer; provided, however, that Customer provided Vendor with reasonable notice prior to the acquisition of a license to such Vendor Third-Party Intellectual Property that Customer may desire such assignment or sublicense and Customer pays any costs associated with such assignment or sublicense;] and

(5) upon Customer's request, with respect to any contracts applicable to the Services being provided to Customer on a dedicated, full-time basis for maintenance, disaster recovery services and other necessary third-party services being used by Vendor to perform the Services as of the date of the expiration or termination of this Agreement, Vendor shall transfer or assign such agreements to Customer or its designee, on terms and conditions acceptable to both parties; provided, however, that Customer provided Vendor with reasonable notice prior to entering into such contracts that Customer may desire such transfer or assignment and Customer pays any costs associated with such transfer or assignment.

ARTICLE 18   INDEMNITIES.

18.01   *Infringement.* Vendor agrees to indemnify, defend, and hold Customer harmless from and against any and all Losses incurred by Customer arising from any **[third party]** claim of **[United States] [SPECIFY COUNTRY/TERRITORY]** patent, trade secret or copyright infringement asserted against Customer by virtue of Customer's use of the Vendor Proprietary Intellectual Property or the Developments; provided, however, that (1) Vendor is given prompt notice of any such claim, (2) Vendor has the right to control and direct the defense of such claim and (3) Customer fully cooperates with Vendor in such defense. Vendor shall have no liability for any claim of infringement that results from or relates to (a) any modification or enhancement to the Vendor Proprietary Intellectual Property or the Developments by Customer, (b) any failure by Customer to implement or install the Vendor Proprietary Intellectual Property or the Developments as directed by Vendor, (c) the combination, operation or use of the Vendor Proprietary Intellectual Property or the Developments with non-Vendor programs, data or documentation and (d) materials, items, resources, or services provided or performed by Customer (whether or not used in connection with or incorporated into the Vendor Proprietary Intellectual Property or the Developments). In the event the Vendor Proprietary Intellectual Property or the Developments, in Vendor's opinion, are likely to or do become the subject of a claim of infringement, Vendor shall have the right at its sole option and expense to (i) modify the Vendor Proprietary Intellectual Property or the Developments to be non-infringing, (ii) obtain for Customer a license to continue using the Vendor Proprietary Intellectual Property or the Developments or (iii) terminate this Agreement and the license granted hereunder, accept return of the Vendor Proprietary Intellectual Property or the Developments and refund to Customer a pro rata portion of the fee paid to Vendor hereunder for that portion of the Vendor Proprietary Intellectual Property or the Developments which is the subject of such infringement, such portion based on a straight line depreciation over a five-year term beginning on the delivery of such portion of the Vendor Proprietary Intellectual Property or the Developments to Customer. **THE FOREGOING STATES CUSTOMER'S SOLE AND EXCLUSIVE REMEDY AND THE ENTIRE LIABILITY AND OBLIGATION OF VENDOR AND VENDOR AGENTS WITH RESPECT TO ANY INFRINGEMENT OR CLAIMS OF INFRINGEMENT BY THE VENDOR INTELLECTUAL PROPERTY, THE DEVELOPMENTS OR THE SERVICES, OR ANY PART THEREOF, OF ANY PATENT, COPYRIGHT, TRADE SECRET, OR OTHER PROPRIETARY RIGHT.**

18.02   *Personal and Property Damage By Vendor.* Vendor agrees to indemnify, defend and hold Customer harmless, from and against any and all Losses incurred by Customer arising from any **[third party]** claim for (1) bodily injuries to, including fatal injury or disease to, Vendor employees and (2) damage to tangible real or personal property of Vendor and Vendor employees arising from or in connection with this Agreement. **[EXCEPT GROSS NEGLIGENCE/INTENTIONAL ACTS?]**

18.03   *Personal and Property Damage By Customer.* Customer agrees to indemnify, defend and hold Vendor and Vendor Agents harmless from and against any and all Losses arising from any claim for (1) bodily injuries to, including fatal injuries or disease to, Customer employees and (2) damage to tangible real or personal property of Customer and Customer employees arising from or in connection with this Agreement. **[EXCEPT GROSS NEGLIGENCE/INTENTIONAL ACTS?]**

18.04   *By Customer.* Customer agrees to indemnify, defend and hold Vendor and Vendor Agents harmless from and against any and all Losses arising from any claim relating to: (1) the infringement by or of Customer Data, the Transferred Assets, the Customer Assets, the Customer Intellectual Property or any other resources or items provided to Vendor or Vendor Agents by Customer or Customer Agents; (2) any amounts, including taxes, interest and penalties which are obligations of Customer pursuant to *Section 11.09*; (3) any products or services provided by Customer or Customer Agents to third parties; (4) any breach or default by Customer in the performance of Customer's obligations under agreements with third parties; and (5) **[any environmental claim arising out of this Agreement or as a result of the Services performed at the Customer Service Locations, unless Vendor has caused the environmental damage by actions unrelated to and unauthorized by this Agreement.]**

18.05   *Indemnification Procedures.* If any third-party claim is commenced against a Party entitled to indemnification under *Section 18.02*, *Section 18.03* or *Section 18.04* (the "*Indemnified Party*"), notice thereof shall be given to the Party that is obligated to provide indemnification (the "*Indemnifying Party*") as promptly as practicable. If, after such notice, the Indemnifying Party shall acknowledge that this Agreement applies with respect to such claim, then the Indemnifying Party shall be entitled, if it so elects, in a notice promptly delivered to the Indemnified Party, but in no event less than 10 days prior to the date on which a response to such claim is due, to immediately take control of the defense and investigation of such claim and to employ and engage attorneys reasonably acceptable to the Indemnified Party to handle and defend the same, at the Indemnifying Party's sole cost and expense. The Indemnified Party shall cooperate, at the cost of the Indemnifying Party, in all reasonable respects with the Indemnifying Party and its attorneys in the investigation, trial and defense of such claim and any appeal arising therefrom; provided, however, that the Indemnified Party may, at its own cost and expense, participate, through its attorneys or otherwise, in such investigation, trial and defense of such claim and any appeal arising therefrom. No settlement of a claim pursuant to this Section that involves a remedy other than the payment of money by the Indemnifying Party shall be entered into without the consent of the Indemnified Party, which consent shall not be unreasonably withheld. After notice by the Indemnifying Party to the Indemnified Party of its election to assume full control of the defense of any such claim, the Indemnifying Party shall not be liable to the Indemnified Party for any legal expenses incurred thereafter by such Indemnified Party in connection with the defense of that claim. If the Indemnifying Party does not assume full control over the defense of a claim subject to such defense as provided in this Section, the Indemnifying Party may participate in such defense, at its sole cost and expense, and the Indemnified Party shall have the right to defend the claim in such manner as it may deem appropriate, at the cost and expense of the Indemnifying Party.

18.06   *Subrogation.* In the event that a Party is obligated to indemnify the other Party pursuant to *Section 18.01*, *Section 18.02*, *Section 18.03* or *Section 18.04* the Indemnifying Party shall, upon payment of such indemnity in full, be subrogated to all rights of the Indemnified Party with respect to the claims and defenses to which such indemnification relates.

18.07 *Exclusive Remedy.* The indemnification rights of each Indemnified Party pursuant to *Section 18.01*, *Section 18.02*, *Section 18.03* or *Section 18.04* shall be the sole and exclusive remedy of such Indemnified Party with respect to the claims to which such indemnification relates.

ARTICLE 19 LIABILITY.
[ADD LIABILITY/DAMAGE PROVISIONS IF APPLICABLE]

ARTICLE 20 MISCELLANEOUS PROVISIONS.
20.01 *Notices.* Except as otherwise specified in this Agreement, all notices, requests, consents, approvals, agreements, authorizations, acknowledgements, waivers, and other communications required or permitted under this Agreement shall be in writing and shall be deemed given when sent by facsimile to the facsimile number specified below or delivered by hand to the address specified below. A copy of any such notice shall also be sent by express air mail on the date such notice is transmitted by facsimile to the address specified below:

    In the case of Customer:
        [ADDRESS]
        Attention:
        Facsimile No.:
    In the case of Vendor:
        [ADDRESS]
        Attention:
        Facsimile No.:

Either Party may change its address or facsimile number for notification purposes by giving the other Party **[SPECIFY TIME PERIOD]** days' notice of the new address or facsimile number and the date upon which it shall become effective.

20.02 *Assignment and Third-Party Beneficiaries.* Customer may not, without the consent of Vendor, assign this Agreement or any of its rights under this Agreement, in whole or in part, and may not delegate its obligations under this Agreement. Any such purported assignment or delegation in contravention of this Section shall be null and void. Each Party intends that this Agreement shall not benefit, or create any right or cause of action in or on behalf of, any person, or entity other than the Parties.

20.03 *Relationship.* The Parties intend to create an independent contractor relationship and nothing contained in this Agreement shall be construed to make either Customer or Vendor partners, joint venturers, principals, Agents or employees of the other. **[Except as expressly set forth in Article ___,]** no officer, director, employee or Vendor Agent retained by Vendor to perform work on Customer's behalf under this Agreement shall be deemed to be an employee of Customer or a Customer Agent. Neither Party shall have any right, power or authority, express or implied, to bind the other. Vendor shall have the sole right to supervise, manage, contract, direct, procure, perform, or cause to be performed, all work to be performed by Vendor under this Agreement.

20.04 *Severability and Waivers.* If any provision of this Agreement is held by a court of competent jurisdiction to be contrary to Law, then the remaining provisions of this Agreement, if capable of substantial performance, shall remain in full force and effect. No delay or omission by either Party to exercise any right or power it has under this Agreement shall impair or be construed as a waiver of such right or power. A waiver by any Party of any breach or covenant shall not be construed to be a waiver of any succeeding breach or any other covenant. All waivers must be signed by the Party waiving its rights.

20.05 *Survival.* **[The terms of [TO BE FILLED IN] shall survive the expiration or termination of this Agreement.][OPTION: BE SILENT]**

20.06 *Governing Law.* This Agreement and the rights and obligations of the Parties under this Agreement shall be governed by and construed in accordance with the Laws of **[SPECIFY LAW].**

20.07 *Sole and Exclusive Venue.* Subject to the provisions of *Article 16* **[and except as required by local law]**, each Party irrevocably agrees that any legal action, suit, or proceeding brought by it in any way arising out of this Agreement must be brought solely and exclusively in **[SPECIFY COURT]** and irrevocably accepts and submits to the sole and exclusive jurisdiction of each of the aforesaid courts in personam, generally and unconditionally with respect to any action, suit or proceeding brought by it or against it by the other Party**[; provided, however, that this Section shall not prevent a Party against whom any legal action, suit or proceeding is brought by the other Party from seeking to remove such legal action, suit or proceeding, pursuant to applicable federal law, to the district court of the United States of America for the district and division embracing the place where the action is pending in the state courts of [SPECIFY], and in the event an action is so removed each Party irrevocably accepts and submits to the jurisdiction of the aforesaid district court] [; provided, however, that this Section shall not prevent a Party from enforcing a judgment or court order in another jurisdiction or court].** Each Party hereto further irrevocably consents to the service of process from any of the aforesaid courts by mailing copies thereof by registered or certified mail, postage prepaid, to such Party at its address designated pursuant to this Agreement, with such service of process to become effective 30 days after such mailing.

20.08 *Export.* Neither Party shall export, directly or indirectly, any information acquired under this Agreement or any product utilizing such information to any country for which the government of the United States of America or any agency thereof or any other Governmental Authority at the time of export requires an export license or other governmental approval without first obtaining such license or approval.

20.09 *Force Majeure.* **[ADD APPLICABLE FORCE MAJEURE PROVISION]**

20.10 *Nonperformance.* To the extent any nonperformance by either Party of its nonmonetary obligations under this Agreement results from or is caused by the failure of the other Party or the other Party's Agents to perform its obligations under this Agreement, such nonperformance shall be excused.

20.11 *Right to Provide Services.* Each Party recognizes that Vendor personnel providing services to Customer under this Agreement may perform similar services for others and this Agreement shall not prevent Vendor from using the personnel and equipment provided to Customer under this Agreement for such purposes. Nothing in this Agreement shall impair Vendor's right to acquire, license or develop for itself or others or have others develop for Vendor similar technology performing the same or similar services as contemplated by this Agreement. Vendor may perform its obligations under this Agreement through the use of Vendor Agents; provided, however, that Vendor shall not be relieved of its obligations under this Agreement by such use of such Vendor Agents.

20.12 *Non-Disparagement.* **[Each Party shall refrain, and shall use commercially reasonable efforts to cause its employees and Agents to refrain, from making negative or disparaging comments about the other Party; provided, however, that Vendor shall not be deemed to be in breach of this Section due to comments made during the first [SPECIFY TIME PERIOD] of the Term by those former employees of Customer who accept Vendor's offer of employment pursuant to *Article 8*.]**

20.13 *Further Assurances.* Each of the Parties acknowledges and agrees that, subsequent to the execution and delivery of this Agreement and without any additional consideration, each of the Parties shall execute and deliver any further legal instruments and perform any actions which are or may become necessary to effectuate the purposes of this Agreement.

20.14 *Solicitation.* During the Term and for **[SPECIFY TIME PERIOD]** after the expiration of this Agreement or termination of this Agreement, Customer shall not solicit **[or hire]** any Vendor employees without Vendor's consent.

20.15 *Limitation Period.* **[Neither Party may bring an action, regardless of form, arising out of this Agreement more than [SPECIFY TIME PERIOD] after the cause of action has arisen or the date such cause of action was or should have been discovered.]**

20.16 *Negotiated Terms.* The Parties agree that the terms and conditions of this Agreement are the result of negotiations between the Parties and that this Agreement shall not be construed in favor of or against any Party by reason of the extent to which any Party or its professional advisors participated in the preparation of this Agreement.

20.17 *Entire Agreement; Amendments; Counterparts.* This Agreement and the Exhibits to this Agreement represent the entire agreement between the Parties with respect to its subject matter, and there are no other representations, understandings, or agreements between the Parties relative to such subject matter. No amendment to, or change, waiver or discharge of, any provision of this Agreement shall be valid unless in writing and signed by an authorized representative of each of the Parties. This Agreement may be executed in any number of counterparts, each of which shall be deemed an original, but all of which taken together shall constitute one single agreement between the Parties.

* * * *

IN WITNESS WHEREOF, each of Customer and Vendor has caused this Agreement to be signed and delivered by its duly authorized representative.

[CUSTOMER]

By: _____
Name:
Title:

[VENDOR]

By: _____

Name:

Title:

EXHIBIT 1   DEFINITIONS

(1) *"Agents"* shall mean Customer Agents or Vendor Agents, as the case may be.

(2) *"Agreement"* shall mean this **[SPECIFY TYPE OF BUSINESS PROCESS SERVICES TO BE OUTSOURCED]** Agreement, dated as of **[SPECIFY DATE],** by and between Vendor and Customer.

(3) **[*"Assumptions"* shall have the meaning set forth in *Section 11.08*.]**

(4) *"Change"* shall have the meaning set forth in *Article 6*.

(5) *"Change Order"* shall mean a document agreed upon by the Parties (1) implementing a Change or (2) adding an Out-of-Scope Service under this Agreement.

(6) *"Confidential Information"* **[OPTION 1: of Customer or Vendor shall mean all information and documentation that is (1) marked as confidential by Customer or Vendor or (2) disclosed verbally by Customer or Vendor and subsequently summarized and designated as confidential in writing by the disclosing Party, in each case, whether disclosed to or accessed by Customer or Vendor in connection with this Agreement, including (a) with respect to Customer and Vendor, the terms of this Agreement and (b) with respect to Vendor, the Vendor Intellectual Property.] [OPTION 2: shall mean (1) with respect to Customer, any information, technical data or know-how of Customer which is identified by Customer as confidential at the time of disclosure, (2) with respect to Vendor, any information, technical data or know-how of Vendor disclosed to or relating to Vendor, including the Vendor Intellectual Property, and (3) with respect to Customer and Vendor, the terms of this Agreement.]**

(7) *"Consents"* shall mean all licenses, consents, authorizations and approvals that are necessary to allow Vendor and Vendor Agents to use Customer's owned and leased assets, including the Customer Data and the Customer Intellectual Property.

(8) *"Contract Year"* shall mean each 12-month period during the Term commencing on the Effective Date and thereafter upon the completion of the immediately preceding Contract Year.

(9) *"Control"* shall mean, with respect to any entity, the possession, directly or indirectly, of the power to direct or cause the direction of the management and policies of such entity, whether through the ownership of voting securities (or other ownership interest), by contract or otherwise.

(10) *"Customer"* shall mean **[CUSTOMER]**, a **[SPECIFY LOCATION OF INC./FORMATION] [corporation/partnership/other],** having its principal place of business at **[SPECIFY ADDRESS].**

(11) *"Customer Agents"* shall mean contractors and agents of Customer.

(12) *"Customer Assets"* shall mean the assets owned or leased by Customer that are listed in *Exhibit 4*, as may be modified by agreement of the Parties from time to time during the Term.

(13) *"Customer Data"* shall have the meaning set forth in *Section 13.01*.

(14) *"Customer Intellectual Property"* shall mean the Customer Proprietary Intellectual Property and the Customer Third-Party Intellectual Property, collectively.

(15) *"Customer Project Manager"* shall have the meaning set forth in *Section 9.01*.

(16) *"Customer Proprietary Intellectual Property"* shall mean the Intellectual Property owned by Customer that is listed in *Exhibit 8*, as may be modified by agreement of the Parties from time to time during the Term.

(17) *"Customer Service Location(s)"* shall mean any service location of Customer set forth in *Exhibit 5*.

(18) *"Customer Third-Party Intellectual Property"* shall mean the Intellectual Property licensed or leased by Customer from a third party that is listed in *Exhibit 8*, as may be modified by agreement of the Parties from time to time during the Term.

(19) *"Default Rate"* shall mean **[SPECIFY]**.

(20) *"Developments"* shall mean **[SEE OPTIONS IN PROPRIETARY RIGHTS RIDERS]**.

(21) *"Effective Date"* shall mean **[INSERT COMMENCEMENT DATE OF SERVICES]**.

(22) *"Fees"* shall mean the fees for the Services set forth in *Exhibit 3*.

(23) **[*"Force Majeure* Event" shall have the meaning set forth in *Section 20.09*.]**

(24) *"Governmental Authority"* shall mean any international, national, provincial, municipal, local, territorial or other governmental department, regulatory authority, judicial or administrative body, domestic, international or foreign.

(25) *"Indemnified Party"* shall have the meaning set forth in *Section 18.05*.

(26) *"Indemnifying Party"* shall have the meaning set forth in *Section 18.05*.

(27) *"Initial Term"* shall have the meaning set forth in *Article 2*.

(28) *"Intellectual Property"* shall mean **[Software]**, methodologies, processes, procedures and algorithms and Related Documentation, in whatever form or media.

(29) *"Law"* shall mean any declaration, decree, directive, legislative enactment, order, ordinance, regulation, rule or other binding requirement of or by any Governmental Authority.

(30) *"Losses"* shall mean any and all damages, fines, penalties, deficiencies, losses, liabilities (including settlements and judgments) and expenses (including interest, court costs, reasonable fees and expenses of attorneys, accountants and other experts or other reasonable fees and expenses of litigation or other proceedings or of any claim, default or assessment).

(31) *"Out-of-Scope Service(s)"* shall mean any **[SPECIFY SERVICES]** service that is not expressly included within the scope of the Services.

(32) *"Parties"* shall mean Customer and Vendor, collectively.

(33) *"Party"* shall mean either Customer or Vendor, as the case may be.

(34) **[*"Performance Credits"* shall mean the performance credits set forth in *Exhibit 6*.]**

(35) *"Project Staff"* shall mean the personnel of Vendor and Vendor Agents who provide the Services.

(36) *"Related Documentation"* shall mean, with respect to Intellectual Property, all materials, documentation, specifications, technical manuals, user manuals, flow diagrams, file descriptions and other written information that describes the function and use of such Intellectual Property, as applicable.

(37) *"Renewal Term"* shall have the meaning set forth in *Article 2*.

(38) *"Service Levels"* shall have the meaning set forth in *Section 5.01*.

(39) *"Services"* shall have the meaning set forth in *Section 3.01*.

(40) **[*"Software"* shall mean the object [and source] code versions of any applications programs, operating system software, computer software languages, utilities, other computer programs and Related Documentation, in whatever form or media, including the tangible media upon which such applications programs, operating system software, computer software languages, utilities, other computer programs and Related Documentation are recorded or printed.]**

(41) *"Term"* shall have the meaning set forth in *Article 2*.

(42) *"Termination Assistance Period"* shall have the meaning set forth in *Section 17.03*.

(43) *"Termination Assistance Services"* shall have the meaning set forth in *Section 17.03*.

(44) [*"Third Party Contracts"* **shall mean the third-party contracts listed in** *Exhibit 9*.]

(45) [*"Third Party Intellectual Property Licenses"*] **shall mean the third-party agreements pursuant to which Intellectual Property Used in connection with this Agreement is licensed to Customer or Vendor.**]

(46) *"Tools"* shall have the meaning set forth in *Section 10.04*.

(47) [*"Transferred Assets"* **shall mean the assets set forth in** *Exhibit 10*.]

(48) *"Use"* shall mean the right to load, execute, store, transmit, display, copy, maintain, modify, enhance, create derivative works, make, and have made.

(49) *"Vendor"* shall mean **[VENDOR]**, a **[SPECIFY LOCATION OF INC./FORMATION] [corporation/partnership/other]** having its principal place of business at **[SPECIFY ADDRESS]**.

(50) *"Vendor Account Manager"* shall have the meaning set forth in *Section 3.03(1)*.

(51) *"Vendor Affiliate"* shall mean any entity that, directly or indirectly, Controls, is Controlled by or is under common Control with Vendor.

(52) *"Vendor Agents"* shall mean Vendor Affiliates and subcontractors, suppliers and agents of Vendor and Vendor Affiliates.

(53) *"Vendor Intellectual Property"* shall mean the Vendor Proprietary Intellectual Property and the Vendor Third-Party Intellectual Property, collectively.

(54) *"Vendor Proprietary Intellectual Property"* shall mean the Intellectual Property owned or developed by or on behalf of Vendor that is used in connection with the Services.

(55) *"Vendor Third-Party Intellectual Property"* shall mean the Intellectual Property licensed or leased by Vendor from a third party that is used in connection with the Services.

PROPRIETARY RIGHTS RIDER (VENDOR FORM)

PROPRIETARY RIGHTS RIDER

*[OPTION 1: VENDOR OWNS NEW DEVELOPMENTS WITH LICENSE
TO CUSTOMER]*
[ADD TO DEFINITIONS:]

"*Developments*" shall mean any Intellectual Property, and any modifications or enhancements to Intellectual Property, developed or acquired in connection with this Agreement (but excluding Tools) by or on behalf of (1) Vendor and Vendor Agents, separately or jointly, or (2) Vendor and Vendor Agents, separately or jointly, and Customer and Customer Agents, separately or jointly.

[ADD TO ARTICLE 10:]

__.03 *Developments.*

(1) All Developments are and shall be owned by Vendor. Vendor shall have all right, title and interest, including worldwide ownership of copyright and patent rights, in and to the Developments and all copies made from it. Customer hereby irrevocably assigns, transfers and conveys, and shall cause Customer Agents to assign, transfer and convey, to Vendor without further consideration all of its right, title and interest in and to such Developments, if any, including all rights of patent, copyright, trade secret, and any other proprietary rights in such materials. **[ADD IF VENDOR WILL LICENSE DEVELOPMENTS TO CUSTOMER: Upon expiration or termination of this Agreement (except for a termination pursuant to *Section 17.01*), Vendor hereby grants to Customer a nonexclusive, nontransferable license to use the Developments in accordance with subSection (2) below [OPTION 1: IF THERE WILL BE A LICENSE FEE: at rates to be agreed upon by the Parties at such expiration or termination] [OPTION 2: IF THERE WILL BE A LICENSE FEE: at Vendor's then-current standard commercial rates].**

(2) **[ADD IF VENDOR WILL LICENSE DEVELOPMENTS TO CUSTOMER:** Customer's use of the Developments upon expiration or termination of this Agreement (except for a termination pursuant to *Section 17.01*) shall be subject to, and Customer shall comply with, the following terms and conditions:

   (a) The Developments shall (i) not be Used directly or indirectly by persons other than an employee of Customer **[or an Approved Service Provider]**, **[(ii) only be operated on equipment owned or leased by Customer which is located on Customer's**

premises] and (iii) only be Used in connection with the internal work of Customer. **[LIMIT RIGHT TO MODIFY/ENHANCE?]** **[*"Approved Service Provider"* shall mean a third party providing services to Customer that has entered into a non-disclosure agreement with Vendor in a form acceptable to Vendor [and that does not compete directly or indirectly with Vendor].]**

(b) Except as set forth in sub-Section (2)(a) above, at no time may the Developments or their components or any modifications thereto be disclosed to third parties or sold, assigned, leased or otherwise disposed of or commercially exploited or marketed in any way, with or without charge. Except as may be necessary for archival purposes, Customer shall not copy, and shall not permit the copying by a third party of, the Developments in whole or in part.

(c) Upon Vendor's request, Customer shall affix to all copies of the Developments in Customer's possession any form of copyright or other proprietary notice specified by Vendor.

The licenses granted pursuant to this Section in respect of a component of the Developments shall terminate if (i) Customer ceases use of such component of the Developments or (ii) Customer breaches the terms of this license. Upon request after termination of this license, Customer (A) deliver to Vendor a current copy of such component (including all Related Documentation and source code in Customer's possession) in the form in use as of such date and (B) destroy or erase all other copies of such component in Customer's possession.]

[OPTION 2: JOINTLY OWNED]
[ADD TO DEFINITIONS:]

"Developments" shall mean all Intellectual Property developed **[for Customer]** in connection with the Services (but excluding Tools) by or on behalf of (1) Vendor and Vendor Agents, separately or jointly, or (2) Vendor and Vendor Agents, separately or jointly, and Customer and Customer Agents, separately or jointly.

[ADD TO ARTICLE 10:]

___.03   *Developments.* **[Subject to the provisions of the Third-Party Intellectual Property, Licenses,] [t] [T]**he Parties shall jointly own the Developments. Neither Party will have a duty of accounting with respect to the Developments, and each Party will take such actions as the other Party reasonably requests to evidence the joint ownership of the Developments. Except as otherwise provided by this Agreement, neither Party will have any obligation to maintain the Developments or to provide the other Party with any modifications or enhancements to the Developments.

[OPTION 3: CUSTOMER OWNS NEWLY CREATED DEVELOPMENTS ONLY]
[ADD TO DEFINITIONS:]

"Developments" shall mean any Intellectual Property **[and other items]** expressly designated as deliverables in Exhibit ___ are developed by Vendor or Vendor Agents.

[ADD TO ARTICLE 10:]

___.03   *Developments.* **[Subject to the provisions of any Third-Party Intellectual Property, Licenses,] [a] [A]**ll Developments shall be owned by Customer. Customer shall have all right, title and interest in and to the Developments. **[Customer hereby grants to Vendor a nonexclusive, irrevocable, worldwide, fully paid-up, royalty-free license to use, and sublicense the use of, the Developments [in connection with the provision of the Services] [for any purpose].]** All other Intellectual Property, materials, data, information and other items developed by, on behalf of or in conjunction with Vendor under this Agreement shall be owned by Vendor. Customer hereby irrevocably assigns, transfers and conveys, and shall cause Customer's subcontractors and agents to assign, transfer and convey, to Vendor without further consideration all of its right, title and interest in and to such Intellectual Property, documentation, materials, data, information and other items, if any, including all rights of patent, copyright, trade secret and any other proprietary rights.

[OPTION 4: CUSTOMER OWNS DERIVATIVE WORKS OF CUSTOMER SOFTWARE; VENDOR OWNS DERIVATIVE WORKS OF VENDOR SOFTWARE; VENDOR OWNS ALL OTHER DEVELOPMENTS WITH LICENSE BACK TO CUSTOMER]
[ADD TO DEFINITIONS:]

"Derivative Work" shall mean Intellectual Property based on one or more preexisting works, including, a condensation, transformation, expansion for adaptation, which, if prepared without authorization of the owner of the copyright of such preexisting work, would constitute a copyright infringement, but excluding Tools.

"Customer Derivative Work" shall mean a Derivative Work for which the preexisting copyright is owned by Customer.

"Developments" shall mean Intellectual Property developed or acquired by or on behalf of (1) Vendor and Vendor Agents, separately or jointly or (2) Vendor and Vendor Agents, separately or jointly and Customer and Customer Agents, separately or jointly, which does not constitute (a) Vendor Intellectual Property, (b) a Customer Derivative Work or a Vendor Derivative Work or (c) Tools.

"Vendor Derivative Work" shall mean Intellectual Property which constitutes a Derivative Work for which the preexisting copyright is owned by Vendor or Vendor Agents.

[ADD TO ARTICLE 10:]

___.03 *Developments*

(1) *Customer Derivative Works.* All Customer Derivative Works are and shall be owned by Customer or its licensors. Customer or its licensor shall own all rights, title and interests in and to the Customer Derivative Works, and Vendor hereby assigns, transfers, and conveys (and shall cause Vendor Agents to so assign, transfer and convey) to Customer without further consideration any rights, title or interests that Vendor may have or acquire in or to the Customer Derivative Works and any copy, translation, modification, adaptation, enhancement, or derivation of the Customer Derivative Works, including any improvement or development thereof. Customer hereby grants to Vendor a nonexclusive, irrevocable, worldwide, fully paid-up, royalty-free license to Use, and sublicense the Use of, the Customer Derivative Works **[in connection with the provision of the Services] [for any purpose]**.

(2) *Vendor Derivative Works.* All Vendor Derivative Works are and shall be owned by Vendor or its licensors. Vendor or its licensor shall own all rights, title, and interests in and to the Vendor Derivative Works, and Customer hereby assigns, transfers and conveys (and shall cause Customer Agents to so assign, transfer and convey) to Vendor without further consideration any rights, title or interests that Customer may have or acquire in or to the Vendor Derivative Works and any copy, translation, modification, adaptation, enhancement, or derivation of the Vendor Derivative Works, including any improvement or development thereof.] **[ADD IF VENDOR WILL LICENSE VENDOR DERIVATIVE WORKS TO CUSTOMER: Upon expiration or termination of this Agreement (except for a termination pursuant to *Section 17.01*),] [Vendor hereby grants to Customer a nonexclusive, nontransferable license to Use the Vendor Derivative Works in accordance with sub-Section (2) below [OPTION 1: IF THERE WILL BE A LICENSE**

FEE: at rates to be agreed upon by the Parties at such expiration or termination] [OPTION 2: IF THERE WILL BE A LICENSE FEE: at Vendor's then-current standard commercial rates]. [LIMIT RIGHT TO MODIFY/ENHANCE?]

(3) *Developments.* All Developments are and shall be owned by Vendor or its licensors. Customer shall not take any actions that jeopardize Vendor's or its licensor's proprietary rights or acquire any right in the Developments[, **except the limited use rights expressly set forth herein**]. Vendor or its licensor shall own all rights, title and interests in and to the Developments, and Customer hereby assigns, transfers and conveys (and shall cause Customer Agents to so assign, transfer and convey) to Vendor without further consideration any rights, title or interests that Customer may have or acquire in or to the Developments and any copy, translation, modification, adaptation, enhancement, or derivation of the Developments, including any improvement or development thereof.] **[ADD IF VENDOR WILL LICENSE DEVELOPMENTS TO CUSTOMER: Upon expiration or termination of this Agreement (except for a termination pursuant to *Section 17.01*), Vendor hereby grants to Customer a nonexclusive, nontransferable license to Use the Developments in accordance with sub-Section (2) below [OPTION 1: IF THERE WILL BE A LICENSE FEE: at rates to be agreed upon by the Parties at such expiration or termination] [OPTION 2: IF THERE WILL BE A LICENSE FEE: at Vendor's then-current standard commercial rates].] [LIMIT RIGHT TO MODIFY/ENHANCE?]**

(4) *License Terms.* **[ADD IF VENDOR WILL LICENSE VENDOR DERIVATIVE WORKS/DEVELOPMENTS TO CUSTOMER**: Customer's use of the Developments upon expiration or termination of this Agreement for any reason (except for a termination pursuant to *Section 17.01*)] shall be subject to, and Customer shall comply with, the following terms and conditions:

(a) The Developments shall (i) not be Used directly or indirectly by persons other than an employee of Customer **[or an Approved Service Provider], [(ii) only be operated on equipment owned or leased by Customer which is located on Customer's premises]** and (iii) only be used in connection with the internal work of Customer. **[LIMIT RIGHT TO MODIFY/ENHANCE?] [*"Approved Service Provider"* shall mean a third party providing services to Customer that has entered into a nondisclosure agreement with Vendor in a form acceptable to Vendor and that does not compete directly or indirectly with Vendor.]**

(b) Except as set forth in sub-Section (2)(a) above, at no time may the Developments or their components or any modifications thereto be disclosed to third parties or sold, assigned, leased, or otherwise disposed of or commercially exploited or marketed in any way, with or without charge. Except as may be necessary for archival purposes, Customer shall not copy, and shall not permit the copying by a third party of, the Developments in whole or in part.

(c) Upon Vendor's request, Customer shall affix to all copies of the Developments in Customer's possession any form of copyright or other proprietary notice specified by Vendor.

The licenses granted pursuant to this Section in respect of a component of the Developments shall terminate if (i) Customer ceases use of such component of the Developments or (ii) Customer breaches the terms of this license. Upon request after termination of this license, Customer shall (A) deliver to Vendor a current copy of such component (including all Related Documentation and source code in Customer's possession) in the form in use as of such date and (B) destroy or erase all other copies of such component in Customer's possession.]

Appendix **6.1**

CUSTOMER SATISFACTION SURVEY CHECKLIST

1. Define general categories that are to be measured by the satisfaction survey. What are the areas of concern that the survey is targeting? Examples of measurements include:
   - Delivery
   - Performance
   - Support
   - Responsiveness
   - Quality
   - Integration
   - Cost
   - Value
   - Business Relationship

2. Determine the frequency that the survey will be distributed.
   - Monthly
   - Quarterly
   - Semi-Annually
   - Yearly
     —Calendar Year
     —Contract Year

3. Develop a mechanism to rate or score the vendor's performance. For example:
   - 0–5 with:
     5 = Excellent
     4 = Very Good
     3 = Good
     2 = Fair
     1 = Poor
     0 = Unacceptable
   - 0–10 with:
     10 = Exceptional
     8 = Exceeds Expectations
     5 = Meets Expectations

3 = Below Expectations

0 = Unacceptable

4. Decide how index will be computed and reviewed. The results should be reviewed with the account managers and published in the monthly account status report.

5. Determine group to be surveyed (e.g., users, executives, both).

6. Examples of topics to be surveyed:

DELIVERY
- Ability to provide products and services that contribute to business success
- Delivery of products that perform as specified
- Ability to roll out new methodologies/technology
- Implementation of updates, changes and enhancements with minimal disruption

PERFORMANCE/SUPPORT
- Ability to meet service levels
- Availability
- Continuous improvement
- Dependable and accurate performance of products and services
- Efficiency
- Open/productive communication between customer/vendor personnel
- Degree to which contractual terms and conditions have been met
- Use of proper resources on a timely basis to satisfy customer's business needs (for example, providing emergency contacts or the assistance in interacting with other organizations to resolve problems)

RESPONSIVENESS
- Willingness to help customers and provide prompt service
- Response to customer questions/requests
- Willingness to take the initiative to identify problems, improvements and new methodologies/technology
- Personal attention
- The timeliness of program change you request

QUALITY
- Quality of equipment and services
- Appearance of staff, equipment, documents, and facilities
- Vendor understanding of customer industry
- Vendor experience
- Vendor expertise/know-how
- Demonstration of interest, understanding, timeliness, and accuracy

INTEGRATION
- Integration with other business processes
- Ability to work across business process lines
- Troubleshooting

COST
- Accurate/fair pricing
- Competitive pricing
- Delivery in cost effective manner
- Ability to keep costs down with minimal impact on quality
- Perception of the quantity and quality of services received for the time, effort, and money invested
- Willingness to share in risk
- Flexibility
- No surprises

VALUE
- Problem identification/resolution
- Ability to identify improvement opportunities
- Application of innovative solutions
- Degree to which vendor demonstrates leadership in customer industry
- Flexibility in approach
- Impact vendor has on customer's businesses
- Information provided regarding new products and services

BUSINESS RELATIONSHIP
- Ability to breed confidence based on professionalism and knowledge of industry and business
- Understanding of and sensitivity to customer's business goals, objectives, and needs
- Ability of vendor and customer to work together in the outsourcing arrangement
- Vendor commitment to customer's success
- Overall rating of vendor's performance

LIST OF REPORTS

EXAMPLES OF REPORTS TO BE PROVIDED
PURSUANT TO BPO AGREEMENT

- Operations Statistics
- Performance Reports
  - Service Volumes
  - Customer Service Metrics
  - MAC Statistics
  - Service Level Achievement
- Billing Report (including Base Fees, Incremental Fees, and Additional Service Fees)
- Charge Back Reports
- Site Activity Reports
- Project Status Reports
- Training
- Asset Management Reports
  - Current Inventory
  - Projected Inventory
- Problem Management Reports
  - Equipment Service Descriptions
  - Software Service Descriptions
  - Facility Service Descriptions
  - Root Cause Analysis
- Change Orders/Management
- Customer Satisfaction Reports
- Benchmarking Reports
- Production Reports

Appendix 7.1

STAY INCENTIVES

I. Examples of Stay Incentives

This appendix includes examples of various types of stay incentives to consider when seeking to increase the likelihood that employees being transferred to the vendor ("Affected Employees") will accept employment with the vendor and remain in the vendor's employ through migration.

	STAY INCENTIVE	SAMPLE CONTRACT LANGUAGE
1.	Lump sum payment to all Affected Employees; same percentage/amount offered to all Affected Employees; payable upon transfer to the vendor	Each Affected Employee will be hired by the vendor at a base salary rate equal to 105% of the base salary rate he or she was receiving as of his or her last date of employment with the customer. The vendor will pay each Affected Employee an additional amount equal to 15% of his or her base salary with customer within 30 days of his or her effective date of employment. Affected Employees designated as part-time will be paid a prorated payment based on the ratio of hours worked per week at customer.
2.	Lump sum payment to all Affected Employees; same percentage/amount offered to all Affected Employees; **payable if the Affected Employee has not quit or been terminated for cause prior to the completion of the migration of the Affected Employee's location**	The vendor will pay each Affected Employee an amount equal to 10% of his or her base salary as of his or her last date of employment with the customer if the Affected Employee has not voluntarily resigned or been terminated for cause prior to the migration completion date for the Affected Employee's location.
3.	Lump sum payment to all Affected Employees; **varied percentage/amount offered to Affected Employees**; payable upon transfer to the vendor	

(Continued)

	STAY INCENTIVE	SAMPLE CONTRACT LANGUAGE
4.	Lump sum payment to all Affected Employees; varied percentage/amount offered to Affected Employees; **payable if the Affected Employee has not quit or been terminated for cause prior to the completion of the migration of the Affected Employee's location**	
5.	Lump sum payment to **selected** Affected Employees; varied percentage/amount offered to selected Affected Employees; payable if the Affected Employee has not quit or been terminated for cause prior to the completion of the migration of the Affected Employee's location	Customer will pay stay bonuses in an amount not to exceed $_____ to selected Affected Employees upon the migration completion date.
6.	Enhanced severance (customer's severance plus a supplemental payment) for all Affected Employees, payable if the Affected Employee does not, prior to completion of the migration, (a) receive an offer to continue in the vendor's employment or (b) is terminated by the vendor (other than for cause)	If an Affected Employee **[does not accept an offer from or]** is terminated by the vendor without cause (a) after completion of the minimum employment period and (b) prior to or on the migration completion date for such Affected Employee's location, such Affected Employee shall receive: • A completion allowance equal to _____ weeks of the Affected Employee's base salary for each full year and partial six-month period of employment with customer; provided that the maximum allowance may not exceed _____ weeks of such Affected Employee's base salary, and • A health benefit allowance equal to the amount of the employer's contribution for the Affected Employee's health insurance during his or her employment, which shall be payable as a part of said employee's COBRA payment to continue such coverage for a period of time equal to the number of weeks calculated above.
7.	Severance "comparable to customer's severance" for all Affected Employees, payable if the Affected Employee does not, prior to completion of the migration, (a) receive an offer to continue in the vendor's employment or (b) is terminated by the vendor (other than for cause)	If an Affected Employee is terminated by the vendor (a) after completion of the minimum employment period and (b) prior to or on the migration completion date for such Affected Employee's location, such Affected Employee shall receive: • A separation allowance equal to _____ weeks of the Affected Employee's base salary for each full year and partial six-month period of employment with customer, provided that the maximum allowance may not exceed _____ weeks of such Affected Employee's base salary.

(Continued)

	STAY INCENTIVE	SAMPLE CONTRACT LANGUAGE
8.	Same as (7), which is only payable if the Affected Employee is not offered another job or is terminated—and a lump sum payment, **payable if the Affected Employee has not quit or been terminated for cause prior to the completion of the migration of the Affected Employee's location**	
9.	Good faith efforts to encourage employees to stay	Customer will encourage Affected Employees to accept employment with the vendor and provide representatives of the vendor with access to such Affected Employees for the purposes of discussing potential employment.
10.	No stay incentive	

II. Alternative Methods

Following are examples of other incentives that may be used by outsourcing customers to increase the likelihood that Affected Employees are available during the migration of systems operations to the vendor:

- Retention of certain key or critical support Affected Employees by customer
- Minimum guarantee period of employment with the vendor (subject only to termination for cause)
- Mandatory notice period of ___ months prior to termination
- Attractive employment/advancement opportunities
- Training
- Continuation of educational tuition advances and reimbursements for Affected Employees
- Payment of relocation expenses

III. Checklist

Following are additional issues to consider prior to implementing a stay incentive program:

- Remember that the structure of incentives being offered to Affected Employees will vary from country to country. Local counsel from each of the locations should review and approve any incentive plan prior to it being announced to Affected Employees.
- Beware of misrepresentation claims: carefully communicate in writing terms of employment to Affected Employees who will receive stay incentives. Do not make oral representations.
- Be careful not to create special classes of employees based on protected classifications, e.g., age, race, sex.
- Prepare an agreement for Affected Employees to sign who are to receive stay incentives.
- Include a release of claims against customer in the agreement.
- Identify customer representative responsible for administering stay incentives.
- Beware of noncompetition provisions in vendor employment agreements.
- Beware of other restrictions in vendor employment agreements (e.g., requirement that certain training expenses be reimbursed if employee leaves the vendor).
- Identify all perks that Affected Employees currently receive and determine whether they will be offered once the Affected Employees are outsourced.
  - Recreational programs
  - Fitness centers
  - Travel programs
  - Banking benefits
  - Discounts
  - Automobiles
  - Transportation
  - Housing
  - Medical Benefits
  - Medical Deductible
  - Dental Benefits
  - Stock Options
  - Vacation
  - Holidays
  - Day Care
  - Special Care
  - Performance Reviews
  - Bonuses
- Discuss incentive plans with the vendor.

Appendix **7.2**

HUMAN RESOURCES: SAMPLE LANGUAGE FOR THE REQUEST FOR PROPOSAL

A. Overview

Customer expects to transfer **[all] [substantially all]** of its employees who are providing **[SPECIFY TYPE OF BUSINESS PROCESS]** services (the "Affected Employees") to the selected vendor. The Affected Employees are currently located in **[SPECIFY LOCATION(S)]**. Customer anticipates that all vendors will offer competitive employment compensation and benefits packages to the Affected Employees. The value of these packages should meet or exceed the current value of compensation and benefits currently enjoyed by each employee. In addition, it is intended that the transfer of the Affected Employees will not result in any severance or redundancy obligations on behalf of Customer.

Each vendor may choose to initiate special programs to generate good will with the Affected Employees. These programs are the responsibility of the vendor organization. Customer will entertain requests from the vendor to assist in the roll-out and implementation of these programs.

B. Offers of Employment
  1. Affected Employees
    1.1 The selected vendor will be required to offer employment to **[all] [substantially all]** of the Affected Employees, including those Affected Employees on disability or other approved leaves of absence. Please describe your plans for offering employment to the Affected Employees.
    1.2 Specify whether any Affected Employees will be offered employment with a subcontractor or affiliate of the vendor (rather than the vendor). If subcontractors or affiliates will be involved, identify the proposed subcontractors and affiliates, as well as the Affected Employees who will be offered employment by such subcontractors and affiliates.
    1.3 Specify whether any offers of employment to the Affected Employees will be of limited duration.

  2. Compensation
    Each offer of employment to an Affected Employee will include initial base salary of not less than the base salary (including bonuses or other incentive pay) that each Affected Employee received from Customer. Please confirm that you will meet this requirement.

3. Positions
    3.1 The selected vendor will be required to offer employment to the Affected Employees in positions comparable to the positions in which such Affected Employees are currently employed. Please confirm that you will meet this requirement.
    3.2 Each Affected Employee will be offered a position that is at the same location as the Affected Employee was employed by Customer prior to that time. Please confirm that you will meet this requirement.

4. Health Benefits
    4.1 Each Affected Employee will be eligible as of his or her start date for enrollment in the vendor's health care plans, including major medical, life insurance, hospitalization, dental, vision, short-term, and long-term disability, pharmacy and personal accident coverage. The vendor will provide each Affected Employee with health care coverage so that on the start date, he or she (and any family and dependents) is (are) covered by such health care plans, and all pre-existing condition exceptions and exclusionary provisions and waiting periods are waived with respect to the Affected Employee (and any family and dependents). The vendor will be responsible for any medical or health expenses incurred by the Affected Employees on or after the start date. Please confirm that you will meet this requirement.
    4.2 **[DISCUSS: CO-PAYMENT/DEDUCTIBLE REIMBURSEMENTS]**

5. Vacation
    5.1 The Affected Employees will be allowed to carry over accrued but unused vacation. Please confirm that you will meet this requirement.
    5.2 The selected vendor will calculate time off for paid vacation and sick leave purposes for each Affected Employee using each Affected Employee's length of service with Customer and the vendor. Please confirm that you will meet this requirement.

6. Savings Benefits
    6.1 Describe how you will handle the Affected Employee's existing savings benefits (including 401(k)).
    6.2 Describe your saving benefit plans.

7. Retirement Benefits
    7.1 Describe how you will handle the Affected Employee's existing retirement benefits.
    7.2 Describe your retirement benefit plans.

8. Severance/Redundancy
    [DESCRIBE HOW CUSTOMER WISHES VENDOR TO HANDLE THIS ITEM]

9. Retiree Medical
    [DESCRIBE HOW CUSTOMER WISHES VENDOR TO HANDLE THIS ITEM]

10. Other Benefits
    The vendor will be responsible for providing (as part of the base fees) equal or substantially comparable benefits to those currently provided to the Affected

Employees. This will be determined on a country-by-country basis and may include such benefits as car, housing and meal allowances. It is the general intent of Customer that the transition to the vendor will not result in any severance or redundancy obligations on behalf of Customer. **[If any such obligations are triggered as a result of the transition, the vendor will be responsible for any severance/redundancy pay.]** Please confirm that you will meet this requirement.

11. Work Hours
    The work days, including daily work hours and holidays, of the Affected Employees located at any Customer's location will be the same as the work hours in effect at that Customer's location. Please confirm that you will meet this requirement.

12. Service Credit
    The Affected Employees will be given credit for prior service with Customer for purposes of determining eligibility and accrual rates for vacation, sick leave, disability benefits, severance, retiree benefits and health plans and other plans, and programs that are service related. Please confirm that you will meet this requirement.

13. Hiring Requirements
    There will not be any conditions (e.g., pre-employment screening) to the offers of employment to the Affected Employees. Please confirm that you will meet this requirement.
    [CONSIDER ISSUES RELATING TO: MINIMUM EMPLOYMENT PERIOD; UNION EMPLOYEES; LOCAL BENEFITS/REQUIREMENTS]

C. Employee Transition
   1. Specify the duration and timing of the employee transition period, the procedures that will be followed and the date on which the Affected Employees accepting offers will start work with the vendor.

   2. The selected vendor will be responsible for filling the positions of any Affected Employees not hired by the vendor with replacements of comparable skill levels. The vendor will be responsible for the salary and benefits of such replacements.

   3. The selected vendor will appoint a human resources representative who will be responsible for the transition of the Affected Employees from Customer to the vendor. The vendor will not replace or reassign the representative until after the Affected Employees' start date with the vendor.

D. Employment Policies and Procedures
   1. Specify any planned reduction/relocation of any of the Affected Employees.

   2. Attach a copy of any employment contract or procedures that would apply to the Affected Employees.

E. Project Staff
   1. The selected vendor will appoint a project executive to supervise the Customer account. Customer must approve of such appointment. In addition, the vendor will not replace or reassign the project executive without Customer's consent. Please confirm that you will meet this requirement.

2. Customer will designate certain members of the vendor's project staff as key employees. The vendor will not be replace or reassign any of the key employees without Customer's consent. Please confirm that you will meet this requirement.

3. The selected vendor will not subcontract any of the services to be provided without Customer's consent. Please confirm that you will meet this requirement. In addition, specify any proposed subcontractors and the services they will provide.

Appendix 7.3

HUMAN RESOURCES: SAMPLE TERMS AND CONDITIONS FOR EMPLOYEE TRANSITIONS IN THE UNITED STATES

Sample Terms and Conditions for
Employee Transitions in the United States[a]

1.01 *Definitions.* Capitalized terms not defined in this Exhibit __ are defined as in the Agreement.

(a) *Affected Employees.* The in-scope employees identified by Customer as being employed by Customer as of the Commencement Date and providing services to Customer that will constitute Designated Services.

(b) *Commencement Date.* The date on which the Parties will commence the transition process pursuant to which employees of Customer will become Transitioned Employees.

(c) *Critical Support Personnel.* All Transitioned Employees who have been designated by Customer and Vendor as being essential to the transition process or to _____ **[a particular project].**

(d) *Effective Date.* The date on which all Transitioned Employees will begin their employment with Vendor, which date shall not be more than __ days after the Commencement Date.

(e) *Out-of-Scope Employees.* The employees identified by Customer as being employed by Customer and providing out-of-scope services to Customer.

(f) *Transitioned Employees.* All employees of Customer who become Vendor employees pursuant to the Agreement and this Exhibit.

(g) *Transition Period.* The period between the Commencement Date and the Effective Date.

1.02 *Hiring Requirements.* Subject to the terms and conditions set forth in this Exhibit, Vendor shall extend offers of employment to the following individuals:

(a) all Affected Employees, regardless of whether any such Affected Employee is on an approved leave of absence as determined under any of the Customer leave of absence policies ("Customer Leave of Absence") during the Transition Period; **[and**

---

[a] Jane L. Hanson, an employment lawyer with Milbank, Tweed, Hadley & McCloy LLP, assisted in the preparation of this Appendix 7.3.

(b) **all Out-of-Scope Employees who are identified by Customer during the Transition Period as being available for hiring consideration by Vendor;** *provided, however,* **that Vendor has a position available for such Out-of-Scope Employee and the employee meets the qualifications of the Vendor position, and** *provided, further,* **that all hiring decisions concerning the Out-of-Scope Employees shall be Vendor's sole responsibility.]**

1.03 *Transition Process.* The process by which any or all of the employees identified in Section 1.02, above, will become Transitioned Employees is as follows:

(a) On or before the Commencement Date, Customer shall provide Vendor with a list of all Affected Employees, which list shall not contain the names of more than ___ Affected Employees, and any employees known to be subject to Section 1.02(b) at the time, together with their base salaries and any salary adjustments scheduled to be made by Customer in _____ **[the first few months after the Effective Date],** in accordance with established merit, salary and promotional adjustment plans for Customer employees.

(b) Vendor shall extend offers of employment to all In-Scope Employees and to any Out-of-Scope Employees who are selected by Vendor, as identified on the list provided by Customer.

[(c) If Vendor has any *nondiscretionary* **hiring requirements that are acceptable to Customer, e.g. drug testing, credit checks and background checks, those requirements should be provided here, with a provision describing what happens to any employee who is rejected.]**

(d) All employees of Customer who receive an offer of employment from Vendor must accept said offer no later than ten (10) business days thereafter; *provided, however,* that any Customer employee to whom an offer of employment may not reasonably be made earlier than ten (10) days before the Effective Date may be required to accept the offer in less than ten (10) business days of the offer.

(e) All employees of Customer who have accepted Vendor's offer of employment shall become Transitioned Employees and shall commence their employment on the Effective Date, unless the Customer employee is on a Customer Leave of Absence, in which event the employee shall commence his or her employment immediately upon returning to work.

(f) Vendor shall make all hiring decision regarding Customer Employees in accordance with the provisions of this Exhibit ___. Vendor shall be solely responsible for making such hiring decisions.

1.04 *Terms of Employment.* Vendor shall employ the Transitioned Employees according to the following provisions:

(a) *Term.* Vendor shall not terminate any Transitioned Employee during the _____ **[e.g., the first six months to a year]** of his or her employment with Vendor, nor shall Vendor terminate any Critical Support Personnel in the first _____**[e.g., the first two years]** of his or her employment, except in either case for cause, as such term is defined or used by Vendor in its applicable policies, procedures and practices; *provided, however,* that all employment decisions regarding Transitioned Employees shall be the sole responsibility of Vendor.

(b) *Positions.* Vendor shall offer employment to each Affected Employee to perform job responsibilities substantially similar to the job responsibilities performed by the Affected Employee at Customer as of the Commencement Date.

(c) *Work Days.* Work days, including work hours and holidays, of Transitioned Employees working at the **[Vendor location]** shall be the same as the work days in effect at the **[Customer location]** as of the date of this Agreement. Vendor agrees to continue using the work schedules being used by Customer on the Commencement Date.

(d) *Holidays.* Vendor shall recognize the holiday schedule of Customer (currently _____ (__) paid holidays) for all Transitioned Employees performing work for the benefit of Customer pursuant to this Agreement.

(e) *Location.* Every Transitioned Employee shall be offered a position at the same location at which the Transitioned Employee was employed by Customer prior becoming a Transitioned Employee or at another commercial facility within a reasonable commuting distance from that location. **[Note: Customer's severance policy should be reviewed, and if necessary amended, in order to avoid creating an event that the employee may claim triggers a severance right, e.g., some policies provide for severance to be paid if an employee declines a transfer or reassignment to a location that is not within a reasonable commuting distance from the employee's current assignment.]**

(f) *Protection of Confidential or Proprietary Information.* All Transitioned Employees shall be deemed to have, or have had, access to considerable confidential and proprietary information of Customer. In order to protect Customer's rights with respect to this information, Vendor shall not (i) reassign any Critical Support Personnel to a similar role with a direct competitor of Customer for a period of at least two (2) years after said employee ceases to be assigned to the Customer account, or (ii) reassign any other personnel assigned to the Customer account, but not designated as Critical Support Personnel, to a similar role with a direct competitor of Customer for a period of at least one (1) year after said employee cease to be assigned to the Customer account. **[Vendor should describe its approach to providing this protection.]**

[(g) *Employment Agreements.* To the extent required, refer to any requirements Customer may have regarding Vendor's honoring prior employment agreements with any of the Transitioned Employees.]

1.05 *Compensation.*

(a) *Base Salary.* Vendor shall pay each Transitioned Employee an initial base salary of not less than the base salary that such Transitioned Employee was receiving from Customer as of the Commencement Date. **[Customer may want to require Vendor to provide salary increases that were scheduled before the Effective Date but would not become effective until afterwards, e.g., plus any adjustments scheduled to be made by Customer _____ [in the first few months after the Effective Date], in accordance with established merit, salary and promotional adjustment plans of Customer, as provided to Vendor by Customer].**

[(b) Add applicable references to bonuses or other employee incentive compensation arrangements.]

1.06 *Employee Benefits.*

(a) *General Provisions.* As of the Effective Date, Transitioned Employees shall be eligible to participate in all employee benefit programs, plans or policies maintained for employees of Vendor ("Vendor Benefit Plans") under the same terms and conditions as apply to employees of Vendor, unless otherwise provided in this Section 1.06. Vendor shall recognize service with Customer by each Transitioned Employee from such employee's date of hire with Customer until the

Effective Date, as may be adjusted for breaks in service under policies of the Customer ("Service") as service for the Vendor for all purposes under Vendor Benefit Plans, unless otherwise provided in this Section 1.06. Vendor shall take any and all such actions as may be necessary, including, but not limited to, adopting additional plans, amending existing Vendor Benefit Plans and contracting with insurance carriers to provide Vendor Benefit Plans to Transitioned Employees in accordance with this Section 1.06.

(b) *Welfare Benefits*. Each Transitioned Employee shall be eligible as of the Effective Date for participation in all Vendor Benefit Plans that are welfare benefits, including **[major medical, life insurance, hospitalization, dental, vision, long term disability, pharmacy, and personal accident coverage].** Vendor shall provide each Transitioned Employee with health care coverage so that on the Effective Date, the Transitioned Employee (and covered dependents) is (are) covered by such health care plans, and all exclusionary provisions and waiting periods are waived with respect to the Transitioned Employee (and covered dependents). **[DISCUSS APPLICATION OF YEAR-TO-DATE DEDUCTIBLES TO VENDOR BENEFIT PLANS]**

(c) *Vacation*. Transitioned Employees shall immediately begin accruing vacation with Vendor in accordance with Vendor's vacation policies on the Effective Date, which shall take into account each employee's Service with the Customer. **[DISCUSS BUYING OUT ACCRUED VACATION]**

(d) *Savings Plans*. **[LANGUAGE IF ACCOUNTS OF TRANSITIONED EMPLOYEES IN CUSTOMER SAVINGS PLAN MAY BE TRANSFERRED OR ROLLED OVER TO VENDOR'S PLAN. SUCH OPTIONS SUBJECT TO AVAILABILITY UNDER THE "SAME DESK RULE".]** Vendor shall allow the Transitioned Employee, at the Transitioned Employee's option, to transfer his or her pre-tax benefits in the **[Customer Savings Plan]** to the **[Vendor Savings Plan]** through (a) a direct transfer from the **[Customer Savings Plan]** to the **[Vendor Savings Plan]** or (b) a distribution from the **[Customer Savings Plan]** to the Transitioned Employee and a roll over from the Transitioned Employee to the **[Vendor Savings Plan]**. Vendor represents to Customer, and shall provide such evidence and information as Customer may reasonably request to confirm, that the **[Vendor Savings Plan]** is in full force and effect and meets all the applicable requirements for qualifications under the Internal Revenue Code. **[DISCUSS VENDOR'S MATCHING CONTRIBUTIONS] [DISCUSS HOW UNVESTED MATCHING CONTRIBUTION WILL BE HANDLED] [DISCUSS HOW EMPLOYEE LOANS WILL BE HANDLED] [ADVANCED CONSULTATION WITH BENEFITS CONSULTANTS TO DETERMINE COMPATIBILITY OF VENDOR'S AND CUSTOMER'S PLANS WHERE ASSET TRANSFER.]**

(e) *Pension Plans*. Transitioned Employees' Service shall be credited for vesting, eligibility and **[benefit accrual]** purposes under the **[Vendor Defined Benefit Plan] [ADVANCED DISCUSSION AND CONSULTATION WITH ACTUARIES NECESSARY TO DETERMINE COSTS]**

(f) *Retiree Medical*. **[DISCUSSION NECESSARY IF RETIREE MEDICAL IS AVAILABLE]**

(g) *Tuition Aid*. Tuition in respect of any course work in which a Transitioned Employee is currently enrolled as of the Effective Date and for which Customer has previously approved reimbursement shall be paid by [Customer/Vendor] upon the Transitioned Employee's presentation of evidence of satisfactory completion thereof. Course work that has been previously approved for reimbursement, but which has not yet begun, shall be reimbursed by [Customer/Vendor]. For purposes of this paragraph, "course work" does not mean a degree program, but refers only to a specific class during a particular term. **[DISCUSS COMPATIBILITY OF TUITION REIMBURSEMENT PLANS]**

(h) *Flexible Spending Accounts.* On the Effective Date, Transitioned Employees shall be eligible to participate in Vendor's flexible spending accounts under the terms and conditions thereof that apply to Vendor employees, including such terms as may apply to employees who begin participation in such flexible spending accounts during a coverage period.

(i) *Severance.* No Transitioned Employee shall be entitled to receive severance payments from Customer on account of any action contemplated by or arising from this Agreement.

(j) *Miscellaneous Benefits.* **[FURTHER DISCUSSION NECESSARY TO DETERMINE THE COMPATIBILITY OF VENDOR'S AND CUSTOMER'S SICK PAY, SHORT TERM DISABILITY, LONG TERM DISABILITY, AND WORKER COMPENSATION PLANS OR POLICIES. FAMILY AND MEDICAL LEAVE SERVICE CREDITS SHOULD ALSO BE DISCUSSED.]**

1.07 *Human Resources Representative.* Vendor shall appoint _____, or such other designated representative selected by Vendor's management, as its Human Resources representative. Vendor's Human Resources representative shall be responsible for the transition of the Customer employees from Customer to Vendor. There shall be no additional charge for the services of this representative.

1.08 *Liability and Indemnification.*
[TO BE INCLUDED IN THE HUMAN RESOURCES EXHIBIT OR IN THE BPO AGREEMENT.]

(a) Customer shall assume liability for all claims asserted by any Affected Employees arising out of their employment with Customer prior to their Effective Date, and Vendor shall assume liability for all claims asserted by any Affected Employee arising out of hiring decisions made by Vendor affecting any Affected Employee and for all claims asserted by any of the Transitioned Employees arising out of their employment with Vendor.

(b) Customer shall indemnify and hold Vendor harmless, to the fullest extent permitted by applicable law, against any liability or expenses (including reasonable attorneys' fees and expenses) incurred or suffered by Vendor as a consequence of Vendor's being made a party or being threatened to be made a party to any action, suit or proceeding commenced by any Affected Employee arising out of or relating to any act or omission by Customer or any employee or agent of Customer with respect to any:

    (1) alleged violation of federal, state, local, international, or other laws or regulations or any common law protecting persons or members of a protected class or category, including without limitation laws or regulations prohibiting discrimination or harassment on the basis of a protected characteristic,

    (2) alleged work-related injury, illness or death, except as may be covered by Customer's workers' compensation plan,

    (3) claim for payment of wages, or

    (4) claim for accrued employee pension or welfare benefit obligations not expressly assumed by Vendor.

(c) Vendor shall indemnify and hold Customer harmless, to the fullest extent permitted by applicable law, against any liability or expenses (including reasonable attorneys' fees and expenses) incurred or suffered by Customer as a consequence of Customer's being made a party or being threatened to be made a party to any action, suit or proceeding commenced by any Affected Employee or any Transitioned Employee arising out of or relating to any act or omission by Vendor or any employee or agent of Vendor with respect to any:

(1) alleged violation of federal, state, local, international, or other laws or regulations or any common law protecting persons or members of a protected class or category, including without limitation laws or regulations prohibiting discrimination or harassment on the basis of a protected characteristic,

(2) alleged work-related injury, illness, or death, except as may be covered by Vendor's workers' compensation plans,

(3) claim for payment of wages, or

(4) claim accrued employee pension or welfare benefits to the extent expressly assumed by Vendor.

[The following to be inserted only if Customer has U.S. government contracts.

1.09 *Department of Labor Regulations.* To the extent applicable, Vendor shall comply with United States Department of Labor regulations regarding:

(a) equal employment opportunity obligations of government contractors and subcontractors (41 C.F.R. § 60-1.4(a)(1)-(7));

(b) employment by government contractors of Vietnam-era and disabled veterans (41 C.F.R. § 60-250.4(a)-(m));

(c) employment of the handicapped by government contractors and subcontractors (41 C.F.R. § 60-741.4(a)-(f));

(d) developing written affirmative action programs (41 C.F.R. §§ 60-1.40, 60-2.1, 60-250.5 and 60-741.5);

(e) certifying no segregated facilities (41 C.F.R. § 60-1.8);

(f) filing annual EEO-1 reports (41 C.F.R. § 60-1.7);

(g) utilizing minority-owned and female-owned business concerns (48 C.F.R. §§ 52-219.9 and 52-219.12); and

(h) any successor regulations thereto which are incorporated by reference herein.]

[NOTE: DISCUSS ADDITIONAL ISSUES, E.G. STOCK OPTIONS; CAR ALLOWANCE; UNION EMPLOYEES]

Appendix **9.1**

CHECKLIST: KEY ISSUES IN INTERNATIONAL BPO TRANSACTIONS[a]

KEY ISSUES IN
INTERNATIONAL BPO TRANSACTIONS

1. *Structure of Agreement*

    Define scope of services for each of the entities receiving services to determine whether to structure the agreement as a single service contract or as a master contract. (A master contract or "MSA" typically contains general terms and conditions applicable to all entities receiving services with schedules of work detailing the specific services to be provided to each of the entities.)

2. *Contract Management*
    - Determine how Customer will manage the contract in each of the locations receiving services and how Customer will centrally manage each of the locations
    - Construct:
        - Customer's internal organizational structure
        - Vendor's organizational structure
        - Mechanism pursuant to which the two structures will interact
    - Define Change Control Procedures
        - Services
        - Assets

3. *Approvals*
    - Specify the levels of approval necessary, for example:
        - Level 1   —   Senior Executives (Parent/Contracting Party)
        - Level 2   —   Management Committee
        - Level 3   —   Global Project Manager
        - Level 4   —   Location/Site Project Manager
        - Level 5   —   (Other)

---

[a] Note: This checklist should be used in connection with the more detailed checklists of key issues in BPO transactions (general services, accounting services, human resource management, warehouse distribution services, and property management services) set forth in Appendices 5.1–5.5.

- Determine whether a specific level of approval is necessary for a particular task (e.g., termination for failure to provide the critical services = Level 1 approval)

4. *Effective Date*
   - When will Vendor assume responsibility for providing services to Customer
   - Determine whether there should be different effective dates for different locations (the term typically runs from the first/last effective date—so that there is a single expiration date)

5. *Entities Receiving Services from the Vendor*
   Determine which entities (intercompany and third party) will be receiving services

6. *Services Being Provided*
   Determine scope of services being provided to each entity and locations from which services will be provided

7. *Vendor/Subcontractors*
   - Will Vendor personnel be responsible for providing services to all locations or will a subcontractor be responsible
   - Determine scope of subcontracting
   - Create mechanisms to restrict subcontracting

8. *Conditions Precedent*
   - Identify (with local counsel) country specific approvals/consents/authorizations that are a condition to the provision of services, for example:
     - Migration
     - Provision of services by a third party
     - Personnel transfer
     - Industry specific approvals (banking, insurance, EC)
   - Determine consequences if condition precedent does not occur (work around, associated costs)

9. *Service Locations*
   Determine from, through and to which countries services will be provided

10. *Local Laws/Regulations*
    - Identify (with local counsel) country-specific laws/regulations affecting transaction
    - Determine consequences of changes in laws/regulations during term of Agreement (work around, associated costs)

11. *Transborder Data Flow*
    Determine compliance requirements relating to TDF laws/regulations

12. *Assets*
    - Identify asset requirements for each entity
    - Will Customer/Vendor be providing assets
    - Determine ownership/license rights during term and upon expiration/termination of Agreement

13. *Agreements to be Reviewed*
    - Assess which third-party contracts will need to be reviewed for each of the affected entities, for example:
        - Contracts covering assets that will be transferred to Vendor
        - Contracts covering assets for which Vendor will have administrative, operational, and/or financial responsibility
    - Issues to consider in Customer review:
        - What are access/transfer rights
        - Will third party vendor consent be necessary
        - Will additional charges/fees be applicable
        - When does agreement terminate/renew
        - Will renewal/termination/cancellation fees be applicable

14. *Performance Standards*
    - Determine performance standard for each of the affected entities and/or global performance standards
    - Determine local/global penalties
    - Determine local/global termination rights if penalties reach certain amounts

15. *Retained Assets/Responsibilities*
    - Determine which assets Customer will retain management, administrative, operational and/or financial responsibility for on a global/local level
    - If Vendor will assume financial responsibility for assets retained by Customer, determine how, by whom and in which currency invoices will be paid (*see also* item #13)

16. *Employee Transfer*
    - Identify number of employees to be transferred and the countries in which employees will be transferred
    - Summarize employee benefits in each affected country
    - Compare Vendor's benefits
    - Review local laws/regulations (re: transfers, benefits, severance, vacation)
    - Develop benefit package on a country by country basis

17. *Project Staff*
    - Identify global/location project managers for Customer/Vendor
    - Identify any other key personnel
    - Specify qualification/reassignment provisions pertaining to project manager/key personnel

18. *Reports*
    - Identify reports that Customer currently prepares on a country by country basis
    - Identify any additional reports that may be required/desired on a country by country basis
    - Determine who will receive which reports on a global/local level

19. *Audits (Processing/Charges)*
    - Determine local audit requirements
    - Determine responsibility for making changes required by internal/external auditors

20. *Pricing*
    - Determine global/location pricing mechanisms
    - Which services will incremental charges apply to
    - When will credits apply
    - How will charges/credits be paid (e.g., net out global charges/credits)

21. *Cost of Living Adjustment*
    - Will COLA apply on a global/location level
    - How will inflation-sensitive countries be handled
    - Will Vendor share in the risk

22. *Method of Payment*
    - Determine when, where and in what currency payment will be made
    - Assess currency risks

23. *Benchmarking*
    - Determine whether benchmarking procedures are appropriate
    - If so, implement on a global/location basis
    - Create mechanism for implementing improvements

24. *Baselines/Baseline Adjustments*
    - Determine whether baselines apply on a global/location level
    - Discuss baseline adjustment mechanisms, for example:
        - Quarterly/annual adjustments
        - Adjustments upon significant change in volume

25. *Improvements*
    - How will significant changes in methodologies/technology be handled
    - What are Vendor's notice obligations regarding improvements in methodologies/technology

26. *Taxes*
    - Determine potential tax liability
    - Allocate responsibility for taxes (sales, use, service, VAT) on a location-by-location basis

27. *Additional Services*
    - How will additional assets be handled on a location-by-location basis
    - Does Customer want the ability to contract with third parties
    - Does Customer want the ability to add/take away entities/locations

28. *Early Termination*
    - How will global/location terminations be handled, including:
        - Termination for convenience (in whole or in part)
        - Termination upon change of control of Customer
        - Termination for change of control of Vendor
        - Termination for breach
        - Termination for nonpayment
        - Termination for failure to provide the critical services
        - Termination due to *force majuere* event
        - Termination due to a disaster
        - Termination upon the occurrence of a regulatory event

- Discuss cross-termination rights (e.g., if more than one location terminated, agreement terminates)

29. *Termination Fees*
    - Determine applicable fees for global/local termination for convenience (in whole or in part)
    - Determine manner and in which currency payment is made

30. *Rights upon Termination*[b]
    - Determine rights to purchase/use Vendor/third-party assets upon termination
    - Have assets been amortized?
    - Determine rights to assign third-party service contracts upon termination
    - Allocate responsibility for transfer/ongoing fees
    - Specify Vendor's obligations to provide assistance upon termination

31. *Business Recovery*
    - Specify disaster recovery/business continuation requirements for each Customer/Vendor location
    - Identify Customer responsibilities
    - Identify Vendor responsibilities
    - Determine consequences if Vendor is not able to restore services within specified period of time

32. *Security Procedures*
    - Specify data security requirements for each Customer/Vendor location
    - Specify physical security requirements for each Customer/Vendor location
    - Identify who will be responsible for maintaining security
    - Determine how changes in security requirements will be handled

---

[b] *See also* "Due Diligence List for Customers Considering Termination" set forth in Appendix 12.2.

GENERAL ASSIGNMENT
AND BILL OF SALE[a]

THIS GENERAL ASSIGNMENT AND BILL OF SALE is entered into this **[NUMBER VARIATION]** day of **[MONTH] [YEAR],** by and between **[***]**, a **[***]** corporation (*"Purchaser"*) and **[***]**, a **[***]** corporation (*"Seller"*).

WITNESSETH:

WHEREAS, Purchaser and Seller are entering into an Agreement dated **[DATE]** (the *"Services Agreement"*); (capitalized terms not defined herein shall have the meanings ascribed to them in the Services Agreement);

WHEREAS, pursuant to the Services Agreement, Seller has agreed to sell and Purchaser has agreed to purchase the Assets on the Effective Date; and

WHEREAS, Seller desires to transfer and assign the Assets and Purchaser desires to accept the transfer and assignment thereof.

NOW, THEREFORE, in consideration of the mutual covenants contained herein and for other good and valuable consideration, the receipt and sufficiency of which are hereby acknowledged, Seller hereby irrevocably sells, transfers, conveys, and assigns to Purchaser all of Seller's right, title, and interest in the Assets, TO HAVE AND TO HOLD the same unto Purchaser, its successors, and assigns, forever.

Purchaser hereby accepts the sale, transfer, conveyance, and assignment of the Assets.

At any time or from time to time after the date hereof, at Purchaser's request and without further consideration, Seller shall execute such other instruments of transfer, conveyance, assignment, and confirmation, provide such materials and information and take such other actions as Purchaser may reasonably deem necessary or desirable in order more effectively to transfer, convey, and assign to Purchaser, and confirm Purchaser's title to, all of the Assets, and, to the full extent permitted by law, to put Purchaser in actual possession and operating control of the Assets and to assist Purchaser in exercising all rights with respect thereto.

This General Assignment and Bill of Sale may be executed in any number of counterparts, each of which will be deemed an original, but all of which together will constitute one and the same instrument.

---

[a] Note: The terms of this general assignment and bill of sale may need to be modified to comply with the requirements of the local jurisdiction. Legal counsel should be consulted prior to entering into or negotiating any purchase or sale transaction.

This General Assignment and Bill of Sale shall be governed by the laws of the State of **[STATE]**. Purchaser and Seller agree that the Federal courts of **[***]** shall have exclusive jurisdiction over disputes under this General Assignment and Bill of Sale, and the parties agree that jurisdiction and venue in such courts is appropriate.

IN WITNESS WHEREOF, the undersigned have caused their duly authorized officers to execute this General Assignment and Bill of Sale on the date first written above.

[PURCHASER]

By: _____
           [NAME]
           [Title:]

[NOTARIZE]

[SELLER]

By: _____
           [NAME]
           [Title:]

[NOTARIZE]

Appendix 10.2

TEAMING AGREEMENT[a]

TABLE OF CONTENTS

---

[a] Note: The provisions in this teaming agreement are for illustrative purposes only. The specific content and scope of a teaming agreement will vary from transaction to transaction. In addition, the terms of the teaming agreement may need to be modified to comply with the requirements of the local jurisdiction. Legal counsel should be consulted prior to entering into any teaming agreement.

Article 12. MISCELLANEOUS PROVISIONS
>   12.1   Assignment.
>   12.2   Notices.
>   12.3   Counterparts.
>   12.4   Headings.
>   12.5   Consents, Approvals and Requests.
>   12.6   Severability.
>   12.7   Waiver.
>   12.8   Publicity.
>   12.9   Entire Agreement.
>   12.10   Amendments.
>   12.11   Governing Law.
>   12.12   Survival.
>   12.13   Third-Party Beneficiaries.
>   12.14   Covenant of Further Assurances.
>   12.15   Solicitation.
>   12.16   *Force Majeure.*

THIS TEAMING AGREEMENT (this *"Agreement"*), dated as of **[DATE]** (the *"Agreement Date"*), by and between **[PRIMARY CONTRACTOR]**, with a principal place of business at **[ADDRESS]** (the "Primary Contractor") and **[SUBCONTRACTOR]**, with a principal place of business at **[ADDRESS]** (the "the Subcontractor") (the Primary Contractor and the Subcontractor each, a "Party"; collectively, the "Parties").

WITNESSETH:

WHEREAS, **[CUSTOMER]** ("Customer") has requested that the Primary Contractor submit a proposal for certain services and products, described more particularly in Exhibit A (the "Services"); and

WHEREAS, the Parties wish to work together, in accordance with the terms and conditions of this Agreement, to develop a quality approach to the provision of the Services and to prepare a proposal describing such approach to be submitted by the Primary Contractor to the Customer (the "Proposal").

NOW, THEREFORE, for and in consideration of the agreements of the Parties set forth below, the Parties hereby agree as follows:

ARTICLE 1. DEFINITIONS

The following defined terms shall have the meanings specified in the portion of this Agreement indicated below:

TERM	DEFINED IN
AAA	Section 9.2
Agreement	Heading
Agreement Date	Heading
Confidential Information	Section 5.1
Customer	Recitals
Force Majeure	Section 12.16
Indemnitee	Section 10.3
Indemnifying Party	Section 10.3
Party(ies)	Heading
Primary Contractor	Heading
Primary Contractor Representative	Section 9.1

ARTICLE 2. TERM

This Agreement shall commence on the Agreement Date and continue until terminated pursuant to Article 7 (the "Term").

ARTICLE 3. RESPONSIBILITIES

3.1   *Primary Contractor.* The Primary Contractor shall have sole responsibility for (1) developing and directing the format and content of the Proposal, including preparing and revising portions of the Proposal, (2) presenting the Proposal to Customer and (3) negotiating a prime contract between Customer and the Primary Contractor (the "Prime Contract") as may be requested by Customer after review of the Proposal.

3.2   *Subcontractor.* The Subcontractor shall (1) provide information and data relating to its performance of certain of the Services identified by the Primary Contractor in [***] (the "Subcontracted Services") and (2) assist the Primary Contractor in the Primary Contractor's development and presentation of the Proposal as requested by the Primary Contractor. The Subcontractor shall provide access to qualified personnel and resources as may be requested by the Primary Contractor.

3.3   *Prime Contract.* If the Primary Contractor enters into the Prime Contract with Customer, the Primary Contractor shall subcontract to the Subcontractor the Subcontracted Services, as may be amended during negotiations with Customer; provided, that (1) the Primary Contractor and the Subcontractor negotiate and execute an appropriate subcontract (the "Subcontracting Agreement"), (2) Customer approves of the Subcontractor and the scope of the work to be performed by the Subcontractor and (3) this Agreement has not been terminated pursuant to Article 7.

3.4   *Subcontracting Agreement.* Within [NUMBER] days after the award to the Primary Contractor of the Prime Contract, the Parties shall commence to negotiate the Subcontracting Agreement. The Subcontracting Agreement shall (1) contain those terms and conditions as may be required in the Prime Contract and (2) reflect the scope and requirements set forth in the Prime Contract.

3.5   *Third Parties.* In the event that the Parties are not able to negotiate the Subcontracting Agreement within [NUMBER] days from award of the Prime Contract to the Primary Contractor, the Primary Contractor may negotiate with and enter into subcontracts with third parties for the performance of the Subcontracted Services or provide such Subcontracted Services itself. The right to subcontract to third parties or provide the Subcontracted Services itself shall be in addition to other rights the Primary Contractor may have. In the event the Primary Contractor subcontracts to a third party or notifies the Subcontractor that it will provide the Subcontracted Services itself, this Agreement shall terminate.

3.6   *Right to Communicate with Customer.* The Subcontractor shall not contact or communicate with Customer or its employees or agents, directly or indirectly, without the Primary Contractor's approval. The Subcontractor shall notify the Primary Contractor immediately if it is approached or contacted by Customer.

ARTICLE 4. RELATIONSHIP

During the Term, the Subcontractor shall not team with any other party or work individually in connection with the preparation of a proposal to be submitted to Customer for the provision of any of the Services. The performance by the Subcontractor of its duties and obligations under this Agreement shall be that of an independent contractor and nothing contained in this Agreement shall create or imply an agency relationship between the Parties, nor shall this agreement be deemed to constitute a joint venture, partnership, or formal business organization between the Parties.

ARTICLE 5. PROPRIETARY RIGHTS

5.1   *Confidential Information.* Each Party shall use at least the same standard of care in the protection of confidential or proprietary information ("Confidential Information") of the other Party as it uses to protect its own Confidential Information. Each Party shall use the Confidential Information of the other Party only in connection with the purposes of this Agreement and shall make such Confidential Information available only to its employees, subcontractors, or agents having a "need to know" with respect to such purpose. In the event of the termination of this Agreement for any reason, all Confidential Information of a Party disclosed to and all copies thereof made by the other Party shall be returned to the disclosing Party or, at the disclosing Party's option, erased or destroyed. The recipient of the Confidential Information shall provide to the disclosing Party certificates evidencing such destruction. The obligations in this Section 5.1 shall not restrict any disclosure by a Party pursuant to any applicable law, or by order of any court or government agency (provided that the disclosing Party shall give prompt notice to the non-disclosing Party of such order). Confidential Information of a Party shall not be afforded the protection of this Agreement if such data was (1) developed by the other Party independently, (2) rightfully obtained by the other Party without restriction from a third party, (3) publicly available other than through the fault or negligence of the other Party or (4) released without restriction to anyone.

5.2   *Proprietary Rights.* All information, documentation, data and other materials developed, created or provided solely by a Party in connection with its obligations under this Agreement ("Work Product") **[shall remain the property of the such Party].** Each Party grants the other Party the right to use its Work Product for the limited purpose of preparing and amending the Proposal and negotiating the Prime Contract and the Subcontracting Agreement. **[DISCUSS HOW WORKS CREATED JOINTLY WILL BE TREATED]**

ARTICLE 6. PROJECT TEAM

6.1   *Subcontractor Representative.* The Subcontractor shall appoint an individual who from the Agreement Date shall serve as the contact person in respect of, and shall be responsible for, the performance of the Subcontractor's obligations under this Agreement (each such individual, the "Subcontractor Representative"). **[The Subcontractor Representative shall work on the Proposal and the Subcontractor's other responsibilities under this Agreement on a full-time** basis.] The Subcontractor's appointment of any Subcontractor Representative shall be subject to the Primary Contractor's consent. The initial Subcontractor Account Representative shall be **[NAME]. [The Subcontractor shall not reassign or replace the Subcontractor Representative until the earlier of (1) the termination of this Agreement and (2) the date on which the Prime Contract and the Subcontracting Agreement are entered into by the appropriate parties.]**

6.2 *Project Staff.* The Subcontractor shall appoint sufficient staff of suitable training and skills to perform the Subcontractor's responsibilities under this Agreement.

ARTICLE 7. TERMINATION

Except as set forth in Section 12.16, this Agreement shall terminate:

(1) if Customer has not awarded a prime contract for the Services within **[NUMBER]** days from the Agreement Date;

(2) if Customer enters into a prime contract for the Services to a party other than the Primary Contractor;

(3) if the Primary Contractor notifies the Subcontractor that the supplies or services to be offered by the Subcontractor are unsatisfactory or do not otherwise meet Customer's requirements;

(4) if the Parties do not enter into the Subcontracting Agreement within **[NUMBER]** days of the date that the Prime Contract is entered into by the Primary Contractor and Customer;

(5) if either Party is ineligible to receive an award or to enter into a contract for the provision of the Services;

(6) if the Primary Contractor enters into the Prime Contract; or

(7) pursuant to Section 3.5.

ARTICLE 8. EXPENSES

Each Party shall bear all of its own expenses incurred in connection with the preparation and negotiation of the Proposal, the Prime Contract and the Subcontracting Agreement.

ARTICLE 9. DISPUTE RESOLUTION

9.1 *Account Representatives.* All disputes shall initially be referred jointly to (1) the Subcontractor Representative and (2) the individual appointed by the Primary Contractor to serve as its primary contact with the Subcontractor (the "Primary Contractor Representative"). If the Subcontractor Representative and the Primary Contractor Representative are unable to resolve the dispute within **[NUMBER]** business days after referral of the matter to them, the parties shall submit the dispute to members of the senior management of both Parties.

9.2 *Arbitration.* If a dispute is not resolved pursuant to Section 9.1, then either Party may, within **[NUMBER]** business days after the completion of the procedures set forth in Section 9.1, upon notice, submit the dispute to [formal binding] arbitration in accordance with this Section 9.2.

(1) The arbitration shall be held in [***] before a panel of three arbitrators. Either the Primary Contractor or the Subcontractor may by notice to the other Party demand arbitration, by serving on the other Party a statement of the dispute, controversy, or claim, and the facts relating or giving rise thereto, in reasonable detail, and the name of the arbitrator selected by it.

(2) Within **[NUMBER]** days after receipt of such notice, the other Party shall name its arbitrator, and the two arbitrators named by the Parties

shall, within **[NUMBER]** days after the date of such notice, select the third arbitrator.

(3) The arbitration shall be governed by the Commercial Arbitration Rules of the American Arbitration Association, as may be amended from time to time (the "AAA"), except as expressly provided in this Section 9.2; provided, however, that the arbitration shall be administered by any organization agreed upon by the parties. The arbitrators may not amend or disregard any provision of this Section 9.2.

(4) The arbitrators shall allow such discovery as is appropriate to the purposes of arbitration in accomplishing fair, speedy and cost-effective resolution of disputes. The arbitrators shall reference the rules of evidence of the Federal Rules of Civil Procedure then in effect in setting the scope and direction of such discovery. **[The arbitrators shall not be required to make findings of fact or render opinions of law.]**

(5) **[The decision of and award rendered by the arbitrators shall be final and binding on the Parties.]** Judgment on the award may be entered in and enforced by any court of competent jurisdiction. The arbitrators shall have no authority to award damages in excess or in contravention of Article 11.

Except (a) for an action to seek injunctive relief to prevent or stay a breach of Article 5 or (b) any action necessary to enforce the award of the arbitrators, the provisions of this Section 9.2 are a complete defense to any suit, action or other proceeding instituted in any court or before any administrative tribunal with respect to any dispute, controversy or claim arising out of or related to this Agreement or the creation, validity, interpretation, breach, or termination of this Agreement.

ARTICLE 10. INDEMNIFICATION

10.1 *By Primary Contractor.* The Primary Contractor shall indemnify the Subcontractor from, and defend the Subcontractor against, any liability or expenses (including attorneys' fees and expenses as incurred) arising out of or relating to (1) any claim by a third party that the Work Product developed, created, or provided by the Primary Contractor infringes upon the proprietary rights of any third party and (2) **[personal injury, death or damage to tangible personal or real property in any way incident to, or in connection with or arising out of the act or omission of the Primary Contractor, its employees, contractors or agents]**. The Primary Contractor shall be responsible for any costs and expenses incurred by the Subcontractor in connection with the enforcement of this Section 10.1.

10.2 *By Subcontractor.* The Subcontractor shall indemnify the Primary Contractor from, and defend the Primary Contractor against, any liability or expenses (including attorneys' fees and expenses as incurred) arising out of or relating to (1) any claim by a third party that the Work Product developed, created or provided by the Subcontractor infringes upon the proprietary rights of any third party, (2) any claim by a third party in respect of services or systems provided by the Subcontractor to a third party and (3) personal injury, death or damage to tangible personal or real property in any way incident to, or in connection with or arising out of the act or omission of the Subcontractor, its employees, contractors, or agents. The Subcontractor shall be responsible for any costs and expenses incurred by the Primary Contractor in connection with the enforcement of this Section 10.2.

10.3 *Indemnification Procedures.* If any third party makes a claim covered by Section 10.1 or Section 10.2 against any indemnitee (an "Indemnitee") with respect to which such Indemnitee intends to seek indemnification under Section 10.1 or Section 10.2, such Indemnitee shall give notice of such claim to the indemnifying party (under Section 10.1 or Section 10.2) (the "Indemnifying Party") including a brief description of the amount and basis therefor, if known. Upon giving such notice, the Indemnifying Party shall be obligated to defend such Indemnitee against such claim, and shall be entitled to assume control of the defense of the claim with counsel chosen by the Indemnifying Party, reasonably satisfactory to the Indemnitee. Indemnitee shall cooperate fully with, and assist, the Indemnifying Party in its defense against such claim. The Indemnifying Party shall keep the Indemnitee fully apprised at all times as to the status of the defense. Notwithstanding the foregoing, the Indemnitee shall have the right to employ its own separate counsel in any such action, but the fees and expenses of such counsel shall be at the expense of such Indemnitee; provided, however (1) if the parties agree that it is advantageous to the defense for the Indemnitee to employ its own counsel or (2) in the reasonable judgment of the Indemnitee, based upon an opinion of counsel which shall be provided to the Indemnifying Party, there is a conflict of interest with respect to such claim, then reasonable fees and expenses of the Indemnitee's counsel shall be at the expense of the Indemnifying Party, provided that the Indemnifying Party approves such counsel. Neither the Indemnifying Party nor any Indemnitee shall be liable for any settlement of any action or claim effected without its consent.

Notwithstanding the foregoing, the Indemnitee shall retain, assume or re-assume sole control over, and all expenses relating to, every aspect of the defense that it believes is not the subject of the indemnification provided for in Section 10.1 or Section 10.2. Until both (a) the Indemnitee receives notice from the Indemnifying Party that it will defend and (b) the Indemnifying Party assumes such defense, the Indemnitee may, at any time after [NUMBER] days from the date notice of claim is given to the Indemnifying Party by the Indemnitee, resist or otherwise defend the claim or, after consultation with and consent of the Indemnifying Party, settle or otherwise compromise or pay the claim. The Indemnifying Party shall pay all costs of the Indemnitee arising out of or relating to that defense and any such settlement, compromise or payment. The Indemnitee shall keep the Indemnifying Party fully apprised at all times as to the status of the defense.

Following indemnification as provided in Section 10.1 or Section 10.2, the Indemnifying Party shall be subrogated to all rights of the Indemnitee with respect to the matters for which indemnification has been made.

ARTICLE 11. DAMAGES
NEITHER PARTY SHALL BE LIABLE FOR, NOR WILL THE MEASURE OF DAMAGES INCLUDE ANY INDIRECT, SPECIAL OR CONSEQUENTIAL DAMAGES OR AMOUNTS FOR LOST INCOME.

ARTICLE 12. MISCELLANEOUS PROVISIONS
12.1 *Assignment.* Neither Party may assign this Agreement in whole or in part without the consent of the other Party; provided, however, that a Party may assign this Agreement pursuant to a change of control, including a merger, corporate reorganization or sale of all or substantially all of its assets. Any

purported assignment in contravention of this Section 12.1 shall be null and void. The consent of either Party to any assignment, or any other assignment permitted hereunder, shall not constitute consent to further assignment. This Agreement shall be binding on the Parties and their respective successors and permitted assigns.

12.2 *Notices.* Except as otherwise specified in this Agreement, all notices, requests, approvals and consents and other communications required or permitted under this Agreement shall be in writing and shall be sent by telecopy to the telecopy number specified below. A copy of any such notice shall also be personally delivered or sent by (1) first class U.S. Mail, registered or certified, return receipt requested, postage prepaid or (2) U.S. Express Mail, Federal Express, or other, similar overnight bonded mail delivery services to the address specified below:

In the case of the Primary Contractor:
Attention: **[NAME]**
Telecopy Number: **[TELECOPY NUMBER]**
In the case of the Subcontractor:
Attention: **[NAME]**
Telecopy Number: **[TELECOPY NUMBER]**

Either Party may change its address or telecopy number for notification purposes by giving the other Party notice of the new address or telecopy number and the date upon which it will become effective.

12.3 *Counterparts.* This Agreement may be executed in any number of counterparts, all of which taken together shall constitute one single agreement between the Parties.

12.4 *Headings.* The article and section headings and the table of contents are for reference and convenience only and shall not be considered in the interpretation of this Agreement.

12.5 *Consents, Approvals, and Requests.* Unless otherwise specified in this Agreement, all consents and approvals, acceptance or similar actions to be given by either Party under this Agreement shall not be unreasonably withheld or delayed and each Party shall make only reasonable requests under this Agreement.

12.6 *Severability.* If any provision of this Agreement is held by a court of competent jurisdiction to be contrary to law, then the remaining provisions of this Agreement will remain in full force and effect.

12.7 *Waiver.* No delay or omission by either Party to exercise any right or power it has under this Agreement shall impair or be construed as a waiver of such right or power. A waiver by any Party of any breach or covenant shall not be construed to be a waiver of any succeeding breach or any other covenant. All waivers must be in writing and signed by the Party waiving its rights.

12.8 *Publicity.* Neither Party shall use the other Party's name or refer to the other Party directly or indirectly in any media release, public announcement or public disclosure relating to this Agreement or its subject matter, including in any promotional or marketing materials, customer lists or business presentations without consent from the other Party for each such use or release.

12.9 *Entire Agreement.* This Agreement and each of the Attachments, which are hereby incorporated by reference into this Agreement, is the entire agreement between the Parties with respect to its subject matter, and there are no other representations, understandings, or agreements between the Parties relative to such subject matter.

12.10 *Amendments.* No amendment to, or change, waiver or discharge of, any provision of this Agreement shall be valid unless in writing and signed by an authorized representative of the Party against which such amendment, change, waiver or discharge is sought to be enforced.

12.11 *Governing Law.* This Agreement shall be interpreted in accordance with and governed by the laws of **[SPECIFY LAW]**.

12.12 *Survival.* The terms of Article 4, Article 5, Article 8, Article 10, Article 11, Section 9.2, Section 12.8, Section 12.11, this Section 12.12 and Section 12.15 shall survive the termination of this Agreement for any reason.

12.13 *Third Party Beneficiaries.* Each Party intends that this Agreement shall not benefit, or create any right or cause of action in or on behalf of, any person or entity other than the Primary Contractor or the Subcontractor.

12.14 *Covenant of Further Assurances.* The Primary Contractor and the Subcontractor covenant and agree that, subsequent to the execution and delivery of this Agreement and without any additional consideration, each of the Primary Contractor and the Subcontractor will execute and deliver any further legal instruments and perform any acts which are or may become necessary to effectuate the purposes of this Agreement.

12.15 *Solicitation.* The Subcontractor shall not solicit any Primary Contractor employees during the Term and for **[NUMBER]** days after the termination of this Agreement for any reason.

12.16 *Force Majeure.* **[ADD APPROPRIATE FORCE MAJEURE LANGUAGE]**

IN WITNESS WHEREOF, each of the Parties have caused this Agreement to be signed and delivered by its duly authorized representative.

[PRIMARY CONTRACTOR]

By: _____
[NAME]
[TITLE]

[SUBCONTRACTOR]

By: _____
[NAME]
[TITLE]

CONSENT LETTER (ASSIGNMENT OF AGREEMENT TO BPO VENDOR)

[DATE]

Re: [NAME OF BPO AGREEMENT] Agreement between [CUSTOMER] and [VENDOR]

[THIRD-PARTY VENDOR]
[ADDRESS]

To whom it may concern:

This is to inform you that Customer ("Customer") and Vendor ("Vendor") have entered into an agreement pursuant to which Vendor will provide certain [SPECIFY TYPE OF BUSINESS PROCESS] and related services to Customer. In connection with this transaction, Customer will transfer or assign to Vendor the agreements between [THIRD PARTY VENDOR] and Customer for [FILL IN] pursuant to the [NAME OF AGREEMENT] (the "Third-Party Agreements"), including all rights and responsibilities thereunder. Please confirm your consent to such transfer or assignment by Customer to Vendor by signing both copies of this letter and returning one signed original to me as soon as possible.

Upon such transfer or assignment, Vendor will be financially responsible for Customer's obligations to you under the Third-Party Agreement and Customer will have no further obligations to you under such Agreement. Vendor will also have managerial and administrative responsibility of the Third-Party Agreements. Therefore, all correspondence and invoices concerning the Third-Party Agreement as of this date should be mailed to the address currently used by Customer, c/o Vendor.

I would appreciate if the signed original was sent no later than [DATE] to the following: [CUSTOMER]

Sincerely yours,

[CUSTOMER]

ACCEPTED AND AGREED:
[THIRD PARTY VENDOR]

By: _____
[TITLE]
Date: _____

CONSENT LETTER (MANAGEMENT OF THIRD-PARTY PRODUCTS/SERVICES)

[DATE]

Re: [NAME OF BPO AGREEMENT] Agreement between [CUSTOMER] and [VENDOR]

[THIRD PARTY VENDOR]
[ADDRESS]

To whom it may concern:

This is to inform you that **[CUSTOMER]** ("Customer") and **[VENDOR]** ("Vendor") have entered into an agreement pursuant to which Vendor will provide certain **[SPECIFY TYPE OF BUSINESS PROCESS]** and related services to Customer. In connection with this transaction, **[Customer will provide Vendor access to] [Vendor will have managerial, administrative and financial responsibility for] [FILL IN]** (the "Third Party Product/Service"). Please confirm your consent to such access/assumption of responsibility by to Vendor by signing both copies of this letter and returning one signed original to me as soon as possible.

Vendor will be **[financially]** responsible for Customer's obligations to you for the Third-Party Product/Service. **[Vendor will also have managerial and administrative responsibility of the agreements relating to the Third-Party Product/Service.]** Therefore, all correspondence and invoices concerning the such agreements as of this date should be mailed to the address currently used by Customer, c/o Vendor.

I would appreciate if the signed original was sent no later than **[DATE]** to the following: **[CUSTOMER]**

Sincerely yours,

[CUSTOMER]

ACCEPTED AND AGREED:
[THIRD PARTY VENDOR]

By: _____
[TITLE]
Date: _____

CUSTOMER CHECKLIST FOR RENEGOTIATING/TERMINATING BPO TRANSACTIONS[a]

I. Overview
   A. Why customers seek to renegotiate/terminate
   B. Common customer objectives
   C. The renegotiation process
   D. Key success factors
   E. Key business issues
   F. Key contract issues
   G. Assessing customer's rights under the contract
   H. Being prepared to terminate

II. Why customers seek to renegotiate/terminate
   A. Publicly announced reasons
      1. Expiration
         • Of outsourcing contract
         • Of initial pilot period
      2. Change in customer's business
         • Reorganization
         • Acquisition of customer by third party
         • Acquisition by customer of other businesses
         • Downsizing of customer's business
         • Expansion of customer's business
         • Insolvency
         • Redirection of customer's product/market
      3. Material deviations from original scope of services
         • Decision to delay/not to implement certain projects/environments

---

[a] Note: This checklist is intended to illustrate the types of legal issues that may arise in connection with renegotiating/terminating business process outsourcing transactions. The issues identified in this checklist, while comprehensive, may not cover all of the issues relevant to a particular transaction. Legal issues will vary depending on the scope of the BPO transaction being renegotiated/terminated. This checklist or any part thereof should only be used after consultation with your legal counsel. You should consult legal counsel prior to entering into or negotiating any outsourcing transaction.

- Customer's desire to implement new projects/environments which materially impact overall delivery of services
- Need to implement new methodologies/technology to maintain service levels/stay competitive (e.g., Year 2000 compliance)

4. Changes in methodologies/technology
   - More efficient methodologies/hardware/software
   - New developments in industry-specific applications

5. Need for significantly more/fewer resources than contemplated by outsourcing contract
   - Need to adjust baselines
   - Additional/reduced resource charges not in line with market

B. Not Publicly Announced
1. Poor performance by vendor (real or perceived)
   - Service outages
   - Failure to meet service levels
   - Failure to provide deliverables/roll out new environments on time
   - Failure to provide quality deliverables
   - Failure to meet cost reduction goals
   - Failure to increase productivity
   - Failure to standardize

2. Overcharging (real or perceived)
   - Fees for base services are in excess of market
   - Fees for new/additional services are in excess of market

3. Poor customer satisfaction

4. Poor customer/vendor relations
   - Cultural disconnect
   - Mismatched project manager
   - Poor vendor responsiveness

5. Change in customer management

6. Desire to bring core services back in-house

7. Disagreement on interpretation of contract
   - Dispute regarding which services are in-scope vs. out-of-scope
   - Dispute regarding vendor responsibility for upgrades/maintenance
   - Dispute regarding vendor responsibility for equipment upgrades/refresh and additional equipment

8. Three-to-five year itch

9. Unrealized expectations
   - Inadequate access to personnel
   - Inadequate access to cutting edge methodologies/technology
   - Failure to achieve cost savings
   - Failure to roll out cutting edge environment

III. Common Customer Objectives
- Reduction of fees
- Addition of new entities (increase volumes)
- Taking away of entities (decrease volumes)
- Obtaining more flexibility/control
- Obtaining certain services from third parties
- Providing certain core services in-house

- Restructuring of contract to reflect actual services being provided
- Obtaining more control over project staff
- Termination of contract without fees/liability
- Recovering past expenses

IV. The Renegotiation Process
1. Define customer's objectives
   - Be as specific as possible
   - Process often dictated by customer's objectives (e.g., reduction of fees vs. restructuring contract to reflect new services being provided)
2. Obtain management support
3. Obtain business process organization support
4. Obtain empowerment from management
5. Identify point people for renegotiations
   - Management
   - Technical
   - Financial
6. Involve legal counsel
7. Involve human resources (if there are personnel issues)
8. Review the contract (all provisions!)—*See Part VIII*
   - Identify any contractual rights to seek renegotiation/termination
   - Identify contractual provisions that customer must follow in connection with renegotiation/termination (e.g., management meetings, notice provisions, dispute resolution)
   - Identify contractual provisions that allow customer to audit/monitor vendor (e.g., audit rights, benchmarking, customer satisfaction)
   - Identify any contractual rights to withhold payments (e.g., offset, withholding, escrow)
   - Identify any contractual provisions that would allow/prohibit vendor from ceasing to perform the services in the event of a dispute/withholding of payments
   - Identify any contractual rights to insource/resource
   - Identify vendor pre-transition obligations to provide information/assistance necessary to facilitate transition (e.g., provide inventories, provide key employee lists)
   - Identify vendor obligations to cooperate with transition of services in-house or to a third party
9. Review all ancillary agreements with vendor
   - Identify any other agreements with vendor
   - Determine whether there are any formal cross-termination rights, as well as the impact of termination on the other agreements
10. Review the file
    - Correspondence
    - Memoranda
    - Amendments
    - Change orders
    - New service orders
    - Invoices
11. Know the history of the deal
    - Customer's original goals in outsourcing

- Vendor's primary commitments
- Concessions by customer
- Concessions by vendor
- Financial engineering
- Vendor promises/representations

12. Document any problems with vendor
- Nonperformance
- Failure to meet service levels
- Failure to provide deliverables
- Vendor relations
- Churning of employees

13. Anticipate vendor's objectives
- Increase profit
- Increase scope
- Increase length of term
- Increase efficiencies/consolidation
- Decrease cost
- Increase presence/expertise in customer's industry
- Decrease scope (i.e., take troubled/unprofitable services out-of-scope)

14. Develop strategy
- Assess customer's current and future business process needs
- Assess strength of any nonperformance/breach claims
- Calculate any credits/fees owing to Customer for nonperformance/delayed performance
- Identify and access alternatives
  - Insource
  - Resource
- Determine Customer's willingness/ability to use a third party

15. Determine impact of termination on other business processes

16. Initiate contact/dialogue with vendor

V. Key Success Factors
1. Practicality of objectives
2. Commitment of management
3. Commitment of organization (time; support)
4. Underlying customer/vendor relationship
5. Profitability of original deal
6. External economic factors
7. Customer leverage
- Ability to go to another vendor
- Ability to provide services in-house
- Publicity
- Ability to document vendor's breach

VI. Key Business Issues
1. What rights does customer have to compel renegotiation?
2. What are the reasons for customer's dissatisfaction?
3. What are the non-contractual leverage points?
4. What is the worst case scenario?
5. Who gains by a public disclosure?

VII. Key Contract Issues
    A.   At signing
        1.   What is it?
- Scope of services
- Entities receiving services

        2.   Who does it?
- Vendor's responsibilities
- Right to use subcontractors
- Customer's responsibilities

        3.   Who owns it?
- Work product/developments
- Documentation
- Data
- Equipment

        4.   How much will it cost?
- Base fees
- Additional/reduced resource charges
- Cost of living adjustments
- Taxes

        5.   What happens if it isn't done?
- Liquidated damages
- Right to insource
- Right to resource/use third parties
- Right to terminate
- Right to obtain damages

    B.   At Renegotiation
        1.   Has there been a default?
        2.   Are there exercisable termination rights?
        3.   Are there exercisable renegotiation rights?
- Due to change in customer's business
- Due to benchmarking results

        4.   Does customer have the right to access/use:
- Methodologies (proprietary and third party)
- Technology (proprietary and third party)
- Tools
- Equipment (owned and leased)
- Data
- Documentation
- Configurations
- Passwords
- Third party services
- Facilities

        5.   Can customer transfer to another vendor without substantial degradation in services?
        6.   What are vendor's assistance/training obligations?
        7.   What rights does customer have to hire project staff?

VIII. Assessing the customer's right under the contract
    A.   Term of agreement
        1.   Is there a pilot period?
        2.   Renewal options

B. Data
    1. Does the contract specify that customer owns data it submits to vendor?
    2. Does customer have the right to recover a copy of its data and software (if applicable) at any time during the term?
    3. Does customer have the right to recover a copy of its data and software (if applicable) upon expiration or termination of the contract for any reason?
    4. What is the cost of recovering data (e.g., delivery charges, storage, media costs)?

C. Intellectual Property
    1. Who owns new developments?
    2. Who owns modifications/enhancements to customer's intellectual property (including methodologies, technology, documentation)?
    3. Who owns modifications/enhancements to vendor's intellectual property (including methodologies, technology, documentation)?
    4. Does customer have the right to use vendor's proprietary intellectual property during the term? Upon expiration or termination?
    5. Does customer's right to use vendor's proprietary intellectual property include software object and source code (if applicable)? Does it include the right to maintain the software?
    6. What are customer's rights to use intellectual property licensed by vendor from a third party during the term? Upon expiration or termination? Is there any associated cost (e.g., transfer/consent fee)?
    7. What are customer's rights to use tools used to provide the services? During the term? Upon expiration or termination?
    8. Who owns work product?
    9. What are customer's rights to require vendor to transfer knowledge (e.g., training, configuration designs) to customer or its designee during the term? Upon expiration or termination?
    10. What are customer's rights to request copies of all work product? To request an inventory?

D. Equipment/Facilities
    1. Who owns equipment acquired in connection with the provision of the services?
    2. Who owns upgrades/enhancements/add-ons to customer's equipment/facilities?
    3. Who owns upgrades/enhancements/add-ons to vendor's equipment/facilities?
    4. Does customer have the right to access/use vendor-owned equipment/facilities during the term? Does customer have a purchase right upon expiration or termination? At what cost?
    5. What are customer's rights to access/use equipment/facilities leased by Vendor from a third party during the term? Upon expiration or termination?
    6. Does vendor occupy any customer space? Has vendor leased any facilities in connection with the provision of services?

E. Third-Party Service Contracts
    1. What are customer's rights to use vendor's subcontractors upon expiration or termination?
    2. What are customer's rights to assume vendor's third-party service contracts upon expiration or termination? Is there any associated cost (e.g., transfer or consent fee)?

F. Service Levels/Customer Satisfaction
    1. Has Vendor met all of its service level obligations?
    2. Can customer request vendor to perform root cause analysis of the service failure?

3. Is there a termination right associated with the failure to meet service levels (in addition to the right to terminate for material breaches)?
4. Does customer have the right to request liquidated damages?
5. Are there any obligations for vendor to conduct customer satisfaction surveys? Has vendor complied? What are the results?

G. Deliverables/Milestones
1. Has vendor provided all deliverables in a timely manner? Has vendor met all required milestones?
2. Is there a termination right associated with the failure to provide deliverables/meet milestones (in addition to the right to terminate for material breaches)?
3. Does customer have the right to request liquidated damages?

H. Fees
1. How is customer charged?
2. Are there fixed rates for additional/reduced resource usage?
3. Can baselines be adjusted?
4. Are there any minimum revenue commitments?
5. Are there any cost of living adjustments?
6. Who is responsible for what taxes?
7. How is termination assistance charged?
8. Does customer have any right to offset/withhold/escrow payments?
9. What are customer's rights to audit? Have such rights been exercised?

I. Benchmarking
1. Is there a benchmarking provision?
2. Has a benchmark been performed? Do the results reveal inconsistencies with industry standards?
3. Do the benchmarking results allow customer to request a readjustment of pricing/services or implementation of new methodologies/technology?

J. Gainsharing
1. Does the contract contain any guaranteed savings?
2. Are there any shared benefits/shared risks?
3. Does the contract contain a profitability index?
4. Are there any cross-marketing opportunities that have been exercised? That should have been exercised?

K. Limitation of Liability
1. What is each party's ultimate liability for failure to perform?
2. What types of damages *cannot* be recovered?
3. What fees are owed in a termination for convenience?

L. Confidential Information
1. What are each party's obligations regarding proprietary data and confidential information?
2. What does the contract say regarding disclosing information to consultants, lawyers, etc.?

M. Dispute Resolution
1. Does the contract establish an informal dispute resolution mechanism?
2. Can action be taken without going to management committee?
3. Has notice been given?

N. Continued Performance
1. Is this a force majeure event?
2. What constitutes a disaster? Are there adequate disaster recovery plans in place?
3. Does vendor have any right to cease performance (e.g., nonpayment)? Are there any protections that would prohibit vendor from ceasing to perform?

O. Right to Renegotiate/Terminate
    1. Renegotiate
- Is there any contractual basis for requesting a renegotiation (e.g., a provision which calls for renegotiations if volumes exceed/go below a certain amount)?
- Has there been any breach?

    2. Termination
- What are termination rights (e.g., convenience, change of control, breach)?
- Is there any basis for termination for breach? What is the cure period?
- Has proper notice been given?
- When are termination fees appliable?

P. Termination/Transition Assistance
    1. What in-scope services is the vendor obligated to perform?
    2. What out-of-scope services is the vendor obligated to perform?
    3. What is the extent of vendor's assistance obligations? Does it include cooperation with third parties? Do third-party vendors need to sign a confidentiality agreement?
    4. What are the costs of termination/transition assistance?
    5. Can the customer hire vendor personnel?

Q. Rights to Resource/Insource
    1. Does customer have any contractual right to source services to a third party?
    2. Does customer have any contractual right to bring any of the services back in-house?

R. Assignment
    1. Does vendor have the unfettered right to assign?
    2. Does customer have the right to assign under certain circumstances (e.g., merger or other corporate reorganization)?

S. Solicitation of Employees
    1. Can customer hire vendor employees during the term? Upon expiration or termination?
    2. Can vendor hire customer employees?
    3. Is there a noncompetition clause? What is its scope?

T. Strategic Alliance/Joint Venture
    1. Has a strategic alliance/joint venture been formed?
    2. What are the cross-negotiation/termination rights (if any)?
    3. Are there any other rights in the strategic alliance/joint venture documents that would impact/affect or have to be amended in connection with renegotiation/termination?

U. Ancillary Agreements
    1. Are there any ancillary agreements (e.g., reengineering, specific projects, consulting, training) that would be impacted by a termination?
    2. What are the termination rights in these agreements?

IX. Be Prepared to Terminate
- Know the contract!
- Review ancillary agreements
- Read the exhibits
- Establish rights to terminate
- Fulfill any notice/dispute resolution requirements
- Prepare for disaster recovery

- Identify key vendor personnel
- Identify key methodologies/technology/tools
- Identify key documentation/manuals
- Identify key equipment/assets
- Prepare to insource/resource

DUE DILIGENCE CHECKLIST FOR CUSTOMERS CONSIDERING TERMINATION

I. Prepare a summary of all termination provisions in the BPO contract
- Include prerequisites and procedures, such as:
    - Acts that may trigger termination right (expiration of pilot period; change of control; default)
    - Required notice periods
    - Any dispute resolution obligations
    - Cure periods
    - For example, *Prerequisite for Termination for Cause.* The customer may terminate for cause if vendor defaults in the performance of any of its material duties or obligations under the BPO contract. The dispute resolution process [is] [is not] a condition precedent to termination for cause. *Procedures for Termination for Cause.* The customer must provide written notice to Vendor of the alleged default. Vendor has ___ days to cure the default. Customer may terminate upon further notice to Vendor if Vendor is unable to cure within the ___-day cure period.
- Read all contract provisions to determine whether there are any termination rights not listed in termination section of the BPO contract
- Examples of possible termination rights:
    - Termination for convenience in the entirety
    - Termination at the end of a pilot phase
    - Partial termination
    - Termination for change of control of customer
    - Termination for change of control of vendor
    - Termination for cause
    - Termination for failing to provide certain critical services
    - Termination for failing to meet service levels on a repeated basis
    - Termination for failing to reinstitute services within the specified time frame in the event of a disaster or *force majeure* event
    - Termination if vendor's liability exceeds damages caps
    - Termination upon the occurrence of a regulatory event
    - Termination upon the termination/expiration of a lease
    - Termination upon the sale of asset
    - Termination upon an event of bankruptcy

II. Analyze whether customer may exercise any of its termination rights
- After which date may customer exercise its termination for convenience right?
- When and under what circumstances may customer exercise its partial termination rights (e.g., only if services will be resourced to a third party; if services are resourced or brought back in-house?)
- Can services be substantially reduced through partial termination? At what stage are services reduced enough to constitute termination in the entirety (e.g., is there a floor of services that must be retained?)
- Has there been any change of control (including corporate reorganization)?
- Does customer have any claims of breach (e.g., have all the service levels been met)?
- Has there been a disaster/*force majeure* event? Has vendor successfully reinstituted critical services?
- Has there been a regulatory event that could trigger termination?
- Has a "key" lease" expired/terminated or has a "key" asset been sold?

III. Assess termination fee payable by customer under each termination provision
- May depend on the type of termination right being exercised (e.g., termination for convenience is typically tied to a termination fee; termination for cause is not typically tied to a termination fee)
- Calculation of the termination fee may be according to:
  - A fixed amount (agreed upon during contract negotiations)
  - A fixed formula (agreed upon during contract negotiations)
  - General statement basing the termination fee on expenditures incurred by vendor and amortized over the contract term (e.g., upfront costs for equipment/technology)
  - Fixed amount plus wind down costs (e.g., costs of relocating employees, resale/relocation costs of equipment; third party contract termination fees)
  - If wind down costs are part of formula/calculation, termination fee may be reduced if customer purchases all or a portion of the assets used to provide the services or if customer hires some or all of the employees that would be relocated
  - Some contracts also allow vendor to recover some percentage of lost profits

IV. Analyze the parties' rights and obligations upon termination
- A. *Termination Assistance*: Vendor is typically contractually obligated to provide reasonable assistance for a minimum period of time after the termination date. Termination assistance services may include:
  - Continued provision of certain services for a period of time
  - Continued processing
  - Parallel processing
  - Testing
  - User acceptance
  - Provision of back-up tapes
  - Provision of operating documentation
  - Freezing of all methodology/technology changes
  - List of procedures to be followed during transition
  - Review of all systems libraries
  - Analysis of space required for databases and systems libraries
  - Unload production and test databases
  - Return of customer equipment

- Return of customer software/tools
- Return of customer data
- Copies of all methodologies/technology used to provide the services
- Generation of reports during transition
- Maintenance of service levels during transition

B. *Transition Assistance*: The BPO contract may require vendor to provide assistance to Customer and its other third party service provider in transitioning services to the third party service provider. Transition assistance may be in addition to termination assistance. Examples of transition assistance services include:
- Making vendor employees available for consultation
- Making vendor subcontractors available for consultation
- Providing copies of all customer owned and licensed methodologies/technology (for software: object and source code)
- Providing access to vendor technology and copies of all vendor methodologies/technology to be licensed to customer or customer's designee
- Providing access to vendor tools and copies of all vendor tools to be licensed to customer or customer's designee
- Providing documentation of customer configurations
- Providing manuals
- Providing procedures
- Providing passwords/security codes
- Providing access to vendor hardware
- Providing access to facilities
- Allowing third-party service provider to hire vendor employees assigned to customer account
- Providing an inventory
  - Equipment
  - Methodologies
  - Software
  - Networks
  - Tools
  - Cabling/lines
  - Documentation
  - Manuals
  - Configurations
  - Procedures
  - Work product
  - Third-party agreements (licenses, leases, service contracts, tariff agreements)
- Identifying which party owns which assets and how ownership was determined (i.e., under which contract provision)
- Identifying whether assets are used in dedicated/shared environment
- Identifying where assets are being used
- Identifying which customer entity the asset is being used for
- List of vendor employees/subcontractors used to provide services
- Identification of key personnel
- List of works in progress, including a status report and report as to the work necessary to complete the project
- List of any contract negotiations in progress, including status report and name and contact person for other negotiating parties
- List of all facilities
- List of all reports generated

C. *Rights with respect to methodologies, technology, equipment, and third-party contracts*
- Does customer have a license to use vendor methodologies/technology upon termination? Are these rights assignable (e.g., to a third-party service provider)?
- Who owns newly developed methodologies/technology? If vendor owns, does customer have a license to use newly developed methodologies/technology upon termination? Are these rights assignable (e.g., to a third-party service provider)?
- Will third-party methodology/technology contracts and third-party maintenance contracts be transferred to customer or customer's designee? Is this at customer's option? Which party is responsible for transfer fees?
- Does customer have the option/obligation to purchase rquipment used to provide the services? How will the purchase price be calculated (e.g., fair market value; book value; the lesser/greater of fair market value and book value)?

D. *Employee issues*
- What are customer's rights to hire vendor employees?
  - Right to rehire employees transferred to vendor by customer
  - Right to hire vendor employees assigned to customer account (is there a restriction on vendor employees primarily assigned to customer's account? Determine time contribution of employees that customer is interested in hiring)
  - Right to hire other vendor employees
- Are there any exceptions from the restrictions on hiring for blind solicitations (e.g., through newspapers)?
- If there is a partial termination, customer should ascertain whether hiring restrictions/allowances only apply upon full termination
- May third-party service providers assuming responsibility for part/all of the services hire any vendor employees previously assigned to customer's account?
- Are there any restrictions on the use by customer or its third-party service provider of vendor's subcontractors?
- What are vendor's rights to hire customer's employees?

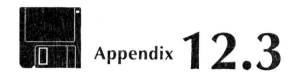

TERMINATION AGREEMENT[a]

TERMINATION AGREEMENT
BETWEEN
CUSTOMER
AND
VENDOR

EXHIBIT LISTING

Exhibit 1	Termination Assistance Agreement
Exhibit 2	Personnel Transition Agreement
Exhibit 3	Termination Payments
Exhibit 4	Assets
Exhibit 5	General Assignment and Bill of Sale
Exhibit 6	Transferred Contracts
Exhibit 7	Consent Letter

THIS TERMINATION AGREEMENT, dated as of **[DATE]** (the "*Termination Date*"), by and between **[NAME OF CUSTOMER]** ("*Customer*") and **[NAME OF VENDOR]** ("*Vendor*") (this "*Termination Agreement*"):

WITNESSETH:

WHEREAS, Customer and Vendor entered into a **[SPECIFY NAME OF BPO AGREEMENT]** dated as of **[DATE]** (the "*Outsourcing Agreement*");

WHEREAS, pursuant to the Outsourcing Agreement, Customer **[transferred certain assets] [and made payments]** to Vendor and Vendor performed the services described in the Outsourcing Agreement;

---

[a] Note: The provisions in this termination agreement are for illustrative purposes only. The specific content and scope of a termination agreement will vary from transaction to transaction. In addition, the terms of the temination agreement may need to be modified to comply with the requirements of the local jurisdiction. Legal counsel should be consulted prior to entering into any termination agreement.

WHEREAS, for good and valuable consideration, Customer and Vendor wish to enter into this Termination Agreement in order to terminate the Outsourcing Agreement and to settle and release the other from agreed upon claims and causes of action.

NOW, THEREFORE, in consideration of the foregoing and the mutual promises, covenants, and undertakings set forth herein, the parties agree as follows:

ARTICLE 1. TERMINATION OBLIGATIONS.

1.01 *Conditions Precedent.* Concurrently with, and as a condition of this Termination Agreement, Customer and Vendor shall execute and deliver a Termination Assistance Agreement in a form substantially similar to *Exhibit 1* **[and a Personnel Transition Agreement in a form substantially similar to *Exhibit 2*].**

1.02 *Payments by [SPECIFY PARTY].* In consideration of the termination of the Outsourcing Agreement and the release of certain claims and causes of actions pursuant to *Article 3*, **[SPECIFY PARTY]** shall pay to **[SPECIFY PARTY]** the payments set forth in *Exhibit 3* (the *"Termination Payments"*).

1.03 *Settlement of Payments.* The Termination Payments shall be made to **[SPECIFY PARTY]** by no later than 5:00 p.m. (_____ Time) on the Termination Date.

1.04 *Assets Transferred.* On the Termination Date, Customer shall pay to Vendor **[SPECIFY DOLLAR AMOUNT]** for the assets described in *Exhibit 4* (the *"Assets"*). **[NOTE: DISCUSS ALLOCATION OF TAXES, IF ANY, RELATED TO TRANSFER OF ASSETS]** On the Termination Date, Vendor shall assign and transfer to Customer good and valid title in and to the Assets free and clear of all liens by delivery of (1) a General Assignment and Bill of Sale, in a form substantially similar to *Exhibit 5* (the *"General Assignment"*), duly executed by each of Customer and Vendor and (2) such other good and sufficient instruments of conveyance, assignment and transfer to be prepared by Customer, in form and substance reasonably acceptable to Vendor, as shall be effective to vest in Customer good title to the Assets.

1.05 *Transferred Contracts.* On the Termination Date, Vendor shall transfer or assign to Customer **[in accordance with Section ___ of the Outsourcing Agreement], [to the extent permitted under the applicable third party agreement]** and except as otherwise provided in *Exhibit 6*, the agreements, including all rights and responsibilities thereunder, for the assets and facilities leased or licensed by Vendor and third party services, **[methodologies and software]** identified in *Exhibit 6*. To the extent that an applicable third party agreement is held in Vendor's name, Vendor shall obtain any necessary consents to assignment pursuant to a letter, in a form substantially similar to *Exhibit 7.*

1.06 *Software and Tools.* On the Termination Date, Vendor shall **[provide access to] [deliver copies of (including object and source code) in the form and on the media designated by Customer]** the software and tools used by Vendor to provide the services under the Outsourcing Agreement prior to the Termination Date **[in accordance with Section ___ of the Outsourcing Agreement] [and the license granted to Customer pursuant to Section ___ of the Outsourcing Agreement shall commence].**

1.07 *Documentation.* On the Termination Date, Vendor shall provide copies of all methodologies, documentation, configurations, manuals, and other information and work product used by Vendor to provide the services under the Outsourcing Agreement **[in accordance with Section ___ of the Outsourcing Agreement].** Vendor represents and warrants that it has provided to Customer all methodologies, documentation, configurations, manuals, and other information and work product necessary to run and maintain Customer's **[SPECIFY BUSINESS PROCESS]** operations.

1.08 *Knowledge Transfer.* Upon Customer's request, Vendor shall meet with those individuals designated by Customer in order to provide training and direction with respect to the operation and maintenance of Customer's **[SPECIFY BUSINESS PROCESS]** operations **[in accordance with Section ___ of the Outsourcing Agreement]**.

1.09 *Return of Customer Data and Other Property.* On the Termination Date, Vendor shall return to Customer all copies (in the form and on the media designated by Customer) of (1) Customer-owned or licensed software and tools, (2) data of Customer and Customer's clients, and (3) Customer-owned or licensed methodologies, documentation, configurations, manuals, and other information and work product **[in accordance with Section ___ of the Outsourcing Agreement]**. Vendor shall promptly erase all files from its computers containing the foregoing information and, upon Customer's request, provide written certification that all such files have been erased.

1.10 *Verification of Payments.* During the 90-day period following the Termination Date, each of Customer and Vendor reserves the right to confirm, validate, and update any information set forth in *Exhibit 4* and *Exhibit 5*. Vendor shall provide any data, information, and access to software reasonably requested by Customer in connection with the validation of information described in this *Section 1.10* consistent with that provided to Customer prior to the Termination Date. If any such information should prove to be inaccurate or incomplete, unless the parties otherwise agree, there shall be an equitable adjustment to the amounts paid or to be paid by Customer to Vendor under this Termination Agreement. Any amounts to be so paid or reimbursed pursuant to an equitable adjustment as aforesaid shall be paid or reimbursed within 30 days of the determination of such amount.

ARTICLE 2. TERMINATION OF OUTSOURCING AGREEMENT.
Effective as of the Termination Date, the Outsourcing Agreement is terminated.

ARTICLE 3. RELEASES.
3.01 *Release of Claims by Customer.* Customer hereby releases Vendor and its parent, affiliates, subsidiaries and their respective directors, officers, employees, agents, assignees, transferees, and successors from any and all claims, causes of action, suits, damages, losses, liabilities, demands, judgments, orders of any kind whatsoever, in law or in equity (*"Claims"*), arising out of or relating to (1) the termination of the Outsourcing Agreement and (2) the following payment obligations **[SPECIFY AMOUNTS OWED BY VENDOR]** incurred prior to the Termination Date. The release set forth in this *Section 3.01* shall not apply to Claims that may arise as a result of (a) Vendor's failure to comply with the terms of this Termination Agreement and, (b) obligations of Vendor which pursuant to the Outsourcing Agreement survive the termination thereof **[NOTE: CONSIDER EXCEPTIONS TO SURVIVAL CLAUSE]**. Customer shall bear its own costs and attorneys' fees arising out of or relating to the negotiation and preparation of this Termination Agreement.

3.02 *Release of Claims by Vendor.* Vendor hereby releases Customer and its parents, affiliates and subsidiaries and its directors, officers, employees, agents, assignees, transferees, and successors from any and all Claims, arising out of or relating to **[(1)]** the termination of the Outsourcing Agreement and (2) the following payment obligations **[SPECIFY AMOUNTS OWED BY CUSTOMER]** incurred prior to the Termination Date. The release set forth in this *Section 3.02* shall not apply to Claims that may arise as a result of (a) Customer's failure to comply with the terms of this Termination Agreement and (b) obligations of Customer which pursuant to the Outsourcing Agreement survive the termination thereof **[NOTE: CONSIDER EXCEPTIONS TO SURVIVAL CLAUSE]**. Vendor shall bear its own costs and attorneys' fees arising out of or relating to the negotiation and preparation of this Termination Agreement.

ARTICLE 4. INDEMNITIES.

4.01 *Indemnity By Customer.* Customer shall indemnify Vendor from, and defend against, any losses, liabilities, and damages (including taxes and related penalties) and all related costs and expenses, including reasonable attorneys' fees and expenses and costs of investigation, litigation, settlement, judgment, appeal, and penalties as relates to either party ("*Losses*"), arising out of or relating to any claim by a third party based on any breach of this Termination Agreement by Customer.

4.02 *Indemnity by Vendor.* Vendor shall indemnify Customer from, and defend against, any Losses arising out of or relating to any claim by a third party based on any breach of this Termination Agreement by Vendor.

[NOTE: CONSIDER ADDING INDEMNITY PROCEDURES]

ARTICLE 5. CONFIDENTIALITY.

All confidential or proprietary information, trade secrets, information relating to customers, prospective customers, business plans, practices, procedures, and documentation ("*Confidential Information*") relating to either party or its parent, affiliates, or subsidiaries shall be held in confidence by the other party to the same extent and in at least the same manner as such party protects its own confidential or proprietary information. Neither party shall disclose, publish, release, transfer, or otherwise make available Confidential Information of the other party in any form to, or for the use or benefit of, any person or entity, except as provided in this *Article 5*, without the other party's approval. Each party shall, however, be permitted to disclose relevant aspects of the other party's Confidential Information to its officers, agents, employees, and subcontractors and to the officers, agents, employees, and subcontractors of its corporate parent, affiliates, or subsidiaries to the extent that such disclosure is reasonably necessary for the performance of its duties and obligations under this Termination Agreement or the determination, preservation, or exercise of its rights and remedies under this Termination Agreement; provided, however, that such party shall take all reasonable measures to ensure that Confidential Information of the other party is not disclosed or duplicated in contravention of the provisions of this Termination Agreement by such officers, agents, employees, and subcontractors. The obligations in this *Article 5* shall not restrict any disclosure by either party pursuant to any applicable law, or by order of any court of competent jurisdiction or governmental agency or to banking regulators in connection with their investigative and audit functions (provided that the disclosing party shall endeavor to give such notice to the non-disclosing party as may be reasonable under the circumstances) and shall not apply with respect to information that is independently developed by the other party, becomes part of the public domain (other than through unauthorized disclosure), is disclosed by the owner of such information to a third party free of any obligation of confidentiality or which either party gained knowledge or possession of free of any obligation of confidentiality. The terms of this Termination Agreement are confidential and shall not be disclosed by either party to any third party except as provided in this *Article 5*.

ARTICLE 6. REPRESENTATIONS AND WARRANTIES.

6.01 *By Customer.* Customer represents and warrants that (1) it has all the requisite power and authority to execute, deliver, and perform its obligations under this Termination Agreement, (2) the execution, delivery, and performance of this Termination Agreement have been duly authorized by Customer and (3) it is not a party to any agreements which would prevent Customer from performing its obligations under this Termination Agreement.

6.02 *By Vendor.* Vendor represents and warrants that (1) it has all the requisite power and authority to execute, deliver, and perform its obligations under this Termination Agreement, (2) the execution, delivery, and performance of this Termination Agreement have been duly authorized by Vendor and (3) it is not a party to any agreements that would prevent Vendor from performing its obligations under this Termination Agreement.

ARTICLE 7. MISCELLANEOUS.

7.01 *Assignment.* Neither party may assign this Termination Agreement without the consent of the other party. Any assignment in contravention of this *Section 7.01* shall be void.

7.02 *Successors and Assigns.* This Termination Agreement shall be binding upon, and shall inure to the benefit of the successors and permitted assigns of each of the parties.

7.03 *Notices.* All notices, requests, approvals, consents, and other communications required or permitted under this Termination Agreement shall be in writing and shall be sent by telecopy to the telecopy number specified below and the party sending such notice shall telephone to confirm receipt. A copy of any such notice shall also be sent by registered express mail or courier with the capacity to verify receipt of delivery on the date such notice is transmitted by telecopy to the address specified below:

[SPECIFY]

Either party may change its address or telecopy number for notification purposes by giving the other party notice of the new address or telecopy number and the date upon which it shall become effective.

7.04 *Survival.* The terms of **[SPECIFY]** shall survive the termination of this Termination Agreement for any reason.

7.05 *Counterparts.* This Termination Agreement may be executed in any number of counterparts, all of which taken together shall constitute one single agreement between the parties.

7.06 *Relationship.* Nothing contained in this Termination Agreement shall create or imply an agency relationship between Customer and Vendor, nor shall this Termination Agreement be deemed to constitute a joint venture or partnership between the parties. Except as expressly set forth in *Article 3*, each party intends that this Termination Agreement shall not benefit or create any right or cause of action in or on behalf of any person other than Customer or Vendor and their respective parents, affiliates, and subsidiaries.

7.07 *Severability.* If any provision of this Termination Agreement is held by a court of competent jurisdiction or any arbitral tribunal to be contrary to law, then the remaining provisions of this Termination Agreement or the application of such provisions to persons or circumstances other than those to which it is invalid or unenforceable shall not be affected thereby, and each such provision of this Termination Agreement shall be valid and enforceable to the extent granted by law.

7.08 *Waiver.* No delay or omission by either party to exercise any right or power it has under this Termination Agreement shall impair or be construed as a waiver of such right or power. A waiver by any party of any breach or covenant shall not be construed to be a waiver of any succeeding breach or any other covenant. All waivers must be in writing and signed by the party waiving its rights.

7.09 *Publicity.* Each party shall submit to the other all advertising, written sales promotion, press releases, and other publicity matters relating to the Outsourcing Agreement or its termination and this Termination Agreement and shall not publish or use such advertising, written sales promotion, press releases, or publicity matters without approval of the other party. Whenever required by reason of legal, accounting or regulatory requirements, a party may disclose all or any part of this Termination Agreement following reasonable notice to the other party, and after satisfying all reasonable means for masking, deleting or otherwise protecting all or portions of this Termination Agreement.

7.10 *Entire Agreement.* This Termination Agreement and the Exhibits, which are hereby incorporated by reference into this Termination Agreement, represent the entire agreement between the parties with respect to its subject matter, and there are no other representations, understandings, or agreements between the parties, whether written or oral, relative to such subject matter.

7.11 *Amendments.* No amendment to, change, waiver, or discharge of, any provision of this Termination Agreement shall be valid unless in writing and signed by an authorized representative of the party against which such amendment, change, waiver or discharge is sought to be enforced.

7.12 *Governing Law.* This Termination Agreement shall be governed, interpreted, and enforced under the laws of the State of **[SPECIFY]**. In connection with any judicial proceeding, Customer and Vendor agree that the Federal and State courts of competent jurisdiction in **[SPECIFY]** shall have exclusive jurisdiction over disputes under this Termination Agreement. The parties agree that jurisdiction and venue in such courts is appropriate.

7.13 *Covenant of Further Assurances.* Each of Customer and Vendor agrees that, subsequent to the execution and delivery of this Termination Agreement and without any additional consideration, each of Customer and Vendor shall execute and deliver any further legal instruments and perform any acts that are or may become necessary to effect the purposes of this Termination Agreement.

7.14 *Interpretation.* "Including" and all usage of the word "including," or the phrase "e.g.," in this Termination Agreement shall mean "including, without limitation." The article and section headings are for reference and convenience only and shall not be considered in the interpretation of this Termination Agreement.

IN WITNESS WHEREOF, the parties have caused this Termination Agreement to be executed by their duly authorized representatives.

Sworn to before me   **[CUSTOMER]**
this _____ day of
_____, _____

_____   By: _____
Notary Public   Name:
                            Title:

Sworn to before me   **[VENDOR]**
this _____ day of
_____, _____

_____   By: _____
Notary Public   Name:
_____   Title:

OUTLINE OF A TERMINATION ASSISTANCE SERVICES AGREEMENT[a]

- Condition Precedent

  Concurrently with, and as a condition of, the Termination Assistance Services Agreement (the "TASA"), Customer and Vendor shall execute and deliver the Termination Agreement **[and the Personnel Transition Agreement]**.

- Term

  The initial term of the TASA shall commence on **[DATE]** and continue until **[DATE]**. The initial term may renew upon notice from Customer for a period of **[NUMBER]** months.

- Transition Services

  Commencing on the effective date of the TASA, Vendor shall perform all functions and services necessary to accomplish the transition of Customer's **[SPECIFY BUSINESS PROCESS]** operations and capabilities back to Customer on or before **[DATE]** (the "Transition Services"). The Transition Services shall include those services listed in Exhibit ___.

- Transition Manager

  As part of the its obligations under the TASA, Vendor shall designate an individual for each of Customer's facilities, functions and services being transitioned. Each such designee shall be responsible for managing and implementing the Transition Services with respect to such facilities, functions or services. Until completion of the Transition Services, Vendor's designees shall review the status of the Transition Services on a weekly basis with designated personnel from Customer's management.

- Transition Schedule

  Vendor shall perform the Transition Services in accordance with the schedule set form in Exhibit ___ (the "Transition Schedule"). If, however:

  (1) Customer desires Vendor to extend the Transition Schedule by more than **[NUMBER]** days, or if the Transition Schedule is extended for more than **[NUMBER]** days as a result of delays caused by Customer, (a) Vendor shall ex-

---

[a] Note: This outline is intended to illustrate the types of legal issues that may arise in connection with the provision of termination assistance services. The provisions included in this outline, while comprehensive, may not cover all of the issues relevant to a particular transaction. Legal issues will vary depending on the type and scope of BPO arrangement being terminated. This outline or any part thereof should only be used after consultation with your legal counsel. You should consult legal counsel prior to entering into or negotiating any termination assistance agreement.

tend the Transition Schedule for the applicable period of time and (b) Customer shall pay to Vendor an amount equal to Vendor's direct and actual costs associated with any such extension of the Transition Schedule; or

(2) the Transition Schedule is extended for more than **[NUMBER]** days as the result of delays caused by Vendor, (a) Customer shall continue to pay the fees under the TASA and (b) Vendor shall pay to Customer an amount equal to Customer's direct and actual costs associated with any such extension of the Transition Schedule.

In the event Customer and Vendor agree to extend the Transition Schedule, or if the Transition Schedule is extended for more than **[NUMBER]** days as a result of delays caused by Customer and Vendor, Customer and Vendor shall negotiate an appropriate adjustment to the fees.

- Projects

  Vendor shall perform all tasks requested by Customer which are included in the Transition Services and any projects requested by Customer for **[SPECIFY BUSINESS PROCESS]** and related services. Vendor is not entitled to decline to perform such Transition Services or projects. Vendor shall receive the designated fees for providing such services or, for services not covered by the designated fees, Vendor shall be entitled to reasonable compensation agreed upon by Customer and Vendor. **[CUSTOMER MAY CONSIDER SETTING FORTH IN AN EXHIBIT LABOR RATES FOR SERVICES AND PROJECTS NOT COVERED BY THE DESIGNATED FEES]**

- Other Services

  Vendor shall provide the following services/assistance to Customer: **[CUSTOMER LIST OTHER SERVICES, SUCH AS:]**

  - Documentation
  - Configuration
  - ID numbers/passwords
  - Access to methodologies/technology/tools
  - Access to hardware
  - Access to facilities
  - Training
  - Assistance to/cooperation with third parties
  - Transfer of knowledge

- Required consents

  All consents to transfer any Vendor or third-party methodologies/technology or services to Customer shall be obtained by Vendor with Customer's cooperation. Vendor shall pay any costs of obtaining the consents.

- Fees

  In consideration of Vendor providing the Transition Services and projects, Customer shall pay to Vendor the designated fees as set forth in Exhibit ___. Except as expressly set forth in the TASA, there shall be no charges or fees payable by Customer in respect of Vendor's performance of its obligations under the TASA.

- Expenses

  Customer shall not be responsible for any of Vendor's expenses incurred in connection with the provision of the Transition Services or projects.

- Payment schedule

  Invoices shall be provided to Customer within **[NUMBER]** days of the provision of service. The fees shall be payable within **[NUMBER]** days of receipt of invoice.

- Milestones

  In connection with the Transition Services, Customer and Vendor shall develop a list of milestones relating to Vendor's obligations pursuant to the TASA that are critical to Customer and, for each milestone, (1) a description of the applicable triggering event from which achievement of that milestone shall be measured, (2) the duration of time from the triggering event for completion of that milestone, and (3) an amount of the designated fees that Customer may defer with respect to that milestone if, as a result of Vendor's failure to perform its obligations pursuant to the TASA, Vendor fails by more than **[NUMBER]** days to achieve such milestone by the specified completion date. Exhibit ___ contains a list of milestones agreed upon by Customer and Vendor.

- Data

    Customer data is the property of Customer and shall be deemed confidential information of Customer. Customer data shall not, without Customer's approval be, (1) used by Vendor other than in connection with providing the Transition Services, (2) disclosed, sold, assigned, leased, or otherwise provided to third parties by Vendor or (3) commercially exploited by or on behalf of Vendor. Vendor hereby irrevocably assigns, transfers, and conveys to Customer without further consideration all of its right, title, and interest in and to Customer data.

- Confidentiality

    All confidential information or proprietary information relating to either party shall be held in confidence by the other party to the same extent and in at least the same manner as such party protects its own confidential or proprietary information. The terms of the TASA are confidential and shall not be disclosed to any third party except as provided in the TASA.

- Customer's Representations and Warranties

    Customer represents and warrants that (1) it has the requisite power and authority to execute the TASA, (2) the execution of the TASA has been duly authorized by Customer, (3) there is no outstanding litigation, arbitration or other dispute to which Customer is a party which, if decided unfavorably to Customer, would have a material adverse effect on Customer's ability to fulfill its obligation under the TASA, and (4) it shall comply with all applicable Federal, state, and local laws and regulations in connection with its obligations under the TASA.

- Vendor's Representations and Warranties

    Vendor represents and warrants that (1) it has the requisite power and authority to execute the TASA, (2) the execution of the TASA has been duly authorized by Vendor, (3) there is no outstanding litigation, arbitration, or other dispute to which Vendor is a party which, if decided unfavorably to Vendor, would have a material adverse effect on Vendor's ability to fulfill its obligation under the TASA, and (4) it shall comply with all applicable Federal, state, and local laws and regulations in connection with its obligations under the TASA.

- Termination

    Customer may terminate the TASA (without any termination fee) effective as of any time upon **[NUMBER]** days' notice to Vendor.

- Liability

    [ADD LIABILITY PROVISION IF APPLICABLE]

- Customer's Indemnities

    Customer indemnifies Vendor from and will defend Vendor against any losses, liabilities and damages, and all related costs and expenses arising out of or relating to any claim by a third party based on any breach of the TASA by Customer.

- Vendor's Indemnities

    Vendor indemnifies Customer from, and will defend Customer against, any losses, liabilities and damages, and all related costs and expense arising out of or relating to any claim (1) by a third party based on any breach of the TASA by Vendor or (2) that the Transition Services or any methodologies/technology, documentation, or work product provided, developed or acquired by Vendor in connection with the TASA infringes another party's proprietary rights.

[ADD ADDITIONAL INDEMNITIES AS APPROPRIATE; E.G., RE: ENVIRONMENTAL, ERISA, AND OTHER COMPLIANCE REQUIREMENTS]

- Insurance

  Vendor shall maintain the following insurance during the term of the TASA: **[LIST INSURANCE REQUIREMENTS]**

- Miscellaneous Provisions
  - Assignments: Neither party may assign the TASA without the consent of the other party.
  - Successors and Assigns: The TASA is binding on and inures to the benefit of successors and permitted assigns.
  - Notices: All notices under the TASA shall be in writing and by telecopy to addresses specified in this provision.
  - Survival: The indemnity, confidentiality, representation, and warranties and survival provisions shall all survive termination of the TASA.
  - Counterparts: The TASA may be executed in counterparts.
  - Relationship of the Parties: The TASA does not create an agency, partnership, or joint venture relationship between the parties.
  - Severability: If any provision of the TASA is held by a court to be contrary to law, the remaining provisions shall be valid and enforceable to the extent granted by law.
  - Waiver: No delay or omission by either party to exercise any right or power it has under the TASA shall be construed as a waiver of such right or power.
  - Publicity: Each party shall submit to the other all publicity relating to the Services Agreement or its termination or the TASA and shall not publish such publicity without the written approval of the other party.
  - Entire Agreement: The TASA and the appendices constitute the entire agreement between the parties with respect to its subject matter.
  - Amendments: No amendment to the TASA will be valid unless properly signed by the party against whom enforcement is sought.
  - Governing Law: The TASA shall be governed by **[STATE]** law.
  - Covenants of Further Assurances: The parties agree to execute any further agreement between the parties with respect to its subject matter.

- Exhibits
  - Exhibit ___ sets forth a detailed list and description of the Transition Services.
  - Exhibit ___ sets forth the Transition Schedule.
  - Exhibit ___ sets forth the designated fees payable by Customer in consideration of Vendor's performance of the Transition Services.
  - Exhibit ___ sets forth a list of milestones relating to the Transition Services to be met by Vendor pursuant to the TASA and includes target completion dates for such Transition Services and amounts of the designated fees that mat be deferred by Customer if such milestones are not met by Vendor.

INDEX

For information about the disk see the **About the Disk** section on page xv.